STATISTICAL
STRATEGIES
FOR
SMALL
SAMPLE
RESEARCH

D088006:3

STATISTICAL STRATEGIES FOR SMALL SAMPLE RESEARCH

RICK H. HOYLE

SAGE Publications
International Educational and Professional Publisher
Thousand Oaks   London   New Delhi

For information:

SAGE Publications, Inc.
2455 Teller Road
Thousand Oaks, California 91320
E-mail: order@sagepub.com

SAGE Publications Ltd.
6 Bonhill Street
London EC2A 4PU
United Kingdom

SAGE Publications India Pvt. Ltd.
M-32 Market
Greater Kailash I
New Delhi 110 048 India

Printed in the United States of America

Library of Congress Cataloging-in-Publication Data

Statistical strategies for small sample research / Rick H. Hoyle,
  editor.
        p. cm.
    Includes bibliographical references and index.
    ISBN 0-7619-0885-4 (c). — ISBN 0-7619-0886-2 (p.)
    1. Social Sciences—Statistical methods. I. Hoyle, Rick H.
HA29.S7844 1999
001.4′22—dc21   98-43490

This book is printed on acid-free paper.

99 00 01 02 03 04 05 7 6 5 4 3 2 1

Acquisition Editor:	C. Deborah Laughton
Editorial Assistant:	Eileen Carr
Production Editor:	Diana Axelsen
Editorial Assistant:	Nevair Kabakian
Typesetter:	Technical Typesetting, Inc.
Book & Cover Designer:	Ravi Balasuriya

Brief Contents

Detailed Table of Contents

2. Maximizing Power in Randomized Designs When N Is Small

Anre Venter and Scott E. Maxwell

6. Exact Permutational Inference for Categorical and Nonparametric Data

Cyrus R. Mehta and Nitin R. Patel

11. Small Samples in Structural Equation State Space Modeling

Johan H. L. Oud, Robert A. R. G. Jansen, and
Dominique M. A. Haughton

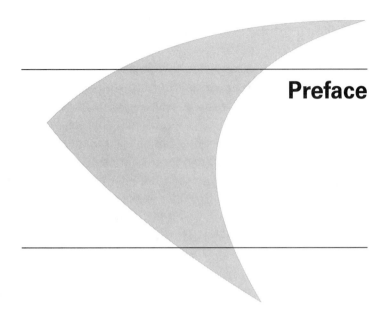

Preface

DURING THE PAST 20 years, the repertoire of statistical methods available to researchers in the social and behavioral sciences has dramatically increased in size. Staples such as analysis of variance and multiple regression have, in some circles, been overshadowed by more general methods such as structural equation modeling and hierarchical linear modeling. It is not a coincidence that these newer, more computationally demanding, statistical methods were developed and rose to prominence during a period when desktop computers evolved from sophisticated typewriters to powerful workstations. Researchers now can readily complete statistical analyses that, until recently, were accessible only to methodologists working in a mainframe environment.

A limiting feature of these emergent statistical methods is their basis in asymptotic theory: Their theoretical underpinnings derive from the behavior of estimators in arbitrarily large samples. Of course, most researchers do not have access to "arbitrarily large" samples. Indeed, many researchers find themselves working in important research arenas that typically do not provide them with more than a few dozen cases. Thus, although newer statistical methods might fit their research question nicely, those methods assume larger samples than they could ever hope to acquire. Such researchers are faced with three unsatisfactory options: (1) Find a way to increase the size of their samples. (2) Use a statistical approach that may not be a good fit to their research questions but is appropriate for small samples. (3) Reorient their research so that their research questions can be addressed by statistical methods appropriate for smaller samples. Often, due to limited resources or limited size of the population under study, it is not possible to increase sample size. And choosing a statistical strategy based on sample size rather than one's research question, or altering one's research question to conform to the assumptions of a statistical method, is to put the proverbial cart before the horse. A more desirable option would be statistical strategies that offer the flexibility and sophistication of large-sample strategies without the requirement of prohibitively large samples.

In this volume, contributors describe and illustrate statistical strategies that are flexible and sophisticated, yet appropriate for analyzing data from small samples. Authors were asked to describe and illustrate strategies that could be applied to data from 150 or fewer cases. Many authors use simulations to evaluate the performance of statistical methods based on asymptotic theory in very small samples, in effect asking, "*Ceteris paribus*, for how small a sample is a particular technique defensible?" Others present strategies for maximizing the yield from small-sample data. Collectively, the authors provide encouragement and viable options for researchers who routinely address research questions using data from small samples.

In Chapter 1, Graham and Schafer provide a didactic introduction to an emerging technique for analyzing incomplete data—multiple imputation. After persuasively arguing that traditional techniques for handling incomplete data such as mean substitution and regression imputation are statistically indefensible, they present results of a simulation study that both illustrates the use of multiple-imputation software and shows that multiple imputation can be used profitably with data sets as small as $N = 50$ and with as much as 50% missing data.

Venter and Maxwell (Chapter 2) consider means of increasing statistical power when sample size cannot be increased. They first consider from a theoretical perspective the sample size necessary to achieve equivalent statistical power for between-subjects, within-subjects, and between-subjects with pretest designs. After showing that, under typical conditions, the within-subjects design fares best, the authors acknowledge that within-subjects designs are not always defensible, and describe strategies for maximizing the power of between-subjects designs when sample size cannot be increased. In particular, they focus on the impact of measurement error in the posttest on statistical power of mean comparisons.

Chapter 3, by Kramer and Rosenthal, focuses on the use of effect size indicators to evaluate hypotheses when sample size is small. After a presentation of strategies for computing effect sizes, the authors discuss how effect sizes are combined across studies with an emphasis on pooling the results of pilot studies. They conclude that, when sample size is small, effect size indicators, perhaps pooled across studies, provide a better basis for judging the significance of a finding than results of traditional statistical tests evaluated with regard to Type I error.

Yung and Chan (Chapter 4) describe and illustrate the application of the bootstrap, a strategy that can prove useful for carrying out statistical tests when sample size is too small to satisfy the assumptions of standard statistics. After contrasting the bootstrap with the more familiar Monte Carlo simulation, the authors detail the logic of hypothesis testing using the bootstrap and illustrate its application using data from a cross-cultural study of factorial invariance. They conclude the chapter with a set of guidelines and a list of useful references relevant for social and behavioral science research.

Hershberger, Wallace, Green, and Marquis take up the issue of pooling effect size indicators from single-case studies in Chapter 5. They review different approaches to deriving an effect size from single-case studies and discuss the strengths and limitations of each. Next, they discuss approaches for combining effect size indicators from single-case research. They conclude with an informative example comparing results based on two methods of indexing effect size in single-case studies and tests of statistical moderation.

In Chapter 6, Mehta and Patel describe a framework for drawing inferences from cross-tabulated data when N is small or observations are sparse in portions of a contingency table. The authors show that, by fixing the margins of an observed contingency table, one can obtain an exact p value for testing the row-by-column interaction rather than relying on approximate p values based on theoretical sampling distributions that are correct only when N is large. They present a number of examples that illustrate the generality and statistical power of the permutation-based exact test compared to more traditional asymptotic tests.

In Chapter 7, Fouladi and Steiger describe why and how to determine whether a correlation or covariance matrix warrants structure analysis such as factor analysis or multiple-regression analysis. After a comprehensive review of statistics for evaluating whether a correlation or covariance matrix is an identity matrix (i.e., coefficients are not different from zero) in the population, they review simulation research that has compared the performance of the various statistics. They conclude that, when N is small relative to the number of variables, the most widely used statistic performs poorly. They recommend three relatively new statistics and illustrate their application in two examples.

Chapter 8, by Hoyle and Kenny, focuses on the effectiveness of tests of simple statistical mediation when sample size is small and the mediator is measured with error. In a Monte Carlo experiment, they evaluate the effects of sample size, degree of reliability of the mediator, collinearity between the predictor and the mediator, and method of analysis on estimates of parameters as well as power of the statistical test. They conclude that, when the mediator is unreliably measured, the magnitude of a mediated effect can be dramatically underestimated. When the mediator is unreliably measured and sample size is small, the likelihood of correctly detecting a mediated effect is very small. Their analysis indicates that, under certain conditions, latent variable modeling is a viable approach to correcting for unreliability in the mediator even when sample size is modest.

In Chapter 9, Nesselroade and Molenaar describe and illustrate dynamic factor analysis, a strategy for modeling temporal processes by analyzing multivariate, time series data from small numbers of individuals. The authors begin by providing several compelling justifications for analyzing process within individuals. They next outline the type of design and data needed for dynamic factor analysis—a strategy that is well suited for small samples and short time series. After a discussion of how subsets of cases with similar dynamic structures are identified, the authors illustrate the identification of "poolable" subsamples and the fitting of dynamic structure models to data from identified subsamples. They conclude with a discussion of the challenges and promise associated with extracting process information from intraindividual data.

Chapter 10, by Marsh and Hau, considers strategies for coping with estimation problems in confirmatory factor analysis (CFA) that arise when N is relatively small. They review findings from a large-scale Monte Carlo experiment by Marsh and colleagues and present findings from two new experiments on the effects of N, indicator-to-factor ratio, and other model features on estimation and fit. They conclude that estimation problems frequently encountered when attempting CFA with small samples (< 100) may be overcome by increasing rather than decreasing the number of indicators (either items or parcels) per factor. They further demonstrate that, by imposing within-factor equality constraints on loadings—even when equality does not hold in the population—estimation problems associated with CFA with small samples can be overcome with minimal biasing of parameter estimates.

In Chapter 11, Oud, Jansen, and Haughton describe the state space model in structural equation modeling terms. Like the dynamic factor model discussed in Chapter 9, the state space model incorporates time and intraindividual change into a model of dynamic process. After detailing the specification of the state space model as a structural equation model, the authors present results of a simulation study aimed at evaluating the performance of the state space model when N is small. They conclude that some forms of the state space model can be estimated and tested with surprising accuracy with data from samples of size 50 and 100.

In the final chapter, Chin and Newsted describe and illustrate the partial least squares (PLS) approach to structural equation modeling (SEM). They begin by contrasting PLS with the more commonplace covariance-based SEM. Next, they detail the PLS algorithm, walking the reader through each step of the estimation process. After outlining the specification of PLS models, the authors take up the issue of sample size requirements. They summarize findings from two Monte Carlo experiments on the performance of PLS with small samples. They conclude that PLS is a viable alternative to covariance-based SEM, particularly when N is small, the number of variables in a model is large, or both.

The strategies described in these chapters do not allow one to make a silk purse from a sow's ear—there are clear limits on what one can do with a very small number of cases. Rather, they suggest means by which research questions typically addressed in large-N studies might be profitably considered in small-sample research as well. Our hope is that the strategies described herein offer encouragement to researchers frustrated by the large-sample requirements of new statistical methods and provide the impetus for additional research on the performance of these methods when N is small and the development of new strategies that increase the options for researchers in the social and behavioral sciences who routinely work with small samples.

Acknowledgments

Most of the work on the volume was completed during a year-long sabbatical leave, and I acknowledge the generous financial support from the College of Arts and Sciences at the University of Kentucky during that period. Also, I was supported, in part, by Grants DA-05312 and DA-09569 from the National Institute on

Drug Abuse and Grant SP-07967 from the Center for Substance Abuse Prevention.

The authors and I gratefully acknowledge the contribution of colleagues who reviewed drafts of chapters: Gerald Adams, Baylor College of Medicine; Jenny Baglivo, Boston College; Donald W. Barclay, University of Western Ontario; Peter M. Bentler, University of California, Los Angeles; Frank Bernieri, University of Toledo; Dale Glaser, Sharp HealthCare; James B. Grace, National Wetlands Research Center; Michael M. Granaas, University of South Dakota; Monica J. Harris, University of Kentucky; Frank M. Howell, Mississippi State University; Yu-Fang Li, University of Maryland at Baltimore; Keith Markus, City University of New York; Shaun McQuitty, University of Northern British Columbia; Jeremy Miles, Derby University; Alex Piquero, Temple University; Doris McGartland Rubio, Saint Louis University; Anne E. Seraphine, University of Texas, Austin; Ronald L. Thompson, University of Vermont; Jerry C. Toops, University of Texas at Arlington; Phillip Wood, University of Missouri. I thank Carl Ferguson, University of Alabama, for permission to use SEMNET as a mechanism for enlisting reviewers.

I am especially grateful to my family, Lydia, Matthew, and Michael, who constitute a small sample to which I am most privileged to belong. The support and encouragement of my wife and the persistent curiosity of my children make possible projects such as this one.

Rick H. Hoyle
Lexington, Kentucky

1

On the Performance of Multiple Imputation for Multivariate Data With Small Sample Size

John W. Graham & Joseph L. Schafer

A Brief History of Missing-Data Procedures

MISSING DATA have long been a problem for researchers in various fields. In the social and behavioral sciences, analyses are typically multivariate, focusing on relationships among variables. In multivariate settings, even modest amounts of missing information on each variable may result in very few cases with complete data on all variables. Until recently, the only incomplete-data techniques accessible to most researchers have been ad hoc methods such as listwise deletion (excluding incomplete cases from consideration) and mean substitution. The often serious shortcomings of these ad hoc procedures are well known and clearly documented (e.g., Graham, Hofer, & Piccinin, 1994; Little & Rubin, 1987).

Following the influential article of Dempster, Laird, and Rubin (1977) on the expectation-maximization (EM) algorithm, researchers with strong technical backgrounds have been implementing and using likelihood-based procedures (Little & Rubin, 1987). Likelihood-based procedures are efficient, making full use of the data available from any incomplete cases; however, they are also model specific, requiring unique implementation for each class of models. Likelihood-based procedures for incomplete data have been implemented for modeling of repeated measures by BMDP (Program 5V) and SAS (PROC MIXED) and for structural equation modeling (SEM) in Mx (Neale, 1991) and Amos (Arbuckle, 1995). For other types of modeling (e.g., logistic regression with partially missing covariates), no specialized software has been available, and researchers have had little choice but to return to ad hoc procedures.

With certain types of multivariate analyses, it may be possible to "fool" a standard statistical package (i.e., one designed to handle only complete data) into performing a correct likelihood-based estimation from incomplete data. Structural equation modeling programs such as LISREL (Jöreskog & Sörbom, 1993) and EQS (Bentler, 1992) can fit models where cases are classified into multiple, possibly heterogeneous groups. A number of authors (Allison, 1987; McArdle & Hamagami, 1991, 1992; Muthén, Kaplan, & Hollis, 1987) have shown how multiple-group procedures can be applied to data with missing values: Each distinct pattern of missing values (by variable) defines a group, and parameters with similar meaning across groups are constrained to be equal. This method requires each missingness pattern to have more cases than variables, and it becomes extremely tedious as the number of missingness patterns grows.

In a similar vein, it is often possible to preprocess an incomplete data set so that, when it is later submitted to a standard statistical package, the resulting estimates are close to what would be obtained under a direct likelihood-based procedure. For example, many SEM programs allow the user to input a sample covariance (or correlation) matrix rather than raw unit-level data. When the unit-level data contain missing values, one can apply an EM algorithm to obtain an estimated covariance matrix, and use that estimated matrix as input to the SEM program (Graham & Donaldson, 1993; Graham et al., 1994). Parameter estimates obtained from this two-step procedure tend to be of very high quality. The standard errors printed by the SEM software accompanying those estimates can be very misleading, however, because standard errors are determined by the sample size; it is not clear what sample size should be ascribed to a covariance matrix estimated by EM. One proposed solution to the standard-error problem is to apply a resampling procedure such as the bootstrap: Generate new pseudo-samples by drawing cases at random (with replacement) from the original sample, and apply the EM algorithm to each one (Efron, 1994; Graham et al., 1994; Graham, Hofer, Donaldson, MacKinnon, & Schafer, 1997). Bootstrapping is conceptually straightforward but computationally tedious. Moreover, its performance may seriously degrade in smaller samples, because the resampling procedure may produce undue replication of data values leading to problems of severe multicollinearity (Rubin, 1994).

In the 1980s, Rubin proposed a new missing-data method called multiple imputation (Rubin, 1987, 1996). Multiple imputation is a simulation-based technique in which each missing datum is replaced by $m > 1$ plausible values; the variation among these values reflects the uncertainty with which the missing data can be predicted from the observed. The m resulting versions of the complete data are analyzed separately by standard complete-data methods, and the results are combined at the end. Multiple imputation is operationally attractive because it allows the user to analyze the data by nearly any method or software package of choice. Moreover, the resulting measures of variability (standard errors and p values) will accurately reflect uncertainty due to missing data as well as ordinary sampling variability.

Until recently, the theoretical and computational tools needed to generate multiple imputations have been nonexistent or inaccessible to most researchers. Schafer (1997) has written a set of general-purpose programs for multiple imputation of continuous multivariate data (NORM), multivariate categorical data (CAT), mixed continuous and categorical data (MIX), and multivariate panel or clustered data (PAN). These programs were initially created as functions operating within the statistical languages S and Splus (Becker, Chambers, & Wilks, 1988). S and Splus are the favorite computational tools of many statisticians but are not widely used by researchers in other fields. In 1997, Schafer's software was rewritten as graphical, standalone applications for PCs running Windows (95/NT). This new generation of programs, which is much easier to learn and use, makes multiple imputation methods accessible to a broader population of researchers and data analysts.

In summary, analyses of incomplete data no longer need to be ad hoc. With the release of these new software tools, listwise deletion and mean substitution can no longer be justified on the grounds that better methods are inaccessible. Direct likelihood-based methods when available (e.g., as in Arbuckle's, 1995, Amos program) and multiple imputation have been shown to yield high-quality estimates and reliable standard errors. These methods offer potentially dramatic improvements over the ad hoc approaches to missing data that have dominated practice far too long.

Application to Small Samples: The Present Chapter

The purpose of this chapter is to investigate the performance of these new missing-data procedures—in particular, multiple imputation using NORM—in realistic analyses where the sample size, N, is relatively small. The statistical theory underlying these tools is based partly on large-sample approximations, and most evaluations to date (e.g., Ezatti-Rice et al., 1995) have dealt with large samples. To what extent are these methods appropriate when one has a relatively small sample? How do they perform when one has as few as 100 or even 50 cases? To help answer the question of how little data is too little, we performed a simulation study to investigate factors that may impact the performance of missing-data procedures with small N.

In the remainder of this chapter, we review from a user's perspective the key ideas of multiple imputation and the use of

NORM software developed by Schafer (1997). We then describe a simulation study designed to test the limits of NORM in a realistic setting where N is small and the data do not conform to assumptions of normality. Our discussion of the simulation results focuses not only on the bias and efficiency of the parameter estimates but on other important issues including the quality of standard errors and statistical power. The chapter concludes with recommendations about the use of multiple imputation in smaller samples.

Overview of Multiple Imputation With NORM

Multiple imputation is conceptually straightforward. Consider first a simple situation where a data set contains several variables $(X_1, X_2, \ldots, X_j)$ that are completely observed and one variable (Y) that is partially missing. If Y is continuous, it would be natural to predict the missing values of Y by multiple regression with $X_1, X_2, \ldots, X_j$ as predictors. One can estimate the coefficients of the regression equation using the cases for which Y is observed, and then use the resulting equation to predict values of Y among the cases for which Y is missing. It may be tempting to use the predicted score, $\hat{Y}$, as an imputed value for the missing Y. This procedure, referred to as "regression imputation" or "conditional mean imputation," does not perform well in practice because the imputed values exhibit too little variability; the standard deviation of Y in the imputed data set will be unnaturally small, whereas its correlations with the Xs will be unnaturally strong. The imputed values of Y are implausible in that they fall *exactly* on the predicted regression line (plane); the method erroneously pretends that all missing values can be predicted from observed data without error.

Multiple imputations reflect the uncertainty of missing-data prediction by restoring the natural levels of variability in the imputed data. This variability comes from two sources: first, the residual variation of Y values above and below the regression line; and second, the variation in estimating the regression line itself. Let us consider how NORM adds these two types of variability when it creates multiple imputations.

NORM restores variability above and below the regression line by drawing residuals at random from a normal error distribution. Each imputation of a missing value of Y is a regression prediction plus a newly drawn normal random residual. An alternative approach would be to draw residuals with replacement from the actual distribution of regression residuals in the present data set, rather than from a normal distribution. In most cases, these two approaches will yield very similar overall results.

The second type of variability added by NORM is uncertainty associated with the regression predictions themselves. The regression line estimated from the observed values of Y is not the regression for the population, but only an estimate of it; this estimate is the best fitting line for the present sample but not for all possible samples. Each set of imputed values for Y relies on a different set of regression predictions within the range of plausibility allowed by the present sample. One possible way to vary the regression predictions is by a resampling procedure such as the bootstrap: Draw a new sample of units with replacement from the current sample and reestimate the regression coefficients with this new sample. NORM adds regression-prediction variability in a conceptually similar, but statistically more elegant way, by a procedure known as data augmentation (Tanner & Wong, 1987).

Data augmentation is an iterative simulation procedure that bears a strong resemblance to EM (see Schafer, 1997, for a more detailed discussion of EM and data augmentation; EM is also discussed in more detail by Graham & Donaldson, 1993, and Graham et al., 1994, 1997). Data augmentation is one member of a family of new simulation procedures known as Markov chain Monte Carlo. The data augmentation procedure in NORM produces a sequence of random covariance matrices, any of which could plausibly represent the population covariance matrix. Successive covariance matrices in this sequence tend to resemble one another, but those that are spaced widely apart are essentially independent. Proper multiple imputations must be based on covariance matrices spaced far enough apart to be essentially independent. Each of these independent covariance matrices provides a new set of regression coefficients and regression predictions for the NORM imputation procedure.

The preceding discussion pertained to a simple situation where missing values occur on only a single variable Y. In reality, NORM handles missing values on any or all variables simultaneously. Imputations created by NORM are based on regression predictions for each unit's missing variables given its observed ones. Variability from both sources—residual variation about the regression predictions and uncertainty in the regression predictions themselves—appear as an automatic byproduct of NORM's data augmentation procedure.

After the multiple imputations are created, the analyst is free to analyze the imputed data sets using almost any technique or software that would be appropriate if the data were complete. With m imputations, the same analysis (e.g., regression modeling) would be performed in an identical manner on each of the m data sets. From each analysis, one would save the estimates of the quantities of interest (e.g., regression coefficients) and their respective standard errors. The m sets of estimates and standard errors are then combined using a simple set of rules described by Rubin (1987) and Schafer (1997).

How many imputations are required? In most situations, accurate and valid inferences can be obtained with only a very small number of imputations such as $m = 3$, 5, or 10. In fact, it is usually not helpful to use a larger value of m. Rubin (1987) showed that the efficiency (on a variance scale) of an estimate based on m imputations is approximately

$$1/(1 + \gamma/m),$$

where γ represents the *fraction of missing information*. With 20% missing information ($\gamma = 0.2$), an estimate based on $m = 3$ imputations will tend to have a standard error only $\sqrt{1 + 0.2/3} = 1.033$ times as wide as one based on an infinite number of imputations. In most applications, the additional time required to create more than a handful of imputations could be better spent elsewhere.

Using the NORM Program

We now describe how one would use the standalone Windows (95/NT) version of NORM to multiply impute and analyze an incomplete data set. This free software and other multiple-imputation programs can be downloaded from our Web site (http://methcenter.psu.edu).

Preparing the Data Set

First, one prepares the data set. NORM reads data from an ordinary text (ASCII) file. Each row or line of the file represents data for a single case or unit; the variables recorded for each unit should be separated by one or more blank spaces or tabs. Missing values throughout the data set are indicated by a single numerical value (e.g., -9 or 99); for obvious reasons, this value should lie out of the legal range for all variables in the data set.

The name NORM is derived from *normal*; this software operates under an assumption that the variables in the data set are jointly normally distributed. Experienced analysts know that with real data normality tends to be an exception rather than the rule. Despite the fact that few data sets conform to this ideal, we believe that normal-based imputation procedures are still useful and widely applicable. As the simulation results in the present chapter illustrate, multiple imputation can be robust against even fairly strong departures from the imputation model. There are two fundamental reasons for this. The first reason is that an incorrect imputation model will not distort the shape of the entire data set, but only the portion of it that is missing. The second reason is that, even when data are clearly not normal, the imputed values generated by NORM still resemble the observed data in terms of their first and second distributional moments (means, variances, and covariances). Many of the statistical procedures in common use (e.g., linear regression, SEM) are little more than summaries of a data set's mean and covariance structure. Multiple imputation of missing data under an incorrect assumption of normality would tend to have little or no adverse effect on these procedures, whereas methods tied to other aspects of distributional shape (e.g., estimation of a variable's 5th or 95th percentile) would tend to be affected more.

Despite the robustness of NORM against departures from normality in the data, we recommend that in practice users perform some exploratory analyses of their data before applying NORM. If a variable is highly skewed, it may be a good idea to apply a sensible transformation (e.g., logarithm or square root) to improve normality prior to imputation, and then transform the imputed values back to the original scale afterward. In many cases, NORM may even be used to impute variables that are binary or ordinal (having three or more ordered categories); the continuous imputed values can then be rounded off to the nearest category.

Describing the Data

Once the data are entered, NORM can generate a printed report showing the number and proportion of observations missing for each variable, and the number of observations exhibiting each unique missing-data pattern.

Running the EM Algorithm

NORM includes an EM algorithm for maximum-likelihood estimation of means, variances, and covariances. Although not absolutely necessary, it is almost always a good idea to run the EM algorithm before attempting to generate multiple imputations. The parameter estimates from EM provide convenient starting values for data augmentation. Moreover, the convergence behavior of EM provides useful information on the likely convergence behavior of data augmentation. If EM converges within a certain number of iterations, say 50, then in nearly all situations it will be sufficient to allow 50 steps of data augmentation between successive imputations.

Running Data Augmentation and Generating Multiple Imputations

The next step is to run data augmentation. One must specify the total number of steps of data augmentation to be executed and how many steps are to be taken between imputations. With moderate rates of missingness (say, no more than 50% or 60% missing values on any variable), it is almost always sufficient to run the algorithm for 1,000 steps, generating one imputation at every 100th step for a total of $m = 10$ imputations. Once these parameters are specified, the data augmentation sequence executes and generates the imputations automatically.

Diagnostics

In practice, it is always wise to verify that the number of steps taken between successive imputations was indeed enough to guarantee statistical independence. NORM allows the user to check this by the "series" option in the data augmentation procedure. If this option is selected, then NORM will store the entire sequence of parameters (means, variances, and covariances) generated by the data augmentation run. By viewing time-series plots and autocorrelation functions for these parameters, it is typically easy to see how many steps of data augmentation are required for the parameters of successive imputations to be independent. NORM creates a visual display of these plots automatically. If one finds that the number of steps was not sufficiently large, then some of the imputations (e.g., every other one) could be discarded and recreated by another data augmentation run.

Analyzing the Data

This step is performed outside of NORM. One does whatever analysis would normally be done, using whatever analysis procedure (e.g., SAS, PROC, REG) that could be applied to complete data. Each data set is analyzed separately as if the imputed values were real data. The same analysis is performed m times. For each of the m analyses, one must create a data file containing two columns: The left column contains the parameter estimates of interest (e.g., regression coefficients), and the right column contains the corresponding standard errors.

Combining the Results

When the m analyses are complete, one returns to NORM to combine the results. NORM performs this step automatically, generating a printed report that resembles a table of coefficients from standard regression software. The table includes overall estimates (which are simply the averages of the m sets of estimates), overall standard errors (which include uncertainty due to missing data), t ratios (the estimates divided by their standard errors), degrees of freedom associated with these ratios, p values, confidence intervals, and the percentage of missing information.

A Simulation With Small N

With large sample sizes, multiple-imputation procedures such as those implemented in NORM are known to perform well in the following respects: (a) The multiple-imputation (MI) parameter estimates are essentially unbiased, averaging close to the population parameter values in repeated application. (b) The MI parameter estimates are efficient, having small standard errors. (c) The 95% MI confidence intervals are accurate, covering the true population values at least 95% of the time. This good performance can be expected provided that the model used to generate the imputations (in the case of NORM, a normal model) is somewhat plausible, as are the assumptions that must be made about the processes that led to missingness.[1] Evidence of good performance, which comes from both theoretical arguments and sim-

---

[1] NORM and the other programs written by Schafer operate under an assumption that the missing data are *missing at random*, in the sense described by Little and Rubin (1987). Missing at random means that the chance an observation is missing may depend only on quantities that are observed, rather than quantities that are missing. For more discussion on the plausibility of the missing-at-random assumption, see Schafer (1997) and Graham et al. (1997).

ulation studies, is described by Rubin (1996) and Schafer (1997) and authors they reference.

Despite this evidence, some questions remain about the performance of MI with smaller samples. To help address these questions, we conducted a limited but realistic simulation study on the performance of MI procedures with small N. In this simulation, we repeatedly drew multivariate samples from a large population, imposed random patterns of missingness, multiply imputed the missing values with NORM, calculated estimates and 95% confidence intervals by the MI procedure, and recorded how these estimates and intervals behaved with respect to the known population values. Details of the simulation are given next.

The Population

To keep the study realistic, we decided to use a large population of real data that did not conform to the modeling assumptions of our imputation method. The data were drawn from the Adolescent Alcohol Prevention Trial (AAPT), a longitudinal study of substance use among middle- and high-school students in the Los Angeles area (Donaldson, Graham, & Hansen, 1994; Donaldson, Graham, Piccinin, & Hansen, 1995; Hansen & Graham, 1991). Students in the AAPT study received yearly questionnaires designed to measure a variety of substance-use attitudes and behaviors. We limited attention to a subset of questionnaire items for which the missingness rates were fairly low. An exploratory factor analysis of these items led us to identify 18 more or less distinct domains of information; all but three of these domains were made up of multiple items. We standardized and averaged the items within each domain containing more than one item. Despite this averaging, the distributions of many variables remained highly nonnormal. Descriptions of the 18 variables and information about their distributions are presented in Tables 1 and 2.

To obtain a clean population with no missing values, we removed individuals with missing values on any variable except GRADES7. This variable was particularly important to us, be-

---

Table 1 Variables Used for Simulation Population

GENDER (single item, 0 = female, 1 = male)

WHITOTHER (single item, 1 = white, 0 = other ethnic groups)

DRUNK7 (drunkenness, four items)

ALCJOKE7 (alcohol self-concept; three items)

ALCINT7 (alcohol intentions; three items) (**.213, .137**)

SMKINT7 (smoking intentions; three items)

SMK7 (smoking; three item)

ALC7 (alcohol use; four items) (**.361, .237**)

MAR7 (marijuana use; four items)

FALC7 (friends' alcohol use; three items)

FDRUNK7 (friends' drunkenness; two items)

FSMK7 (friends' smoking; three items)

FMAR7 (friends' marijuana use; three items)

COLA7 (cola drinking; two items)

COFFEE7 (coffee drinking; two items) (**.078, .059**)

ADULTS7 (contact with adult alcohol use; two items) (**.051, .028**)

GRADES7 (single item measuring school performance) (**-.024, -.010**)

ALC8 (alcohol use at 8th grade; four items)

RANDOM (normally distributed random variable) (**.001, .000**)

Note. Except where noted, these measures were taken at 7th grade, and were continuous composites of two or more items. True (population) parameter values (*b*-weights) for 6 key predictors are shown in bold for the 6- and 18-predictor models, respectively.

---

cause in AAPT it is related both to substance use and to unplanned missingness.[2] Unfortunately, GRADES7 also had a very high rate of missingness because it was omitted by design from one-third of the questionnaires; removing individuals without GRADES7 would have substantially reduced the size of the population. To keep this variable in the simulation study and to keep the population sufficiently large, we decided to impute the miss-

---

[2] Students with lower grades tended to have poorer reading skills and completed the questionnaires more slowly; running out of time was a major cause of missing data in AAPT. Students with lower grades also exhibited higher rates of substance use.

Table 2 Distribution Information for Simulation Population Variables

	M	SD	Skew	Kurtosis
GENDER	.475	.499	.10	−1.99
WHITOTHER	.462	.499	.15	−1.98
DRUNK7	−.029	.760	3.18	11.90
ALCJOKE7	−.023	.764	.75	−.05
ALCINT7	−.011	.813	1.40	1.48
SMKINT7	−.023	.761	2.53	7.43
SMK7	−.037	.789	4.58	24.99
ALC7	−.015	.828	3.15	11.92
MAR7	−.027	.734	6.55	49.13
FALC7	−.019	.819	1.98	3.21
FDRUNK7	−.029	.835	3.96	18.47
FSMK7	−.036	.815	2.72	7.26
FMAR7	−.030	.790	6.87	55.88
COLA7	−.013	.909	.03	−.43
COFFEE7	−.007	.893	1.08	.60
ADULTS7	−.009	.845	.57	−.27
GRADES7	5.967	1.525	−.83	.61
ALC8	−.002	.861	2.60	7.29

ing values of GRADES7 using a nonparametric method known to survey statisticians as a "predictive mean-match hot deck" (Little & Rubin, 1987). This hot-deck procedure was intended to preserve the natural, nonnormal distribution of the variable and its relationships to other variables.

By imputing the missing values of GRADES7 and omitting cases with missing values on any of the other variables, we were left with a clean population data set with 18 variables and 9,461 individuals. To this data set we added a 19th variable (RANDOM) entirely unrelated to the others. This variable, which we artificially generated by drawing from a standard normal distribution, was added to investigate the performance of MI with respect to Type I error rates (see the following discussion).

Sampling Method

Once the population was created, we proceeded to generate artificial samples of size $N = 500$, 100, and 50. In each simulation round, the sample of $N = 500$ was drawn by simple random sampling without replacement. The sample was then degraded by imposing missing values using the procedure described later. Out of this larger sample, the first 100 and the first 50 cases were then taken as the samples of $N = 100$ and $N = 50$, respectively.

Rates and Patterns of Missingness

On each sample, we imposed missing values at a moderate (25%) and a high (50%) rate in a manner intended to mimic the unplanned missingness found in AAPT. As in AAPT, this missingness was related to the variable GRADES7. For each student in a sample, we first created a "propensity for missingness" by drawing a random variate from a beta distribution, a continuous probability distribution whose values lie between 0 and 1.0. The shape of this beta distribution varied with GRADES7: Those with lower grades tended to have higher propensities for missingness (near 1.0), and those with higher grades tended to have lower propensities for missingness (near 0). Missingness decisions were then made for each variable by drawing independent Bernoulli random variates (weighted coin flips) with success probability equal to the individual's propensity.[3] This was done for each variable except GRADES7. The GRADES7 variable was never made missing, because we wanted to ensure that the missing data would satisfy the missing-at-random assumption made by NORM. Some evidence suggests that in AAPT the missing-at-random assumption is somewhat plausible (Graham

---

[3] In previous simulation work (Graham et al., 1994), samples were degraded by a one-step procedure in which a certain percentage of values were made missing for each variable, independent of all other variables. This one-step procedure is somewhat unrealistic because it tends to produce very few sample cases with complete data. In reality, missingness is not independent across variables; persons who are likely to respond to one questionnaire item are also likely to respond to other questionnaire items.

et al., 1997). The shapes of the beta distributions were adjusted to give an overall per-variable missingness rate (for all variables except GRADES7) of either 25% or 50%.

Imputation and Analysis

Data from large studies like AAPT are analyzed in a wide variety of ways. To keep matters simple, we limited the scope of our analyses to multiple linear regression. With each sample, we performed two regression analyses. In the smaller (six-predictor) analysis, ALC8 was regressed on six other variables: ALCINT7, ALC7, GRADES7, COFFEE7, ADULTS7, and RANDOM (see Table 1 for the meanings of these variables). The degree to which these six variables were related to ALC8 ranged from no association at all (RANDOM) to a strong association (ALC7), so that the magnitude of the b-weight (i.e., the regression coefficient) constituted a naturally varying experimental factor. In the larger (18-predictor) analysis, ALC8 was regressed on the same 6 variables plus the 12 remaining ones. Because of intercorrelations, adding the 12 remaining variables attenuated the b-weights for the original 6 variables. The population b-weights for these 6 predictors, for both 6- and 18-predictor models, are shown in Table 1.

Prior to regression, the missing values in each sample were multiply imputed $m = 10$ times using the NORM program. The imputation procedure corresponded to how NORM would probably be used in practice. For the 6-predictor regression, the imputation procedure involved all 7 variables (6 predictors plus ALC8); for the 18-predictor regression, the procedure used all 19. Each application of NORM involved only those sample cases that would appear in the subsequent regression model. For example, in the 18-predictor regression with high (50%) missingness and a sample size of $N = 50$, imputation was performed on the data matrix with 50 rows, 19 columns, and 50% missingness on all variables (except GRADES7). Thus, each round of the simulation required 12 runs of the NORM imputation procedure to cover all possible combinations of regression model (6-predictor, 18-predictor), missingness rate (25%, 50%), and sample size ($N = 50, 100, 500$).

NORM is an interactive package, and fundamental decisions such as the number of imputations to generate, number of steps of data augmentation to allow between imputations, and so forth are typically influenced by examination of the data at hand. In a simulation, however, the precise way in which NORM was to be used needed to be specified ahead of time. We decided to use the following procedure. For each data set, NORM would be applied to the raw sample without any transformation of variables. Initial parameter estimates would be obtained by running the EM algorithm. These estimates would then serve as starting values for a single run of data augmentation. The data augmentation procedure would be run for 500 steps, with imputations generated at every 50th step for a total of $m = 10$ imputations. Each run of EM and data augmentation would be carried out under NORM's "ridge prior" option, with the value of the ridge hyperparameter set to 1.0.[4] After imputation, no editing would be performed except that imputed values for the two binary variables (GENDER and WHITOTHER) would be rounded off to the nearest category. The same regression model would be fit to each of the $m = 10$ imputed data sets, and the 10 sets of estimated b-weights and standard errors would be combined using the MI procedure as implemented in NORM.

---

[4] By default, the EM and data augmentation procedures in NORM operate under "noninformative" prior assumptions about the parameters. For most applications of NORM, the use of a noninformative prior is recommended; however, in certain situations when the data are sparse—for example, with small samples, large numbers of variables, and/or high rates of missingness—the data may exhibit extreme multicollinearity, which can cause the default procedures to fail. To guard against this possibility, we automatically applied a ridge prior in both the EM and the data augmentation phases. Using a ridge prior is similar to adding to the data a small number of fictitious cases for which all variables are uncorrelated. The additional prior information tends to be very beneficial in stabilizing the model and improving the functioning of EM and data augmentation. The amount of added information is controlled by the ridge prior's hyperparameter; setting the hyperparameter to 1.0 is equivalent to adding just one fictitious observation or row to the data. Using a ridge prior will introduce a small amount of bias, shifting the observed correlations slightly toward 0. When the hyperparameter is much smaller than the sample size (as it is here), the impact of this bias is minimal.

Running the Simulation

The entire simulation procedure—drawing the samples of $N = 50$, 100, and 500, imposing missing values at low and high rates, and multiple imputation and regression analysis for the 6-predictor and 18-predictor models—was carried out 1,000 times. For each regression b-weight, we stored the final MI estimates and standard errors, the degrees of freedom associated with the t ratio, and the estimated fraction of missing information. Based on this information, we also recorded whether or not the 95% MI interval covered or contained the true population b-weight, and whether one would reject the null hypothesis that the population b-weight is 0 against a two-sided alternative (i.e., whether the standard p value associated with the t ratio was less than or equal to 0.05).

Criteria of Performance

The performance of MI or any other statistical inference procedure ought be measured by a variety of criteria. We concentrated on four: bias, efficiency, coverage, and rejection rates.

Bias

One hopes that a statistical procedure would produce estimates that are relatively unbiased. In this study, unbiasedness means that the MI estimates of the regression b-weights would, on average, reproduce the true values in the population. Our measure of bias is simply the average over the 1,000 simulation rounds of the difference between the MI estimate of a b-weight and its corresponding value in the population.

Efficiency

In addition to small bias, one should also strive for estimates that are efficient, having relatively little variability around the true parameter values. Our measure of efficiency was the average width of the 95% MI confidence interval, which is essentially four times the value of the standard error; a wider interval implies less efficiency.

Coverage

Good statistical procedures will not only produce accurate estimates, but honest measures of how reliable those estimates are. A procedure for constructing a 95% confidence interval is honest if the resulting intervals contain the true parameter values about 95% of the time. With 1,000 iterations in our simulation procedure, this means that about 950 of the MI intervals for the regression b-weights should cover (include) their respective population b-weights.

Rejection Rates

Another issue closely related to coverage pertains to rates of rejection of null hypotheses. For the null hypotheses that were true (i.e., those pertaining to the predictor RANDOM, whose population b-weight is indeed 0), one would hope for rejection about 50 times out of 1,000, because a conventional hypothesis-testing procedure is designed to hold Type I error rates at 5%. For the null hypotheses that are false (those pertaining to all other predictors), one would want the null hypothesis to be rejected as often as possible; rejection rates for these hypotheses measure statistical power.

Of course, efficiency and statistical power should increase with the sample size N and decrease with the rate of missingness. Multiple imputation (or any other missing-data procedure, for that matter) should not be expected to make up for deficiencies in the observed data. Multiple imputation does not create or recover any information that has already been lost by nonresponse; it merely provides a convenient way of representing the missing-data uncertainty and measuring it in a computational environment dominated by complete-data methods.

Simulation Results

Performance of Multiple Imputation

To keep matters simple, we present results for the b-weights of just three predictors of the response variable ALC8: RANDOM, which is entirely unassociated with the response; ALC7, which is strongly associated with the response; and COFFEE7, whose association is weak but nonzero. Results for the b-weights of other variables were entirely consistent with the results for these three predictors. For brevity, we are using a single set of tables to report the results from both the 6-predictor and the 18-predictor regressions, but the reader should keep in mind that these b-weights actually represent two different parameters; the b-weights for the 6-predictor model in the population are not the same as those for the 18-predictor model.

Alongside the performance of MI with a moderate (25%) and high (50%) rate of missingness, we also report the performance of the conventional regression modeling procedure applied to the complete sample before any values were removed. In practice, it is not usually possible to achieve 0% missing values, and the MI procedure with 25% or 50% missingness will naturally be less accurate and less powerful than this. Nevertheless, the 0% situation serves as a useful benchmark to help separate the effects of missing data from the effects of small N and from the effects of the nonnormal data themselves. Many statistical procedures for *complete* data depend on a large sample size for good performance. For example, the likelihood-based procedures in conventional SEM software require a fairly large sample for their estimates to be approximately unbiased and for their standard errors to be accurate. In the present context of multiple linear regression, it is well known that the ordinary least squares estimates retain their unbiasedness when the data are not normal, but the standard errors that arise from normal-model theory may not be accurate unless the sample size is large. If an MI interval fails to have good coverage, it is important to identify whether that failure is associated with the imputation method or if it is due to inappropriate large-sample approximations in the analysis of the complete data.

Results for the b-weight of the variable RANDOM (population $b = 0.001$ and 0.000 for the 6- and 18-predictor models, respectively) are shown in Table 3. The MI estimates showed no appreciable bias for any combination of missingness or sample size. All biases were negligible in comparison to the average width of the 95% confidence intervals. As expected, the intervals for smaller sample sizes were wider than those for larger sample sizes. Also as expected, the intervals became wider as the rates of missingness increased.

The lower half of Table 3 shows the proportion of times the 95% MI confidence interval for the b-weight covered the true population value and the proportion of times the null hypothesis $b = 0$ was rejected. (Because the population b-weights for this variable are indeed 0, the two proportions must add up to 1.) The coverage rates are quite close to 95% and the actual Type I error rates are thus close to the target of 5%. The one notable exception is that when the data are very sparse—in the cell with $N = 50$, 50% missingness, and 18 predictors—the coverage and Type I rates are 98.3% and 1.7%, respectively. Many analysts (including ourselves) would agree that it would be unwise to attempt to fit an 18-predictor model with only 50 cases and large amounts of missing data. Yet, under these very extreme conditions, the MI procedure tends to be conservative, leading to Type I error rates below the nominal level. This suggests that one could perhaps find a procedure that would be more efficient, but the one who applies MI with $m = 10$ is not going to be misled; he or she will falsely reject the true null hypothesis at no more than the advertised rate of 5%.

The results for ALC7—the variable with the highest b-weight—appear in Table 4. Biases for the MI estimates are larger than they were for the variable RANDOM. Biases for many of the MI estimates here are also noticeably larger than for the corresponding estimates with no missing data (0%). The fact that the biases increase as missingness increases suggests that MI is indeed introducing bias. This is not surprising because the predictor (ALC7) and the response (ALC8) are both highly skewed;

Table 3 Simulation Results for Normal Random Variable (RANDOM)						
	6-Predictor Model			*18-Predictor Model*		
	% Missing			*% Missing*		
Sample Size	*0*	*25*	*50*	*0*	*25*	*50*
Bias in Parameter Estimates						
50	−.0036	−.0008	−.0026	.0017	.0046	−.0029
100	−.0019	−.0036	−.0034	−.0015	−.0046	−.0051
500	−.0000	.0001	−.0013	.0006	.0008	−.0016
Average Width of MI 95% Confidence Interval						
50	.41	.50	.71	.42	.53	.82
100	.28	.35	.48	.28	.34	.50
500	.12	.16	.22	.12	.15	.21
Proportion of Times True Value Included in 95% Confidence Interval						
50	.946	.927	.941	.948	.937	.983
100	.950	.941	.938	.946	.931	.932
500	.956	.949	.957	.966	.954	.950
Proportion of Times Null Hypothesis (b = 0) Was Rejected						
50	.054	.073	.059	.051	.063	.017
100	.052	.060	.061	.054	.069	.068
500	.044	.053	.046	.034	.047	.050

Note. The true (population) parameter value for this variable was .00096 and .00015 for the 6- and 18-predictor models, respectively.

imputing under a normal model is bound to distort the estimates to a degree. These biases, however, are all quite small in relation to the average width of the 95% interval estimates. The amount of bias introduced by MI in these small-sample settings is of little or no practical importance.

Table 4 Simulation Results for ALC7 (Alcohol Use at 7th Grade)						
	6-Predictor Model			*18-Predictor Model*		
	% Missing			*% Missing*		
Sample Size	*0*	*25*	*50*	*0*	*25*	*50*
Bias in Parameter Estimates						
50	.0132	.0475	.0643	.0566	.0595	.0044
100	.0062	.0207	.0557	.0326	.0538	.0714
500	.0021	.0119	.0238	.0057	.0122	.0397
Average Width of MI 95% Confidence Interval						
50	.76	1.05	1.63	1.17	1.66	2.14
100	.49	.66	.98	.66	.92	1.37
500	.21	.27	.38	.25	.34	.51
Proportion of Times True Value Included in 95% Confidence Interval						
50	.769	.755	.840	.819	.878	.976
100	.746	.754	.769	.791	.796	.869
500	.763	.759	.758	.780	.772	.801
Proportion of Times Null Hypothesis (b = 0) Was Rejected						
50	.480	.413	.301	.263	.181	.039
100	.708	.585	.460	.429	.355	.219
500	.998	.984	.885	.866	.733	.547

Note. The true (population) parameter value for this variable was .36114 and .23728 for the 6- and 18-predictor models, respectively.

The coverage and rejection rates at the bottom of Table 4 do not sum to 1, because the null hypotheses $(b = 0)$ are no longer true. The coverage of many of the MI intervals falls substantially below 95%. This failure, however, appears to be entirely due to the fact that the corresponding intervals with no missing data (0%) have severe undercoverage. This undercoverage shows the inability of ordinary linear regression to produce high-quality standard errors and interval estimates with data that are grossly nonnormal. Surprisingly (or perhaps not), the coverages of the MI intervals for 25% and 50% missingness are actually *better* than the coverages for 0% missingness (although the intervals are naturally wider). This curious result, which has been observed in other MI simulation studies as well, seems to be an artifact of the normal imputation model; the imputed values generated by NORM are more consistent with the assumptions of a linear regression model than are the observed data.

The rejection rates at the bottom of Table 4, which are now measures of power, show that statistical power rapidly degrades as the sample size decreases and the rates of missingness increase. This predictor (ALC7) is obviously strongly related to the response (ALC8). One would hope that even with a small sample, a significant relationship between these two predictors could be detected. Yet, with a sample size of 50 in a 6-predictor model, we have only a 48% chance of observing a statistically significant result. With high (50%) rates of missingness, the chance drops down to only 30%. This illustrates a key point of data imputation: You don't get something for nothing. When data are missing for a variable, one necessarily has less power to detect true effects involving that variable; imputation cannot recover information lost by nonresponse.

The results for the third predictor, COFFEE7, are shown in Table 5. Biases for the MI estimates were again somewhat larger than for the undegraded (0%) data set, but negligible in comparison to the average width of the confidence intervals. The MI intervals and the corresponding complete-data (0%) intervals showed similar patterns of coverage; undercoverage, although noticeable in most cells, is much less severe than for the ALC7 results in Table 4, because this variable is not nearly as skewed. Power to detect a significant effect for this predictor, as might be expected, was very low for small sample sizes, because the relationship between COFFEE7 and ALC8 in the population is very weak. The further loss of power due to missing data is not beyond what would be expected.

Table 5 Simulation Results for COFFEE7 (Coffee Use at 7th Grade)

Sample Size	6-Predictor Model % Missing			18-Predictor Model % Missing		
	0	25	50	0	25	50
	Bias in Parameter Estimates					
50	−.0007	−.0067	−.0122	−.0081	−.0142	−.0195
100	−.0101	−.0104	−.0155	−.0085	−.0158	−.0207
500	−.0016	−.0036	−.0036	−.0027	−.0057	−.0050
	Average Width of MI 95% Confidence Interval					
50	.50	.64	.92	.57	.74	1.10
100	.34	.44	.61	.36	.46	.68
500	.15	.19	.27	.15	.20	.28
	Proportion of Times True Value Included in 95% Confidence Interval					
50	.907	.897	.902	.925	.908	.974
100	.898	.908	.898	.914	.901	.935
500	.913	.903	.889	.907	.904	.903
	Proportion of Times Null Hypothesis (b = 0) Was Rejected					
50	.129	.123	.111	.111	.091	.029
100	.159	.135	.121	.128	.114	.077
500	.508	.332	.242	.324	.233	.176

Note. The true (population) parameter value for this variable was .07781 and .05899 for the 6- and 18-predictor models, respectively.

Performance of Complete Cases Analysis

We had originally intended to compare the MI results with results from the most common ad hoc approach: analysis of cases containing no missing data. However, the complete cases analysis performed so poorly in our simulation that we did not even present the results. Often (e.g., $N = 50$ and 50% missing), the number of cases with no missing data fell below the number of variables in the model, making estimation impossible. Of course, the poor performance of complete cases analysis in our simulation was in part an artifact of the method by which we created our missing data. However, situations like these are rather common. For example, in two recent studies with empirical data, we had the situation in which we had relatively small amounts of missing data (e.g., approximately 85% of all data points were nonmissing), but very few (15%) complete cases (Graham et al., 1997; Hawkins et al., 1997). In those two empirical studies, as with our simulation, analysis with complete cases was simply not an option.

Discussion and Conclusions

The results of our simulation strikingly illustrate a single point: The biggest problem of analyses with small N is that one simply has too little data to form conclusions about all but the largest of effects. The results also show that missing data only make the problem worse, leading to an effective sample size even smaller than before. The good news, however, is that, provided one has sufficiently strong effects, multiple imputation using NORM can be an excellent solution to the missing-data problem, even with sample sizes as low as 50, even with as much as 50% missing from most variables, and even with relatively large and complex models.

In short, the limitations of analysis with small sample size lie in the small sample size itself, not with the multiple-imputation procedure. The effects of missing data in this situation are little different from a simple reduction in sample size. Multiple imputation cannot compensate for having collected too little data. It can, however, allow the researcher to make effective use of all the data that were collected.

Author Note: This research was supported in part by NIDA Grant P50 DA 10076.

References

Allison, P. D. (1987). Estimation of linear models with incomplete data. In C. Clogg (Ed.), *Sociological methodology 1987* (pp. 71–103). San Francisco: Jossey Bass.

Arbuckle, J. L. (1995). *Amos users' guide*. Chicago: SmallWaters.

Becker, R. A., Chambers, J. M., & Wilks, A. R. (1988). *The new S language: A programming environment for data analysis and graphics*. Pacific Grove, CA: Wadsworth and Brooks/Cole Advanced Books and Software.

Bentler, P. M. (1992). *EQS structural equations program manual*. Los Angeles: BMDP Statistical Software.

Dempster, A. P., Laird, N. M., & Rubin, D. B. (1977). Maximum likelihood from incomplete data via the EM algorithm (with discussion). *Journal of the Royal Statistical Society, B39*, 1–38.

Donaldson, S. I., Graham, J. W., & Hansen, W. B. (1994). Testing the generalizability of intervening mechanism theories: Understanding the effects of adolescent drug use prevention interventions. *Journal of Behavioral Medicine, 17*, 195–216.

Donaldson, S. I., Graham, J. W., Piccinin, A. M., & Hansen, W. B. (1995). Resistance skills training and onset of alcohol use: Evidence for beneficial and potentially harmful effects in public schools and in private Catholic schools. *Health Psychology, 14*, 291–300.

Efron, B. (1994). Missing data, imputation, and the bootstrap (with discussion). *Journal of the American Statistical Association, 89*, 463–479.

Ezatti-Rice, T. M., Johnson, W., Khare, M., Little, R. J. A., Rubin, D. B., & Schafer, J. L. (1995). A simulation study to evaluate the performance of model-based multiple imputations in NCHS health examination surveys. *Proceedings of the Annual Research Conference*, 257–266. Washington, DC: Bureau of the Census.

Graham, J. W., & Donaldson, S. I. (1993). Evaluating interventions with differential attrition: The importance of nonresponse mechanisms and use of followup data. *Journal of Applied Psychology, 78*, 119–128.

Graham, J. W., Hofer, S. M., Donaldson, S. I., MacKinnon, D. P., & Schafer, J. L. (1997). Analysis with missing data in prevention research. In K. Bryant, M. Windle, & S. West (Eds.),

The science of prevention: Methodological advances from alcohol and substance abuse research (pp. 325–366). Washington, DC: American Psychological Association.

Graham, J. W., Hofer, S. M., & Piccinin, A. M. (1994). Analysis with missing data in drug prevention research. In L. M. Collins & L. Seitz (Eds.), *Advances in data analysis for prevention intervention research*. National Institute on Drug Abuse Research Monograph Series (#142). Washington, DC: National Institute on Drug Abuse.

Hansen, W. B., & Graham, J. W. (1991). Preventing alcohol, marijuana, and cigarette use among adolescents: Peer pressure resistance training versus establishing conservative norms. *Preventive Medicine, 20,* 414–430.

Hawkins, J. D., Graham, J. W., Maguin, E., Abbott, R., Hill, K. G., & Catalano, R. F. (1997). Exploring the effects of age of alcohol use initiation and psychosocial risk factors on subsequent alcohol misuse. *Journal of Studies on Alcohol, 58,* 280–290.

Jöreskog, K. G., & Sörbom, D. (1993). *LISREL 8 user's reference guide*. Chicago: Scientific Software.

Little, R. J. A., & Rubin, D. B. (1987). *Statistical analysis with missing data*. New York: Wiley.

McArdle, J. J., & Epstein, D. (1987). Latent growth curves within developmental structural equation models. *Child Development, 58,* 110–133.

McArdle, J. J., & Hamagami, F. (1991). Modeling incomplete longitudinal and cross-sectional data using latent growth structural models. In L. M. Collins & J. Horn (Eds.), *Best methods for analysis of change: Recent advances, unanswered questions, future directions* (pp. 276–304). Washington, DC: American Psychological Association.

McArdle, J. J., & Hamagami, F. (1992). Modeling incomplete longitudinal and cross-sectional data using latent growth structural models. *Experimental Aging Research, 18,* 144–166.

Muthén, B., Kaplan, D., & Hollis, M. (1987). On structural equation modeling with data that are not missing completely at random. *Psychometrika, 52,* 431–462.

Neale, M. C. (1991). *Mx: Statistical modeling.* [Available from M. C. Neale, Box 3, Department of Human Genetics, Medical College of Virginia, Richmond, VA.]

Rubin, D. B. (1987). *Multiple imputation for nonresponse in surveys*. New York: Wiley.

Rubin, D. B. (1994). Comment on "Missing data, imputation, and the bootstrap" by B. Efron. *Journal of the American Statistical Association, 89*, 475–478.

Rubin, D. B. (1996). Multiple imputation after 18+ years. *Journal of the American Statistical Association, 91*, 473–489.

Schafer, J. L. (1997). *Analysis of incomplete multivariate data.* New York: Chapman and Hall.

Tanner, M. A., & Wong, W. H. (1987). The calculation of posterior distributions by data augmentation (with discussion). *Journal of the American Statistical Association, 82*, 528–550.

2

Maximizing Power in Randomized Designs When *N* Is Small

Anre Venter & Scott E. Maxwell

THE MOST TYPICAL RESPONSE to concerns about low statistical power has traditionally been to increase sample size. This trend continues despite the growing body of literature illustrating a variety of options such as increasing power by accounting for sources of error variance in the dependent measure. Recent concerns about increased research costs and competition for limited research funds have prompted a renewed emphasis on this issue (Allison, Allison, Faith, Paultre, & Pi-Sunyer, 1997; Kraemer, 1991; McClelland, 1997). Besides, even when it is possible to increase the sample size, some of these options may more effectively increase statistical power.

Although there are many general and specific design and analysis strategies that influence power, this chapter focuses on ways in which multiple measures of subjects' responses over time can enhance power. The most obvious such design, the within-subjects design, in which each subject receives every treatment, is described first. Although usually more powerful than the between-subjects design, this design requires some thought about possible confounding carryover effects. Clearly, it is not suitable for research in which the treatment or manipulation may have some permanent effect on the subjects. However, when used appropriately, it is extremely useful and is widely used in the field of cognitive psychology, for example.

Then we present three options that maximize power in a conventional randomized pretest-posttest between-subjects design. First, the standard pretest-posttest analysis of covariance (ANCOVA) is compared to a lengthened posttest-only analysis of variance (ANOVA) design. Second, the optimal allocation of assessment time between the pretest and posttest is examined. Finally, the value of additional time points in the pretest-posttest design is considered. There are other options for increasing power in a between-subjects design like blocking and stratification that control for intrasubject variability by creating matched subgroups of subjects. Kraemer (1991) provides an excellent review of these options.

Our general approach to comparing the power and precision of various designs is to compare the magnitude of the noncentrality parameters (or, equivalently, mean differences relative to error variances). While Monte Carlo simulations are often useful for evaluating power considerations, they are unnecessary here because the error variances or noncentrality parameters of interest are derived analytically. The only other factor of theoretical importance is degrees of freedom; however, Arvey and Cole (1989) have shown that, except in studies with exceedingly small sample sizes, the effect of differences in degrees of freedom alone tends to be inconsequential.

The two major sections of this chapter are defined by design differences, within-versus between-subjects designs. Specific methods of analysis are discussed as they flow from the more fundamental design themes. More generally, the manner in which analyses are conducted can also influence statistical power. Rosenthal and Rosnow (1985) show how contrast analyses with focused 1-degree-of-freedom tests can provide more statistical power and clearer substantive interpretation of results as compared to omnibus analyses. Readers are encouraged to familiarize themselves with this approach as a general way to test their questions of interest more effectively.

Within- Versus Between-Subjects Designs

Introduction

The single most effective way of increasing power to detect treatment effects in randomized designs is typically to employ a within-subjects design, where treatment condition constitutes a within-subjects factor. This type of within-subjects design has two major advantages over a between-subjects comparison of treatment effects. First, in a between-subjects design, each individual participates in only a single treatment condition, so only a single score on the dependent variable is obtained for each subject. In a within-subjects design, however, each person participates in every condition, yielding as many scores as there are treatment conditions. Thus, when subjects are at a premium, more data points are obtained from a fixed number of subjects in the within-subjects design than in the between-subjects design. Second, each subject in the within-subjects design serves as his or her own control, which usually reduces error variance—often substantially. These two advantages of the within-subjects design mutually increase power and frequently lead to a sizable advantage over the between-subjects design.

In later sections of this chapter, we describe modifications to the between-subjects design that can produce some of the same advantages offered by the within-subjects design. Before considering these modifications, however, in this section we compare the relative power of the within- and between-subjects designs. Specifically, we first present a statistical model for scores on the dependent measure. From this model, we derive expressions comparing the power and precision of the two types of designs.

After this section of algebraic derivations, we present a numerical example that concretely illustrates the impact of the previously derived abstract principles on realistic experimental data. Our specific examples focus on two-level designs for conceptual simplicity, but the pattern of results holds more generally for designs with multiple levels of each factor.

The Statistical Model and Assumptions

Senn (1993) provides a useful discussion of the relative precision of the within- and between-subjects designs. Much of our presentation follows his framework, although our approach adopts a somewhat different perspective and we use a different notational system. Following Senn, a statistical model for scores is given by

$$Y_{ijk} = \mu + \alpha_j + \beta_k + \pi_{ij} + \varepsilon_{ijk}, \tag{1}$$

where Y_{ijk} is the score on the dependent variable.

Before explaining the parameters on the right-hand side of the equation, it may be useful to begin with a description of the subscripts that appear on both sides of the equation. The i and j subscripts denote the score for person i in treatment condition j. In the within-subjects design, we will assume that half of the subjects receive Treatment Condition 1 followed by Treatment Condition 2, whereas the other half receive the treatments in the opposite order. Thus, in this design, the k subscript denotes whether Y is observed at Time 1 or at Time 2. All individuals in the between-subjects design are observed at a single time point, so k always equals 1 in this design.

The parameters of the model have a standard analysis of variance interpretation in both types of design. In particular, μ denotes a grand mean term common to all observations. The α_j parameter represents the effect associated with treatment condition j. Thus, in both types of designs, the primary emphasis is on estimating the difference between the effects of the two treatments, which can be represented as $\alpha_1 - \alpha_2$. The β_k parameters represent the effect of time, or period, as it is often referred to in within-subjects designs. Thus, the β_k parameters allow for change over time, irrespective of treatment effects. Notice that the between-subjects design includes only a single time period, so the β_k parameters become unnecessary in this design. The π_{ij} parameter represents the effect of person i in group j. In other words, this parameter reflects systematic individual differences between subjects. Finally, the ε_{ijk} represents any other unaccounted for sources of variance and for this reason is considered to be error within the context of the model.

Several assumptions are implicit in this model. First, the model assumes the absence of carryover effects. Second, the means of both π_{ij} and ε_{ijk} are assumed to equal 0. Third, these same two effects are assumed to be independent of one another, and, fourth, all errors are assumed to be independent of one another. We make three other important assumptions in our derivations. First, all error variances are assumed to be homogeneous. Second, for simplicity, we will assume that the same number of individuals is assigned to each group. Third, we also assume random assignment to treatment groups in the between-subjects design and to treatment sequences in the within-subjects design.

Relative Power and Precision of the Designs

This model formulation provides the opportunity to compare the relative power and precision of the two types of design. It is useful first to focus on the underlying population cell means. Table 1 shows these means based on Equation 1, where the dot subscript indicates that in all cells the mean is obtained by averaging over subjects.

Table 1 Population Cell Means for the Two Types of Designs

	Time Period	
Group	1	2
1	$\mu_{.11} = \mu + \alpha_1 + \beta_1$	$\mu_{.22} = \mu + \alpha_2 + \beta_2$
2	$\mu_{.21} = \mu + \alpha_2 + \beta_1$	$\mu_{.12} = \mu + \alpha_1 + \beta_2$

In the between-subjects design, the treatment effect can be estimated by calculating the difference between the group sample means at Time 1. The formal estimator can be written as

$$(\hat{\alpha}_1 - \hat{\alpha}_2)_{\mathrm{B}} = \bar{Y}_{.11} - \bar{Y}_{.21}, \tag{2}$$

where the B subscript emphasizes that this estimate comes from the between-subjects design. Examination of Table 1 shows that the expected value of this estimator equals $\alpha_1 - \alpha_2$, yielding an unbiased estimate of the population mean difference between the two treatment conditions.

The corresponding estimator in the within-subjects design is given by

$$(\hat{\alpha}_1 - \hat{\alpha}_2)_{\mathrm{W}} = \left[(\bar{Y}_{.11} - \bar{Y}_{.22}) + (\bar{Y}_{.12} - \bar{Y}_{.21})\right]/2, \tag{3}$$

where the W subscript emphasizes that this estimate comes from the within-subjects design. It follows from Table 1 that the expected value of this estimator also equals $\alpha_1 - \alpha_2$, so the estimator in the within-subjects design is also unbiased under the constraints of the model, which assumes the complete absence of carryover effects in the population.

The previous two paragraphs show that, in the absence of carryover effects, the between- and within-subjects designs provide the same expected estimate of the treatment effect. In the long run, the average estimate of the treatment effect will thus be identical in the two designs; however, they differ in the degree of precision of the estimate in any specific sample. This difference can be shown by examining the variance of the estimated treatment difference in each of the two designs.

From Equation 2, it follows that the variance of the estimated treatment effect in the between-subjects design equals

$$\mathrm{var}(\hat{\alpha}_1 - \hat{\alpha}_2)_{\mathrm{B}} = \mathrm{var}(\bar{Y}_{.11} - \bar{Y}_{.21}). \tag{4}$$

Given the model shown in Equation 1, the variance of a sample mean can be written as

$$\mathrm{var}(\bar{Y}_{.11}) = \mathrm{var}(\bar{Y}_{.21}) = 2(\sigma_\pi^2 + \sigma_\varepsilon^2)/n_{\mathrm{B}}, \tag{5}$$

where σ_{π}^2 and σ_{ε}^2 represent the variance associated with the π_{ij} and ε_{ijk} parameters, respectively, and n_B represents the total sample size summed over the two treatment groups in the between-subjects design. Because subjects in the two treatment groups are independent of one another in the between-subjects design, the variance of the difference between means equals the sum of the variances, yielding

$$\text{var}(\hat{\alpha}_1 - \hat{\alpha}_2)_{\text{B}} = 4(\sigma_{\pi}^2 + \sigma_{\varepsilon}^2)/n_{\text{B}}. \tag{6}$$

A parallel set of steps can be derived for the within-subjects design. In particular, the variance of the treatment effect in the within-subjects design follows from Equation 3, and is given by

$$\text{var}(\hat{\alpha}_1 - \hat{\alpha}_2)_{\text{W}} = \text{var}\{[(\bar{Y}_{.11} - \bar{Y}_{.22}) + (\bar{Y}_{.12} - \bar{Y}_{.21})]/2\}. \tag{7}$$

This expression can be simplified by realizing that the analysis proceeds by subtracting the Treatment 2 score for each subject from the same subject's Treatment 1 score. For the half of the total sample of n_W individuals receiving Treatment 1 first, straightforward algebra shows that the variance of their mean difference score is given by

$$\text{var}(\bar{Y}_{.11} - \bar{Y}_{.22}) = 4\sigma_{\varepsilon}^2/n_{\text{W}}, \tag{8}$$

where n_W is the total sample size for the within-subjects design. An equivalent expression emerges for subjects receiving the treatments in the opposite order. Combining Equations 7 and 8 yields

$$\text{var}(\hat{\alpha}_1 - \hat{\alpha}_2)_{\text{W}} = 2\sigma_{\varepsilon}^2/n_{\text{W}}. \tag{9}$$

Two points deserve special attention. First, the variance shown in Equation 9 is lower than that in Equation 8 because the treatment effect is averaged over the $n_W/2$ subjects in Group 1 and the $n_W/2$ subjects in Group 2, producing a more precise estimate than that of either group separately (note that this averaging also controls for a period effect in the absence of carryover). Second, the difference score controls for systematic individual differences, so the variance of the treatment effect depends only on σ_ε^2 (and, of course, sample size) in the within-subjects design, whereas σ_π^2 also contributes to imprecision in the between-subjects design.

The relative power and precision of the between-subjects and within-subjects designs can be evaluated by comparing Equations 6 and 9. In particular, the power and precision of the two types of designs will be equal when the two variance expressions are equal to one another. Setting the expressions in Equations 6 and 9 equal to one another shows that equal power and precision will occur when

$$n_W = n_B \sigma_\varepsilon^2 / 2(\sigma_\pi^2 + \sigma_\varepsilon^2). \tag{10}$$

This equation can be simplified, because the ratio of σ_π^2 to $(\sigma_\pi^2 + \sigma_\varepsilon^2)$ can be shown from Equation 1 and the aforementioned assumptions to equal the correlation between the pair of scores in the within-subjects design. This correlation, which we denote by ρ in the population, is akin to a reliability coefficient, which helps explain why ρ and not ρ^2 equals the ratio of variance components. As a result, Equation 10 can be rewritten as

$$n_W = n_B(1 - \rho)/2. \tag{11}$$

Equation 11 explicitly reveals the two advantages mentioned earlier in the chapter for the within-subjects design. First, suppose that there were no systematic individual differences on the dependent variable, in which case the population correlation between scores under the two treatment conditions would equal 0. Even here, Equation 11 shows that the within-subjects design requires only one half as many subjects as the between-subjects design to achieve equal power and precision. The reason for this advantage is once again that each subject contributes two data points in the within-subjects design, but only one data point in the between-subjects design. Second, for most dependent measures in the behavioral sciences, there will be noticeable individual differences. Equation 11 shows that as ρ increases, the relative number of subjects required by the within-subjects design decreases. For example, if ρ equals 0.5, the within-subjects design requires only one fourth as many subjects as the between-subjects design. Only in the unlikely event that scores are negatively correlated would the within-subjects design require more than one half as many subjects as the between-subjects design.

Equation 11 shows that the within-subjects design can produce the same power and precision as the between-subjects design while requiring fewer subjects. However, not only is the within-subjects design susceptible to carryover effects, but, in addition, it requires greater time involvement from each subject. In this respect, the comparison reflected in Equation 11 might well be deemed unfair. A more appropriate comparison would compare the within-subjects design to a between-subjects design where a pretest measure was administered to each subject. Notice that the pretest-posttest design would require two assessments per individual, which then makes it more directly comparable to the within-subjects design. This realization then naturally leads to the question of whether a pretest assessment in the between-subjects design produces the same power and precision as does the additional assessment in the within-subjects design.

Senn (1993) showed that, under the assumptions of the model in Equation 1, the variance of the estimated treatment effect using analysis of covariance (ANCOVA) in the pretest-posttest design is given by

$$\text{var}(\hat{\alpha}_1 - \hat{\alpha}_2)_{\text{PP}} = 4(1 - \rho^2)(\sigma_\pi^2 + \sigma_\varepsilon^2)/n_{\text{PP}}, \tag{12}$$

where ρ is the pretest-posttest correlation (which, according to the model, also equals the correlation between scores in the two treatment conditions in the within-subjects design), and the PP subscript serves as a reminder that the equation pertains to a pretest-posttest design. Comparing Equation 12 with Equation 6 for the posttest-only between-subjects design shows that the inclusion of the pretest reduces the required sample size by a factor of $(1 - \rho^2)$. For example, when the pretest correlates 0.5 with the posttest, the inclusion of the pretest reduces the required sample size by 25%.

The pretest-posttest and the within-subjects designs will be equally powerful and precise when the variances shown in Equations 9 and 12 are equal to one another. Rearranging terms and remembering that ρ equals the ratio of σ_π^2 to $(\sigma_\pi^2 + \sigma_\varepsilon^2)$ yields

$$n_W = n_{PP}/2(1 + \rho). \tag{13}$$

Although the inclusion of the pretest reduces the required sample size in the between-subjects design, Equation 13 shows that under our model assumptions the pretest-posttest design still requires more subjects than does the within-subjects design. For example, when ρ equals 0.5, Equation 13 shows that the within-subjects design requires only one third as many subjects as does the pretest-posttest design. Once again, part of the advantage of the within-subjects design results from having twice as many data points per subject, but there is still a further advantage that the treatment condition comparison entirely controls for individual differences in the within-subjects design, whereas even using a pretest as a covariate only partially controls for individual differences in the between-subjects design.

The fact that ANCOVA only partially controls for individual differences suggests another possible strategy. Subtracting the pretest from the posttest completely removes σ_π^2 as a source of variance in the estimated treatment effect, just as in the within-subjects design. In fact, the variance of the mean difference score (i.e., posttest minus pretest) within each group is simply $4\sigma_\varepsilon^2/n_{PP}$, just as in the within-subjects design (see Equation 8). However, unlike the within-subjects design where difference scores are averaged over groups, in the pretest-posttest design the differences must be compared between groups. As a consequence, the variance of the estimated treatment effect becomes

$$\text{var}(\hat{\alpha}_1 - \hat{\alpha}_2) = 8\sigma_\varepsilon^2/n_{PP}. \tag{14}$$

Comparing Equation 14 to Equation 9 shows that this approach requires four times as many subjects as the within-subjects design to achieve equal precision. Comparing Equation 14 to Equation 12 shows that the analysis of difference scores in the pretest-posttest design yields less precision than the ANCOVA in the same design, except in the limiting case where ρ equals 1. To achieve the same precision, the difference score analysis would require $2/(1 + \rho)$ as many subjects as the ANCOVA.

Despite its failure to control completely for individual differences, ANCOVA is more precise because, unlike the difference score, it estimates the regression coefficient of the pretest so as to minimize within-group variance.

Table 2 illustrates practical implications of the previous abstract derivations. Suppose an investigator desires a power of .80 to detect a medium size effect in a two-group comparison. A posttest-only between-subjects design would require a total of 128 subjects to achieve the desired power (Cohen, 1988). The table shows the total sample size required by the previously compared designs under previously stated assumptions. Naturally, analyses based on either a pretest or a within-subjects design require fewer subjects for larger values of ρ. Most striking are the large sample size requirements of the difference score approach in the pretest-posttest design when ρ is low and the small sample size requirements of the within-subjects design when ρ is moderate or large.

Numerical Example

Table 3 shows hypothetical data for 20 subjects that we use to illustrate the previously derived abstract results comparing three types of designs and accompanying analyses: posttest-only between-subjects design, pretest-posttest between-subjects design (analyzed with both ANCOVA and difference scores), and

Table 2 Sample Sizes Required to Detect a Medium Size Effect With Pretest-Posttest Data				
ρ	*Posttest-Only*	*ANCOVA*	*Difference Score*	*Within Subjects*
0.8	128	46	51	13
0.6	128	82	102	26
0.4	128	108	154	38
0.2	128	123	205	51
0.0	128	128	256	64

Table 3 Hypothetical Data for 20 Subjects				
i	*Pre*	*Treatment 1*	*Treatment 2*	*Period 1*
1	19	19	45	19
2	28	40	50	40
3	53	66	78	66
4	44	32	41	32
5	45	60	64	60
6	50	35	52	35
7	37	47	68	47
8	23	43	49	43
9	47	34	74	34
10	61	63	65	63
11	49	68	62	62
12	11	51	46	46
13	32	53	53	53
14	26	41	43	43
15	57	66	52	52
16	36	44	38	38
17	44	25	49	49
18	56	48	81	81
19	40	55	69	69
20	35	42	51	51

within-subjects design. The table shows scores for three measures for every subject: a score on a pretest, a score under Treatment 1, and a score under Treatment 2. Although none of the three designs under consideration uses all three of these measures, these data can nevertheless be regarded as the available scores associated with each subject. By choosing a design, an experimenter is effectively choosing a subset of these data that will become known as a result of the experiment. For example, an experimenter choosing a within-subjects design would not observe the pretest scores shown in Table 2. Similarly, an experimenter choosing a between-subjects design would observe only the Treatment 1 score or the Treatment 2 score for each subject.

Five other points need to be made. First, these data were generated in accordance with Equation 1 and the assumptions previously described for the model. Second, in the within-subjects design, the first 10 subjects are assumed to receive Treatment 1 first, followed by Treatment 2. The second 10 subjects receive Treatment 2 first, followed by Treatment 1. Furthermore, a period effect of 5 points is assumed, so $\beta_1 = -2.5$ and $\beta_2 = 2.5$ in terms of the parameters of the model shown in Equation 1. Third, both the posttest-only and pretest-posttest between-subjects designs would use only those treatment condition scores obtained from Time 1. Thus, for the first 10 subjects, the dependent variable would be the scores shown in the Treatment 1 column, whereas, for the second 10 subjects, the dependent variable would be the scores shown in the Treatment 2 column. For simplicity, these scores are duplicated in a separate column labeled "Period 1." Fourth, the data were generated from a population where ρ equals 0.5, reflecting a moderate influence of systematic individual differences. Fifth, the data were generated from a population where the difference between the two treatments (i.e., $\alpha_1 - \alpha_2$) equals 10 points. In the long run, all three design and analysis approaches would thus produce an average estimate of the treatment effect equal to 10 points.

Table 4 shows the results that would be obtained for each design from analyses of the Table 3 data. Notice, as expected, that all three designs produce an estimated treatment difference of close to 10 points; however, the designs differ dramatically in the precision of this estimate. For a fixed sample size, the within-subjects design produces a much narrower confidence interval than either of the other two designs. Including a pretest and using ANCOVA produces a somewhat narrower confidence interval than the posttest-only design, but the pretest-posttest confidence interval is still substantially wider than that of the within-subjects design. Also notice that, as expected, analyzing difference scores instead of using ANCOVA in the pretest-posttest design produces a wider confidence interval, although the difference is only moderate for these data. The corresponding F and p values display the same overall pattern, consistent with the power differences expected to occur with repeated sampling. Of course, it should be emphasized that the pattern of results obtained for the Table 3 data is not guaranteed to occur in each and every sample; however, in the long run, the within-subjects design will yield the greatest precision and power, the pretest-posttest design will be intermediate (when analyzed by ANCOVA), and the posttest-only design will be last.

Qualifications

Several qualifications should be made explicit. First, the analysis of within-subjects designs becomes complicated whenever there are more than two levels of the within-subjects factor because of possible violations of the sphericity assumption. Readers are referred to Algina (1994), Keselman, Lix, and Keselman (1996), Maxwell and Arvey (1982), and Maxwell and Delaney (1990) for further details. Second, other presumed assumptions of the model may be inaccurate in some applications. For example, the pretest-posttest correlation may not equal the correlation between scores obtained from different treatment conditions, changing the relative power and precision of the pretest-posttest design. Most important, the assumption that carryover does not

---

Table 4 Comparison of Three Designs and Corresponding Analyses for Table 3 Data

---

Posttest-Only Between-Subjects Design

95% CI for $\alpha_1 - \alpha_2 = -10.50 \pm 13.20$, $F = 2.78$, $p = .113$

Pretest-Posttest Between-Subjects Design (ANCOVA)

95% CI for $\alpha_1 - \alpha_2 = -11.76 \pm 11.09$, $F = 5.01$, $p = .039$

Pretest-Posttest Between-Subjects Design (Difference Scores)

95% CI for $\alpha_1 - \alpha_2 = -12.60 \pm 11.89$, $F = 4.96$, $p = .039$

Within-Subjects Design

95% CI for $\alpha_1 - \alpha_2 = -9.90 \pm 6.27$, $F = 11.01$, $p = .004$

---

occur may be questionable in some applications of the within-subjects design. The presence of carryover can bias the resultant estimate of the treatment effect, potentially overriding any precision and power advantage. For this reason, many behavioral investigations all but demand the use of between-subjects designs, despite the loss in precision and power. The remainder of this chapter explores methods for increasing precision and power in the between-subjects design.

Between-Subjects Designs

The preceding section makes it apparent that in terms of advantages in precision and power the within-subjects design generally should be the design of choice. However, it is often the case that the questions of interest do not lend themselves to a within-subjects design. This section delineates three options that can maximize statistical power in a randomized between-subjects design without requiring an increase in sample size.

The Statistical Model and Assumptions

First, some general points of note. Following Equation 1, the statistical model for the scores on the dependent measure in the between-subjects design is given by

$$Y_{ijk} = \mu + \alpha_j + \pi_{ij} + \varepsilon_{ij}, \tag{15}$$

where Y_{ij} is the score of person i in group j. Note that Equation 15 differs from Equation 1 only in that there is no need for the β_k parameter, as there is only a single time period. As before, μ denotes a grand mean common to all observations, and the α parameter represents the effect associated with being in either the treatment or the control group. The difference between the groups is then given by $\alpha_1 - \alpha_2$. In this design, half of the subjects are randomly assigned to the treatment condition, the other half to the control condition. McClelland (1997) and others have shown that power can be increased by unequal allocation of subjects to treatments; however, we will assume equal alloca-tion throughout primarily because the benefits of unequal allo-cation would be comparable for the various designs considered here. Again, the π_{ij} parameter is the effect of person i in group j, reflecting the systematic individual differences between subjects. The ε_{ij} parameter represents the remaining unexplained vari-ance, which, in terms of this model, is considered to be error variance.

As before, the same assumptions are implicit in this model. Namely, the means of both π_{ij} and ε_{ij} are assumed to equal 0, these two effects are assumed to be independent of each other, and, finally, all errors are assumed to be independent of one an-other. In addition, there are a number of general assumptions that are made in the remainder of this chapter. First, the rela-tionship between the pretest and posttest is assumed to be ac-curately depicted by the usual ANCOVA model. This model as-sumes the relationship to be linear with homogeneous regression slopes and error variances across groups (Maxwell, 1994). Sec-ond, the reliability coefficients of the pretest and posttest are as-sumed to be equal to each other if the tests are of equivalent length. In many cases, the same measurement instrument is used as the pre- and posttest, making this assumption plausible. It should also be noted that we are not assuming that the pretest-posttest correlation is equal to the common reliability of the pre- and posttests. Maxwell (1994) notes that this will hold in the special case in which the true scores on the pre- and posttests cor-relate perfectly. However, the derivations presented in this sec-tion allow for a less-than-perfect correlation between the pretest and posttest true scores.

Posttest-Only Versus Pretest-Posttest Design

Unless the sample size is very small, the pretest-posttest AN-COVA will be at least as powerful as the posttest-only ANOVA. Whenever the pretest and posttest are even slightly correlated, the decrease in error variance accompanying ANCOVA will typ-ically more than compensate for the loss of one denominator de-gree of freedom. Although this may make the pretest-posttest design preferable from a purely statistical perspective, it may not do so from a cost-benefit perspective. McClelland (1997) points out that the efficiency of the design should also be considered. In this regard, it is quite apparent that often the pretest-posttest design requires the additional expenditure of time and effort on the part of both the experimenter and the subject (Maxwell, Cole, Arvey, & Salas, 1991). This increased cost is most apparent in the additional effort required to obtain a pretest measure. The question is whether the increased cost of the pretest-posttest design is outweighed by the benefits enjoyed in enhanced statistical power.

One alternative solution is not to use a pretest, but rather to double the length of the posttest, thereby increasing its reliability. Nicewander and Price (1983) have shown that, when this increased reliability is a result of decreased error variance, statistical power is enhanced. In other words, if the test items are parallel, share a common between-groups variance, and do not correlate perfectly, power is increased (Maxwell et al., 1991). The question now becomes: What happens if we use a single lengthened posttest as opposed to a pretest-posttest design? Obviously, using both of these may be ideal but would involve the most expenditure of time and effort. The critical issue, then, is whether doubling the posttest overcomes the power differential between the pretest-posttest and the posttest-only design. If it does, the expenditure of time and effort may be decreased without losing power.

The first step requires deriving expressions that compare the relative precision and power of the two designs. In both the pretest-posttest ANCOVA and the posttest-only ANOVA, power is a function of the numerator and denominator degrees of freedom as well as the noncentrality parameter of the noncentral F distribution. Maxwell et al. (1991) showed that the noncentrality parameter ϕ for ANCOVA in a one-way randomized between-subjects design with a levels can be written as

$$\phi = \sqrt{\frac{n \sum_{j=1}^{a} \alpha_j^2}{a\sigma_\varepsilon^2(1 - \rho_{XY}^2)}}. \tag{16}$$

Note that n is the sample size per group, α_{ij} is the deviation of group j from the grand mean, a is the number of levels of the factor, σ^2 is the within-group variance on the dependent variable, and ρ_{XY} is the within-group population correlation between the pretest (X) and the posttest (Y). This noncentrality parameter is closely related to measures of effect size in that $f = \phi/n$, where f denotes Cohen's (1988, p. 275) standardized effect size for ANOVA and ANCOVA. Thus, for a fixed sample size, the noncentrality parameter is directly proportional to the standardized effect.

Maxwell et al. (1991) also derived the noncentrality parameter for the lengthened posttest, which is as follows:

$$\phi_Z = \sqrt{\frac{n'k \sum_{j=1}^{a} \alpha_j^2}{a\sigma_\varepsilon^2[1 + (k-1)\rho_{YY'}]}}. \tag{17}$$

$\rho_{YY'}$ in Equation 17 refers to the within-group reliability of the original unlengthened posttest measure. Maxwell et al. pointed out that their derivation of Equation 17 was partly based on the perspective of items on a test. They noted, however, that Rowley (1976, 1978) showed that regarding k as the lengthening factor for the number of observation periods in a behavioral assessment produces the same result. In this instance, then, $\rho_{YY'}$ reflects the stability of behavior during the assessment period and may often have a lower numerical value than other reliability indices such as interobserver agreement.

Notice that the power of the pretest-posttest ANCOVA and lengthened posttest-only ANOVA designs will be equal if and only if their noncentrality parameters are equal to each other as follows:

$$\sqrt{\frac{n \sum_{j=1}^{a} \alpha_j^2}{a\sigma_\varepsilon^2(1 - \rho_{XY}^2)}} = \sqrt{\frac{n'k \sum_{j=1}^{a} \alpha_j^2}{a\sigma_\varepsilon^2[1 + (k-1)\rho_{YY'}]}}. \tag{18}$$

This can be reduced and rewritten to become

$$\frac{n'}{n} = \frac{(k-1)\rho_{YY'} + 1}{k(1 - \rho_{XY}^2)}. \tag{19}$$

This equation provides the general condition under which the pretest-posttest ANCOVA and the lengthened posttest-only ANOVA will have the same power.

For the purpose of this chapter, we are assuming that the sample size is fixed (predetermined) at the same number regardless of design, in which case the ratio n'/n is equal to 1. The issue then becomes whether there are any conditions under which the posttest-only ANOVA will be more powerful than the pretest-posttest ANCOVA. Under this constraint that n'/n is equal to 1, Equation 19 simplifies to

$$1 = \frac{(k-1)\rho_{YY'} + 1}{k(1 - \rho_{XY}^2)}. \tag{20}$$

Recall that the first alternative of particular interest involves using a single posttest that is doubled in length. Thus, the posttest (in the posttest-only design) now is twice as long as it was in the pretest-posttest design. Note that the two designs have the same total assessment time (e.g., the same total number of test items). For example, subjects could answer two 5-item questionnaires (pre and post) or a single 10-item questionnaire (post only). To achieve this doubling of length, k, the lengthening factor, must equal 2. When $k = 2$ and the ratio of $n'/n = 1$, Equation 20 simplifies to

$$1 = \rho_{YY'} + 2\rho_{XY}^2. \tag{21}$$

Before presenting a numerical example, a conceptual perspective on the relative merits of the ANCOVA versus the doubled posttest ANOVA is offered. The ANOVA model contains two important sources of error, namely, measurement error and error due to systematic individual differences, both of which contribute to within-group variability. Power can potentially be enhanced by reducing the influence of either of these two sources of error. Lengthening the posttest reduces the error of measurement, whereas the ANCOVA controls for systematic individual differences. Obviously, power will be enhanced the most by reducing the error from the source that is most influential in any given situation. If measurement error dominates, both ρ_{XY} and

$\rho_{YY'}$ are small, and lengthening the posttest is the most effective strategy; however, if systematic individual differences dominate, ρ_{XY} and $\rho_{YY'}$ are both likely to be large, and covarying the pretest measure will be the most effective strategy.

Equation 21 shows that the ANOVA design with the doubled posttest and the ANCOVA design with the original-length posttest will be equally powerful if and only if the value of $\rho_{YY'} + 2\rho_{XY}^2$ is equal to 1.0. Whenever $\rho_{YY'} + 2\rho_{XY}^2$ is greater than 1.0, the ANOVA will be more powerful than the ANCOVA. Conversely, whenever this sum is less than 1.0, the ANCOVA will be more powerful. Readers are referred to the article by Maxwell et al. (1991) for more detail in this regard.

Hypothetical data[1] for 20 subjects were generated in accordance with Equation 15 and the assumptions described for the model. These data are used to illustrate the comparisons discussed in this section of the chapter. The data consist of 15 measures for each subject, of which 5 are pretest scores and the remaining 10 are posttest scores. These 10 posttest items constitute the population from which 5 items are to be selected for the posttest in the pretest-posttest ANCOVA analysis. Thus, in this design, each subject is administered the 5 pretest items, then the treatment or control, followed by the 5 posttest items sampled out of the possible 10. The same set of 5 posttest items is administered to all the subjects in this particular design. In the lengthened posttest-only design, there is no pretest. Subjects are administered the treatment or control followed by all 10 of the posttest items.

These data were generated from a population where the difference between the treatment and control groups (i.e., $\alpha_1 - \alpha_2$) equals 20 points. In addition, the population values used to generate these data were $\rho_{XY} = 0.31$ and $\rho_{YY'} = 0.47$. Note that these population values ($\rho_{YY'}$ and ρ_{XY}) are lower than what might be observed in reliability indices of interobserver agreement, for instance. Table 5 shows the means and standard deviations for the data used in each of the designs. Of interest to us presently

---

[1] Requests for the data should be addressed to A. Venter, Department of Psychology, University of Notre Dame, Notre Dame, IN 46556.

Table 5 Means and Standard Deviations for the Between-Subjects Design Data

	Time	
Group	Pretest	Posttest
Posttest-Only		
Control		99.31
		(17.88)
Treatment		120.69
		(17.33)
Standard Pretest-Posttest Design (Equal Length)		
Control	98.98	101.64
	(17.31)	(18.54)
Treatment	99.36	122.12
	(16.14)	(13.60)
Two-Item Pretest Eight-Item Posttest (Unequal Length)		
Control	99.95	100.94
	(14.91)	(13.97)
Treatment	100.55	119.38
	(14.34)	(11.54)

are the descriptive statistics for the equal-length pretest-posttest design and the 10-item posttest-only design. Notice that the treatment and control groups differ by about 20 points on the posttest in the pretest-posttest design (viz., 20.48 points, which is the difference between 122.12 and 101.64). In the lengthened-posttest design, this group difference on the posttest is similar (viz., 21.38 points, which is the difference between 120.69 and 99.31). As we would expect, minimal group differences exist at the pretest in the pretest-posttest design. Table 6 illustrates the results obtained from each of the analyses of the data. The slight advantage of the pretest-posttest ANCOVA over the ANOVA on the doubled posttest in this sample is consistent with the population values used to generate the data.

Unequal Allocation of Assessment Units
Between the Pretest and Posttest

In the pretest-posttest design described previously, the assessment units were split equally between the pretest and posttest periods; however, utilizing a pretest-posttest design in which the posttest is somewhat longer than the pretest could provide even greater statistical power under certain conditions. This unequal-length pretest-posttest design constitutes the second between-subjects alternative of interest. Note that again we are assuming that the total assessment time or number of items is of some fixed duration. The general issue now is whether there is some way to allocate these units (time or items) between the pretest and posttest assessments in such a way as to maximize the statistical power to detect a treatment effect.

This question implies, at one extreme, a choice between the pretest-posttest design and the lengthened posttest-only design that was tested previously. However, it may be possible to enjoy the benefits of both types of designs by lengthening the posttest by a factor less than 2 and using the remaining assessment time to administer a pretest. Even though the pretest will then be shorter than the posttest, this design affords the opportunity to reduce both measurement error and systematic individual differences while holding total assessment time constant. In terms of these two sources of error, it is worth noting that, up to a point at least, this technique will be more effective if the data are characterized more by measurement error than systematic individual differences.

Recall that in the numerical pretest-posttest example presented earlier, the posttest consisted of five items and the pretest consisted of five parallel items. Now consider lengthening the posttest using the constraint that the total assessment time must remain constant. Thus, for each item added to the posttest, one item must be removed from the pretest. Maxwell (1994) shows that the lengthening factor k is related to the proportion P of units allocated to the posttest by the simple expression:

$$P = k/2. \tag{22}$$

For example, a value of $k = 1.5$ (alternatively, $P = .75$) would correspond to allocating 25% to the pretest and 75% of the assessment units to the posttest. Notice that $k = 1$ would result in 50% of the items being allocated to the pretest and 50% to the posttest (i.e., the standard pretest-posttest design), and $k = 2$ would result in 0% of the items being allocated to the pretest and 100% to the posttest (corresponding to our lengthened posttest-only design).

Maxwell derives a formula for the optimal choice of P from the noncentrality parameter ϕ for the pretest-posttest design in which the posttest is lengthened by the factor k and the pretest shortened by the factor $2 - k$. The optimal value of P is given by

$$P_0 = \frac{1 + \rho_{YY'}}{2(\rho_{XY} + \rho_{YY'})}. \tag{23}$$

Recall that in the numerical example $\rho_{XY} = 0.31$ and $\rho_{YY'} = 0.47$. Using these values in Equation 23 provides us with the optimal P value of .80. This indicates that the statistical power to detect a treatment effect in this population would be maximized by allocating 20% of the assessment units to the pretest and 80% to the posttest. Recall that in the numerical example the total number of assessment units was fixed to be equal to 10, either 5 in the pretest and 5 in the posttest, or 10 in the posttest. Applying $P = .80$ to the numerical example produces a pretest consisting of two units and a posttest consisting of eight units.

Table 5 shows the means and standard deviations for the data used in each of the designs. Of interest to us presently are the descriptive statistics for the unequal-length pretest-posttest design. These indicate that the treatment and control groups differ by about 20 points on the posttest (viz., 18.44 points, which is the difference between 119.38 and 100.94). Again, as expected, minimal group differences exist at the pretest.

Referring to Table 6, we can compare the results obtained from this unequal-length pretest-posttest design to both the standard pretest-posttest design with equal-length pre- and posttests

Table 6 Comparisons of the Three Types of Between-Subjects Design Analyses

Posttest-Only Design

95% CI for $\alpha_1 - \alpha_2 = -21.38 \pm 16.54$, $t = 2.72$, $p = .014$

Standard Pretest-Posttest Design

95% CI for $\alpha_1 - \alpha_2 = -20.41 \pm 15.49$, $t = 2.78$, $p = .013$

Two-Item Pretest Eight-Item Posttest Design

95% CI for $\alpha_1 - \alpha_2 = -18.40 \pm 12.41$, $t = 3.13$, $p = .006$

and the lengthened posttest-only design. The ANCOVA on the unequal-length pretest-posttest design produced a narrower confidence interval than the equal-length pretest-posttest ANCOVA and the lengthened posttest-only design. Although specific samples may produce results in which the lengthened posttest has slightly more precision than the design with eight posttest units and two pretest units, with repeated sampling allocating 20% to the pretest and 80% of the units to the posttest would produce the most precision of any of the designs; however, its advantage over the lengthened-posttest design is small even in the population for these values of ρ_{XY} and $\rho_{YY'}$, so the advantage would not necessarily be evident in any single sample.

Maxwell (1994) noted that, when the pretest and posttest measures are equally reliable (as has been assumed in this chapter), the optimal allocation of assessment units ranges anywhere between a 50%/50% split and a 0%/100% split favoring the posttest. Although the parameter values needed to calculate the optimal allocation of assessment units are often not known, Maxwell points out that for the most commonly occurring parameter values in behavioral research, a 25%/75% split favoring the posttest will typically produce results only slightly suboptimal. Not only will this 25%/75% split be only slightly inferior to the optimal design, it will often also be much superior to the weaker of the two standard designs (equal pretest-posttest and lengthened-posttest designs), which might mistakenly be chosen because of insufficient knowledge of likely population values.

The Intensive Design

Kraemer and Thiemann (1989) proposed that statistical power can be increased in data containing both systematic individual differences and measurement error by adopting a two-tiered approach. First, subjects' responses across the period of treatment are measured repeatedly with intermediate time points falling between the pretest and posttest. Time is coded 0 at the pretest and 1 at the posttest with the intermediate time points coded in fractions. Second, a regression line is fit to the responses of each subject as a function of time, and a slope is calculated for each individual subject. Then an average slope calculated for each of the groups (control and treatment) serves as the outcome measure.

Kraemer and Thiemann (1989) showed that, with random assignment, comparing groups on their endpoint scores (i.e., posttest scores), change scores, or slopes all test the same null hypothesis; however, as soon as measurement error or sampling error is introduced, these three outcome measures differ in their precision. The advantage of the slope is that, as a weighted sum of unreliably positively correlated observations, it tends to be more reliable than any one of its component observations. In addition, given that the slope calculation requires just two time points and that multiple measurements are collected in this design, those subjects with missing data need not be absolutely discarded from the analysis. In either endpoint or change score analysis, missing data points typically result in the loss of that subject's data and a drop in power.

Kraemer and Thiemann (1989) noted that, when test-retest reliability is high and weak individual differences exist at the pretest, the lower cost of the endpoint design in terms of time and effort may make it more preferable; however, as the test-retest reliability becomes weaker, the pretest and slope measures become more useful. Furthermore, the slope is interpretable as a measure of consistent directional trend, which facilitates the examination of potentially different patterns of responses across time between subjects. The endpoint and prepost change scores would not allow for this practice. Interestingly, Kraemer and Thiemann's approach can be viewed as a special case of multilevel modeling, also referred to as hierarchical linear modeling (Bryk & Raudenbush, 1987).

General Conclusion

We presented a variety of methods that can increase the power and precision to detect intervention effects. Although social and behavioral scientists in some areas of research have long benefited from the use of within-subjects designs to enhance power and precision, recent research has presented researchers with a variety of alternatives for improving power and precision in between-subjects designs. We described conditions under which some of these alternatives are likely to be most useful, but further research is needed to delineate fully specific parameter values most conducive to any particular design. However, as the range of options expands, it is important that behavioral researchers realize that they can increase power and precision not just by increasing their sample size but also by wisely choosing their design.

In conclusion, this chapter is not, nor was it intended to be, exhaustive in its review of strategies for managing and improving power within randomized designs attempting to detect treatment effects. Throughout the chapter, we have tried, wherever possible, to provide readers with references providing other strategies or more detail about those that we have reviewed. With this in mind, additional sources that may be particularly useful for other discussions of strategies for increasing power or simply for calculating power in specific designs include publications by Allison et al. (1997), Cohen (1988), Kraemer (1991), Levin (1997), McClelland (1997), O'Brien and Muller (1993), and Satorra and Saris (1985).

References

Algina, J. (1994). Some alternative approximate tests for a split plot design. *Multivariate Behavioral Research, 29*, 365–384.

Allison, D. B., Allison, R. L., Faith, M. S., Paultre, F., & Pi-Sunyer, F. X. (1997). Power and money: Designing statistically powerful studies while minimizing financial costs. *Psychological Methods, 2*, 20–33.

Arvey, R. D., & Cole, D. A. (1989). Evaluating change due to training. In I. L. Goldstein (Ed.), *Training and development in organizations: Frontiers of industrial and organizational psychology* (pp. 89–117). San Francisco: Jossey-Bass.

Bryk, A. S., & Raudenbush, S. W. (1987). Application of hierarchical linear models to assessing change. *Psychological Bulletin, 101*, 147–158.

Cohen, J. (1988). *Statistical power analysis for the behavioral sciences* (2nd ed.). Hillsdale, NJ: Erlbaum.

Keselman, J. C., Lix, L. M., & Keselman, H. J. (1996). The analysis of repeated measurements: A quantitative research synthesis. *British Journal of Mathematical and Statistical Psychology, 49*, 275–298.

Kraemer, H. C. (1991). To increase power in randomized clinical trials without increasing sample size. *Psychopharmacology Bulletin, 27*, 217–224.

Kraemer, H. C., & Thiemann, S. (1989). A strategy to use soft data effectively in randomized controlled clinical trials. *Journal of Consulting Clinical Psychology, 57*, 148–154.

Levin, J. R. (1997). Overcoming feelings of powerlessness in "aging" researchers: A primer on statistical power in analysis of variance designs. *Psychology and Aging, 12*, 84–106.

Maxwell, S. E. (1994). Optimal allocation of assessment time in randomized pretest-posttest designs. *Psychological Bulletin, 115*, 142–152.

Maxwell, S. E., & Arvey, R. D. (1982). Small sample profile analysis with many variables. *Psychological Bulletin, 92*, 778–785.

Maxwell, S. E., Cole, D. A., Arvey, R. D., & Salas, E. (1991). A comparison of methods for increasing power in randomized between-subjects designs. *Psychological Bulletin, 110*, 328–337.

Maxwell, S. E., & Delaney, H. D. (1990). *Designing experiments and analyzing data: A model comparison perspective.* Belmont, CA: Wadsworth.

McClelland, G. H. (1997). Optimal design in psychological research. *Psychological Methods, 2,* 3–19.

Nicewander, W. A., & Price, J. M. (1983). Reliability of measurement and the power of statistical tests: Some new results. *Psychological Bulletin, 94,* 524–533.

O'Brien, R. G., & Muller, K. E. (1993). Unified power analysis for t-tests through multivariate hypotheses. In L. K. Edwards (Ed.), *Applied analysis of variance in behavioral science.* New York: Marcel Dekker.

Rosenthal, R., & Rosnow, R. L. (1985). *Contrast analysis: Focused comparisons in the analysis of variance.* New York: Cambridge University Press.

Rowley, G. L. (1976). The reliability of observational measures. *American Educational Research Journal, 13,* 51–59.

Rowley, G. (1978). The relationship of reliability in classroom research to the amount of observation: An extension of the Spearman–Brown formula. *Journal of Educational Measurement, 15,* 165–180.

Satorra, A., & Saris, W. E. (1985). Power of the likelihood ratio test in covariance structure analysis. *Psychometrika, 50,* 83–90.

Senn, S. (1993). *Cross-over trials in clinical research.* New York: Wiley.

3

Effect Sizes and Significance Levels in Small-Sample Research

Sharon H. Kramer & Robert Rosenthal

MOST SOCIAL SCIENCE RESEARCHERS have, at some point, discovered that small samples can present big problems. However, there are occasions when we are simply unable to avoid using small samples in our research. For example, the phenomenon we are studying may be rare; or we may have limited resources to allocate to pay subjects; or we may be conducting a pilot study. This chapter focuses on the effect size estimate and its particular usefulness and importance to situations of small-sample research. We first look at issues of effect size within a single study, discussing several different types of effect sizes, providing tools that can facilitate interpretation of effect sizes, and showing the value of computing contrasts within studies. We then look across studies showing the usefulness of considering effect sizes, first, when comparing two studies to answer questions of replication, and, second, when looking across many studies

when conducting a meta-analysis. Finally, although the sugges-
tions, strategies, and recommendations described in this chapter
are particularly useful when faced with the problems presented by small samples, they should not be disregarded, but rather,
they should be strongly encouraged, even when samples are not
small.

Effect Sizes: An Introduction

When research is conducted, the researcher is generally interested in the answer to the question: What is the relationship between any variable X and any variable Y? To answer this question thoroughly, two estimates are needed: (1) an estimate of the
level of significance at which we can reject the null hypothesis,
expressed by a p value associated with a significance test such as
t, F, Z, or χ^2; and (2) an estimate of the degree of departure from
the null hypothesis, or, in other words, an estimate of the magnitude of the relationship between variables X and Y, expressed by
an effect size estimate such as r or d. (Specific examples of different types of effect sizes are discussed in greater detail below.)

Relationship Between Effect Sizes and Significance Tests

The relationship between an effect size and a significance test
is given by the following basic equation (Rosenthal & Rosnow,
1991):

$$\text{Test of Significance} = \text{Size of Effect} \times \text{Size of Study.} \qquad (1)$$

Table 1 provides several examples of this relationship.

As the equations in Table 1 illustrate, as any study increases
its sample size, it will obtain more significant results (except in
the unusual case where an effect size is truly zero in which case
a larger study will not produce a result any more significant than
a smaller study). An effect size, however, would not be affected
by the size of the sample used in the study. Consider the following example of two studies investigating the impact of a new
recruiting program on hiring minority job applicants.

Table 1 Examples of the Relationship Between Effect Sizes and Tests of Significance

Test of Significance	=	Size of Effect	×	Size of Study	
	=		×		(1)
$\chi^2(1)$	=	ϕ^2	×	N	(2)
Z	=	ϕ	×	$\sqrt{N}$	(3)
t	=	$\dfrac{r}{\sqrt{1-r^2}}$	×	$\sqrt{df}$	(4)
t	=	d	×	$\dfrac{\sqrt{df}}{2}$	(5)
F	=	$\dfrac{r^2}{1-r^2}$	×	df_{error}	(6)
t^a	=	d	×	$\sqrt{df}$	(7)

[a] Nonindependent observations.

Table 2 Two Studies Investigating the Impact of a New Recruiting Program on Minority Hiring: Effect Size Estimate Is Unaffected by Increased Sample Size

	Study A		Study B	
	Minorities	Nonminorities	Minorities	Nonminorities
Program	Hired	Hired	Hired	Hired
New	200	100	2	1
Old	100	100	1	1

Study A	Study B
$N = 500$	$N = 5$
$\chi^2(1) = 13.89$	$\chi^2(1) = .139$
$p = .00019$	$p = .70^a$
$\phi = .17$	$\phi = .17$

[a] From the Fisher exact test (see Appendix).

In the first study of Table 2, 200 of the 300 applicants hired under the new program were minorities, whereas 100 of the 200 were minorities under the old program. The results of this experiment showed a clearly significant p value ($p = .00019$) and an associated effect size of $\phi = .17$, where ϕ is the special case of Pearson's r for two dichotomous variables. In the second study, two of the three applicants who were hired under the new recruiting program were minorities, whereas only one of the two was a minority under the old program. Due to the small sample size, the results of this experiment were far from significant ($p = .70$, from a Fisher exact test; see Appendix), yet the associated effect size is the same as that found with the substantially larger, more significant, study ($\phi = .17$). As we see from the equations in Table 1, effect size is unchanged by the reduction in the sample size from 500 to 5.

Types of Effect Size Estimates

Table 3 shows three families of effect size indicators. The first effect size shown, Cohen's d, is part of a family of three effect size indicators which are all standardized mean differences. Each of these three indicators, d, Δ, and g, use the difference between the

Table 3 Three Families of Effect Size Indicators	
Effect Size Indicator	Definition
Standardized Differences Between Means	
Cohen's d	$(M_1 - M_2)/s_{pooled}$
Glass' Δ	$(M_1 - M_2)/s_{control\ group}$
Hedges' g	$(M_1 - M_2)/s_{pooled}$
Differences Between Proportions	
Cohen's g	$P - .50$
d'	$P_1 - P_2$
Cohen's h	$\arcsin P_1 - \arcsin P_2$
Product Moment Correlation Coefficient (r) and Functions of r	
Pearson's r	$\sum(Z_x Z_y)/N$
Fisher's Zr	$1/2 \log_e[(1 + r)/(1 - r)]$
Cohen's q	$Zr_1 - Zr_2$

means of two groups as their numerators, differing only in the estimate of the standard deviation used in their denominators.

The next three indicators are all examples of differences between proportions (P). Cohen's g is the difference between an obtained proportion and a proportion of .50. The effect size d' is the difference between two obtained proportions (P_1 and P_2) and Cohen's h is the difference between the obtained proportions after they have been transformed to angles.

The final three effect sizes shown in Table 3 include the Pearson product moment correlation coefficient (r) and related estimates. Fisher's Zr is a transformation of r (see footnote 4 for a discussion of Fisher's Zr). Although it could be employed as an effect size estimate, it is not done so typically because it is not as easily interpreted as r. Cohen's q is an effect size that estimates the magnitude of the difference between two effect sizes. (For a more detailed discussion of these different types of effect sizes, see Cohen, 1977, 1988; Rosenthal, 1991, 1994; Rosenthal, Rosnow, & Rubin, 1997. For a discussion of effect size indicators that compare medians rather than means, see Kraemer & Andrews, 1982; Krauth, 1983.) Additionally, when sample sizes in a given study are very small, some useful adjustments to various effect sizes are available. These are summarized elsewhere along with references for readers wanting more detail (Rosenthal, 1994).

The effect size r is sometimes preferred for a number of reasons. First, by rearranging Equation 4 in Table 1 to

$$r = \sqrt{\frac{t^2}{t^2 + df}}, \tag{8}$$

r can be easily computed from t. Second, it can be used when both variables are continuous, when one variable is dichotomous and the other is continuous (in which case it is expressed as the point biserial r), when both variables are dichotomous (the phi coefficient, ϕ), and when both variables are ranked (Spearman rho, ρ). Third, because many outcome variables are used in the social sciences, using correlational (r) effect sizes (and the other effect sizes shown in Table 3) allows for sensible comparisons across studies that would not be possible using the various outcome variables that often do not have intrinsic meaning, such as regression coefficients or unstandardized differences.

Effect Sizes in Small-Sample Studies

Although it is always important to calculate and consider the practical importance of an effect size when analyzing the results of a study, it is particularly valuable when dealing with a study that has a small sample. Quite commonly, small samples will lead to results that do not reach the conventional level of significance—p values of less than .05, which might mistakenly lead the researcher to accept the null hypothesis of no relationship. Yet, by considering the effect size, the researcher might uncover a potentially interesting and valuable relationship that might have yielded more significant results if only more subjects were added to the study.

Table 4 highlights some of the issues presented by considering effect sizes as well as significance levels when interpreting the results of a study. If we were to dichotomize effect sizes and significance levels into "large" and "small,"[1] there are four possible outcomes of p levels and effect sizes. If we obtained a combination of a large level of significance (a large p) and a small effect size, as in the lower right cell of Table 4, we would not have a dilemma for both pieces of evidence are in rough agreement. Similarly, if we obtained the opposite, a small level of significance and a large effect size, as in the upper left cell of Table 4, we would easily conclude that we have successfully detected an effect. However, suppose we were confronted with a large or nonsignificant p and a large effect size, as in the lower left cell in Table 4; what should we conclude? If we concluded on the basis of the significance level that there was "nothing going on," we might be making a serious mistake. A small sample size

---

[1] This dichotomization is done here for illustrative purposes, but should not be taken as an endorsement of a yes/no type of approach to data analysis. Both effect sizes and p values should usually be regarded as points on a continuum rather than as values falling above or below a line of acceptance/rejection.

Table 4 Four Possible Outcomes of Effect Sizes and Significance Levels for a Given Study

Significance Level	Effect Size	
	Large	Small
Small	No inferential problem	Mistake statistical significance for practical importance
Large	Mistakenly conclude "nothing going on"	No inferential problem

may have led to our nonsignificant results and failure to detect the effect that would have been detected with a larger sample. It would probably be wise to continue our investigation with a larger sample before we were comfortably to conclude that the null hypothesis is true. On the other hand, what should we conclude if we obtained a very significant result (a small p) but a small effect size, as in the upper right cell in Table 4? We might embrace the results of our study as "highly significant" and very important when in fact the only reason we reached significance is due to a large sample size. Our results might actually have little practical importance regardless of their significant outcome.[2]

---

[2] It is important to point out that a very small effect size may sometimes have great practical importance. For example, a recent study of the effects of aspirin on reducing heart attacks was found to have an effect size of $r = .034$ (Steering Committee of the Physicians' Health Study Research Group, 1988). This might seem at first like a small and unimportant effect, yet based on this result the study was prematurely terminated since it had become clear that the benefits to patients were so substantial. When this small r is converted to a binomial effect size display (Rosenthal & Rubin, 1982) in which the correlation is shown as the difference in outcome rates between the experimental and the control group, taking aspirin is displayed as associated with a 3.4% decrease in heart attacks, a small but clearly important effect. (For details on computing a binomial effect size display, see Rosenthal & Rubin, 1982; Rosenthal et al., 1997.)

Counternull Value of an Effect Size

A relatively new statistic that helps the researcher avoid the common mistake of accepting nonsignificant results as evidence for a null effect size (e.g., an effect size of .00[3]) is the counternull (Rosenthal & Rubin 1994). The counternull provides an effect size value that is equally as likely to be true as the null effect size of .00. For example, assume that we were examining the effects of a rare type of trauma on later levels of psychopathology for a small number of patients ($N = 10$). Our study yielded a nonsignificant p value ($p = .20$) with an effect size of $r = .44$. To help us avoid the erroneous interpretation of the nonsignificant results as being evidence for a .00 relationship between our two variables, the counternull shows that it is as equally as likely that the true effect size is a very large $r = .74$ as that it is $r = .00$.[4]

Whereas the previous example illustrates the potential danger of treating a nonsignificant result as indicating a null effect size, the following example illustrates that we should also not necessarily treat a significant nonnull value of an effect size as being scientifically important. This might be an example of a re-

---

[3] Generally, the null value of the effect size would be .00. An example in which it is not might be the case of a study testing a new treatment against a placebo control. If an earlier developed treatment is believed to have an average effect size of, for example, $r = .40$, then the null hypothesis is that the new treatment is not different from the earlier developed treatment and the null effect size would be $r = .40$, not $r = .00$ (Rosenthal et al., 1997).

[4] If the null effect size is assumed to be $r = .00$, the counternull can be computed quite simply by first finding Fisher's Zr equivalent of the obtained r. In the example in the text, the obtained r of .44 converts to a Fisher Zr of .47. This value is then doubled (.94) and the r associated with that value ($r = .74$) is the counternull. It is necessary to first convert r to Fisher's Zr because, as the population value of r gets farther from zero, the distribution of rs sampled from that population becomes more and more skewed. Fisher's Zr is a transformation of r that is distributed nearly normally (Fisher, 1928). When dealing with effect size estimates of d or g, both of which have symmetric sampling distributions, their counternull values are simple twice their observed values. If the null effect size is nonzero, then the counternull is calculated by

$$2(ES_{\text{obtained}} - ES_{\text{null}}) = \text{Counternull}. \tag{9}$$

sult that would fall into the upper right cell of Table 4. Suppose a very large clinical trial were conducted to test the effects of a new expensive fiber intended to lower postprandial blood glucose levels. The results were clearly significant ($p = .002$), but the effect size was only $r = .03$. In this example, the null value of the effect size is again .00 and the counternull is .06.[5] Thus, despite the fact that the clinical trial showed the new fiber to be statistically significant, the decrease in blood glucose, even if as large as the counternull would suggest, may still be just too small (especially relative to its expense) to warrant its recommendation over the old fiber treatment.

Effect Sizes in Contrasts Within a Study: Three Types of rs

The examples discussed to this point have all dealt with focused tests, for example, comparisons of two groups employing t tests or χ^2 with 1 degree of freedom (df). These each yield a level of significance and single effect size associated with that significance test. However, often we may be studying more than two groups and will be computing analyses such as F tests that can have more than one df in their numerator. Consider, for example, a study in which the performance of 50 children, 5 groups of 10 at each of 5 different age levels (5, 8, 11, 14, 17), is measured on a new physical coordination task. The mean performance times for each group are 25, 30, 40, 50, and 55, respectively. The analysis of variance (ANOVA) computed on the 50 individual scores found an overall $F(4, 45) = 1.03$, $p = .40$. Should the researcher conclude that age does not make a difference in performance? Clearly, there seems to be a linear relationship in these data. In fact, if we correlate the five groups' means with a set of linear lambda weights of -2, -1, 0, $+1$, $+2$, the resulting correlation is $r = .99$. This r is called an r_{alerting} (Rosenthal et al., 1997) because it "alerts" us that there is a linear relationship in our data and that we should investigate further using contrasts. The r_{alerting} is particularly helpful when we have a number of group means and

---

[5] An r of .03 has a corresponding Fisher Zr of .03, which is then doubled (.06). The counternull value associated with this is then an r of .06.

want a quick and general overview of whether our hypothesized trend is supported by the data. "Omnibus" or "diffuse" tests, such as the $F(4, 45)$ computed previously, are usually of little value, and focused tests such as contrasts are especially important to compute. Not only do contrasts yield more precise interpretable effect sizes, but, especially important when doing small-sample research, they give us greater statistical power than do omnibus tests.

In the example just given, the r_{alerting} alerted us that we would be wise to compute a contrast to test the hypothesis that performance is linearly associated with age. One way to compute this contrast[6] is to use the following equation, which includes the r_{alerting} of .99 that we found earlier:

$$r^2_{\text{alerting}} \times F_{\text{omnibus}} \times df_{\text{numerator}} = F_{\text{contrast}}. \tag{10}$$

Applying this equation, we find that $(.99)^2 \times 1.03 \times 4 = 4.04$, which is our $F_{\text{contrast}}(1, 45)$ associated with a p of .05. By computing a contrast in this example, we went from a rather large p value of .40 to a much smaller p of .05.

The effect size associated with this F_{contrast} is referred to as the r_{contrast} and can be calculated by

$$r_{\text{contrast}} = \sqrt{\frac{SS_{\text{contrast}}}{SS_{\text{contrast}} + SS_{\text{error}}}} \tag{11}$$

or, alternatively, if the sums of squares (SSs) are not available, by using Equation 8. Because $t^2 = F$ when F has 1 degree of freedom in the numerator (which is always the case with an F_{contrast}), applying Equation 8, we find the r_{contrast} to be

$$\sqrt{\frac{4.04}{4.04 + 45}} = .29,$$

which tells us that there is a substantial linear relationship of age with children's performance.

---

[6] For details on computing contrasts, see Rosenthal et al. (1997).

Table 5 Three Types of *rs* That Can Be Computed From a
Contrast Analysis

Type of r	Definition
$r_{alerting}$	Correlation of aggregate means with lambda weights $$= \sqrt{\frac{SS_{contrast}}{SS_{contrast} + SS_{noncontrast}}}$$
$r_{contrast}$	Correlation of individuals' scores with lambda weights partialing out other between-group variation $$= \sqrt{\frac{SS_{contrast}}{SS_{contrast} + SS_{error}}}$$
$r_{effect\ size}$	Correlation of individuals' scores with lambda weights $$= \sqrt{\frac{SS_{contrast}}{SS_{contrast} + SS_{noncontrast} + SS_{error}}}$$

In addition to the $r_{contrast}$ and the $r_{alerting}$ already discussed, there is also a third type of r that can be considered when computing contrasts—the $r_{effect\ size}$ (see Table 5).

The $r_{effect\ size}$ is what we intuitively think of as an effect size correlation; it is the correlation between individuals' scores and their group membership scores (i.e., their lambda weights). When there are only two groups, the $r_{effect\ size}$ is the same as the $r_{contrast}$; however, when more than two groups are compared, the $r_{contrast}$ will be larger than the $r_{effect\ size}$ because the $r_{contrast}$ is a partial correlation, a correlation between the subjects' scores on the outcome variable and the lambdas associated with their groups after eliminating all between-group sources of variation other than the contrast in question (Rosenthal et al., 1997). In other words, the $r_{effect\ size}$ presents a more conservative estimate of the size of the effect of the phenomenon of interest because it regards as noise or error the other between-group sources of variation that might be in the system. The $r_{contrast}$, however, presents a purer view of the size of the effect of the phenomenon of interest, disregarding these other between-group sources of variation. For instance, in the example cited previously, other variables such as children's sex and socioeconomic status might also make a difference on the effect of age on performance times. However, if we were not very interested in the impact of these other variables but wanted a pure test-tube sort of view of only the relationship between age and performance, we could obtain this estimate from the $r_{contrast}$. In general, it is most valuable when performing contrasts to compute and to report all three of the types of rs for the unique information each can give.

Effect Sizes Across Studies

The Nature of Replication

Overemphasis on significance levels and underemphasis on effect sizes present problems not only when interpreting the results of single studies as discussed previously, but also potential difficulties when looking across pairs of studies. The question of whether a study has successfully replicated an earlier study has commonly been interpreted to mean that the later study has succeeded in rejecting the null at the same critical p level (e.g., $p < .05$). This presents a particular obstacle with small-sample studies, which, because of their small chance of reaching significance, would routinely show a failure to replicate larger studies.

Consider the following example: Study A found that a new intervention was able to improve a given outcome at a $p < .05$ level of significance, whereas Study B failed to reach the same level of significance. These results would commonly be interpreted to mean that Study B has failed to replicate Study A. However, on closer inspection, it is shown that both studies had found the same effect size of $r = .30$. Study B failed to replicate Study A's results simply due to a lower level of power than Study A; however, in terms of effect size, it perfectly replicated the earlier study's results.

One reason for our common failure to understand replication is that p levels are erroneously understood as the likelihood of successful replication. Thus, if Study A finds a result significant at .05, it is assumed that there is a 95% likelihood of replication. In fact, this .05 is the likelihood of making a Type I error, but the likelihood of replication lies with the power of the study. If we assume that this study is typical of studies in the behavioral sciences, then its power would be around .50 (Cohen, 1962; Sedlemeier & Gigerenzer, 1989). Thus, even though there is a substantial effect of $r = .30$, and even though Study B has, in truth, perfectly replicated Study A, there was actually only a 50% chance that Study B would also find Study A's $p < .05$ results or only a 25% chance (.50 × .50 = .25) that both studies would find results significant at the .05 level (Rosenthal, 1993).

Consideration of effect sizes in questions of the success of replications is thus essential for all studies, especially for studies with small samples. Focusing on effect sizes would help prevent the researcher from dismissing a study as failing to replicate simply because it had low power. By focusing on effect sizes rather than exclusively on the significance level, studies with small samples are given a fairer chance to show replicational success. Furthermore, this approach also allows us to see the degree of failure to replicate. For example, a study that found an effect size of $r = .15$ compared to a study with an effect size of $r = .20$ found a failure to replicate by only .05 units in r. This can be compared to another set of studies that might have had a failure to replicate by a larger degree, for example, .30 units in r.[7] The first set could be said to show more successful replication than the second set, a comparison of degree that would not be feasible when only looking at dichotomous p-level replications of accepting or rejecting the null hypothesis (Rosenthal, 1993, 1995).

---

[7] An additional method for comparing the two effect sizes to index the success of replication is to first convert the rs to Fisher Zrs and then compare them using the equation

$$\frac{Zr_1 - Zr_2}{\sqrt{\frac{1}{N_1 - 3} + \frac{1}{N_2 - 3}}} = Z, \tag{12}$$

where N is the number of subjects in each study (Rosenthal, 1991; Rosenthal & Rubin, 1982; Snedecor & Cochran, 1989).

Meta-Analysis

In addition to being interested in whether one study successfully replicates another, we are often interested in looking across many studies or at whole bodies of research to see whether the studies are consistent in their findings. A rapidly growing tool that allows us to address these kinds of questions is meta-analysis. Meta-analysis, or the analysis of analyses, is the quantitative cumulation of research results addressing a specific research question. The term was first used in a research synthesis of several hundred studies, all asking the question of whether psychotherapy works better than a control condition (Glass, 1976; Glass, McGaw, & Smith, 1981; Smith, Glass, & Miller, 1980). Glass first located studies that asked this question, then found the effect size for each study, and then statistically described the findings of all the studies combined. Since that time, nearly 2,000 meta-analyses have been conducted in the social and health sciences (Bausell, Li, Gau, & Soeken, 1995; Hunter & Schmidt, 1997).

Meta-analysis focuses on the effect size as well as the level of significance within each study. Thus, similar to the previous discussion under the topic of replication, meta-analysis has often shown a group of studies that seem to have contradictory results to be, in fact, quite similar. By focusing on effect sizes across studies rather than statistical significance, an illusion of conflict has often been cleared away (Cohen, 1994). Because of this, meta-analysis has been recognized not only for its important contributions to furthering research in many fields, but it has also proven to be an effective tool for social and public policy making (Hunter & Schmidt, 1997).

Combining Studies: Pooling Pilots. One way in which meta-analysis can be used strategically for small-sample research is that it allows the researcher to combine the results of many studies that each have a small number of subjects, any of which might not have reached significance on their own, but which together might. Often in clinical research, the number of patients available is so small that all the researcher is able to do is to conduct pilot studies, none of which will ever reach a significance level of

$p < .05$ because of the small N; however, the researcher is able to combine the results of these individual studies meta-analytically. This is a phenomenon that often presents itself in the cancer research field, in which small pilot samples are often used to test the effects of experimental chemotherapy treatments. Commonly, the number of subjects in these studies is less than 20, and p levels rarely reach significance at the .05 levels. Meta-analyses looking at the overall effects of several of these studies combined have been appearing with increasing frequency in medical journals.

Another example of pooling pilots in medical research appeared in *Science* (Cohen, 1993). In two pilot studies, experimental monkeys were vaccinated using SIV (akin to HIV), whereas control monkeys were not. In the first pilot, six monkeys were available—three vaccinated and three controls. The results showed two of the three vaccinated monkeys and none of the three controls in better health ($p = .20$, one-tailed). In the second pilot, 11 animals were available and two of five experimentals and none of six controls wound up in better health ($p = .18$, one-tailed). Although the results of neither of these pilot studies were significant, if treated meta-analytically, they show clear benefits of vaccination ($p = .11$).[8]

Simpson's Paradox. The question might be raised: If we are dealing with several studies, all of which only utilize a small number of subjects, why not simply combine the raw data and then find the overall effect size of this one data set rather than calculating each study's effect size and then meta-analytically combining the effect sizes? The answer to this question has been called Simpson's paradox or Yule's paradox after the researchers who looked at this problem many years ago (Simpson, 1951; Yule, 1903). Consider the data in Table 6 of two studies each reporting the number of deaths in a study comparing a new treatment to a control treatment. The two studies each obtain a strong effect

---

[8] Meta-analytic procedures for combining and comparing studies will not be presented in this chapter. For more detail about these procedures, the reader may wish to consult Cooper and Hedges (1994), Kramer and Rosenthal (1998), and Rosenthal (1984, 1991). For more details on pooling pilots, see Rosenthal (1995).

favoring the treatment condition ($r = .33$); however, when the raw data from the two studies are pooled, as in column 3, the effect disappears. Although both studies used 200 subjects, 75% of the patients in Study 1 received the new treatment, whereas 75% of the patients in Study 2 received the control treatment. Thus, when combining the raw data, the inequalities of the row and column totals lead to this paradox of the disappearing effects. From Simpson's paradox, we see the potential danger of pooling raw data and the importance of computing effect sizes separately for each study and then combining the effect sizes meta-analytically.

Meta-Analysis With a Small Number of Studies

Meta-analyses can be done with as few as two studies or with as many studies as are located. In general, the procedures are the same and, assuming a thorough search for studies was conducted, having only a few studies should not be of great concern.

File Drawer Analysis. One analysis the meta-analyst may wish to consider, particularly if the number of located studies is small, is the file drawer analysis (Rosenthal, 1979). The file drawer analysis addresses the concern that there is a greater likelihood that published studies will have more significant results than unpublished studies and, therefore, they might not be representative of the population of studies that have been conducted. Thus, if a researcher had located 15 studies but was

Table 6 An Illustration of Simpson's Paradox: The Effects of Pooling Raw Data From Tables of Counts

	Study					
	1		*2*		*1 and 2 Pooled*	
Condition	*Alive*	*Dead*	*Alive*	*Dead*	*Alive*	*Dead*
Treatment	50	100	50	0	100	100
Control	0	50	100	50	100	100
	$r = .33$		$r = .33$		$r = .00$	

concerned that there might be a large number of unlocated studies that, if analyzed, would show primarily null results, the file drawer analysis would provide the answer to exactly how many more studies' averaging null results would need to be tucked away in file drawers before one could conclude that the results of the 15 studies were due to sampling bias.

Confounded Moderators. The one problem that may present itself when conducting a meta-analysis with only a small number of studies is that of detecting moderator variables. Moderator variables are variables hypothesized to moderate or alter the magnitude of a relationship, such as gender of the subjects or duration of therapy. First, when the sample size in a meta-analysis is viewed as the number of studies, the power to detect a given moderating variable relationship in the meta-analysis may be low (Hunter & Schmidt, 1990, 1997). Second, with small numbers of studies, the moderators may be confounded with each other. Consider the following example: A meta-analysis of 20 studies examining the effects of culture on management styles showed that, although, overall, managers from Eastern countries involved subordinates more in decision making than managers from Western countries, this relationship was moderated by gender. However, on closer examination, the moderating variable of gender was found to be strongly correlated with size of company because the subsample of studies that looked at female managers also happened to be smaller companies. In a meta-analysis, it is impossible to disentangle these effects completely. The researcher should be guided by theory in approaching the analysis and should be cautious in the interpretation of results as suggestive of a causal relationship (Hall, Tickle-Degnen, Rosenthal, & Mosteller, 1994).

Conclusion

One of the most common problems presented by small-sample research is the low power to achieve statistically significant results. Yet, it would seem that the real problem is not so much one of low power but of researchers' continued reliance on statistical significance rather than on effect size estimates. As this chapter has shown, effect size estimates are unaffected by the size of the study and are essential to determining the practical importance of a study. Calculation and consideration of effect sizes is a particularly important issue when the study has only a small number of subjects but should also be valued regardless of the number of subjects both when analyzing the results of an individual study or when considering the results of more than one study.

References

Bausell, R. B., Li, Y., Gau, M., & Soeken, K. L. (1995). The growth of meta-analytic literature from 1980 to 1993. *Evaluation and the Health Professions, 18*, 238–251.

Cohen, J. (1962). The statistical power of abnormal-social psychological research: A review. *Journal of Abnormal and Social Psychology, 65*, 145–153.

Cohen, J. (1977). *Statistical power analysis for the behavioral sciences* (Rev. ed.). New York: Academic Press.

Cohen, J. (1988). *Statistical power analysis for the behavioral sciences* (2nd ed.). Hillsdale, NJ: Erlbaum.

Cohen, J. (1993). A new goal: Preventing disease, not infection. *Science, 262*, 1820–1821.

Cohen, J. (1994). The earth is round (*p* < .05). *American Psychologist, 49*, 997–1003.

Cooper, H. M., & Hedges, L. V. (Eds.). (1994). *The handbook of research synthesis*. Newbury Park, CA: Sage.

Fisher, R. A. (1928). *Statistical methods for research workers* (2nd ed.). London: Oliver & Boyd.

Glass, G. V. (1976). Primary, secondary, and meta-analysis of research. *Educational Researcher, 5*, 351–379.

Glass, G. V., McGaw, B., & Smith, M. L. (1981). *Meta-analysis in social research*. Beverly Hills, CA: Sage.

Hall, J. A., Tickle-Degnen, L., Rosenthal, R., & Mosteller, F. (1994). Hypotheses and problems in research synthesis. In

H. M. Cooper & L. V. Hedges (Eds.), *The handbook of research synthesis* (pp. 17–28). Newbury Park, CA: Sage.

Hunter, J. E., & Schmidt, F. L. (1990). *Methods of meta-analysis: Correcting error and bias in research findings.* Newbury Park, CA: Sage.

Hunter, J. E., & Schmidt, F. L. (1997). Cumulative research knowledge and social policy formulation: The critical role of meta-analysis. *Psychology, Public Policy and Law, 2,* 324–347.

Kraemer, H. C., & Andrews, G. (1982). A nonparametric technique for meta-analysis effect size calculation. *Psychological Bulletin, 94,* 404–412.

Kramer, S. H., & Rosenthal, R. (1998). Meta-analytic research synthesis. In A. S. Bellack & M. Hersen (Eds.), *Comprehensive clinical psychology* (Vol. 3) (pp. 351–368). New York: Pergamon Press.

Krauth, J. (1983). Nonparametric effect size estimation: A comment on Kraemer and Andrews. *Psychological Bulletin, 94,* 190–192.

Rosenthal, R. (1979). The "file drawer problem" and tolerance for null results. *Psychological Bulletin, 86,* 638–641.

Rosenthal, R. (1984). *Meta-analytic procedures for social research.* Beverly Hills, CA: Sage.

Rosenthal, R. (1991). *Meta-analytic procedures for social research* (Rev. ed.). Newbury Park, CA: Sage.

Rosenthal, R. (1993). Cumulating evidence. In G. Keren & C. Lewis (Eds.), *A handbook for data analysis in the behavioral sciences: Methodological issues* (pp. 519–559). Hillsdale, NJ: Erlbaum.

Rosenthal, R. (1994). Parametric measures of effect size. In H. M. Cooper & L. V. Hedges (Eds.), *The handbook of research synthesis* (pp. 231–244). Newbury Park, CA: Sage.

Rosenthal, R. (1995). Progress in clinical psychology: Is there any? *Clinical Psychology: Science and Practice, 2,* 133–150.

Rosenthal, R., & Rosnow, R. L. (1991). *Essentials of behavioral research: Methods and data analysis* (2nd ed.). New York: McGraw-Hill.

Rosenthal, R., Rosnow, R. L., & Rubin, D. B. (1997). *Contrasts and effect sizes in behavioral research: A correlational approach.* Unpublished manuscript, Harvard University, Cambridge, MA.

Rosenthal, R., & Rubin, D. B. (1982). A simple, general purpose display of magnitude of experimental effect. *Journal of Educational Psychology, 74*, 166–169.

Rosenthal, R., & Rubin, D. B. (1994). The counternull value of an effect size: A new statistic. *Psychological Science, 5*, 329–334.

Sedlemeier, P., & Gigerenzer, G. (1989). Do studies of statistical power have an effect on the power of studies? *Psychological Bulletin, 105*, 309–316.

Simpson, E. H. (1951). The interpretation of interaction in contingency tables. *Journal of the Royal Statistical Society, B13*, 238–241.

Smith, M. L., Glass, G. V., & Miller, T. I. (1980). *The benefits of psychotherapy*. Baltimore: Johns Hopkins University Press.

Snedecor, G. W., & Cochran, W. G. (1989). *Statistical methods* (8th ed.). Ames: Iowa State University Press.

Steering Committee of the Physicians' Health Study Research Group. (1988). Preliminary report: Findings from the aspirin component of the ongoing physicians' health study. *New England Journal of Medicine, 318*, 262–264.

Yule, G. U. (1903). Notes on the theory of association of attributes in statistics. *Biometrika, 2*, 121–134.

Appendix

A Note About Calculating r and Small Samples

When computing rs from the results of studies that have small samples, the researcher needs to be vigilant about computing an exact p value in order to avoid mistakenly calculating an inflated r value associated with that p. For example, Table 7 shows a table of counts with the results of a study of left-handed and right-handed individuals with unilateral brain damage who have been compared as to their short-term memory loss. The results show a $\chi^2(1) = 3.52$, $p = .06$, and associated effect size of $\phi = .42$. (Recall that ϕ is an r for dichotomous data.) Yet, with expected frequencies as low as those in this example (i.e., 1.4 and 2.6), it is more appropriate to compute a p value from a more accurate test such as a Fisher exact test (Rosenthal & Rosnow, 1991). Computing this test yields a p of .101 from which we can obtain an effect size estimate of $\phi = .29$, a smaller but more accurate effect size estimate than the ϕ of .42 that we obtained from the less accurate p value computed directly from the χ^2.

Table 7 A Comparison of 16 Left- and 4 Right-Handed Brain-Damaged Individuals' Short-Term Memory Loss		
	Brain Damage	
Handedness	Memory Loss	No Memory Loss
Left-handed	4	12
Right-handed	3	1
$\chi^2(1) = 3.52$, $p = .06$, $Z = 1.88$, $\phi = .42$[a]		
p from Fisher exact test $= .101$, $Z = 1.28$, $\phi = .29$[a]		

[a] $\phi = \sqrt{(Z)^2/N}$.

4

Statistical Analyses Using Bootstrapping: Concepts and Implementation

Yiu-Fai Yung & Wai Chan

BOOTSTRAPPING, first introduced by Efron (1979), is a simple but powerful tool with a very wide range of application in statistics and applied research. In view of the increasing popularity of the bootstrap method in the social and behavioral sciences, this chapter is dedicated to illustrating the basic concepts of the bootstrap. To this end, two main examples are used. First, we present a hypothetical example in which the bootstrapping results are compared with those from a Monte Carlo experiment. Similarities and differences between these two techniques are worth investigation, and are beneficial to the understanding of the basic logic of the bootstrap. Some bootstrapping strategies are discussed along the way. The second example is a real data problem concerning the replicability of personality structures across two populations. We show how the bootstrap method can be implemented to answer various related research questions.

Next, we suggest some useful guidelines on implementing the bootstrapping procedure. We hope that, after grasping the basic ideas, readers will be able to implement their own bootstrap methods to address specific research questions. Although an extensive review of the literature is not intended, further readings are suggested at the end of the chapter.

A Monte Carlo Experiment on Reaction Time

In many ways, bootstrapping is like a Monte Carlo experiment. Both involve drawing random samples from well-defined distributions. Some researchers even equate the bootstrap with the Monte Carlo method itself. Although there is no need to argue whether these two methods are indeed different, it is useful to make the distinction in this chapter so as to pinpoint the different starting points of these two methods.

Let us consider a hypothetical cognitive experiment in which reaction time is measured. In many cases, it may not be unusual for the distribution of reaction times to be nonnormal with a small skew at the upper end of the distribution. Such a positive skew may represent sporadic shifts of cognitive states or other unexpected environmental factors during the cognitive experiment. To minimize the potential influence of the extreme scores, researchers may prefer the median to the mean as a measure of central tendency. As an example, a theoretical population distribution of reaction times for such a situation is depicted in Figure 1. In this figure, the majority of reaction times are centered at 600 ms; there is also a nonnegligible portion of reaction times centered at 750 ms. This distribution is clearly nonnormal. In fact, the hypothetical distribution depicted is exactly a mixture of two normal distributions: 80% of the reaction times are normally distributed with mean 600 ms and standard deviation 30 ms; the remaining 20% are normally distributed with mean 750 ms and standard deviation 50 ms. The overall mean and standard deviation are 630 ms and 69 ms, respectively. The population median, which is less "pulled" by the skew, is 610 ms.

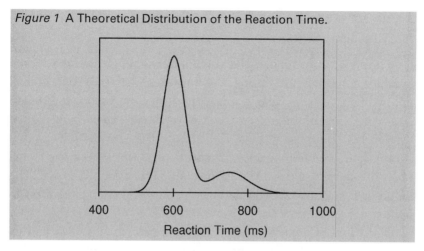

Figure 1 A Theoretical Distribution of the Reaction Time.

Two independent random samples with $N = 51$ and $N = 31$, respectively, are drawn from the hypothetical population in Figure 1. The distributions of reaction times for both samples are shown by means of histograms in Figure 2. The median reaction times are 614 ms and 628 ms, respectively, for $N = 51$ and $N = 31$. A typical statistical question concerns the standard errors (SEs) of these median values. Although there is indeed a rather restrictive formula for calculating the SE of the median based on asymptotic theory,[1] it may be more revealing to answer this question conceptually. That is, the SE of the sample median is the standard deviation of the median values of all possible samples of size N drawn from the population. This conceptual definition suggests an empirical evaluation of the SE via a so-called Monte Carlo experiment. The procedure of the Monte Carlo experiment is as follows:

1. *Population.* Define a population distribution for sampling.
2. *Sampling.* Draw, with replacement, N independent observations from the population. These N observations comprise a random sample. The median for this sample is computed.
3. *Evaluation.* Repeat the sampling above R times. Then, there will be a total of R values for the sample median. Compute

---

[1] The formula for the standard error of the sample median based on asymptotic theory can be found, for example, in Ferguson (1996). Essentially, the formula involves the evaluation of the population density function at the median. Therefore, it is not distribution free and is not very convenient to use in samples.

the *SE* of the sample median as the standard deviation of the *R* median values.

Here we may ignore the technicalities of drawing random samples from the population. As long as the distribution is well defined (e.g., in this case, a mixture of two known normal densities), the sampling stage of the Monte Carlo experiment can be carried out. Suppose we set $N = 51$, and the number of repeated samples, *R*, is set to 3,000. Theoretically, the larger the value of *R*, the more accurate the empirical evaluation of the *SE*. The value of *R* set here should be large enough for the current problem.

The Monte Carlo results for the median with $N = 51$ are illustrated in Figure 3, where the frequency distribution of the 3,000 sampled median values is represented by a smoothed curve. Subject to numerical accuracy and the efficiency of the design of the Monte Carlo experiment, this curve, in theory, represents the *true* sampling distribution of the median under the conditions specified. By applying the usual formula for computing the standard deviation of these 3,000 median values (with $R - 1$ in the denominator), the *SE* of the median is found to be 7.07. Similarly, we can evaluate the *SE* of the sample mean. The mean values of the random samples are recorded, and the corresponding sam-

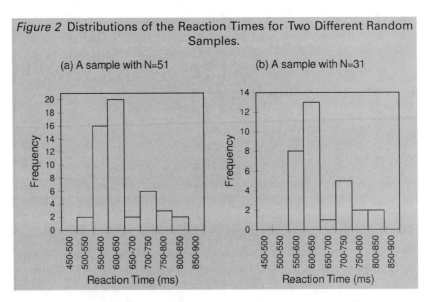

Figure 2 Distributions of the Reaction Times for Two Different Random Samples.

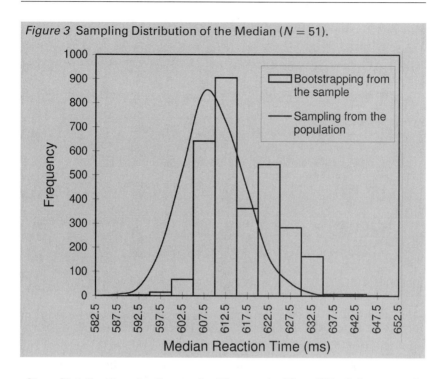

Figure 3 Sampling Distribution of the Median ($N = 51$).

pling distribution is shown in Figure 4. The *SE* of the sample mean is 9.61, which is clearly larger than the *SE* of the median. Or, without calculating the *SE*s, we can get the same impression by comparing the sampling distribution curves in Figures 3 and 4. Assuming these curves are drawn on the same scale, as they are here, the sampling distribution of the mean is much flatter and dispersed than that of the median, indicating that the sample median is statistically more stable than the sample mean in the current situation. This is perhaps another reason for us to choose the median over the mean as a measure of central tendency for these reaction times.

In Monte Carlo experiments, we do not need to apply sophisticated statistical theories such as the central limit theorem to derive analytically the sampling characteristics of the statistics of interest. The statistics may be as simple as the median, or they may be more complicated. For example, we may consider a so-called "balance index,"

$$BI = Mean/Median - 1,$$

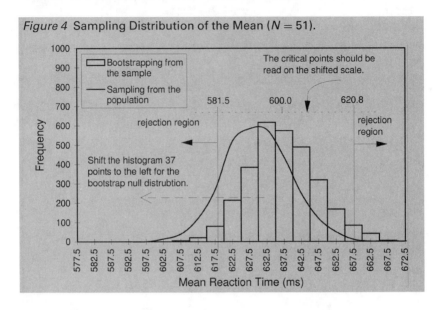

Figure 4 Sampling Distribution of the Mean (*N* = 51).

for the reaction time example. This index could be used to measure the degree to which reaction times are balanced around the median point, with a zero value indicating complete balance. An example of a nonzero BI is that for the population distribution shown in Figure 1, where BI = 630/610 − 1 = .033, indicating the existence of a small portion of outlying reaction times at the upper end that cannot be balanced out by the much faster reaction times at the lower end. Even though the BI is not a very complicated measure, deriving its sampling distribution analytically can be quite involved.[2] However, the Monte Carlo sampling procedure described can still be applied easily. As before, the BI is measured in each random sample and its *SE* is simply the standard deviation of the sampled BI values. In this example, the *SE* of the BI is .011. One could continue the Monte Carlo experiment to explore the sampling properties at another sample size level, say, *N* = 31. The results for this sample size are shown in Ta-

---

[2] To derive the asymptotic variance of the BI, the asymptotic joint distribution of the mean and the median must first be found under a specified family of population distributions. Depending on the family of population distribution, this may or may not be a straightforward task. The so-called delta method is then applied for obtaining the asymptotic variance.

ble 1, together with the previous Monte Carlo results for $N = 51$ and other results yet to be discussed.

What if the Population Distribution Is Not Known? The Bootstrap Method

Readers might argue that the Monte Carlo experiment described previously is impractical. Because the population information must be known in order to carry out the Monte Carlo experiment, how is it possible to apply the method when random samples are all one has at hand? Fortunately, this question is answered by the bootstrap. The bootstrap procedure is summarized as follows:

1. *Pseudo-Population.* Define a pseudo-population distribution for resampling. This pseudo-population is usually defined as the distribution of the sample data or of some appropriate transformation of the data.
2. *Resampling.* Draw, with replacement, N independent random observations from the pseudo-population. These N observations comprise a bootstrap resample. Compute the statistics of interest for the resample.
3. *Evaluation.* Repeat the resampling above B times. Then, there will be B sets of (bootstrapped) values for the statistics of interest. The distribution of bootstrapped values is the bootstrap sampling distribution of the statistics.

The bootstrapping procedure described here is strikingly similar to what has been presented for the Monte Carlo experiment; the two methods use similar simulation techniques. There is a critical difference, though. Instead of requiring the actual population distribution for sampling, the bootstrap needs only the distribution of a pseudo-population for resampling. That is, the bootstrap resampling starts with Figure 2, rather than Figure 1. The question is, does it work?

Let us explore this using the sample data for Figure 2(a), where $N = 51$. How do we resample data from this pseudo-population? First, we divide the interval $(0, 1)$ into 51 equal bins and associate each bin with an individual label of a data point in the pseudo-population as follows:

Individual label:	1	2	......	50	51	
	| — |	— |	......	| — |	— |	
Boundary of bin:	0	.02	.039	.961	.98	1

Next, a uniform random number, which is available in most computer programming languages, is drawn and its value is noted. The individual data point associated with the bin into which the random value falls is sampled. With 51 independent uniform random numbers, a resample of size $N = 51$ from the pseudo-population is drawn. As a consequence of the resampling with replacement procedure, this will not exclude the possibility of drawing the same individual data point more than once in a resample.

Bootstrapping, with $B = 3,000$, yields two bootstrap sampling distributions, one of the median and one of the mean. They are shown as histograms in Figures 3 and 4. The corresponding numerical results are shown in Table 1. The number of B used here enables us to compare the bootstrap sampling distributions shown in Figures 3 and 4 directly with that from the Monte Carlo experiment, in which we also set $R = 3,000$ replications. In Figure 4, except for a location shift, the shape of the sampling distribution for the mean obtained from bootstrapping is quite similar to the "true" sampling distribution. Although the middle range of the bootstrap sampling distribution for the median in Figure 3 shows a little irregularity, the overall spread of the distribution is still quite similar to that of the true distribution. Therefore, we can expect the bootstrap SE estimates to be very good for this sample of size 51. In fact, the bootstrap SE estimates, as shown in Table 1, are quite close to the corresponding true SE values.

For the sample mean, a well-known formula for estimating its SE is $s/\sqrt{N}$, where s is the sample standard deviation. Applying this formula to the current sample yields an SE estimate of 10.09, which is also very close to the true value. For the median, an asymptotic-theory-based SE formula is also available. Unfortunately, to apply this formula, the distribution family for the population must be known. For example, if the distribution

Table 1 Estimation of Standard Errors Using the Monte Carlo Method, Bootstrapping, and Formulas Based on Asymptotic Theory		
	Sample Size	
	N = 51	N = 31
Monte Carlo Experiment (Sampling From the Population)		
Mean	9.61	12.17
Median	7.07	9.06
Balance index	.011	.014
Bootstrapping (Resampling From the Sample)		
Mean	9.89	13.70
Median	7.61	14.71
Balance index	.011	.016
Using Existing Formula		
Mean	10.09	13.90
Median (assuming normal distribution)	12.65	17.42
Balance index	(unavailable)	(unavailable)

is that of the normal family, the SE of the median can be estimated by multiplying the SE of the mean by $\sqrt{\pi/2}$. The SE formula under other distributions may be much more complicated and difficult to apply. If we were to apply indiscriminately the normal-theory-based asymptotic formula, the SE estimate for the median is 12.65, which is far from the true value of 7.07. As for the BI, the corresponding SE formula based on the asymptotic theory is yet to be derived.

For the sample data ($N = 31$) with its distribution depicted in Figure 2(b), another set of bootstrapping results is obtained in Table 1. The bootstrap SE estimates for the mean and the BI are still close to the corresponding true values; however, the bootstrap SE of the median is not good. The estimated SE of the median obtained using the normal-theory-based asymptotic formula is even worse, though the SE of the mean estimated using this method looks fine.

What Makes the Bootstrap Work?

We have demonstrated some successful applications of the bootstrap for estimating SEs, especially when $N = 51$. Even though no population information has been assumed when bootstrapping, we observe that sampling distributions of the statistics, at least with regard to the overall shape, can still be estimated reasonably by the bootstrap. The critical reason for this success lies in the fact that similar starting points have been used by the bootstrap and the Monte Carlo experiment. If we compare Figure 2(a) with Figure 1, most readers will agree that they display very similar distributional form, although the former only approximates the latter. Therefore, sampling or resampling from these similar distributions may yield similar sampling distributions, as shown in Figures 3 and 4.

However, we would like to remind readers that the reaction time example is not intended as a proof of the success or failure of the bootstrap. It simply illustrates the basic concepts of the bootstrap. Although we cannot draw very solid conclusions from the results of just a few random samples, it is still legitimate to state that whenever we have a "good" sample like the one in Figure 2(a), we expect the bootstrap to work well. But how likely is it to have a good sample for bootstrapping? A general rule is: The larger the N, the more likely it is that the distribution of a random sample resembles the true population distribution. This can be illustrated by comparing the histograms in Figure 2. For example, no observations fall into the interval $500-550$ ms for the sample of size $N = 31$. This lack of information at the lower end of the sample distribution impairs its resemblance to the population distribution. When we have more observations, as with the sample of size $N = 51$, the histogram in Figure 2(a) is more refined and provides better information at every point of the distribution, including those points in the interval 500–550 ms.

In sum, the success of the bootstrap depends on how well the sample distribution resembles the population distribution. This, in turn, depends on the sample size N, in favor of large N. This explains the differential results for the two sample size levels in Table 1. However, this also sounds like the bootstrap is just another asymptotic method. So why do we think the bootstrap is better than existing asymptotic techniques? Fortunately, evidence for the superiority of the bootstrap for small sample size is available; this will be discussed later.

Sometimes a bootstrap application may appear a failure when, in fact, it could have worked properly if some adjustment were made. An example of this involves a bootstrap test. Recall our reaction time example and suppose we wanted to test the following hypothesis about the population mean reaction time: $H_0: \mu = 600$. The mean for the sample of size 51 is 637 ms. Can we construct a bootstrap test based on the bootstrap sampling distribution obtained in Figure 4? A naive (and incorrect) way is to pick the 2.5th and 97.5th percentiles of the histogram as the critical points for a two-sided test of the null hypothesis at $\alpha = .05$. Because there are 3,000 bootstrap mean values, the 75th and the 2,925th smallest bootstrap mean values are picked as the critical points. To locate the ith smallest bootstrap value at the pth percentile, the relationship $p/100 = i/B$ is used. The critical values found are 618.5 and 657.8. The corresponding rejection region is shown in Figure 4. Because our sample mean 637 ms does not fall inside the critical region, we do not reject the null hypothesis that $\mu = 600$. This poses a problem. Recall that the bootstrap SE of the mean for the current sample was found to be 9.89. A sample mean of 637 ms with this relatively small SE should have been very strong evidence against the assertion that this sample has been drawn from a population with mean 600 ms (i.e., the sample value is more than 3 SEs above the hypothesized value of 600). However, we still fail to reject the null hypothesis. Or, have we failed to use the bootstrap appropriately?

The reason for the contradictory evidence is that the null hypothesis has not been accommodated at the starting point of bootstrapping. When defining the pseudo-population for boot-strapping, we must realize which sampling distribution we actu-ally want. In the case of null hypothesis testing, what we really want is the *null* distribution of the statistic (or the test statis-tic). Applied to the current problem, the sampling distribution of the mean under $\mu = 600$, but not any other value, is intended; however, the above naive construction of the rejection region is based on resampling from a pseudo-population with mean equal to 637 ms, which is also the sample mean value. It is thus almost sure that this sample mean value of 637 will be located some-where in the middle of the naive bootstrap sampling distribution (see Figure 4), yielding a test that has very little chance of reject-ing the null hypothesis—or a test that has very little power—no matter how wrong the null hypothesis in fact is.

To rectify this problem, the null hypothesis needs to be ac-commodated when defining the pseudo-population. A simple re-centering procedure can be done for the current problem. That is, we first subtract 37 ms from every score in the original sam-ple. The pseudo-population is then defined by this set of modified scores, which is distributed exactly like the original sample, ex-cept that its mean is located at 600 ms, instead of 637 ms. In this way, the null hypothesis is satisfied in the pseudo-population. Then, we can proceed to the resampling stage. Equivalently, the above recentering procedure can be done by shifting the naive bootstrap sampling distribution 37 points to the left (or shifting the scale 37 points to the right) so the "new" critical points are 37 points less than before. They become 581.5 and 620.8, respective-ly (see Figure 4). Because the observed mean 637 ms is located at the far side of the new upper rejection region, we now feel re-lieved to reject the null hypothesis $\mu = 600$ at the .05 significance level.

A Study of Factor Replicability Using the Bootstrap

We now proceed to a real data example to demonstrate the tech-niques of constructing bootstrap tests for correlation structures and of interval estimation. The data considered here are from the normative study of the Chinese Personality Assessment Inventory (CPAI), a multiphasic inventory for measuring common personality traits and for clinical assessment (Cheung et al., 1996; Cheung, Leung, Song, Zhang, & Zhang, 1993). Here we consider the 22 personality scales of the CPAI only. These scales are developed for constructs specifically related to the Chinese as well as constructs commonly found in Western cultures. Participants in the study were from either Hong Kong (HK) or the People's Republic of China (PRC). Under several decades of British colonial rule until recently, Hong Kong is considered to be a relatively westernized society departing from its traditional Chinese cultural roots. An interesting question here concerns the factor replicability across the HK and the PRC populations. That is, if we factor-analyze the personality scales respectively for these two regions, will they exhibit the same personality structures (i.e., the same factor matrices)?

When the factor matrices under comparison are obtained from exploratory factor analyses, one way to evaluate factor replicability is through the use of orthogonal Procrustes rotation (see, e.g., Cliff, 1966; Schönemann, 1966). This method permits an orthogonal rotation of one of the factor matrices to agree maximally with the target factor matrix. To assess the degree of similarity between the rotated and the target factor matrices, so-called congruence coefficients have been proposed (Korth & Tucker, 1975, 1976). McCrae, Zonderman, Costa, Bond, and Paunonen (1996) suggested several variations of these coefficients. Two of them are considered here. The *total congruence coefficient* measures the overall similarity between the rotated and the target factor matrices, and the *factor congruence coefficient* measures the degree of similarity of individual factors. The value of each congruence coefficient is between 0 and 1, with 1 indicating perfect replicability of a factor (or factors) across regions. From the values of the sample congruence coefficients, we would like to construct some bootstrap tests concerning the factor replicability in the populations. In this respect, the bootstrap method proposed by Chan, Ho, Leung, Chan, and Yung (1997) is considered (see McCrae et al., 1996, for an alternative method).

The current data set consists of 100 responses from participants from each region. They were randomly selected from the much larger original normative sample of the CPAI. The factor matrix for the PRC sample is set as the target to which the factor matrix for HK is rotated. Following the findings of Cheung et al. (1996), a four-factor model is fitted to the data for each sample. The total congruence coefficient is .89. The individual factor congruence coefficients are .98, .97, .91, and .38, respectively, for the four factors. Do these values indicate strong evidence for factor replicability in the populations?

Because the congruence coefficients are complicated functions of the Procrustes rotation, sampling theory about them is difficult to derive using standard asymptotic techniques. However, the bootstrap testing procedure can still be implemented. From the example of testing the population mean reaction time, readers are now alerted to the importance of creating a good starting point for implementing the bootstrap test of factor replicability. What is the appropriate modification of the data that accommodates the null hypothesis in the current situation? Chan et al. (1997) provide a solution for this.[3] Using the null hypothesis of complete factor replicability, Chan et al. proposed that the sample data be transformed in a way such that the resultant correlation matrices for the pseudo-populations are exactly the same. It follows that the factor solutions for the pseudo-populations must also be the same and hence complete factor replicability is satisfied. Technical details can be found in Chan et al.[4] Similar techniques are also used in various sources (e.g.,

---

[3] The solution provided by Chan et al. (1997) could be argued to be too restrictive in two senses. First, complete replicability of all factors may be unrealistic in most practical situations. Research on developing bootstrap methods that only assume the replicability of a subset of factors is in progress. Second, a congruence coefficient of 1 for defining factor replicability may be too restrictive as a criterion. Further improvement on this is needed, and we leave this an open issue. Nonetheless, the proposed bootstrap method serves as a viable alternative, at least when no better method seems to be available.

[4] Creating pseudo-populations using Chan et al.'s (1997) procedure in the current context is summarized in the following steps:

1. Factor-analyze, respectively, the sample *correlation* matrices for the PRC (the target) and the HK samples using the principal component method with

Beran & Srivastava, 1985; Bollen & Stine, 1993; Yung & Bentler, 1996; Zhang, Pantula, & Boos, 1991).

Bootstrapping with $B = 1,000$ was conducted. In each bootstrap replication, we resampled $N = 100$ observations from each pseudo-population independently. Then, the factor matrix of the HK resample was Procrustes-rotated toward the target factor matrix of the PRC resample. Various congruence coefficients were computed. Thus, 1,000 bootstrap values were obtained for each congruence coefficient. Because a factor congruence coefficient of 1 indicates perfect replicability, the rejection region for the null hypothesis of factor replicability is set entirely at the lower end of the bootstrap sampling distribution. This is illustrated in Figure 5, where the bootstrap sampling distributions for the first and the third factor congruence coefficients are shown. First, let us start with the result for the total congruence coefficient. The sample value .89 of this coefficient is located in the critical region of the bootstrap sampling distribution, indicating that the hypothesis of complete factor replicability is not supported. It implies that the two regions studied may not share exactly the same personality structure. To locate which factor might

---

normal varimax rotation. The fitted correlation matrices for the PRC and the HK samples are denoted as P_1 and P_2, respectively.

2. Find the sample covariance matrices, S_1 and S_2, respectively, for the PRC and the HK samples. The corresponding diagonal matrices that contain the standard deviations of the variables on the main diagonals are denoted by D_1 and D_2, respectively. They can be formed easily by taking the square roots of the variances in S_1 and S_2.

3. Let the original data matrices be Y_1 and Y_2, respectively, for the PRC and the HK samples. The following transformation of the data matrices are applied:

$$Z_1 = Y_1 S_1^{-1/2} \hat{\Sigma}_1^{1/2} \quad \text{and} \quad Z_2 = Y_2 S_2^{-1/2} \hat{\Sigma}_2^{1/2},$$

where $\hat{\Sigma}_1 = D_1 P_1 D_1$ and $\hat{\Sigma}_2 = D_2 P_1 D_2$; and a matrix of the form $A^{1/2}$ is the Cholesky decomposition of A, which can be obtained readily in most high-level computer languages for matrix operations (e.g., SAS/IML, SAS Institute, 1985). The pseudo-populations for bootstrapping are now defined by the modified data Z_1 and Z_2. Notice carefully that both $\hat{\Sigma}_1$ and $\hat{\Sigma}_2$ are associated with the fitted correlation matrix P_1 for the PRC sample. It can then be shown that Z_1 and Z_2 will have the same correlation matrix P_1 and, hence, lead to the same factor matrix when factor-analyzed.

have contributed to the overall discrepancy in the factor structure, we examine the bootstrap tests of individual factor congruence coefficients.[5] For example, in Figure 5(a) the observed value
.98 for the first factor congruence coefficient does not fall inside
the critical region. It supports the replicability of the first factor across the regions. Similarly, replicability of the second factor
is confirmed using the bootstrap test. However, replicability of
the third and the fourth factors is not supported by the bootstrap
test. It is interesting to note that, despite the seemingly large
congruence coefficient for the third factor (i.e., .91), the bootstrap
test does not support the factor's replicability (but see footnote 5).
This is illustrated in Figure 5(b).

Another use of the factor-analytic results is to form composites for measuring the underlying constructs in future samples.
For example, we might use the composite (summed) score of the
items for a particular scale as a measure of the corresponding

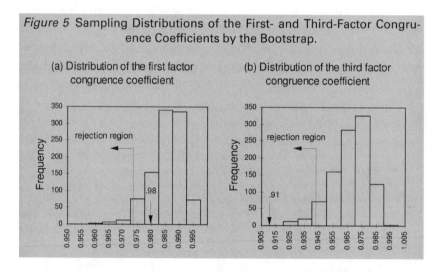

Figure 5 Sampling Distributions of the First- and Third-Factor Congruence Coefficients by the Bootstrap.

[5] The analysis conducted here may not be the most appropriate one. Log-
ically speaking, when testing each individual factor congruence coefficient, one
assumes that only the factor being examined is replicable across the populations, but the replicability of other factors may or may not be true. Instead, the
proposed bootstrap procedure apparently assumes a complete replicability of all
factors, which is more restrictive than needed in some cases. As noted in footnote 3, this procedure is conducted because a more appropriate procedure is still
under development. We hope the present bootstrap tests can still provide some
crude information about the replicability of individual factors.

factor. To measure the reliability of the composite, Cronbach's alpha coefficient is used. For example, for the first factor, the alpha coefficients for the PRC and the HK composites are .83 and .77, respectively. Their difference is .06. Do these alpha coefficients exceed a certain level of reliability if sampling variability is taken into account? And do these two composite measures formed for the two regions share the same reliability? We tackle these problems by setting up bootstrap confidence intervals.

The simplest bootstrap confidence interval (CI) construction is via the use of the standard normal formula $t \pm z \times SE$, where t is the sample statistic of interest and z is the critical value of the standard normal variate associated with the desired confidence level. In the current situation, three different sample statistics (t) are of interest: the two alpha coefficients of the composites for the two regions and their difference. Bootstrapping with $B = 2,000$ replications from the pseudo-populations defined by the *unmodified* sample data is done. In each bootstrap replication, we have a pair of random samples, respectively, from the two pseudo-populations. All three statistics are computed in each bootstrap replication. The SE estimate for each statistic is computed as the standard deviation for the corresponding 2,000 bootstrap values. The bootstrap SEs for the two alpha coefficients are .027 and .036, respectively, for the PRC and the HK composites. The bootstrap SE for the difference in alpha coefficients is .045. With $z = 1.96$, the 95% CI about the alpha coefficient for the PRC composite is bounded by .778 and .884, and that for the HK composite is bounded by .700 and .834. Therefore, if a minimum level at. 70 is desirable, the reliabilities of these composites are satisfactory because both CIs are located at or above this minimum point. The 95% CI about the difference of the alpha coefficients is bounded by $-.028$ and .150. That 0 is covered by this CI indicates that the reliability of the two composites for the two populations may in fact be the same.

There are many other ways to construct confidence intervals using bootstrapping. Some require fewer assumptions than others. The standard intervals discussed previously are considered to be very restrictive, because normal approximation of the sampling distribution is assumed. A slightly less restrictive method is the so-called percentile method. The CI using this method is obtained by simply referring to the relevant percentiles of the bootstrap sampling distribution.[6] For constructing a two-sided 95% CI using $B = 2,000$ bootstrap replications, for example, the 50th (2.5th percentile) and the 1,950th (97.5th percentile) smallest values in the bootstrap sampling distribution are used as the limits of the CI. It is found that the 95% CIs about the alpha coefficients are .768–.874 and .687–.827, respectively, for the PRC and the HK composites. The 95% CI about the difference of the alpha coefficients is −.021–.154. These results are very similar to those of the standard intervals; however, a notable difference is that, unlike the standard intervals, bootstrap percentile intervals are generally not symmetric around their corresponding sample values.

Still another popular variation of the bootstrap CI is the bias-corrected and accelerated (BCa) method (Efron, 1987). Basically, the BCa method utilizes some mathematical properties that—if they exist—will improve the sampling properties of the confidence intervals. The coverage probability using the BCa method has been shown to be highly accurate (Hall, 1988). The formula for obtaining BCa intervals can be found in Efron and Tibshirani (1993, pp. 184–186). Essentially, the BCa intervals achieve better accuracy of the coverage probability by adjusting the pair of percentile points used in the percentile method. For example, recall that, for the 95% CIs, the 50th (2.5th percentile) and the 1,950th (97.5th percentile) smallest values in the bootstrap distribution are used. For the BCa method, however, the 59th (2.95th percentile) and 1,957th (97.9th percentile) smallest values are used as the limits of the 95% CI about the difference of the alpha coefficients. The resultant BCa CI is −.018–.157, which does not depart much from the previous result. Similarly, the 95% BCa CIs for the PRC and HK composites are .777–.879 and .694–.829, respectively. As also observed with the percentile

---

[6] Though the bootstrap percentile method for CI construction appears to use the bootstrap sampling distribution directly, its justification is quite different from that of obtaining bootstrap *SE*s. This issue is quite involved and cannot be made precise here. See Schenker (1985) for a discussion of the assumptions of various bootstrap methods for CI construction.

method, the 95% BCa CI about the alpha coefficient of the HK composite covers some range of values slightly below .70, casting doubt on whether this minimum level of reliability is actually attained in the population.

Implementing a Bootstrap Procedure: Some Suggested Guidelines

There are several advantages of using the bootstrap for statistical analyses, most of which can be understood through its resemblance to Monte Carlo experiments. In a Monte Carlo experiment, we study the "true" sampling properties of statistics of interest through random sampling. This strategy is adaptable to any statistic, no matter how complicated it is. It is also adaptable to any population distribution, provided that the distribution is known. Statistical analyses using bootstrapping inherit all such flexibility of Monte Carlo experiments, but without requiring a known population distribution. In bootstrapping, the population information is estimated from the sample. This additional flexibility of the bootstrap is traded with the quality of the end products. That is, one can only *estimate* the true sampling properties using the bootstrap. Therefore, the performance of the bootstrap also depends on the sample size, N. How large an N is required? This issue is treated immediately below, as one of the suggested guidelines for implementing a bootstrap procedure:

1. *Sample Size.* The bootstrap possesses desirable asymptotic properties and better convergence to its purported properties, when compared with traditional asymptotic methods based mostly on normal approximations (see, e.g., Bickel & Freedman, 1981; Hall, 1988; Singh, 1981). Asymptotic justification of the bootstrap is important to the extent that it helps characterize the statistical properties in precise terms. Researchers in the social and behavioral sciences, however, worry more about statistical properties of the bootstrap under realistic sample sizes. Simulation studies of the finite sample properties of the bootstrap are available in different areas. Some results indicate that

the bootstrap can work reasonably well even with $N = 20$ (e.g., Boos & Brownie, 1989; Stine, 1985; Zhang et al., 1991). Others show a sample size ranging from 50 to 400 may be needed for the bootstrap to work well (e.g., Chan et al., 1997; Ichikawa & Konishi, 1995; Yung & Bentler, 1994; Yung, Chan, & Bentler, 1998). That bootstrap methods compare favorably over older methods in these studies may lead to the belief that statistical inferences based on bootstrapping under realistic sample sizes can generally be trusted, at least in some specific areas of applications. But counterevidence has also been presented (e.g., Rasmussen, 1987, 1988; Schenker, 1985). Therefore, when implementing a bootstrap procedure, we urge researchers to consult simulation studies of the bootstrap that are closely related to their problem areas. Useful information about the sample size needed to attain reliable bootstrapping results can thus be obtained.

2. *Number of Samples.* Theoretically, the larger the B, the more accurate the numerical evaluation of the bootstrap sampling distribution. Practically, it is quite satisfactory to set B at several hundred when estimating standard errors. Hypothesis testing and interval construction require a much larger B because individual percentile points of the bootstrap sampling distribution must be accurately evaluated. For example, when testing a two-sided hypothesis at an $\alpha = .05$, the 2.5th and the 97.5th percentiles will be used as the critical values. To be accurate, one must allow enough bootstrap values at both ends of the bootstrap sampling distribution, say, 50. Therefore, $B = 2,000$ is a minimum. To be more careful, one may need an even larger B for constructing the BCa intervals because the percentiles that are actually used may differ from the prescribed percentiles.

3. *Nonparametric Versus Parametric Bootstrapping.* Thus far, what we have described extensively is the so-called nonparametric bootstrap, which does not assume any knowledge about the distribution family of the data. Resampling is done by selecting individual data points in the pseudo-population. In contrast, when implementing a parametric bootstrap procedure, the parameters of the assumed population distribution are estimated. Resampling is then done by drawing random samples from the pseudo-population defined by the assumed distribution with the

parameter estimates. As long as the knowledge about the distribution form is well established and there is a good estimation procedure for the associated parameters, the parametric bootstrap can be recommended. With these conditions satisfied, the parametric bootstrap procedure may compensate for the statistical instability in very small samples. Otherwise, it is much safer to use the nonparametric bootstrap when little information about the distribution is available.

4. *The Pseudo-Population for Bootstrapping.* We remind readers that when defining the pseudo-populations in bootstrap tests, the null hypothesis must be accommodated. Some examples are given in this chapter. More examples of this principle can be found in Hall and Wilson (1991); see also Bollen and Stine (1993).

5. *Which Statistics Should Be Bootstrapped?* Not all statistics share equally good sampling properties when applying the bootstrap. An important class of statistics is that of pivots. A pivot is a statistic with a sampling distribution independent of the population parameter values (e.g., Studentized t). Bootstrap tests and confidence intervals could be improved by bootstrapping the (approximate) pivotal quantities instead of the original statistics. Unfortunately, this advanced topic is beyond the scope of the present chapter. Readers are referred to publications by Efron and Tibshirani (1993) and Hall and Wilson (1991).

Further Readings

We have explored some basic concepts of bootstrapping and have discussed in some detail its implementation for estimating standard errors, testing hypotheses, and constructing confidence intervals. We did not cover all interesting applications of the bootstrap. For example, a significant omission is bias estimation using bootstrapping.[7] Other topics such as power estimation

---

[7] Bias correction using the bootstrap may not be recommendable in practice. Although correcting biases may lead to slightly more accurate estimates, it may at the same time increase the standard errors of the bootstrap-corrected estimates (see Efron & Tibshirani, 1993).

(e.g., Beran, 1986; Yung & Bentler, 1996) and adjusting multiple-testing p values (Westfall & Young, 1993) are areas where the bootstrap can find useful applications. We hope this chapter has motivated readers to explore these areas in the future.

For a much more thorough but somewhat technical introduction to the bootstrap, the textbook by Efron and Tibshirani (1993) is highly recommended. Other introductory articles include those by Banks (1989), Efron and Gong (1983), and Efron and Tibshirani (1986). For bootstrap applications in the social and behavioral sciences, readers may find the articles by Dietz, Frey, and Kalof (1987), Lambert, Wildt, and Durant (1991), Langeheine, Pannekoek, and Van de Pol (1996), and Stine (1989) useful. A series of articles (Efron, 1988; Lunneborg, 1985; Rasmussen, 1987, 1988; Sievers, 1996; Strube, 1988) debating whether the bootstrap can do a better job estimating the sampling distribution of the correlation coefficient could serve as useful readings in clarifying the role of the bootstrap in contributing to better statistical inferences. For readers with an interest in bootstrap applications to structural equation modeling and factor analysis, the following articles would be relevant: Bollen and Stine (1990, 1993), Boomsma (1986), Chatterjee (1984), Ichikawa and Konishi (1995), and Yung and Bentler (1994, 1996). For applications of the bootstrap to discrete data, see, for example, Langeheine et al. (1996) and Yung et al. (1998).

Author Notes: The authors wish to thank Adam Hafdahl, Rick Hoyle, David Thissen, and an anonymous reviewer for their comments on an earlier draft of the chapter. The authors also extend their thanks to Ringo Ho who helped analyze the CPAI data for the factor replicability example, and to Fanny M. C. Cheung who provided the CPAI data.

References

Banks, D. L. (1989). Bootstrapping II. In S. Kotz & N. L. Johnson (Eds.), *Encyclopedia of statistical science* (Supp. vol., pp. 17–22). New York: Wiley.

Beran, R. J. (1986). Simulated power functions. *Annals of Statistics*, *14*, 151–173.

Beran, R. J., & Srivastava, M. S. (1985). Bootstrap tests and confidence regions for functions of a covariance matrix. *Annals of Statistics*, *13*, 95–115.

Bickel, P., & Freedman, D. (1981). Some asymptotic theory for the bootstrap. *Annals of Statistics*, *9*, 1196–1217.

Bollen, K. A., & Stine, R. (1990). Direct and indirect effects: Classical and bootstrap estimates of variability. In C. C. Clogg (Ed.), *Sociological methodology* (pp. 115–140). Oxford: Blackwell.

Bollen, K. A., & Stine, R. (1993). Bootstrapping goodness of fit measures in structural equation models. In K. A. Bollen & J. S. Long (Eds.), *Testing structural equation models* (pp. 111– 135). Newbury Park, CA: Sage.

Boomsma, A. (1986). On the use of bootstrap and jackknife in covariance structure analysis. *Compstat 1986*, 205–210.

Boos, D. D., & Brownie, C. (1989). Bootstrap methods for testing homogeneity of variances. *Technometric*, *31*, 69–82.

Chan, W., Ho, R. M., Leung, K., Chan, D. K., & Yung, Y. F. (1997). *Evaluating the big five model with procrustes rotation: A bootstrap procedure.* Manuscript submitted for publication.

Chatterjee, S. (1984). Variance estimation in factor analysis: An application of the bootstrap. *British Journal of Mathematical and Statistical Psychology*, *37*, 252–262.

Cheung, F. M., Leung, K., Fan, R. M., Song, W. Z., Zhang, J. X., & Zhang, J. P. (1996). Development of the Chinese Personality Assessment Inventory. *Journal of Cross-Cultural Psychology*, *27*, 181–199.

Cheung, F. M., Leung, K., Song, W. Z., Zhang, J. X., & Zhang, J. P. (1993). *The Chinese Personality Assessment Inventory.* Hong Kong: The Chinese University of Hong Kong.

Cliff, N. (1966). Orthogonal rotation to congruence. *Psychometrika*, *31*, 33–42.

Dietz, T., Frey, R. S., & Kalof, L. (1987). Estimation with cross-national data: Robust and nonparametric methods. *American Sociological Review*, *52*, 380–390.

Efron, B. (1979). Bootstrap methods: Another look at the jackknife. *Annals of Statistics*, *7*, 1–26.

Efron, B. (1987). Better bootstrap confidence intervals (with discussion). *Journal of the American Statistical Association*, *82*, 171–200.

Efron, B. (1988). Bootstrap confidence intervals: Good or bad? *Psychological Bulletin, 104,* 293–296.

Efron, B., & Gong, G. (1983). A leisurely look at the bootstrap, the jackknife and cross-validation. *American Statistician, 37,* 36–48.

Efron, B., & Tibshirani, R. (1986). Bootstrap measures for standard errors, confidence intervals, and other measures of statistical accuracy. *Statistical Science, 1,* 54–77.

Efron, B., & Tibshirani, R. J. (1993). *An introduction to the bootstrap.* New York: Chapman and Hall.

Ferguson, T. S. (1996). *A course in large sample theory.* London: Chapman and Hall.

Hall, P. (1988). Theoretical comparison of bootstrap confidence intervals. *Annals of Statistics, 16,* 927–985.

Hall, P., & Wilson, S. (1991). Two guidelines for bootstrap hypothesis testing. *Biometrics, 47,* 757–762.

Ichikawa, M., & Konishi, S. (1995). Application of the bootstrap methods in factor analysis. *Psychometrika, 60,* 77–93.

Korth, B., & Tucker, L. T. (1975). The distribution of chance congruence coefficients from simulated data. *Psychometrika, 40,* 361–372.

Korth, B., & Tucker, L. T. (1976). Procrustes matching by congruence coefficients. *Psychometrika, 41,* 521–535.

Lambert, Z. V., Wildt, A. R., & Durant, R. M. (1991). Approximating confidence intervals for factor loadings. *Multivariate Behavioral Research, 26,* 421–434.

Langeheine, R., Pannekoek, J., & Van de Pol, F. (1996). Bootstrapping goodness-of-fit measures in categorical data analysis. *Sociological Methods and Research, 24,* 492–516.

Lunneborg, C. E. (1985). Estimating the correlation coefficient: The bootstrap approach. *Psychological Bulletin, 98,* 209–215.

McCrae, R. R., Zonderman, A. B., Costa, P. T., Bond, M. H., & Paunonen, S. V. (1996). Evaluating replicability of factors in the revised NEO Personality Inventory: Confirmatory factor analysis versus Procrustes rotation. *Journal of Personality and Social Psychology, 70,* 552–566.

Rasmussen, J. L. (1987). Estimating the correlation coefficient: Bootstrap and parametric approaches. *Psychological Bulletin, 101,* 136–139.

Rasmussen, J. L. (1988). "Bootstrap confidence intervals: Good or bad": Comments on Efron (1988) and Strube (1988) and further evaluation. *Psychological Bulletin, 104,* 297–299.

SAS Institute. (1985). *SAS/IML user's guide: Version 5.* Cary, NC: SAS Institute.

Schenker, N. (1985). Qualms about bootstrap confidence intervals. *Journal of the American Statistical Association, 80,* 360–361.

Schönemann, P. H. (1966). A generalized solution of the orthogonal Procrustes problem. *Psychometrika, 31,* 1–10.

Sievers, W. (1996). Standard and bootstrap confidence intervals in the correlation coefficient. *British Journal of Mathematical and Statistical Psychology, 49,* 381–396.

Singh, K. (1981). On the asymptotic accuracy of Efron's bootstrap. *Annals of Statistics, 9,* 1187–1195.

Stine, R. A. (1985). Bootstrap prediction intervals for regression. *Journal of the American Statistical Association, 80,* 1026–1031.

Stine, R. A. (1989). An introduction to bootstrap methods: Examples and ideas. *Sociological Methods and Research, 8,* 243–291.

Strube, M. J. (1988). Bootstrap type I error rates for the correlation coefficient: An examination of alternate procedures. *Psychological Bulletin, 104,* 290–292.

Westfall, O. H., & Young, S. S. (1993). *Pesampling-based multiple testing.* New York: Wiley.

Yung, Y. F., & Bentler, P. M. (1994). Bootstrap-corrected ADF test statistics in covariance structure analysis. *British Journal of Mathematical and Statistical Psychology, 47,* 63–84.

Yung, Y. F., & Bentler, P. M. (1998). Bootstrapping techniques in analysis of mean and covariance structures. In G. A. Marcoulides & R. E. Schumacker (Eds.), *Advanced structural equation modeling: Issues and techniques* (pp. 195–226). Mahwah, NJ: Erlbaum.

Yung, Y. F., Chan, W., & Bentler, P. M. (1996). Designing bootstrap tests using the assumed information: Applications to cross-classifications. In W. Liebrand, R. Hegselmann, & A. Nowak (Eds.), *Computer modeling and the study of dynamical social processes.* London: Sage.

Zhang, J., Pantula, S. G., & Boos, D. D. (1991). Robust methods for testing the pattern of a single covariance matrix. *Biometrika, 78,* 787–795.

5

Meta-Analysis
of Single-Case Designs

Scott L. Hershberger, Dennis D. Wallace,
Samuel B. Green, & Janet G. Marquis

IN THIS CHAPTER, we are concerned with developing a comprehensive approach to the meta-analysis of results from single-case experimental designs. Single-case experimental designs come in many different forms (for a review of these designs, see Kazdin, 1982). Nonetheless, all share one common feature: Subjects are repeatedly measured on a dependent variable under treatment and nontreatment conditions. The repeated-measurement aspect of these studies introduces meta-analytic challenges not present in between-subjects designs. We briefly describe three major challenges below, but more fully discuss them as we progress in the chapter:

- *Within-Phase Model Development.* Meta-analysts for single-case designs must develop models within phases that not only include parameters for level, but may also include parameters for linear or nonlinear trends and autoregressive/moving average components. Although complex models may be more appropriate for these analyses, the number of data points within a phase is frequently too small to estimate the parameters for these models.

- *Treatment/Replicability Effects.* They then must consider how best to represent the effect of the treatment (effect size), taking into account both the magnitude of change between baseline and treatment phases and the replicability across baseline-treatment phases. Ideally, these computations should be tailored to the specific design characteristics of the study—an extremely difficult task given the wide variation in these single-case designs.
- *Summarization.* Finally, meta-analysts must select methods for combining effect sizes and assessing whether effect sizes differ as a function of study characteristics (moderator variables). Analysts are likely to encounter problems such as determining appropriate standard errors for effect sizes and combining dependent effect sizes within studies.

Since the early 1980s, several researchers have offered methods that address one or more of these challenges (Allison & Gorman, 1993; Busk & Serlin, 1992; Center, Skiba, & Casey, 1985/86; Faith, Allison, & Gorman, 1996; Gingerich, 1984; Gorsuch, 1983; Scruggs, Mastropieri, & Casto, 1987; Skiba, Casey, & Center, 1986; White, Rusch, Kazdin, & Hartmann, 1989). Although these authors have contributed toward the solution of some of these difficult problems, additional work is required before meta-analyses more effectively summarize the results of studies that use the many design variations employed by single-case methodologists.

In this chapter, we present an approach for conducting single-case meta-analyses that considers the three problems discussed previously: within-phase model development, treatment/replicability effects, and summarization. Initially, we discuss the choice of predicted scores within phases to estimate treatment differences and an appropriate statistical model to determine these scores. We next define treatment effect sizes and methods to assess the replicability of these effect sizes. Then we present an approach to analyzing effect sizes across multiple studies. We conclude with an example meta-analysis of six single-case studies.

Treatment Effect Sizes for Single-Case Designs and Their Replicability

The treatment effect size for studies using single-case designs can be defined in multiple ways; however, all definitions—those in the literature and those proposed here—involve comparing the results on the dependent variable for the B treatment phase with the results on the dependent variable for the A baseline phase and dividing by some factor to yield a unitless index. First, we discuss different methods for comparing results for the A and B phases. Next, we consider various divisors for creating an effect size index. Finally, we suggest an index that assesses the degree of replicability of the treatment effects for the multiple AB phases.

Choice of Scores to Represent A and B Phases for Computing Effect Sizes

In this section, we discuss various issues associated with choosing scores to represent the A and B phases for computing effect sizes. Initially, we introduce the concept of a point of comparison and discuss long-term and short-term estimates of treatment effects as a function of the chosen point of comparison. These estimates may be calculated using simple means or a more complex regression model (general linear model). In the last part of this section, we provide details on computing estimates based on the general linear model.

Point of Comparison. Ideally, we want to represent the difference between the A and the B phases, holding all other variables constant including time. Accordingly, we should use the data within the A and the B phases to compute a difference between a predicted score for the nontreatment condition and a predicted score for the treatment condition at the same point in time, the point of comparison. The predicted score for the nontreatment condition, $\hat{y}_{Ap}$, estimates the value of the dependent variable if the baseline had been extended to point of comparison p beyond the end of the A phase. The predicted score for the treatment condition, $\hat{y}_{Bp}$, estimates the value of the dependent variable for the same time point p but based on the data within the B phase.

Meta-analysts should explicitly define the point of comparison that is of interest scientifically. The choice of the point of comparison for the estimation of $\hat{y}_{Ap}$ and $\hat{y}_{Bp}$ should be dictated by the research question. If the choice is not clearly defined by the meta-analyst, it will be unclear whether the selected effect size index adequately addresses the research questions. Some experimenters may be interested in knowing how effective a treatment would be after a particular number of trials of treatment of the B phase, and then the point of comparison would be at this trial. However, most experimenters are likely to be interested in the effectiveness of a treatment after it has been applied over an extended period of time (i.e., in the long run) and are less interested in its effectiveness before the full benefits of the treatment are known. In this instance, the point of comparison p might be considered as some point beyond the end of phase B.

Long-Run Estimates. The ability to evaluate the effectiveness of a treatment in the long run is dependent on the quality of research data. With well-behaved experimental data, the observed behavior shows little or no trend and is relatively stable (i.e., little variablity) at the end of each phase. Based on these data, we are likely to feel relatively confident that the behavior would continue at similar levels if the phases were extended a number of trials, although extrapolation is always dangerous. If we are interested in estimating the effectiveness of the treatment in the long run, we might estimate $\hat{y}_{Bp}$ using the mean of scores at the end of phase B; the behavior is stable over this time period and would be expected to be similar for trials beyond it. The other score for the computation of an effect size, $\hat{y}_{Ap}$, can be estimated using the mean of the stable scores at the end of phase A. The assumption underlying the use of the estimate of $\hat{y}_{Ap}$ is that the level of behavior would be the same if the baseline were extended to the point of comparison, that is, to some trial beyond the end of phase B. This assumption is reasonable for most experimentally collected data, in which researchers carefully plan the length of the baseline period so as to ensure the behavior stabilizes by the end of it, but is less reasonable for archival or nonexperimentally collected data.

$\hat{y}_{Ap}$ and $\hat{y}_{Bp}$ can be estimated by computing the mean of the scores for the stable portions at the end of the A and the B phases, respectively. Alternatively, the mean could be calculated using only the last three data points within a phase. This alternative avoids making subjective decisions about which data points should be included in the portion considered to be stable and maintains a consistency in the number of data points used across phases and studies.

With many applied single-case studies, it is impractical or impossible to require behavior to be stable and to be neither increasing nor decreasing in trend with each phase. In addition, phases are frequently sufficiently brief that it is difficult to assess the nature of the trend. Given the uncertainty of the data, we cannot feel as confident about what the level of behavior would be if a phase were extended and, therefore, should feel more uncomfortable estimating an effect size based on means at the end of the A and B phases. One possible solution to take into account within-phase trends would be to estimate $\hat{y}_{Ap}$ and $\hat{y}_{Bp}$ using regression models. The simplest approach would be to fit a linear equation to the data points separately for each phase. These equations could then be used to estimate the $\hat{y}_{Ap}$ and $\hat{y}_{Bp}$ at some chosen point beyond the B phase.

Unfortunately, there are problems with regression estimates for $\hat{y}_{Ap}$ and $\hat{y}_{Bp}$ based on a linear equation. In theory, models that allow for nonlinear time functions may be preferable for many studies (Huitema, 1985). For example, for an ABAB design, we might expect a rapid decrease in the frequency of the aberrant behavior initially in a B phase and a less rapid decrease as the treatment continues. Or, in the second A phase, we might anticipate a more rapid return to the baseline at the beginning of the phase and then asymptoting to some level if the phase is of sufficient length. The type of trend, linear or nonlinear, should be assessed using standard statistical methodology. For example, the R^2 for a nonlinear trend model can be compared to the R^2 for a linear trend model to determine if the more complex model is necessary. Although nonlinear trends might occur within phases, the number of observations within phases may be too few for many single-case studies to allow for the estimation of these complex statistical models.

Besides parameters that allow for nonlinear time relationships, time series parameters (e.g., autoregressive or moving average parameters) could be added to the model to take into account serial correlations (autocorrelation) among the scores. Alternatively, this serial correlation could be removed prior to the estimation of the model. A number of arguments have been put forward for ignoring time series parameters. First, positive autocorrelation introduces bias into the standard errors of the parameters of the regression equation but not into the estimates of the parameters (Harvey, 1989). Second, it is rare that single-case experimental designs are of sufficient length to estimate the autocorrelation parameters accurately (Marascuilo & Busk, 1988). Finally, Huitema (1985) argues that with the type of variables often examined in single-case designs, the autocorrelation is minimal. Although autocorrelation may be minimal in many single-case studies, it still seems reasonable to assess whether time series parameters are necessary if data are sufficient.

Another difficulty with regression approaches—with or without nonlinear terms and time series parameters—is that their predicted scores ($\hat{y}_{Ap}$ and $\hat{y}_{Bp}$) may be impossible (e.g., a negative frequency or a percent greater than 100) or highly unlikely (a frequency three standard deviations higher than any score in the phases). To the extent that the point of comparison requires extrapolation beyond the available data, $\hat{y}_{Ap}$ and $\hat{y}_{Bp}$ are likely to be poor estimates, with limitations in both accuracy and precision.

In summary, the long-run perspective requires estimates of behavior for both phases at some point beyond the end of phase B. These estimates can be computed using the means at the end of phases or the predicted scores from regression models. Both types of estimates are problematic because they require extrapolation that cannot be justified empirically or theoretically unless the data are stable around a constant level within both phases. Rather than computing long-run estimates, we could reduce the amount of extrapolation by choosing some point at or prior to the last data point in the B phase as the point of comparison. By choosing a different point of comparison, however, we are no longer addressing the same research question about the effectiveness of a treatment in the long run. If meta-analysts are interested in only the long-run effects of a treatment, then they may have to eliminate studies that fail to meet the within-phase stability conditions. They may even have to abandon doing a meta-analysis if too few studies meet these conditions.

Short-Run Estimates. If the meta-analyst is interested in a research question that can be answered with short-run estimates, then a convenient point of comparison may be the last time point in the B phase. We focus our discussion of short-run estimates using the point of comparison as the end of the B phase, although other points could be chosen within the B phase depending on the research question.

As with long-run estimates, within-phase regression models can be used to estimate $\hat{y}_{Ap}$ and $\hat{y}_{Bp}$. Extrapolation is not required in estimating $\hat{y}_{Bp}$ when p is the last point in the B phase. However, all the other potential problems that were described for regression models in computing long-run estimates may apply for short-run estimates, including extrapolation in the estimation of $\hat{y}_{Ap}$.

Rather than use regression estimates, a simple alternative would be to estimate $\hat{y}_{Ap}$ by computing a mean for the last few data points within the A phase and similarly to estimate $\hat{y}_{Bp}$ by calculating a mean for the last few data points in the B phase. The mean of the last three data points of phase A is not likely to be a good estimate of $\hat{y}_{Ap}$, but it still might be a better estimate than one based on a regression equation. For example, we might prefer a mean estimate of $\hat{y}_{Ap}$ if a steeply sloped straight line fit the data for an A phase and if the point of comparison required extrapolation well beyond the end of phase A or yielded an out-of-range prediction. The mean of the last three data points of phase B might also be a better estimate of $\hat{y}_{Bp}$ in some cases, although no extrapolation is necessary for the regression estimate within this phase. We should use the mean as an estimate to the degree that a linear equation does not fit the data.

General Linear Model for Estimating $\hat{y}_{Ap}$ and $\hat{y}_{Bp}$. Although it is probably apparent how to compute estimates based on means, it is less clear how the estimates might be calculated based on regression models. Because single-case studies invariably include replication of AB phases, the regression models should incorporate estimates for these replicates. For simplicity, we illustrate the use of regression models with only ABAB designs.

First, we want to develop for each pair of AB phases a prediction model for the $\hat{y}_{Ap}$s and $\hat{y}_{Bp}$s that allows for different linear trends within each of the four phases. We will present the prediction equation as a general linear model (GLM) and, more specifically, as an extension of the cell means model (Milliken & Johnson, 1984). The cell means model includes an indicator variable for each cell in a design. All observations within a cell receive a "1" on the indicator variable for that cell, whereas all other observations receive a "0" on this variable. A variable with 1s for all observations is included in some GLMs to estimate an intercept parameter. However, the 1s variable is redundant to the indicator variables in the cell means model in that the sum of the scores for the indicator variables is equal to the score in the 1s variable for all observations. Consequently, no 1s variable is included in the model, and the intercept parameter is not estimated. Because all observations within a cell have a score of 1 on their indicator variable and a score of 0 on all other indicator variables, the weight parameter associated with a model with indicator variables must be the means for the cells of a study.

For the ABAB design, we develop a cell means model by treating each phase as a cell, and, accordingly, we include four indicator variables, x_1 through x_4, in the equation predicting the behavior scores y with some amount of error, ε:

$$y = B_1x_1 + B_2x_2 + B_3x_3 + B_4x_4 + \varepsilon. \tag{1}$$

The least squares estimates of B_1 through B_4 are the means for the four phases, and the predicted score for any observation is the mean for the phase associated with this observation.

The cell means model is an inadequate prediction model if the y scores show some trend over time within phases. Under these conditions, the model must be expanded to include additional parameters that incorporate these trends. Assuming the trends are linear within phases for the ABAB design, we would need to include four additional predictors in the model, one for each phase. These predictors are generated by first creating a trials variable, t. The scores in the trials variable are the trial numbers $1, 2, 3, \ldots, N$ in our ABAB design, where N is the total number of data points in all phases. Next, cross-product variables, $x \cdot t$, are created by multiplying the trials variable by each of the indicator variables. These cross-product variables—four of them in the case of the ABAB design—are then included in the prediction equation:

$$y = B_1 x_1 + B_2 x_2 + B_3 x_3 + B_4 x_4$$
$$+ B_5 x_1 t + B_6 x_2 t + B_7 x_3 t + B_8 x_4 t + \varepsilon. \tag{2}$$

Note that the trials variable itself is not included in the model. The trials variable is not included because it is redundant to the four cross-product terms; that is, the sum of the scores for the cross-product variables is equal to the score in the trials variable for all observations. (The redundancy between the cross-product variables and the trials variable is comparable to the redundancy between the indicator variable and the 1s variables.)

To understand Equation 2, it is helpful to reorganize terms:

$$y = B_1 x_1 + B_5 x_1 t + B_2 x_2 + B_6 x_2 t$$
$$+ B_3 x_3 + B_7 x_3 t + B_4 x_4 + B_8 x_4 t + \varepsilon. \tag{3}$$

For any phase, the model equation simplifies to the linear regression equation for this phase. For example, for observations in the first phase, x_1 is equal to 1 and x_2 through x_4 are equal to 0, and the equation simplifies to the linear regression equation for this phase:

$$y = B_1 + B_5 t + \varepsilon. \tag{4}$$

Similarly, B_2 and B_6, B_3 and B_7, and B_4 and B_8 are the intercept and slope parameters for the second, third, and fourth phases in the ABAB design, respectively. Because Equation 3 represents the trends within each of the phases (cells), we refer to this model as a cell trends model.

Potentially, Equation 3 could be expanded to allow for quadratic or even higher order polynomials. In addition, time series components could be added to the model. The utility of these more complex models could be evaluated using standard statistical methods. Difficulties are likely to be encountered due to the small number of data points in many studies.

Choice of Divisors for an Effect Size Index for AB Phases

Once $\hat{y}_{Ap}$ and $\hat{y}_{Bp}$ are computed using means or regression estimates, a number of indices for effect size could be computed. For example, if all studies of interest examine the same dependent variable scaled in the same manner, an effect size index could be simply the difference between the two estimates:

$$ES_1 = \hat{y}_{Bp} - \hat{y}_{Ap}. \tag{5}$$

Alternatively, if the metric for the dependent variable varies across studies, as is typically the case, these estimates could be divided by a within-phase variability index to obtain a unitless index:

$$ES_2 = \frac{\hat{y}_{Bp} - \hat{y}_{Ap}}{S}. \tag{6}$$

Choices for S could include the standard deviation of scores within the A phase or the pooled standard deviation of scores within the A and the B phases. The former standard deviation is probably preferable in most cases if our suspicions are correct that in most studies the within-phase standard deviations are heterogeneous across phases.

The choice among scores to use in computing the standard deviation S is dependent on which estimators are used in computing $\hat{y}_{Ap}$ and $\hat{y}_{Bp}$. If they are estimated using means based on the last three data points, then the denominator for ES_2 would be the standard deviation of the y scores for the last three data points within the A phase. Alternatively, if they are estimated using linear regression estimates, then the denominator for ES_2 would be the standard deviation of the y residual scores within the A phase:

$$S = \sqrt{\frac{\sum_{i=1}^{N_A}(y_i - \hat{y}_i)^2}{n_A - 2}}, \tag{7}$$

where $\hat{y}_i$ is a predicted score based on a linear regression equation for individual i and n_A is the number of scores in the A phase. The divisor assumes that the regression equation is linear and subtracts 2 from n_A because the equation includes two parameters, a slope and an intercept.

Another index that takes into account the difference in metric of dependent variables across studies is the proportion change index:

$$ES_3 = \frac{\hat{y}_{Bp} - \hat{y}_{Ap}}{\hat{y}_{Ap}}. \tag{8}$$

This index may reflect more accurately the way in which many single-case researchers discuss the effect of a treatment. They tend to make statements like the following: "The treatment reduced (increased) the frequency (duration) of behavior by 20%." By choosing ES_3 for a meta-analysis, researchers are assuming that a change in behavior of a particular amount is less if the level of behavior in the baseline phase was high rather than low.

Treatment and Replication Effects for Multiple AB Phases for a Study

An important requirement of single-case methodology is that studies include multiple AB phases to evaluate replicability of treatment effects. The replicates may be within subjects, as with an ABAB design, or between subjects, as with multiple-baseline-across-cases designs. How to incorporate multiple effect sizes from a single study in a meta-analysis is a difficult issue that has been discussed extensively in the literature (see Gleser & Olkin, 1994).

For simplicity, we will take the mean of effect sizes across AB phases to obtain an overall effect size. However, it may be useful to compute a replication effect that could be used as a moderator variable. A replication effect across AB phases, RE, can be computed as follows:

$$RE = \sqrt{\sum_{j=1}^{m} \frac{(ES_j - \overline{ES})^2}{m - 1}}, \tag{9}$$

where ES_j is an effect size for the jth pair of AB phases, $\overline{ES}$ is the mean of the ES_js, and m is the number of replications of AB phases. RE is small to the extent that the effect sizes for AB phases replicate.

In the next section, we discuss methods for combining an effect size index in order to arrive at some overall effect size estimate, as well as methods for explaining the heterogeneity among estimates of this effect size through the introduction of moderator variables. We have restricted our discussion on these methods to a single index, ES_2 as defined in Equation 6.

Combining Effect Size Measures and Evaluating Moderator Variables

Effect sizes as computed in the previous section provide normalized results that allow us to combine information across studies to address scientific questions of interest. If all studies measured the same underlying phenomenon perfectly, combining effect sizes would be easy. However, most single-case studies used in meta-analyses are not exact replicates; methodologic features including type of design, specific intervention structure, number of within-treatment phases, number of treatment replications, and effect or outcome measures, vary widely. Furthermore, meta-analyses have multiple scientific objectives ranging from characterizing the efficacy of a particular intervention or class of interventions to comparing the efficacy of two or more different interventions, to evaluating the effect of subject or investigator characteristics on the efficacy of a class of interventions. In light of this diversity, the methodology for combining effect sizes from the different studies must be able to provide overall estimates of treatment effectiveness and the precision of those estimates as well as assessments of the magnitude and direction of effects of other variables or factors on treatment effectiveness. Some authors have suggested a multiple-step process in which point estimates and confidence intervals for those estimates are developed first, then heterogeneity of the effect size estimates is assessed, and finally the effects of moderator variables are examined (Faith et al., 1996). As noted by Faith et al., moderator variables may be methodologic (e.g., study design, degree of treatment integrity, overall study quality, etc.) or substantive (e.g., study population, treatment intensity). Although we agree these three issues must be addressed in a comprehensive meta-analysis, we prefer an integrated model-based approach to analyses as described by Shadish and Haddock (1994), Hedges (1994), and Raudenbush (1994). In the following discussion, we summarize that methodology heuristically, with references to the literature for readers who desire more statistical rigor.

Conceptually, the problems encountered in analyzing effect sizes are analogous to those found in analyzing response variables—computing mean responses, determining whether response means vary across levels of another factor, and assessing relationships between the response levels and other continuous variables. Such analyses are often addressed statistically through the use of linear model approaches such as analysis of variance (ANOVA) and regression. We propose similar approaches for analyzing effect sizes, with the effect size from each study treated as the observation unit. We note here that the modeling procedure we are proposing could be adapted relatively easily to consider the replications within each study as the unit of analysis, accounting for the within-study correlation using a mixed-model procedure. To be consistent with the literature on meta-analysis for single-case designs and to use procedures familiar to most readers, we have chosen to use the study as the unit of analysis for this presentation.

Although the analyses are analogous to those used in standard models, they differ from ordinary least squares linear modeling. Univariate linear models typically assume variance homogeneity across the independent observations. However, because of differences in design, study size, and characteristics of individual subjects used in the studies, effect sizes will not have equal variances. To account for variance heterogeneity, each observation is weighted in the analysis with the inverse of the variance used as the weight. This weighting scheme is reasonable in that it produces efficient statistical estimates and it gives larger weight to those studies with greater precision in effect size estimates.

Two alternatives are available for constructing models for studying the variation in values of an effect size index across studies: fixed effects models and random (or more appropriately mixed) effects models. Details of the differences in these models are described by Shadish and Haddock (1994) and Raudenbush (1994). The key difference is that the fixed effects models assume the effect sizes ES_i from the individual studies are a random sample from the same population with true population effect size Ξ and that the ES_i differ from the true Ξ across studies only because of sampling variance. In contrast, mixed effects models assume the subjects used in the different studies are a random sample from a population and that each subject has some "true" effect size θ_i with those subject-specific effect sizes distributed around Ξ, the true population mean effect size; in this model, the estimates ES_i differ from Ξ because of a combination of sampling variance and variance of the effect sizes across the population of potential subjects. Historically, single-case-study meta-analyses have used fixed effects approaches, in part because tools for mixed model computation were limited. However, for most single-case studies, the mixed effects model is more conceptually appealing, and computations for this model can readily be accomplished for meta-analyses with small numbers of studies using the algorithms presented by Raudenbush (1994) or for larger studies with statistical software designed for mixed model analyses such as the mixed model procedures in SAS (PROC MIXED) and BMDP (5V) or with a hierarchical linear modeling package.

Consequently, we choose to use a mixed model approach, but procedures that we describe can readily be adapted to the fixed effects approach described by Hedges (1994) if a researcher determines that a particular study is addressed more appropriately with a fixed effects model.

The mixed model approach described by Raudenbush (1994) requires an estimate of the effect size variance v_i for each study in the meta-analysis. Because the effect size estimates are random variables based on a sample from the subject or subjects used in a particular study, they are not measured exactly, but have sampling error. The variance v_i is simply the square of the standard error of the estimated effect size.

When ES_2 is calculated from regression estimates, an exact estimate of the variance is unavailable. Consequently, we develop heuristic estimates of the v_i using procedures described in the following paragraphs. Although these procedures are conceptually reasonable, further research is needed on their statistical properties, particularly the small-sample properties. Consequently, they should be used primarily to develop descriptive summaries of meta-analytic results, rather than for formal statistical inference.

In each replicate of the study, the numerator of the effect size estimate is simply a linear combination of the parameter estimates from the regression model. For example, for the first replication of an ABAB design the numerator of the effect size estimate is

$$ES \text{ numerator} = (\hat{B}_2 + \hat{B}_6 t) - (\hat{B}_1 + \hat{B}_5 t), \tag{10}$$

where the B_i are estimates from the regression model and the t is a fixed constant. The estimate of the variance of this estimate is a quadratic form that involves the estimated variance/covariance matrix of the regression coefficients, which can be obtained from any standard statistical package. For the previous form, the estimate of the variance is

$$\begin{aligned} V = {} &\mathrm{Var}(\hat{B}_2) + t^2\,\mathrm{Var}(\hat{B}_6) + 2t\,\mathrm{Cov}(\hat{B}_2, \hat{B}_6) \\ &+ \mathrm{Var}(\hat{B}_1) + t^2\,\mathrm{Var}(\hat{B}_5) + 2t\,\mathrm{Cov}(\hat{B}_1, \hat{B}_5). \end{aligned} \tag{11}$$

Note that, under model assumptions (no serial correlation in the errors in each subject's series of observations), the estimates in the two phases are independent. As discussed widely in the single-case meta-analytic literature, the issue of within-subject correlation is an area for further research. As research develops in this area, the variance estimates noted previously can be modified to account for correlation of the regression estimates in different phases. Next, an estimate of the variance was obtained for the phase A standard deviation, S_A, under the assumption that S^2/σ^2, the ratio of the computed variance to the true variance is approximately distributed as a chi-square random variable with $n_A - 1$ degrees of freedom, where n_A is the number of observations in phase A. For sample sizes of 3 or greater, a reasonable estimate of the variance of S_A is approximately $0.5S_A^2$. Again, these variance estimates are based on asymptotic properties of the model, and further research is needed on their small-sample properties. The variance of the ratio in each phase was estimated using a standard formula for the variance of the ratio of independent variables (Kish, 1965):

$$\mathrm{Var}\left(\frac{Y}{X}\right) \approx \frac{1}{X^2}\left[\mathrm{Var}(Y) + \left(\frac{Y}{X}\right)^2 \mathrm{Var}(X)\right]. \tag{12}$$

Finally, the variance of the mean effect size across replications of a study was estimated by dividing the sum of the variances for each phase by m^2, where m is the number of replications in the study.

The preceding approach assumes that the regression approach was used to generate effect size estimates. If the last-three-data-points approach is used, estimation of variance simplifies. The estimate of the numerator variance is simply the sum of S_A^2 and S_B^2 divided by 3 and the equation for the ratio simplifies to

$$\mathrm{Var}(ES) \approx \frac{1}{S_A^2}\left[\frac{S_A^2 + S_B^2}{3} + \frac{(\overline{Y}_A - \overline{Y}_B)^2}{2}\right]. \tag{13}$$

To conduct a meta-analysis using either effect size estimation method, compute the estimated variance for each study used in the meta-analysis, and use those mean effect sizes and their variances in a linear model analysis appropriate for the questions being asked by the study. For example, if the primary objective of the analysis is to generate an overall estimated effect size with confidence intervals, use a model with a single grand mean. If the objective is to assess whether the effect is a function of the length of time over which the treatment phase of the study was extended, use a regression model with effect size regressed against the minimum treatment time in the study.

An Example Meta-Analysis

We now illustrate all steps involved in conducting a meta-analysis based on the results of six single-case experimental studies concerned with treating aberrant, self-injurious behaviors in children. We first discuss in detail the computation of effect sizes and replicability effects for one of these six studies and then present these indices for all six studies. Finally, we show how to assess moderator variables and combine treatment effects for these studies.

Computation of Effect Sizes and Replicability Effects for a Single Study

We illustrate the computation of the effect size ES_2 (Equation 6) and replicability effect RE (Equation 9), with an example using an ABAB design. The data for this study are presented in Table 1. In computing these effects, we will estimate $\hat{y}_{Ap}$ and $\hat{y}_{Bp}$ using both a regression approach and the means for the last three data values in each phase. The example using the ABAB design is from a study by Vollmer, Iwata, Smith, and Rodgers (1992). They were concerned with reducing the frequency of an individual's "aberrant behaviors." The number of observations in the ABAB phases were 12, 8, 7, and 24, respectively.

We now apply the GLM using our example study with an ABAB design. First, we regress the y scores on the four indicator

Table 1 Data from Vollmer et al. (1992) Illustrating Meta-Analysis

Baseline (A$_1$)	4.0	7.0	8.0	6.0	7.5	3.0	10.0	4.5	4.0	4.5	5.0	5.5
Treatment (B$_1$)	1.0	1.0	1.0	2.0	3.5	1.0	1.0	1.0				
Baseline (A$_2$)	3.0	0.0	11.0	6.0	2.0	7.0	15.0					
Treatment (B$_2$)	1.0	1.0	0.0	0.0	8.0	3.0	0.0	1.0	1.0	2.0	0.0	0.0
	3.0	1.0	1.0	1.0	5.0	1.0	0.0	1.0	1.0	0.5	2.0	1.0

variables as shown in Equation 1. The R^2 from this regression is .72. These regression results are compared with the results obtained from regressing the y scores on the indicator variables and the cross-product variables as shown in Equation 2; the R^2 is .78. Because the R^2 increased .06 (the R^2 change is significant, $p < .05$), we choose the more complex model including the individual phase trends. This regression equation is

$$\hat{y} = 6.61x_1 + 1.14x_2 - 28.86x_3 + 2.09x_4$$
$$- .13x_1t + .02x_2t + 1.46x_3t - .02x_4t.$$

There are two phase comparisons in the ABAB design (A$_1$ versus B$_1$ and A$_2$ versus B$_2$), and, therefore, two effect sizes are calculated. First, the effect size for the first pair of AB phases is calculated. If the final trial of the B$_1$ phase (the 20th observation) is the point of comparison, we estimate $\hat{y}_{Bp}$ by substituting into the equation a 1 for x_2, a 0 for all other xs, and a 20 for t and obtain a value of 1.54. To estimate $\hat{y}_{Ap}$, we substitute a 1 for x_1, a 0 for all other xs, and a 20 for t and obtain a value of 4.01. The standard deviation of the residuals for A$_1$ is 2.07, and, therefore, ES_2 is -1.19:

$$ES_2 = \frac{\hat{y}_{Bp} - \hat{y}_{Ap}}{S} = \frac{1.54 - 4.01}{2.07} = -1.19.$$

Similar calculations can be carried out for the second pair of AB phases. For these phases, the point of comparison is the last trial of the B$_2$ phase, the 51st observation. We estimate $\hat{y}_{Bp}$ by substituting into the equation a 1 for x_4, a 0 for all other xs, and a 51 for t and obtain a value of 30.30. To estimate $\hat{y}_{Ap}$, we substitute a 1 for x_3, a 0 for all other xs, and a 51 for t and obtain a value of 1.30. The standard deviation of the residuals for A_1 is 3.02, and, therefore, ES_2 is -9.61:

$$ES_2 = \frac{\hat{y}_{Bp} - \hat{y}_{Ap}}{S} = \frac{1.30 - 30.30}{3.02} = -9.61.$$

To obtain an overall estimate of the effect size for this study, we compute a mean effect size, which for this study is -5.40. We would be most convinced that we understood the effect of the treatment on the subject's behavior if the effect size replicated perfectly across pairs of AB phases (e.g., -5.40 for the first AB phases and -5.40 for the second AB phases). The RE index (Equation 9) reflects the degree that the effect sizes yield dissimilar results. For the ABAB example, the RE index indicates that effect sizes differed considerably across pairs of AB phases:

$$RE = \sqrt{\sum_{j=1}^{m} \frac{(ES_j - \overline{ES})^2}{m - 1}}$$

$$= \sqrt{\frac{(-1.19 - (-5.40))^2 + (-9.61 - (-5.40))^2}{2 - 1}} = 5.95.$$

We next compute the same indices, but using the mean of the last three data points within phases to estimate $\hat{y}_{Ap}$ and $\hat{y}_{Bp}$. The last three observations in A_1 are: 4.5, 5.0, and 5.5, which have a mean of 5 and a standard deviation of .5, whereas the last three observations in B_1 are 1, 1, and 1, which have a mean of 1. ES_2, therefore, is $(1 - 5)/.5 = -8.00$. Similarly, the last three observations in A_2 are 2, 7, and 15, with a mean of 8.00 and a standard deviation of 6.56, whereas the last three observations in B_2 are .5, 2, and 1, with a mean of 1.17. The effect size is then $(1.17 - 8)/6.56 = -1.04$. The overall effect size is the mean of these two effect sizes, $(-8.00 - 1.04)/2 = -4.52$. The replicability effect based on these effect sizes is again large:

$$RE = \sqrt{\sum_{j=1}^{m} \frac{(ES_j - \overline{ES})^2}{m-1}}$$

$$= \sqrt{\frac{(-8.00 - (-4.52))^2 + (-1.04 - (-4.52))^2}{2-1}} = 4.92.$$

The estimates of $\hat{y}_{Ap}$ and $\hat{y}_{Bp}$ based on the means for the last three points within a phase and those based on the regression model differ dramatically, although the overall effect size and the replicability estimates are remarkably similar. They differ because the estimates based on the means do not take into account trends within phases. For example, the slope for the second A phase of 1.46 was positive and strong, indicating a fast rate in returning to the baseline. This slope was used to estimate what the behavior level would have been had the baseline been extended to the end of the second B phase (i.e., $\hat{y}_{Ap}$). Although a straight line with a strong positive slope may be appropriate for the A_2 data, it probably does not represent what would have occurred if the baseline had been extended. In all likelihood, the slope would have declined over time. In fact, the obtained estimate of 30.30 is very large, larger than any of the obtained scores. Because we are skeptical about extrapolation for these data, the mean of the last three data points might be a better estimate of $\hat{y}_{Ap}$.

Computation of Effect Sizes and Replicability Effects for Six Studies

The results of a meta-analysis of five additional single-case experimental studies concerned with treating aberrant, self-injurious behaviors in children, as well as the one just presented, are shown in Table 2. These six studies fall into two design types: the ABAB design and the multiple-baseline design. Effect sizes computed within each phase, the variances of these effect sizes, their replicability, and an overall effect size are reported for each study, using both a regression and a last-three-data-points approach. Obviously, a great deal of heterogeneity exists

Table 2 Meta-Analysis Results for Six Studies

Study	Design Type	Replication	Assessment Time	Regression Approach			Last-Three-Data-Points		
				ES_2	Variance of ES_2	RE	ES_2	Variance of ES_2	RE
Albin et al. (1995)	ABAB	1	13	−2.52	5.47		−2.50	3.46	
		2	28	−2.53	134.94		−8.09	33.38	
		Overall		−2.52	35.10	.01	−5.30	9.21	3.95
Smith et al. (1993)	ABAB	1	32	−2.81	16.82		−4.35	9.79	
		2	59	−1.87	59.02		−5.03	12.99	
		Overall		−2.34	18.96	.66	−4.69	5.70	.48
Vollmer et al. (1992)	ABAB	1	20	−1.19	1.74		−8.00	32.33	
		2	51	−9.61	20.06		−1.04	.88	
		Overall		−5.40	5.45	5.95	−4.52	8.31	.49
Vollmer et al. (1993)	Multiple baseline	1	40	−25.68	443.21		−5.16	13.64	
		2	50	−16.93	231.43		−8.19	33.85	
		3	49	−6.68	.81		−2.88	4.49	
		Overall		−16.43	75.05	9.51	−5.41	5.77	2.84
Zarcone et al. (1994)	Multiple baseline	1	41	−8.20	1177.46		−10.10	51.78	
		2	23	0.33	6.01		4.23	20.44	
		Overall		−3.93	295.87	5.57	−2.93	18.05	10.14
Zarcone et al. (1993)	Multiple baseline	1	49	9.04	35.97		−2.33	3.15	
		2	46	−15.97	454.81		−4.91	13.33	
		3	27	−1.28	115.65		−5.00	12.83	
		Overall		−2.74.	67.38	12.57	−4.08	3.26	1.51

among the effect size estimates, whether computed through the regression or last-three-data-points approaches. Even more important, large differences exist between the results obtained by the two approaches. Even though examining the overall effect sizes computed by both approaches does not lead one to conclude that one method tends to produce higher effect size estimates than the other, the two approaches can give very discrepant results; for example, for the Vollmer, Iwata, Zarcone, Smith, and Mazaleski (1993) study, the overall effect size based on regression is -16.43, whereas the overall effect size based on the last-three-data-points is -5.63. However, it appears that ABAB designs produce more consistency between the two approaches than multiple-baseline designs.

Combining Effect Sizes and Assessing Moderator Variables

Next, we computed the mean effect size based on the six example studies and its standard error, both in aggregate and for different types of studies, and addressed two questions using those six studies. First, is effect size related to replicability, where we consider two groups, replicability less than 10, and replicability greater than 10? Second, is effect size related to mean time during the treatment phase of the study? To address these questions, we computed by hand the variance estimates for each of the six studies and then used restricted maximum-likelihood methods implemented in the SAS procedure MIXED as described by Raudenbush (1994) to analyze the data. To implement the procedure in MIXED, we used the WEIGHT statement with the reciprocal of the study variances as the weight and assumed a single random effects variance component for study in the RANDOM statement.

The estimate of the mean effect size was obtained using the MODEL statement, "model es=;", which generates a means model. The results indicate that the mean effect size is -4.9 with a standard error of 1.3, which yields an approximate 95% confidence interval for the effect size of $(-7.7, -2.3)$. Because this confidence interval is in standard deviation units of the A phase, the effects in these studies appear to be quite large. Considering the two study types separately, the effect size for the ABAB design was −4.48 (1.35) and for the multiple-baseline design it was −8.46 (3.90). Although the magnitude of these effect sizes differs substantially, the sample sizes here are insufficient to demonstrate a difference statistically.

To address the first of the two questions, the six studies were divided into three replicability classes with Studies 1 and 2 having high replicability, Studies 3 and 5 having moderate replicability, and Studies 4 and 6 having low replicability, and a mixed model ANOVA was run. For the three levels of replicability, the resultant estimates of mean effect size in each level with their standard errors were −2.4 (2.3), −5.4 (1.5), and −9.3 (4.0) from high to low replicability, respectively. Obviously, these results suggest a trend, but because we have only six observations, the results provide no statistical evidence of a difference in these means. Finally, a linear regression model was used to assess whether mean sample size for the two B phases was related to effect size. The slope estimate was −0.08 with a standard error of 0.2, again providing no statistical evidence of a relationship between effect size and mean sample size for the two B phases.

We replicated the example using the last-three-data-points approach. The mean effect size aggregated across study type was −4.6 with a standard error of −0.29 yielding a 95% confidence interval of (−5.2, −4.0), reflecting the smaller variability associated with this approach. For the two study types, the effect size for the ABAB design was −4.8 (0.48) and for the multiple-baseline design it was −4.4 (0.41) showing little evidence of a difference as a function of design. For the three levels of replicability, the resultant estimates of mean effect size in each level with their standard errors were −4.3 (0.31), −5.1 (0.28), and −2.9 (0.62) from high to low replicability, respectively. These results differ substantially from those obtained using the regression approach with no apparent trend as a function of replicability. Finally, for the assessment of the relationship between mean sample size across the two B phases and effect size, the slope estimate was 0.002 with a standard error of 0.04, again providing no statistical evidence of a relationship between effect size and mean sample size across the two B phases.

Conclusions

In this chapter, we presented an approach to conducting meta-analyses of the results from single-case experimental designs. This approach may be applied to the results of nearly any single-case experimental design. Certainly, other approaches have been suggested, but our approach has the strength of conducting meta-analyses within a comprehensive framework while keeping in mind the major goal of the studies' authors: To assess the effectiveness of treatments on behavior accurately. Any meta-analytic strategy that fails to incorporate the perspective of the behavioral analyst in evaluating study results is probably doomed to failure either from interpreting incomplete information (e.g., a failure to note the replicability of the treatment effect across the phases) or from ignoring important information (e.g., a failure to note the presence of trends within phases).

Author Notes: Scott Hershberger was instrumental in originating the project. All authors contributed significantly to the final version of the chapter, which is an integration of their thoughts and writings. This research was partially supported by Grant HD-02528 from the National Institute of Child Health and Human Development to the Life Span Institute of the University of Kansas.

References

Albin, R. W., O'Brien, M., & Horner, R. H. (1995). Analysis of an escalating sequence of problem behaviors: A case study. *Research in Developmental Disabilities, 16*, 133–147.

Allison, D. B., & Gorman, B. S. (1993). Calculating effect sizes for meta-analysis: The case of the single case. *Behavior, Research, and Therapy, 31*, 621–631.

Busk, P. L., & Serlin, R. C. (1992). Meta-analysis for single-case research. In T. R. Kratochwill & J. R. Levin (Eds.), *Single-case research design and analysis: New directions for psychology and education* (pp. 187–212). Hillsdale, NJ: Erlbaum.

Center, B. A., Skiba, R. J., & Casey, A. (1985/86). A methodology for the quantitative synthesis of intra-subject design research. *Journal of Special Education, 19*, 387–400.

Faith, M. S., Allison, D. B., & Gorman, B. S. (1996). Meta-analysis of single-case research. In R. D. Franklin, D. B. Allison, & B. S. Gorman (Eds.), *Design and analysis of single-case research* (pp. 245–277). Mahwah, NJ: Erlbaum.

Gingerich, W. J. (1984). Meta-analysis of applied time-series data. *Journal of Applied Behavioral Science, 20*, 71–79.

Gleser, L. J., & Olkin, I. (1994). Stochastically dependent effect sizes. In H. Cooper & L. V. Hedges (Eds.), *The handbook of research synthesis* (pp. 339–355). New York: Russell Sage.

Gorsuch, R. L. (1983). Three methods for analyzing limited time-series (N of 1) data. *Behavioral Assessment, 5*, 141–154.

Harvey, A. C. (1989). *Forecasting, structural time series models and the Kalman filter*. Cambridge: Cambridge University Press.

Hedges, L. V. (1994). Fixed effects models. In H. Cooper & L. V. Hedges (Eds.), *The handbook of research synthesis* (pp. 285–321). New York: Russell Sage.

Huitema, B. E. (1985). Autocorrelation in applied behavior analysis: A myth. *Behavioral Assessment, 7*, 107–118.

Kazdin, A. E. (1982). *Single-case research designs: Methods for clinical and applied settings*. New York: Oxford University Press.

Kish, L. (1965). *Survey sampling*. New York: Wiley.

Marascuilo, L. A., & Busk, P. L. (1988). Combining statistics for multiple-baseline AB and replicated ABAB designs across subjects. *Behavioral Assessment, 10*, 69–85.

Milliken, G. A., & Johnson, D. F. (1984). *Analysis of messy data* (Vol. I). Belmont, CA: Wadsworth.

Raudenbush, S. W. (1994). Random effects models. In H. Cooper & L. V. Hedges (Eds.), *The handbook of research synthesis* (pp. 301–321). New York: Russell Sage.

Scruggs, T. E., Mastropieri, M. A., & Casto, G. (1987). The quantitative synthesis of single-subject research: Methodology and validation. *Remedial and Special Education, 8*, 24–33.

Shadish, W. R., & Haddock, C. K. (1994). Combining estimates of effect size. In H. Cooper & L. V. Hedges (Eds.), *The handbook of research synthesis* (pp. 262–280). New York: Russell Sage.

Skiba, R. J., Casey, A., & Center, B. A. (1986). Nonaversive procedures in the classroom behavioral problems. *Journal of Special Education, 19*, 459–481.

Smith, R. G., Iwata, B. A., Vollmer, T. R., & Zarcone, J. R. (1993). Experimental analysis and treatment of multiply controlled self-injury. *Journal of Applied Behavior Analysis, 26*, 183–196.

Vollmer, T. R., Iwata, B. A., Smith, R. G., & Rodgers, T. A. (1992). Reduction of multiple aberrant behaviors and concurrent development of self-care skills with differential reinforcement. *Research in Developmental Disabilities, 13*, 287–299.

Vollmer, T. R., Iwata, B. A., Zarcone, J. R., Smith, R. G., & Mazaleski, J. L. (1993). The role of attention in the treatment of attention-maintained self-injurious behavior: Noncontingent reinforcement and differential reinforcement of other behavior. *Journal of Applied Behavior Analysis, 26*, 9–21.

White, D. M., Rusch, F. R., Kazdin, A. E., & Hartmann, D. P. (1989). Applications of meta-analysis in individual subject research. *Behavioral Assessment, 11*, 281–296.

Zarcone, J. R., Iwata, B. A., Mazaleski, J. L., & Smith, R. G. (1994). Momentum and extinction effects on self-injurious escape behavior and noncompliance. *Journal of Applied Behavior Analysis, 27*, 353–360.

Zarcone, J. R., Iwata, B. A., Vollmer, T. R., Jagtiani, S., Smith, R. G., & Mazaleski, J. L. (1993). Extinction of self-injurious escape behavior with and without instructional fading. *Journal of Applied Behavior Analysis, 26*, 353–360.

6

Exact Permutational Inference for Categorical and Nonparametric Data

Cyrus R. Mehta & Nitin R. Patel

MODERN STATISTICAL METHODS rely heavily on nonparametric techniques for comparing two or more populations. These techniques generate p values without making any distributional assumptions about the populations being compared. They rely, however, on asymptotic theory that is valid only if the sample sizes are reasonably large and well balanced across the populations. For small, sparse, skewed, or heavily tied data, the asymptotic theory may not be valid. See Agresti and Yang (1987) for some empirical results, and Read and Cressie (1988) for a more theoretical discussion.

One way to make valid statistical inferences in the presence of small, sparse, or imbalanced data is to compute exact p values and confidence intervals, based on the permutational distribution of the test statistic. This approach was first proposed by Fisher (1925) and has been used extensively for the single 2×2 contingency table. In the past, exact tests were rarely attempted for tables of higher dimension than 2×2, primarily because of the formidable computing problems involved in their execution. Two developments over the past 10 years have removed this obstacle. First, the easy availability of immense quantities of computing power in homes and offices has revolutionized our thinking about what is computationally affordable. Second, many new, fast, and efficient algorithms for exact permutational inference have recently been published. Thus, problems that would previously have taken several hours or even days to solve now take only a few minutes. It only remained to incorporate these algorithms into user-friendly, well documented statistical packages. Now this step also has been accomplished. In this chapter, we present a unified framework for exact nonparametric inference, anchored in the permutation principle. We illustrate with several examples that exact statistical inference can be accomplished for a very broad class of nonparametric problems by permuting the entries in a contingency table subject to fixed margins. The examples deal with inference on unordered, singly ordered, and doubly ordered $r \times c$ contingency tables, a single $2 \times c$ contingency table, stratified 2×2 contingency tables, and stratified $2 \times c$ contingency tables. These examples are all analyzed by the StatXact-3 (1995) software package. Both exact and asymptotic inference is performed so that one may assess the accuracy of the asymptotic methods. Numerical algorithms for solving these permutation problems are referenced. Finally, we list various software, textbook, and Internet resources for performing exact permutational inference.

Exact Permutation Tests for $r \times c$ Contingency Tables

In this section, we introduce the main ideas underlying permutation tests through a detailed treatment of the $r \times c$ contingency table. For a broad class of statistical tests, the data can be rep-

Table 1 Layout for a Generic $r \times c$ Contingency Table

Rows	Col_1	Col_2	$\cdots$	Col_c	Row_Total
Row_1	x_{11}	x_{12}	$\cdots$	x_{1c}	m_1
Row_2	x_{21}	x_{22}	$\cdots$	x_{2c}	m_2
$\vdots$	$\vdots$	$\vdots$	$\cdots$	$\vdots$	$\vdots$
Row_r	x_{r1}	x_{r2}	$\cdots$	x_{rc}	m_r
Col_Total	n_1	n_2	$\cdots$	n_c	N

resented in the form of a single $r \times c$ contingency table, **x**, as displayed in Table 1. The entry in each cell of this $r \times c$ table is the number of subjects falling in the corresponding row and column classifications. The row and column classifications may be based on either *nominal* or *ordered* variables. Nominal variables take on values that cannot be positioned in any natural order. An example of a nominal variable is profession—medicine, law, business. In some statistical packages, nominal variables are also referred to as *class* variables or *unordered* variables. Ordered variables take on values that can be ordered in a natural way. An example of an ordered variable is drug dose—low, medium, high. Ordered variables may, of course, assume numerical values as well (e.g., the number of cigarettes smoked per day).

Unconditional Sampling Distributions

The exact probability distribution of **x** depends on the sampling scheme that was used to generate **x**. When both the row and the column classifications are categorical, Agresti (1990) lists three sampling schemes that could give rise to **x**: full multinomial sampling, product multinomial sampling, and Poisson sampling. Under all three schemes, the probability distribution of **x** contains unknown parameters relating to the individual cells of the $r \times c$ table.

Under full multinomial sampling, a total of N items are sampled independently, and x_{ij} of them are classified as belonging to row category i and column category j, each with probability π_{ij}. Thus, the probability of observing the table $\mathbf{x}$ is

$$\Pr(\mathbf{x}) = \prod_{i=1}^{r} \prod_{j=1}^{c} \frac{N! \pi_{ij}^{x_{ij}}}{x_{ij}!}. \tag{1}$$

Full multinomial sampling might arise, for example, if one were to sample N hospital patients and classify them according to their race (white, black, other) and their major medical insurance (Blue Cross, HMO, other). One would be interested in testing the null hypothesis that race and insurance plan were independent. Formally, let $\pi_{i.}$ be the marginal probability of falling in row category i, and $\pi_{.j}$ be the marginal probability of falling in column category j. The null hypothesis of no row by column interaction assumes that

$$\pi_{ij} = \pi_{i.} \pi_{.j}.$$

Under product multinomial sampling, a predetermined number, m_i, of items are sampled independently from population i, and x_{ij} of them are classified as falling into category j. Let π_{ij} be the conditional probability that an item will fall into category j given that it was sampled from population i. Thus, the probability of observing table $\mathbf{x}$ is

$$\Pr(\mathbf{x}) = \prod_{i=1}^{r} \prod_{j=1}^{c} \frac{m_i! \pi_{ij}^{x_{ij}}}{x_{ij}!}. \tag{2}$$

Product multinomial sampling might arise, for example, if r drug therapies were being tested in a clinical trial, m_i patients were treated with drug i, and each patient fell into one of c possible categories of response. One would be interested in testing, the null hypothesis that the probability of falling into response category j was the same for all i; that is, the drugs are all equivalent in terms of response. Formally, let π_{ij} be the probability that an individual treated with drug i manifests the response j. The null hypothesis of no row-by-column interaction assumes that $\pi_{ij} = \pi_j$ for all $j = 1, 2, \ldots, c$, independent of i.

Under Poisson sampling, cell (i,j) of the contingency table accumulates events at a Poisson rate of π_{ij} so that the probability of observing table $\mathbf{x}$ is

$$\Pr(\mathbf{x}) = \prod_{i=1}^{r} \prod_{j=1}^{c} \frac{(N\pi_{ij})^{x_{ij}} \exp{(-N\pi_{ij})}}{x_{ij}!}. \tag{3}$$

Poisson sampling might arise, for example, if the entry in cell (i,j) represented the number of induced abortions in district i in year j. One would be interested in testing the null hypothesis that the abortion rate did not change from year to year within a district. Formally, the null hypothesis of no row-by-column interaction would assume that the Poisson parameter $\pi_{ij} = \pi_{i.}\pi_{.j}$, where $\pi_{i.}$ is the marginal rate for district i and $\pi_{.j}$ is the marginal rate for year j.

Notice that the previous probability distributions for $\mathbf{x}$ depend on a total of rc unknown parameters, π_{ij}, $i = 1, 2, \ldots, r$, $j = 1, 2, \ldots, c$. Because statistical inference is based on the distribution of $\mathbf{x}$ under the null hypothesis of no row-by-column interaction, the number of unknown parameters is reduced (π_{ij} being replaced by $\pi_{i.}\pi_{.j}$ or π_j depending on the sampling scheme) but not eliminated. Unknown nuisance parameters still remain in Equations 1, 2, and 3 even after assuming that the null hypothesis is true. Asymptotic inference relies on estimating these unknown parameters by maximum likelihood and related methods. In exact inference, however, we eliminate nuisance parameters by conditioning on their sufficient statistics. This is discussed next.

Conditional Sampling Distribution

The key to exact permutational inference is getting rid of all nuisance parameters from the probability distribution of $\mathbf{x}$. This is accomplished by restricting the sample space to the set of all $r \times c$ contingency tables that have the same marginal sums as the observed table $\mathbf{x}$. Specifically, define the reference set

$$\Gamma = \left\{ \mathbf{y} : \mathbf{y} \text{ is } r \times c; \ \sum_{j=1}^{c} y_{ij} = m_i; \ \sum_{i=1}^{r} y_{ij} = n_j; \text{ for all } i, j \right\}. \quad (4)$$

Then one can show that, under the null hypothesis of no row-by-column interaction, the probability of observing $\mathbf{x}$ conditional on $\mathbf{x} \in \Gamma$ is

$$\Pr(\mathbf{x} \mid \mathbf{x} \in \Gamma) \equiv P(\mathbf{x}) = \prod_{i=1}^{r} \prod_{j=1}^{c} \frac{n_j! m_i!}{N! x_{ij}!}. \quad (5)$$

Equation 5, which is free of all unknown parameters, holds for categorical data whether the sampling scheme used to generate $\mathbf{x}$ is full multinomial, product multinomial, or Poisson (see, e.g., Agresti, 1992, section 3).

Because Equation 5 contains no unknown parameters, exact inference is possible. The nuisance parameters were, however, eliminated by conditioning on the margins of the observed contingency table. Now some of these margins were not fixed when the data were gathered. Thus, it is reasonable to question the appropriateness of fixing them for purposes of inference. The justification for conditioning at inference time on margins that were not naturally fixed at data sampling time has a long history. Fisher (1925) first proposed this idea for exact inference on a single 2×2 contingency table. At various times since then, prominent statisticians have commented on this approach. The principles most cited for conditioning are the *sufficiency principle*, the *ancillarity principle*, and the *randomization principle*. An informal intuitive explanation of these three principles follows.

Sufficiency Principle. The margins of the contingency table are sufficient statistics for the unknown nuisance parameters. Thus, conditioning on them affords a convenient way to eliminate nuisance parameters from the likelihood function. For example, if the data are generated by product multinomial sampling, the row margins, m_i, would ordinarily be considered fixed but the column margins, n_j, would be considered random variables. The null hypothesis of interest states that $\pi_{ij} = \pi_j$ for all i. There are thus c unknown nuisance parameters, $(\pi_1, \pi_2, \ldots, \pi_c)$, in the likelihood function (Equation 2) under the null hypothesis. By the sufficiency principle, these nuisance parameters are eliminated if we condition on $(n_1, n_2, \ldots, n_c)$, their sufficient statistics. It follows that by restricting our attention to $r \times c$ tables in Γ we are implicitly conditioning on $(n_1, n_2, \ldots, n_c)$, because the other set of margins, $(m_1, m_2, \ldots, m_r)$, are fixed naturally by the sampling scheme. Similar sufficiency arguments can be made for full multinomial and Poisson sampling.

Ancillarity Principle. The principle underlying hypothesis testing is to compare what was actually observed with what could have been observed in hypothetical repetitions of the original experiment, under the null hypothesis. In these hypothetical repetitions, it is a good idea to keep all experimental conditions unrelated to the null hypothesis unchanged as far as possible. The margins of the contingency table are representative of nuisance parameters whose values do not provide any information about the null hypothesis of interest. In this sense, they are ancillary statistics. Fixing them in hypothetical repetitions is the nearest we can get to fixing the values of the nuisance parameters themselves in hypothetical repetitions, because the latter are unknown.

Randomization Principle. The case for conditioning is especially persuasive if the r rows of the contingency tables represent r different treatments, with m_i subjects being assigned to treatment i by a randomization mechanism. Each subject provides a multinomial response that falls into one of the c columns. Thus, n_j represents the total number of responses of the jth type. Now, under the null hypothesis, the r treatments are equally effective. Therefore, the response that a patient provides is the same, regardless of the treatment to which that patient is randomized. Thus, the value of n_j is predetermined and may be regarded as fixed. The statistical significance of the observed outcome is judged relative to its permutational distribution in hypothetical repetitions of the randomization rule for assigning patients to treatments.

An excellent exposition of the conditional viewpoint is available in Yates (1984). For a theoretical justification of the sufficiency and ancillarity principles, refer to Cox and Hinkeley (1974) and Reid (1995). For a detailed exposition of the randomization principle, highlighting its applicability to a broad range of problems, refer to Edgington (1995). Throughout this chapter, we shall adopt the conditional approach. It provides us with a unified way to perform exact inference and thereby compute accurate p values and confidence intervals for $r \times c$ contingency tables, stratified 2×2 contingency tables, stratified $2 \times c$ contingency tables, and logistic regression.

Exact p Values

Having assigned an exact probability $P(\mathbf{y})$ to each $\mathbf{y} \in \Gamma$, the next step is to order each contingency table in Γ by a test statistic or "discrepancy measure" that quantifies the extent to which that table deviates from the null hypothesis of no row-by-column interaction. Let us denote the test statistic by a real-valued function D: $\Gamma \longrightarrow \mathcal{R}$ mapping $r \times c$ tables from Γ onto the real line $\mathcal{R}$. The functional form of D for some important nonparametric tests is specified in the following section.

The p value is defined as the sum of null probabilities of all the tables in Γ which are at least as extreme as the observed table, $\mathbf{x}$, with respect to D. In particular, if $\mathbf{x}$ is the observed $r \times c$ table, the exact p value is

$$p = \sum_{D(\mathbf{y}) \geqslant D(\mathbf{x})} P(\mathbf{y}) = \Pr\left\{ D(\mathbf{y}) \geqslant D(\mathbf{x}) \right\}. \tag{6}$$

Classical nonparametric methods rely on the large-sample distribution of D to estimate p. For $r \times c$ tables with large cell counts, it is possible to show that the distribution of D converges to a chi-squared distribution with appropriate degrees of freedom. Thus, p is usually estimated by $\tilde{p}$, the chi-squared tail area to the right of $D(\mathbf{x})$. Modern algorithmic techniques have made it possible to compute p directly instead of relying on $\tilde{p}$, its asymptotic approximation. This is achieved by powerful recursive algorithms (e.g., Mehta & Patel, 1983, 1986) that are capable of generating the actual permutation distribution of D instead of relying on its asymptotic chi-squared approximation. We shall see later that p and $\tilde{p}$ can differ considerably for contingency tables with small cell counts.

The main advantage of using p rather than $\tilde{p}$ is that it is guaranteed to bound the Type I error rate of the hypothesis-testing procedure to any desired level. Suppose, for example, that you wish to restrict the overall Type I error rate of all your hypothesis tests to 5%. If you use $p \leqslant .05$ as your criterion for rejection each time you test a null hypothesis, the long-run Type I error rate of your hypothesis-testing procedure is guaranteed to never exceed 5%. Moreover, this guarantee is provided unconditionally even though each p value is calculated conditionally by restricting attention to a specific reference set Γ. To see this, let

$$\delta(\Gamma) = \Pr(p \leqslant .05 \mid \Gamma).$$

That is, $\delta(\Gamma)$ is the conditional Type I error rate of a hypothesis-testing procedure in which you repeatedly generate $r \times c$ tables from the same reference set, Γ, under the null hypothesis, and reject whenever $p \leqslant .05$. By the way p is defined in Equation 6, it is clear that, under the null hypothesis, $\delta(\Gamma) \leqslant .05$. Now the unconditional Type I error rate, where Γ may be different each time you execute the test, is

$$\delta = \sum \delta(\Gamma) \Pr(\Gamma), \tag{7}$$

the sum being taken over all possible reference sets, Γ. Notice that Equation 7 is a weighted sum of terms of the form $\delta(\Gamma)$, where each such term is less than or equal to .05, the weights, $\Pr(\Gamma)$, are positive, and they sum to 1. Thus,

$$\delta \leqslant .05.$$

That is, the guaranteed protection against the Type I error of an exact conditional hypothesis test also applies unconditionally. Note, however, that this guarantee does not hold if you use $\tilde{p}$ rather than p in the decision to reject the null hypothesis, because $\Pr(\tilde{p} \leqslant .05 \mid \Gamma) \leqslant .05$ holds only asymptotically.

Application to a Variety of $r \times c$ Problems

As stated previously, the reference set Γ is ordered by the test statistic D. Here we define D for three important classes of problems: tests on unordered $r \times c$ contingency tables, tests on singly ordered $r \times c$ contingency tables, and tests on doubly ordered $r \times c$ contingency tables. In each case, we illustrate the methods with one or more examples.

Tests on Unordered $r \times c$ Tables. When both the row and the column classifications of the table are nominal, the table is said to be unordered and the Fisher, Pearson, and likelihood ratio statistics are the most appropriate. Tests based on these three statistics are known as omnibus tests for they are powerful against any general alternative to the null hypothesis of no row by column interaction.

Fisher's exact test orders each table, $\mathbf{y} \in \Gamma$, in proportion to its hypergeometric probability, $P(\mathbf{y})$, given by Equation 5. Fisher (1925) originally proposed this test for the single 2×2 contingency table. The idea was extended to tables of higher dimension by Freeman and Halton (1951). Thus, this test is also referred to as the Freeman-Halton test. Asymptotically, under the null hypothesis of no row-by-column interaction, $-2 \log \gamma P(\mathbf{y})$ has a chi-squared distribution with $(r-1)(c-1)$ degrees of freedom, where γ is a normalizing constant (Mehta & Patel, 1986).

The Pearson test orders the tables in Γ according to their Pearson chi-squared statistics. Thus, for each $\mathbf{y} \in \Gamma$, the test statistic is

$$D(\mathbf{y}) = \sum_{i=1}^{r} \sum_{j=1}^{c} \frac{(y_{ij} - m_i n_j / N)^2}{m_i n_j / N}. \tag{8}$$

Asymptotically, under the null hypothesis of no row-by-column interaction, the Pearson statistic has a chi-squared distribution with $(r-1)(c-1)$ degrees of freedom.

The likelihood ratio test orders the tables in Γ according to the likelihood ratio statistic. Specifically, for each $\mathbf{y} \in \Gamma$, the test statistic is

$$D(\mathbf{y}) = 2 \sum_{i=1}^{r} \sum_{j=1}^{c} y_{ij} \log \left(\frac{y_{ij}}{m_i n_j / N} \right). \tag{9}$$

In many textbooks, this statistic is denoted by G^2. Asymptotically, under the null hypothesis of no row-by-column interaction, $D(\mathbf{y})$ has a chi-squared distribution with $(r-1)(c-1)$ degrees of freedom.

Example 1: Oral Lesions in a House-to-House Survey. Data were obtained on the location of oral lesions, in house-to-house surveys in three geographic regions of rural India, by Gupta, Mehta, and Pindborg (1980). Consider a hypothetical subset of these data displayed in Table 2 as a 9×3 contingency table in which the counts are the number of patients with oral lesions per site and geographic region.

The question of interest is whether the distribution of the site of the oral lesion is significantly different in the three geographic regions. The row and column classifications for this 9×3 table are clearly unordered, making it an appropriate data set for the Fisher, Pearson, or likelihood ratio test. The exact and asymptotic p values are displayed in Table 3. There are striking differences between the two methods. The exact analysis suggests that the

Table 2 Oral Lesions Data

Site of Lesion	Kerala	Gujarat	Andhra
Labial mucosa	0	1	0
Buccal mucosa	8	1	8
Commissure	0	1	0
Gingiva	0	1	0
Hard palate	0	1	0
Soft palate	0	1	0
Tongue	0	1	0
Floor of mouth	1	0	1
Alveolar ridge	1	0	1

Table 3 Exact and Asymptotic *p* values for Oral Lesions Data

Type of Inference	Three tests of independence		
	Pearson	Fisher	Likelihood Ratio
Value of $D(\mathbf{x})$	22.1	19.72	23.3
Asymptotic *p* value	.1400	.2331	.1060
Exact *p* value	.0269	.0101	.0356

row and column classifications are dependent, but the asymptotic analysis fails to show this.

Tests on Singly Ordered $r \times c$ Tables. When there is a natural ordering of the columns of the $r \times c$ table, but the row classifications are based on nominal categories, appropriate tests are the Kruskal-Wallis test (Hollander & Wolfe, 1973) and its generalization, the one-way analysis of variance (ANOVA) test (Miller, 1981). For example, suppose that the r rows represent r different drug therapies, and the c columns represent c distinct ordered responses (such as no response, mild response, moderate response, severe response, etc.). One is interested in testing the null hypothesis that the r drugs have the same multinomial response rates. The Kruskal-Wallis and generalized one-way ANOVA tests are more powerful than the Fisher, Pearson, and likelihood ratio tests for testing this null hypothesis against ordered alternatives that imply that some of these r drugs are more responsive than others. These tests take advantage of the natural ordering of the columns by assigning a rank or column score to all the observations in a column. The test statistic is obtained as a quadratic function of an r-dimensional vector whose components are formed by summing the column scores of the observations in each of the r rows and standardizing each sum. For the Kruskal-Wallis, test the observations in a column are assigned their mid-rank and the special case, $r = 2$, yields the Wilcoxon rank-sum test. For the generalized one-way ANOVA test, any monotone scores may be assigned. By suitable choice of these scores, one can construct a large number of tests, including the normal scores, exponential scores, and log-rank tests as special cases. The test statistics for all these tests are given in Chapter 18 of *StatXact-3 User Manual* (StatXact-3, 1995). Asymptotically, they are all distributed as chi-square with $(r - 1)$ degrees of freedom under the null hypothesis of no row-by-column interaction.

Example 2: Pilot Study of Five Chemotherapy Regimens. The tumor regression rates of five chemotherapy regimens, cytoxan (CTX) alone, cyclohexyl-chloroethyl nitrosurea (CCNU) alone, methotrexate (MTX) alone, CTX + MTX, and CTX + CCNU + MTX, were compared in a small clinical trial. Tumor regression was measured on a three-point scale: no response, partial response, or complete response. The results are shown in Table 4.

Small pilot studies like this one are frequently conducted as a preliminary to planning a large-scale randomized clinical trial. For such data, the Kruskal-Wallis test may be used to determine whether or not the five drug regimens are significantly different with respect to their tumor regression rates. The observed value of the Kruskal-Wallis statistic for this table is 8.682. Referring this value to a chi-squared distribution with 4 degrees of freedom yields an asymptotic p value of .0695, which is not significant at the .05 level. However, based on the permutation distribution of the Kruskal-Wallis statistic, the exact p value is .039, which is statistically significant.

Doubly Ordered $r \times c$ Contingency Tables. When the $r \times c$ contingency table has a natural ordering along both its rows and its

Table 4 Chemotherapy Pilot Study Data			
Chemotherapy	*No Resp.*	*Partial Resp.*	*Complete Resp.*
CTX	2	0	0
CCNU	1	1	0
MTX	3	0	0
CTX + CCNU	2	2	0
CTX + CCNU + MTX	1	1	4

columns, the Jonckheere-Terpstra test (Hollander & Wolfe, 1973) and the linear-by-linear association test (Agresti, Mehta, & Patel, 1990) have more power than the Kruskal-Wallis test or the various $(r-1)$-degree-of-freedom generalized ANOVA tests. For example, suppose the r rows represent r distinct drug therapies at progressively increasing doses and the c columns represent c ordered responses. Now one would be interested in detecting alternatives to the null hypothesis in which drugs administered at larger doses are more responsive than drugs administered at smaller doses. The Jonckheere-Terpstra and linear-by-linear association test statistics cater explicitly to such alternatives for they are better able to pick up departures from the null hypothesis in which the response distribution shifts progressively toward the right as we move down the rows of the contingency table. The Jonckheere-Terpstra statistic is the normalized sum of $r(r-1)/2$ Wilcoxon rank-sum statistics formed by taking all possible pairs of rows from the r rows of the observed $r \times c$ contingency table and computing a Wilcoxon rank-sum statistic for each resulting $2 \times c$ contingency table. The linear-by-linear association statistic is obtained by standardizing $\sum_{i,j} u_i v_j x_{ij}$, where the u_is are arbitrary row scores and the v_js are arbitrary column scores. The row scores often represent progressively increasing doses of a treatment, whereas the column scores often represent progressively increasing levels of response to treatment. If the u_is and v_js represent the original raw data, the linear-by-linear test is a test of significance for Pearson's correlation coefficient. On the other hand, if the raw data are replaced by Wilcoxon mid-rank scores, we have a test of Spearman's correlation coefficient. Refer to Chapter 19 of the *StatXact-3 User Manual* (StatXact-3, 1995) for the precise functional forms of the Jonckheere-Terpstra and the linear-by-linear test statistics. Under the null hypothesis of no row-by-column interaction, these test statistics are normally distributed. The special case, $r = 2$, yields the family of two-sample linear rank tests. For these tests, row scores are irrelevant, but a large number of different column scores, covering most of the important nonparametric tests, are listed in Chapters 9 and 15 of the *StatXact-3 User Manual* (StatXact-3, 1995).

Example 3: Testing for a Dose-Response Relationship. Patients were treated with a drug at four dose levels (100 mg, 200 mg, 300 mg, 400 mg) and then monitored for toxicity. The data are shown in Table 5. Notice that there is a natural ordering along the rows as well as the columns of this 4×4 contingency table. Thus, the Jonckheere-Terpstra test and the linear-by-linear association test are appropriate for determining if the increase in drug dose leads to greater toxicity.

We first perform the Jonckheere-Terpstra test. The exact two-sided p value of .1134 closely matches the corresponding asymptotic two-sided p value of .1210, indicating that the dose-response relationship between drug dose and toxicity is not statistically significant.

Next, we perform the linear-by-linear association test, whose test statistic is of the form $D(\mathbf{x}) = \sum_{i,j} u_i v_j x_{ij}$, using the equally spaced scores, $u = i$, $v_j = j$ for $i, j = 1, 2, \ldots, 4$. Now the exact two-sided p value is .0866 and the corresponding asymptotic two-sided p value is .0812, confirming that the dose-response relationship is at best marginally statistically significant. The linear-by-linear association test does give us some added flexibility over the Jonckheere-Terpstra test, however. We are free to choose the row and column scores arbitrarily. Suppose, for instance, that the toxic event "Drug Death" was deemed to be catastrophic and orders of magnitude more serious than a "Severe Toxicity." In that case, it might be reasonable to maintain the equally spaced row scores,

Table 5 Dose-Response Drug Toxicity Data

Drug Dose	Drug Toxicity				Row_Score
	Mild	Moderate	Severe	Drug Death	
100 mg	100	1	0	0	u_1
200 mg	18	1	1	0	u_2
300 mg	50	1	1	0	u_3
400 mg	50	1	1	1	u_4
Column_Score	v_1	v_2	v_3	v_4	

$u_i = i$, $i = 1, 2, \ldots 4$, but assign unequally spaced column scores $v_1 = 1$ for "Mild Toxicity," $v_2 = 2$ for "Moderate Toxicity," $v_3 = 3$ for "Severe Toxicity," and $v_4 = 10,000$ for "Drug Death." Because of this severe discontinuity in the column scores, the asymptotic theory breaks down. Now the two-sided asymptotic p value is .1604, implying that there is no association between drug dose and toxicity, whereas the two-sided exact p value is .0372, implying that the dose-response relationship is indeed statistically significant.

Example 4: Space Shuttle, *Challenger.* Professor Richard Feynman in his delightful book *What Do You Care What Other People Think* (1988) recounted at great length his experiences as a member of the presidential commission, formed to determine the cause of the explosion of the space shuttle, *Challenger*, in 1986. He suspected that the low temperature at take-off caused the O-rings to fail. On page 137 of his book, he has published the data on temperature versus the number of O-ring incidents, on 24 previous space shuttle flights. These data are shown in Table 6.

These data may be represented as a contingency table whose rows are the number of O-ring incidents and whose columns are the temperatures at take-off. Thus, both the rows and the columns are ordered, and the linear-by-linear association test may also be used to test the association between temperature and O-ring incidents. Using the number of O-ring incidents as the row scores (the u_is) and the take-off temperatures as the column scores (the v_js), the exact two-sided p value is .005. The

---

Table 6 Space-Shuttle O-Ring Data

O-Ring Incidents	Temperature (Fahrenheit)								
None	66	67	67	67	68	68	70	70	72
	73	75	76	76	78	79	80	81	
One	57	58	63	70	70				
Two	75								
Three	53								

---

corresponding asymptotic two-sided p value is .007. These results are extremely significant and confirm the conclusion that the O-rings were indeed implicated in the explosion of the space shuttle.

Now, suppose we were to ignore the fact that both temperature and O-ring incidents are ordered variables. In that case, we might test for row by column association with the Pearson chi-square test described earlier. This test would be considerably less powerful than the linear-by-linear association test. This is reflected in its exact p value, which has increased to .267 (asymptotic p value, .191). Suppose next that we were to ignore the fact that the number of O-ring incidents is an ordered variable but continued to treat temperature as an ordered variable. Then the Kruskal-Wallis test would be appropriate. This test is more powerful than the Pearson chi-square test, but less powerful than the linear-by-linear association test for this data set. The exact Kruskal-Wallis p value, .015, lies between the exact Pearson and exact linear-by-linear association p values. It is also interesting to observe that the asymptotic Kruskal-Wallis p value is .048, suggesting that the corresponding large-sample theory has behaved poorly for this data set.

Example 5: Leukemia Among Hiroshima Atomic Bomb Survivors. A cohort of Hiroshima atomic bomb survivors was followed to determine the relationship between deaths from leukemia during 1950–1970 and estimated radiation dosage from the bombing. Subjects were stratified according to their age at the time of the bombing. A subset of the data, children in the 0–9 age group exposed to radiation doses ranging from 0–99 rads, are shown in Table 7. Cases are subjects who died from leukemia during the follow-up. Controls are subjects who did not die from leukemia during the follow-up.

Two additional dose groups, 100–199 rads and 200+ rads, are excluded from the present analysis. Their inclusion increased the standardized value of the test statistic from 3 to 16, strongly suggesting that their effect on the risk of leukemia is nonlinear and should be considered in a more general model. The full data set is on page 285 of Agresti (1984).

Table 7 Leukemia Deaths Among Hiroshima/Nagasaki Atomic Bomb Survivors

Survival Status	Radiation Dose (rads)			
	0	1–9	10–49	50–99
Case	0 (0%)	7 (.07%)	3 (.1%)	1 (.14%)
Control	5,015	10,752	2,989	694
Total	5,015	10,759	2,992	695

In absolute terms, the leukemia death rates are rather low. Only 11 deaths were observed in a cohort of size 19,461, amounting to a death rate of 0.06%. However, the rates increase from 0% in the lowest dose group to 0.14% in the highest. It is therefore interesting to ask whether this increasing trend is real or merely due to chance fluctuations in the data. Our intuition cannot help much with these extremely low death rates, and we must resort to a formal statistical test of significance.

One way to determine if there is a statistically significant association between leukemia deaths and radiation exposure is to perform the Cochran-Armitage trend test. This is a special case of the linear-by-linear association test in which there are only two rows. The test statistic is of the form $D(\mathbf{x}) = \sum_{i,j} u_i v_j x_{ij}$ in which $(u_1, u_2) = (1, 0)$ are the row scores, and the column score, v_j, is the mid-range of the jth radiation dose. For these data, $v_1 = 0$ rad, $v_2 = 4.5$ rads, $v_3 = 30$ rads, and $v_4 = 75$ rads. Previously, the only way to perform this trend test was to assume that the test statistic, D, is normally distributed. Figure 1 displays the true permutation distribution of the test statistic. The test statistic is not even close to normal. Its distinct values are unequally spaced; and the distribution has an unusually long right tail, extending all the way out to $D = 825$ even though $E(D) = 107.6$. In addition, the distribution is multimodal. Not surprisingly, the exact and asymptotic p values for the Cochran-Armitage trend test differ. The results are shown in Table 8.

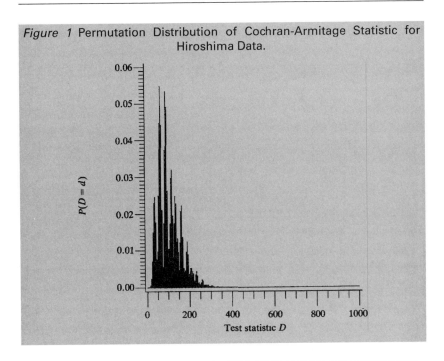

Figure 1 Permutation Distribution of Cochran-Armitage Statistic for Hiroshima Data.

Table 8 Exact and Asymptotic *p* values for Hiroshima Data

p Values	One-Sided	Two-Sided
Exact	.0653	.0682
Asymptotic	.0465	.0929

Example 6: Extending the Theory to Continuous Data.
The methods described previously extend naturally to continuous data. In principle, such data can also be represented as contingency tables but the columns of these tables will sum to 1. Thus, these methods provide a unified approach to handling nonparametric data for both the categorical case and the more traditional continuous case. For example, consider the two-sample problem involving continuous data displayed in Table 9. The two groups are "Males" and "Females." The continuous variable being compared in the two groups is "Monthly income." These data can be represented by the 2×8 contingency table, displayed as Table 10, which may then be permuted in the usual way for exact

Table 9 Two-Sample Continuous Data Represented the Traditional Way

M	M	M	M	F	F	F	F
2,010	3,100	2,555	2,095	1,990	2,122	1,875	2,550

Table 10 Two-Sample Continuous Data Represented as a 2×8 Contingency Table

Rows	Col_1	Col_2	Col_3	Col_4	Col_5	Col_6	Col_7	Col_8	Row_Total
Male	0	0	1	1	0	0	1	1	4
Female	1	1	0	0	1	1	0	0	4
Col_Total	1	1	1	1	1	1	1	1	8
Col_Score	1,875	1,990	2,010	2,095	2,122	2,550	2,555	3,100	

inference, yielding an exact two-sided Wilcoxon-Mann-Whitney p value of .3429 (and corresponding asymptotic p value of .2482). The same idea extends to continuous K-sample data with or without stratification and with or without censoring.

Exact Inference for Stratified Contingency Tables

The general treatment of multidimensional contingency tables is developed in Agresti (1992). A detailed discussion of three-way tables is also available in Landis, Heyman, and Koch (1978). At present, exact small-sample inference has been implemented only for two special cases of the above: stratified 2×2 contingency tables and stratified $2 \times c$ contingency tables.

Stratified 2×2 Contingency Tables

A very important class of exact nonparametric tests and confidence intervals is defined on data in the form of s 2×2 contingency tables. The ith such table is displayed in Table 11. We

Table 11 Layout for the ith of s 2 $\times$ 2 Contingency Tables			
Rows	Col_1	Col_2	Row_Total
Row_1	x_{i1}	x_{i2}	m_{i1}
Row_2	x'_{i1}	x'_{i2}	m_{i2}
Col_Total	n_{i1}	n_{i2}	N_i

may regard the two columns of each table as arising from two independent binomial distributions. Specifically, let (x_{i1}, x_{i2}) represent the number of successes in (n_{i1}, n_{i2}) Bernoulli trials, with respective success probabilities (π_{i1}, π_{i2}). The odds ratio for the ith table is defined as

$$\Psi_i = \left(\frac{\pi_{i2}}{1 - \pi_{i2}} \right) \Big/ \left(\frac{\pi_{i1}}{1 - \pi_{i1}} \right). \tag{10}$$

Stratified 2 $\times$ 2 contingency tables arise commonly in prospective studies with binary endpoints as well as in retrospective case-control studies. Thus, although we have specified that the two columns of the 2 $\times$ 2 table represent two independent binomial distributions, this is just a matter of notational convenience. We could equivalently assume that the two rows represent the disease status (present or absent) and the two columns represent the exposure status (not exposed or exposed) in the ith of s matched sets.

Homogeneity Test. We shall be interested in deriving an exact test for the null hypothesis that

$$\Psi_1 = \Psi_2 = \cdots = \Psi_s = \Psi. \tag{11}$$

This is known as the homogeneity test. Let **x** denote the observed collection of s 2 $\times$ 2 contingency tables, where the ith table in this collection is displayed in Table 11, and define

$$t = x_{11} + x_{21} + \cdots + x_{s1}. \tag{12}$$

Let Ω denote a reference set of collections of s 2 $\times$ 2 contingency tables whose margins are fixed at the values that were actually observed:

$$\Omega = \left\{ \begin{array}{ll} \mathbf{y}: & y_{i1} + y_{i2} = m_{i1}; \quad y'_{i1} + y'_{i2} = m_{i2} \\ & y_{i1} + y'_{i1} = n_{i1}; \quad y_{i2} + y'_{i2} = n_{i2} \end{array} \right\}. \tag{13}$$

Define the more restricted reference set

$$\Omega_t = \{\mathbf{y} \in \Omega: y_{11} + y_{21} + \cdots + y_{s1} = t\}. \tag{14}$$

Zelen (1971) has shown that under the null hypothesis of homogeneity (Equation 11),

$$\Pr(\mathbf{x} \mid \mathbf{x} \in \Omega_t) = \frac{\prod_{i=1}^{s} \prod_{j=1}^{2} \binom{n_{ij}}{x_{ij}}}{\sum_{\mathbf{y} \in \Omega_t} \prod_{i=1}^{s} \prod_{j=1}^{2} \binom{n_{ij}}{y_{ij}}}. \tag{15}$$

An exact test for the homogeneity of odds ratios can thus be constructed by ordering all elements $\mathbf{y} \in \Omega_t$ according to the test statistic

$$D(\mathbf{y}) = -\log \Pr(\mathbf{y} \mid \mathbf{y} \in \Omega_t)$$

and computing the exact p value

$$p = \sum_{D(\mathbf{y}) \geqslant D(\mathbf{x})} \Pr(\mathbf{y} \mid \mathbf{y} \in \Omega_t).$$

This test is known as Zelen's exact test. A statistic proposed by Breslow and Day (1980) is approximately distributed as chi-square with $(s - 1)$ degrees of freedom under the null hypothesis.

Example 7: Site-by-Treatment Interaction. The binary response data tabulated in Table 12 compare a new drug with a control drug at 22 hospital sites. The data can be thought of as twenty-two 2×2 contingency tables, one for each site. If you examine the 2×2 tables carefully, you notice that site 15 appears to be different from the others. Whereas all the other sites have a low response rate for both the new drug and the control drug, the response rate of the control drug is 79% at site 15. The homogeneity test can tell you whether the observed difference at site 15 is a real difference or whether it is just a chance fluctuation due to a small sample. Because of the sparseness in the data, the asymptotic (Breslow-Day) statistic might not yield an accurate p value. The exact (Zelen) test is preferred. The exact p value is .0135. Thus, we reject the null hypothesis that there is a common odds ratio across the 22 sites. The data strongly suggest that the odds ratio at site 15 is different from the other odds ratios. The asymptotic (Breslow-Day) p value is much larger (.0785) and is only marginally significant.

Table 12 Site-by-Treatment Interaction Data				
	New Drug		Control Drug	
Test Site	Response	No	Response	No
1	0	15	0	15
2	0	39	6	32
3	1	20	3	18
4	1	14	2	15
5	1	20	2	19
6	0	12	2	10
7	3	49	10	42
8	0	19	2	17
9	1	14	0	15
10	2	26	2	27
11	0	19	2	18
12	0	12	1	11
13	0	24	5	19
14	2	10	2	11
15	0	14	11	3
16	0	53	4	48
17	0	20	0	20
18	0	21	0	21
19	1	50	1	48
20	0	13	1	13
21	0	13	1	13
22	0	21	0	21

Common Odds Ratio Inference. Next, under the assumption of homogeneity, we shall be interested in computing an exact confidence interval for the common odds ratio, Ψ, and in testing that it equals 1. Exact inference about Ψ is based on the conditional distribution of

$$T = y_{11} + y_{21} + \cdots + y_{s1} \tag{16}$$

given $\mathbf{y} \in \Omega$. It is shown in Mehta, Patel, and Gray (1985) that

$$\Pr(T = t \mid \mathbf{y} \in \Omega) = \frac{C_t \Psi^t}{\sum_u C_u \Psi^u}, \tag{17}$$

where

$$C_t = \sum_{\mathbf{y} \in \Omega_t} \prod_{i=1}^{s} \prod_{j=1}^{2} \binom{n_{ij}}{y_{ij}}, \tag{18}$$

and the denominator of Equation 17 is simply the normalizing constant obtained by summing over all possible values of u in the range $t_{\min} \leqslant u \leqslant t_{\max}$.

To test the null hypothesis that $\Psi = 1$ and to compute an exact confidence interval for this common odds ratio, we need the coefficients C_t for all possible values of t. Network algorithms for this and related computations are described in Mehta et al. (1985). Once these coefficients have been obtained, the conditional distribution of t for any value of Ψ can be generated by Equation 17 and hypothesis tests and confidence intervals may thereby be obtained as shown in the previously cited references.

Asymptotic inference for Ψ is usually based on the popular Mantel-Haenszel method (Mantel & Haenszel, 1959).

Example 8: Minority Discrimination in Hiring. The court case of *Hogan v. Pierce* (Gastwirth, 1984) involved the minority hiring data displayed in Table 13. The most notable feature of these data is that at each hiring opportunity not a single black was hired, whereas small numbers of whites were hired. This makes it impossible to use the usual large-sample maximum likelihood or Mantel-Haenszel methods for estimating the odds of being hired for whites relative to blacks. These methods simply

	Whites		Blacks	
Date of Hire	Hired	Not	Hired	Not
7/74	4	16	0	7
8/74	4	13	0	7
9/74	2	13	0	8
4/75	1	17	0	8
5/75	1	17	0	8
10/75	1	29	0	10
11/75	2	29	0	10
2/76	1	30	0	10
3/76	1	30	0	10
11/77	1	33	0	13

Table 13 Minority Hiring Data

fail to converge. Only the exact method provides a valid answer and it shows that the odds of being hired for a white relative to the odds for a black are no lower than 2.3 to 1, with 95% confidence.

Stratified $2 \times c$ Contingency Tables

In this section, we discuss inference on stratified $2 \times c$ tables where the ith of s such tables is displayed as Table 14. This collection of s $2 \times c$ tables, denoted by $\mathbf{x}$, can accommodate two situations: two multinomial populations and c binomial populations. For both cases, we assume that data are stratified into s independent strata. Inference is conditional on ordering all three-way collections of s $2 \times c$ tables in the conditional reference set

$$\Lambda = \left\{ \mathbf{y} \colon y_{ij} + y'_{ij} = n_{ij}, \ \forall ij; \ \sum_{j=1}^{c} y_{ij} = m_{i1}, \ \sum_{j=1}^{c} y'_{ij} = m_{i2}, \ \forall i \right\} \quad (19)$$

according to some discrepancy measure $D(\mathbf{y})$. We shall be concerned in this section with the special case where the c columns of

---

Table 14 Layout for the ith of s $2 \times c$ Contingency Tables					
Rows	Col_1	Col_2	$\cdots$	Col_c	Row_Total
Row_1	x_{i1}	x_{i2}	$\cdots$	x_{ic}	m_{i1}
Row_2	x'_{i1}	x'_{i2}	$\cdots$	x'_{ic}	m_{i2}
Col_Total	n_{i1}	n_{i2}	$\cdots$	n_{ic}	N_i
Col_Score	v_{i1}	v_{i2}	$\cdots$	v_{ic}	

each $2 \times c$ contingency table have a natural ordering. In this case, an appropriate (unstandardized) discrepancy measure is the linear rank test statistic

$$D(\mathbf{y}) = \sum_{i=1}^{s} \sum_{j=1}^{c} v_{ij} y_{ij}, \tag{20}$$

where the v_{ij}s are arbitrary column scores.

Two Multinomial Populations. The two rows of stratum i represent two independent multinomial populations. Each observation falls into one of c ordinal response categories. Thus, x_{ij} is the number of stratum-i observations, out of a total of m_{i1}, falling into ordered category j for population 1, and x'_{ij} is the number of stratum-i observations, out of a total of m_{i2}, falling into ordered category j for population 2. The Wilcoxon rank-sum test, the Normal scores test, the Savage test, and the log-rank test are examples of tests that are applicable to such data. The v_{ij} scores for these tests are defined in Chapter 15 of the *StatXact-3 User Manual* (StatXact, 1995).

Several Binomial Populations. The c columns of stratum i represent c independent binomial populations with row 1 representing successes and row 2 representing failures. For population j in stratum i, there are x_{ij} successes and x'_{ij} failures in n_{ij} independent Bernoulli trials. The Cochran-Armitage trend test and the permutation test with arbitrary scores are applicable to such data, and determine whether the success rates of the c populations are the same, as against the alternative that they follow an increasing or decreasing trend. The scores $v_{i1}, v_{i2}, \ldots, v_{ic}$ typically represent doses, or levels of exposure, affecting the success rates of the c binomial populations. Often, one uses the equally spaced scores $v_{ij} = j$ for all i.

We shall assume throughout that there exists no three-factor interaction between rows, columns, and strata. An exact test of this hypothesis requires us to include interaction terms in a general logistic regression framework and test that they equal zero. This is an extension of the exact test of homogeneity for s 2×2 contingency tables and will not be discussed here. Given that there is no three-factor interaction, however, we are interested in testing the null hypothesis that the row and column classifications in each stratum are independent. This is known as the hypothesis of conditional independence. One can show that, for both the two multinomial and the c binomial settings under the null hypothesis of conditional independence, the probability of observing $\mathbf{y}$ given $\mathbf{y} \in \Lambda$ is

$$\Pr(\mathbf{y} \mid \mathbf{y} \in \Lambda) = \frac{\prod_{i=1}^{s} \prod_{j=1}^{c} \binom{n_{ij}}{y_{ij}}}{\prod_{i=1}^{s} \binom{N_i}{m_{i1}}}. \tag{21}$$

The exact one-sided p value for testing the null hypothesis of conditional independence is therefore

$$p_1 = \sum_{D(\mathbf{y}) \geqslant D(\mathbf{x})} \Pr(\mathbf{y} \mid \mathbf{y} \in \Lambda). \tag{22}$$

The exact two-sided p value is defined by reflecting the observed value of the test statistic an equal distance away from its mean in the opposite tail. See *StatXact-3 User Manual* (1995) for details.

Example 9: Testing for Trend in Animal Carcinogenicity Studies. The data for this example were provided by the U.S. Food and Drug Administration (FDA). Animals were treated with four dose levels of a carcinogen and then observed (at necropsy) for the presence or absence of a tumor type. The data were stratified by survival time (in weeks) into the four time intervals 0–50, 51–80, 81–104, and terminal sacrifice. Because there were no tumors found in the first time interval, this stratum may be excluded from data entry. The data for the remaining three strata are displayed in Table 15.

We use the stratified Cochran-Armitage trend test (Breslow & Day, 1980, p. 148) to determine if there is a dose-response relationship between the level of carcinogen and the presence of tumors. The test statistic is defined by Equation 20, where v_{ij} is the dose level of carcinogen and y_{ij} is the number of animals with tumors, at the jth dose level in the ith stratum. The results are shown in Table 16. There are large differences between the exact and the asymptotic one-sided p values, and they lead to different conclusions about the significance of the dose-response

Table 15 FDA Animal Toxicology Data

Stratum 1: 51–80 Weeks of Survival

Disease Status	Dose of Carcinogen				
	None	1 unit	5 units	50 units	Total
Tumor present	0	0	0	1	1
Tumor absent	7	10	6	8	31

Stratum 2: 81–104 Weeks of Survival

Disease Status	Dose of Carcinogen				
	None	1 unit	5 units	50 units	Total
Tumor present	0	1	0	1	2
Tumor absent	11	9	13	14	47

Stratum 3: Sacrificed at End of 104 Weeks

Disease Status	Dose of Carcinogen				
	None	1 unit	5 units	50 units	Total
Tumor present	1	1	1	2	5
Tumor absent	29	26	28	20	103

Table 16 One- and Two-Sided p Values for FDA Data

p Values	One-Sided	Two-Sided	Double One-Sided
Exact	.0651	.0769	.1302
Asymptotic	.0410	.0820	.0820

Figure 2 Distribution of Trend Test Statistic for FDA Data.

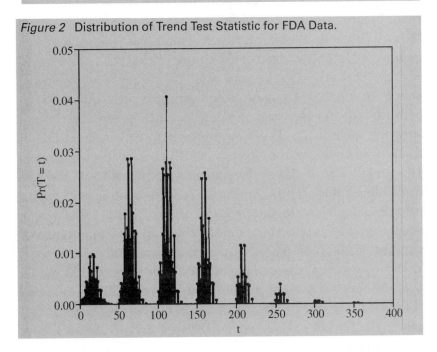

relationship. They also show that the usual practice of doubling the one-sided p value is unnecessarily conservative with asymmetric distributions. The most interesting finding of all, however, is that the distribution of the linear rank statistic (Equation 20) has multiple towers. A normal approximation would be seriously misleading. This is shown in Figure 2.

Computational Issues

Computing Equation 6 is a nontrivial task. The size of the reference set grows exponentially so that explicit enumeration of all the tables in Γ soon becomes computationally infeasible. For example, the reference set of all 5×6 tables with row sums of $(7, 7, 12, 4, 4)$ and column sums of $(4, 5, 6, 5, 7, 7)$ contains 1.6 billion tables. Yet, the tables in this reference set are all rather sparse and unlikely to yield accurate p values based on large-sample theory. Network algorithms have been developed by Mehta, Patel, and co-workers (Mehta & Patel, 1983, 1986; Mehta et al., 1985; Mehta, Patel, & Senchaudhuri, 1992; Mehta, Patel, & Tsiatis, 1984), to enumerate the tables in Γ implicitly. In these algorithms, the reference set is represented by a network of nodes and arcs. A sequence of connected arcs from the starting node to the terminal node constitutes a path through the network. Each such path represents one and only one table in Γ. The length of a path equals the value of the test statistic for the table to which that path corresponds. The probability of the path equals the probability of the corresponding table. Thus, the problem of computing an exact p value is equivalent to the problem of identifying paths whose lengths equal or exceed a specified value and summing the probabilities of all these paths. This can be accomplished by well-known operations research techniques such as backward induction and forward probing through the network. These methods are very efficient and make it feasible to compute exact p values.

Alternate approaches are provided by Baglivo, Olivier, and Pagano (1988), Cheung and Klotz (1997), Pagano and Halvorsen (1981), Pagano and Tritchler (1983), Streitberg and Rohmel (1986), and Vollset, Hirji, and Elashoff (1991). Sometimes a data set is too large even for implicit enumeration, yet it is sufficiently sparse that the asymptotic results are suspect. For such situations, a Monte Carlo estimate and associated 99% confidence interval for the exact p value may be obtained. In the Monte Carlo method, tables are sampled from Γ in proportion to their hypergeometric probabilities (Equation 5), and a count is kept of all the sampled tables that are more extreme than the observed table. For details, refer to Agresti, Wackerly, and Boyett (1979), Mehta, Patel, and Senchaudhuri

(1988), Patefield (1981), and Senchaudhuri, Mehta, and Patel (1995).

Software and Related Resources for Exact Inference

We have presented the essential idea behind exact permutational inference, described one numerical algorithm, referenced others, and shown through several examples that exact inference is a valuable supplement to corresponding asymptotic methods. Several additional examples may be obtained by visiting Cytel Software Corporation's Web site (http://www.cytel.com).

Software support for these methods is available in many standard packages including *LogXact-2* (1996), SAS (1995), SPSS (1995), and *StatXact-3 User Manual* (1995).

Some of the newer textbooks on nonparametric methods, for example, Agresti (1990), Edgington (1995), Good (1993), Manly (1991), and Sprent (1993), devote considerable space to exact and Monte Carlo methods of inference for categorical data. A useful survey paper, in which a unified treatment of exact inference for categorical data is presented through the log-linear model, was recently published by Agresti (1992). A complete collection of references to statistical methodology, numerical algorithms, commercial software, shareware, and textbooks on exact permutational inference can be obtained by visiting the Exact-Stats Web site (http://www.mailbase.ac.uk/lists-a-e/exact-stats).

References

Agresti, A. (1984). *Analysis of ordinal categorical data.* New York: Wiley.

Agresti, A. (1990). *Categorical data analysis.* New York: Wiley.

Agresti, A. (1992). A survey of exact inference for contingency tables (with discussion). *Statistical Science, 7* (1), 131–177.

Agresti, A., Mehta, C. R., & Patel, N. R. (1990). Exact inference for contingency tables with ordered categories. *Journal of the American Statistical Association, 85* (410), 453–458.

Agresti, A., Wackerly, D., & Boyett, J. M. (1979). Exact conditional tests for cross-classifications. *Psychometrika, 44,* 75–83.

Agresti, A., & Yang, M. (1987). An empirical investigation of some effects of sparseness in contingency tables. *Communications in Statistics, 5,* 9–21.

Baglivo, J., Olivier, D., & Pagano, M. (1988). Methods for the analysis of contingency tables with large and small cell counts. *Journal of the American Statistical Association, 83,* 1006–1013.

Breslow, N. E., & Day, N. E. (1980). The analysis of case-control studies. *IARC Scientific Publications No. 32.* Lyon, France.

Cheung, Y. K., & Klotz, J. H. (1997). The Mann Whitney Wilcoxon distribution using linked lists. *Statistica Sinica, 7,* 805–813.

Cox, D. R., & Hinkley, D. V. (1974). *Theoretical statistics.* London: Chapman and Hall.

Edgington, E. S. (1995). *Randomization tests* (3rd ed.) New York: Marcel Dekker.

Fisher, R. A. (1925). *Statistical methods for research workers.* Edinburgh: Oliver and Boyd.

Freeman, G. H., & Halton, J. H. (1951). Note on an exact treatment of contingency, goodness of fit and other problems of significance. *Biometrika, 38,* 141–149.

Gastwirth, J. L. (1984). Combined tests of significance in EEO cases. *Industrial and Labor Relations Review, 38* (1).

Good, P. (1993). *Permutation tests.* New York: Springer.

Gupta, P. C., Mehta, F. R., & Pindborg, J. (1980). *Community Dentistry and Oral Epidemiology, 8,* 287–333.

Hollander, M., & Wolfe, D. A. (1973). *Nonparametric statistical methods.* New York: Wiley.

Landis, R., Heyman, E. R., & Koch, G. G. (1978). Average partial association in three-way contingency tables: a review and discussion of alternative tests. *International Statistical Review, 46,* 237–254.

LogXact-2. (1996). *Software for exact logistic regression.* Cambridge, MA: Cytel Software Corporation.

Manly, B. F. J. (1991). *Randomization and Monte Carlo methods in biology.* London: Chapman and Hall.

Mantel, N., & Haenszel, W. (1959). Statistical aspects of the analysis of data from retrospective studies of disease. *Journal of the National Cancer Institute, 22,* 719–748.

Mehta, C. R., & Patel, N. R. (1983). A network algorithm for performing Fisher's exact test in $r \times c$ contingency tables. *Journal of the American Statistical Association, 78* (382), 427–434.

Mehta, C. R., & Patel, N. R. (1986). A hybrid algorithm for Fisher's exact test on unordered $r \times c$ contingency tables. *Communications in Statistics, 15* (2), 387–403.

Mehta, C. R., Patel, N. R., & Gray, R. (1985). On computing an exact confidence interval for the common odds ratio in several 2×2 contingency tables. *Journal of the American Statistical Association, 80* (392), 969–973.

Mehta, C. R., Patel, N. R., & Senchaudhuri, P. (1988). Importance sampling for estimating exact probabilities in permutational inference. *Journal of the American Statistical Association, 83* (404), 999–1005.

Mehta, C. R., Patel, N. R., & Senchaudhuri, P. (1992). Exact stratified linear rank tests for ordered categorical and binary data. *Journal of Computational and Graphical Statistics, 1,* 21–40.

Mehta, C. R., Patel, N. R., & Tsiatis, A. A. (1984). Exact significance testing to establish treatment equivalence for ordered categorical data. *Biometrics, 40,* 819–825.

Miller, R. G. (1981). *Simultaneous statistical inference.* New York: Springer.

Pagano, M., & Halvorsen, K. (1981). An algorithm for finding exact significance levels of $r \times c$ contingency tables. *Journal of the American Statistical Association, 76,* 931–934.

Pagano, M., & Tritchler, D. (1983). On obtaining permutation distributions in polynomial time. *Journal of the American Statistical Association, 78,* 435–441.

Patefield, W. M. (1981). An efficient method of generating $r \times c$ tables with given row and column totals. (Algorithm AS 159). *Applied Statistics, 30,* 91–97.

Read, R. C., & Cressie, N. A. (1988). *Goodness-of-fit statistics for discrete multivariate data.* New York: Springer.

Reid, N. (1995). The roles of conditioning in inference (with discussion). *Statistical Science, 10* (2), 138–157.

SAS Institute. (1995). *SAS/Stat user's guide, Version 6.11.* Cary, NC: SAS Institute.

Senchaudhuri, P., Mehta, C. R., & Patel, N. R. (1995). Estimating exact p values by the method of control variates, or Monte

Carlo rescue. *Journal of the American Statistical Association,* *90* (430), 640–648.

Sprent, P. (1993). *Applied nonparametric statistical methods* (2nd ed.). London: Chapman and Hall.

SPSS. (1995). Chicago: SPSS.

StatXact-3. (1995). *Software for exact nonparametric inference.* Cambridge, MA: Cytel Software Corporation.

Streitberg, B., & Rohmel, R. (1986). Exact distributions for permutation and rank tests. *Statistical Software Newsletter, 12,* 10–17.

Vollset, S. E., Hirji, K. F., & Elashoff, R. M. (1991). Fast computation of exact confidence limits for the common odds ratio in a series of 2 × 2 tables. *Journal of the American Statistical Association, 86,* 404–409.

Yates, F. (1984). Test of significance for 2 × 2 contingency tables. *Journal of the Royal Statistical Society, A147,* 426–463.

Zelen, M. (1971). The analysis of several 2 × 2 contingency tables. *Biometrika, 58* (1), 129–137.

7

Tests of an Identity Correlation Structure

Rachel T. Fouladi & James H. Steiger

FEW WOULD DENY that the objective of research is increased understanding. One way in which researchers try to meet this objective is by searching for patterns of association. Often, researchers engaging in nonexperimental research find it useful to describe the patterns of association in their data in terms of the structure of the correlation or the covariance matrix of the variables under study. In covariance and correlation structure analytic research, two veins of research are popular: exploratory and confirmatory.

In exploratory structure analytic research, the researcher gathers observational data for several variables on one or more occasions and then attempts to uncover the pattern of relations among the set of variables. In confirmatory research, the researcher gathers the observational data and then attempts to determine whether a hypothesized structure adequately describes the pattern of relations among the variables. Whether engaging in exploratory or confirmatory structure analytic research, the researcher is generally advised to assess whether the observed covariances or correlations are within sampling error of zero, before proceeding with further analysis of the data (Cohen & Cohen, 1983; Cooley & Lohnes, 1971; Dziuban & Shirkey, 1974a, 1974b; McDonald, 1985; Tobias & Carlson, 1969).

This chapter provides a survey of procedures available to test the null hypothesis that the population covariances and correlations are zero, reviews the Monte Carlo literature on the Type I error control and power of these procedures under conditions of multivariate normality and nonnormality, and provides a detailed discussion of two examples illustrating the application of these procedures.

Why Test the Identity Correlation Structure Model?

Consider the situation where data are collected on p variables with the population covariance matrix $\Sigma = \{\sigma_{ij}\}$ and the population correlation matrix $\mathbf{P} = \{\rho_{ij}\}$. Let N be the number of participants in a study. Let the sample covariance matrix be denoted by $\mathbf{S} = \{s_{ij}\}$ and the sample correlation matrix denoted by $\mathbf{R} = \{r_{ij}\}$.

The test of the null hypothesis that the population covariances and correlations are zero, $H_0: \sigma_{ij}$ or $H_0: \rho_{ij}$ for all $i \neq j$, is sometimes termed a test of the diagonality of the population covariance structure, $H_0: \Sigma = Diag$, or a test of the identity population correlation structure, $H_0: \mathbf{P} = \mathbf{I}$, where $\mathbf{I}$ is an identity matrix, which is a diagonal matrix where all values on the diagonal equal 1.0. Testing for the presence of an identity correlation structure is equivalent to addressing the question: Is there any statistically significant nonzero linear relationship among the set of variables? This question is of particular importance, to the extent that it suggests (1) whether there is anything in the structure of the data on which it is worth conducting further analysis or (2) whether further structure analysis of the data is even appropriate.

Cohen and Cohen (1983, pp. 57–59) write, "Circumstances occasionally arise in which the chilling thought crosses (or should cross) the mind of the investigator that none of the correlations [or covariances] among a set of ... variables departs from zero in the population .... It follows, of course that when this null hypothesis cannot be rejected at conventional significance levels, any further analysis involving these correlations [or covariances] runs the serious risk of being an exercise in garbage processing." They also caution that: "This is most likely to occur in exploratory studies where N is relatively small ...."

McDonald (1985, p. 24) gives an example of a correlation matrix from a population in which all the correlations are zero; he shows that a factor analysis of this matrix yields "plausible and very silly results" and writes that, "We could protect ourselves from such foolishness by first calculating the chi-square for $\mathbf{P} = \mathbf{I}$."

Basilevsky (1994, p. 185) writes, "When all random variables are uncorrelated it does not make sense to perform a PCA [principal component analysis] since the variables already possess an independent (uncorrelated) distribution. In practice, however, sample covariances (correlations) are not likely to be identically zero, and sample dispersion matrices will not be perfectly diagonal. A PCA of accidentally correlated data will in reality yield meaningless results, and it is often a good idea to first test for complete independence of the random variables."

It is not unusual for visual inspection of a sample correlation matrix to reveal a number of moderate-to-large correlations; however, with a small sample size, these correlations and indeed all of the correlations may very well be within sampling error of zero. Thus, a sample correlation matrix, which looks very different from identity, could, under small sample conditions, easily have been derived from a population in which all of the variables were uncorrelated. To the extent that further structure analysis would be "an exercise in garbage processing" or "yield meaningless results," then testing for the absence of an identity correlation structure in one's data is particularly important under small sample conditions.

Available Test Procedures

Many different procedures are available to test the null hypothesis that the identity correlation structure is an adequate model of the structure of the variables in the population. Failure to reject the identity correlation structure null hypothesis is taken to suggest that further structure analysis of the data would be inappropriate, and rejection of the null hypothesis is taken to suggest that further structure analysis would be appropriate.

Current statistical practice and recommendations focus on three procedures for a test of identity correlation structure: (1) the Bartlett modified maximum-likelihood test, sometimes termed "Bartlett's test of sphericity" (SPSS, 1997); (2) a statistic described by Steiger (1980a, 1980b) using the Fisher transforms of the sample correlations; and (3) tests of the difference in fit between a nonidentity and a baseline or identity correlation structure model as prescribed in contemporary structure analytic literature (Bollen, 1989). However, these are not the only techniques by which to determine whether there is any statistically significant nonzero relationship among a set of variables. There are also exact procedures and other asymptotic test procedures, some of which have much better small-sample performance than the procedures currently used.

Exact Test Procedure

Mathai and Katiyar (1979), in an important but largely overlooked paper, derived an exact test procedure. This exact procedure includes a statistic, which under conditions of multivariate normality, has a sampling distribution of a known specified form. Because their exact procedure requires evaluation of special mathematical functions that are very difficult to compute, computer software is essential for its implementation. This software is not currently available. Consequently, asymptotic procedures are our next best option.

Asymptotic Test Procedures

Asymptotic procedures include statistics with sampling distributions that converge to a given form under certain conditions. All of the statistical techniques commonly used to test whether the observed covariances and correlations are within sampling error of zero are asymptotic in sample size. As such, these statistics have sampling distributions that converge to a specified distribution as sample size increases. For some statistics, this rate of convergence is slow; for others, the rate of convergence is faster. Clearly, if one is operating under small-sample conditions, the test statistic with fastest convergence will be preferred.

A wide variety of asymptotic test statistics are available for testing the identity correlation structure. A number of the procedures are surveyed in the following discussion; Table 1 details the names, formulas, and asymptotic reference distributions for the test statistics described in the following sections.

Test Statistics Based on the Maximum-Likelihood Approach. Under the condition of multivariate normality, the maximum-likelihood (ML) approach can be used for a test of the identity correlation structure null hypothesis (Box, 1949; Wilks, 1935). As shown in Table 1, the resultant large-sample maximum-likelihood test statistic (ML) can be expressed as the product of $N - 1$ and the natural logarithm of the determinant of the sample correlation matrix, and is distributed asymptotically in N as a χ^2 with $p(p - 1)/2$ degrees of freedom.

Bartlett (1950, 1954) and Box (1949) suggested simple changes in the multiplier of ML in order to obtain statistics more appropriate for use with smaller sample sizes. The test statistic resultant from their proposed modifications is commonly referred to as Bartlett's test (herein denoted B), which is also distributed asymptotically in N as a χ^2 with $p(p - 1)/2$ degrees of freedom.

More recent modifications are typified by more complex changes in the function. Mudholkar, Trivedi, and Lin (1982; Mudholkar & Trivedi, 1980/81) proposed an asymptotically standard normal statistic (MTL) through a series of linear and nonlinear transformations of B; even though the authors have stated that they can provide a computer program to perform the nec-

Table 1 Test Statistics, Formulas, and Asymptotic Distributions

	Statistic	Formula	Distribution
ML	Maximum likelihood	$-(N-1)\ln|\mathbf{R}|$	$\chi^2_{p(p-1)/2}$
B	Bartlett	$-\left(N-1-\dfrac{2p+5}{6}\right)\ln|\mathbf{R}|$	$\chi^2_{p(p-1)/2}$
MTL	Mudholkar-Trivedi-Lin	$\left[\dfrac{B}{p(p-1)/2}\right]^h$	$N(0,1)$
FSN	Fouladi-Steiger normal	$\left[\dfrac{aB+b}{p(p-1)/2}\right]^h$	$N(0,1)$
GLS	Generalized least squares	$(N-1)\sum_{i>j}r_{ij}^2$	$\chi^2_{p(p-1)/2}$
L	"Lawley"	$\left(N-1-\dfrac{2p+5}{6}\right)\sum_{i>j}r_{ij}^2$	$\chi^2_{p(p-1)/2}$
S80	Steiger/Burt	$(N-3)\sum_{i>j}z_{ij}^2$	$\chi^2_{p(p-1)/2}$
FSF1	Fouladi-Steiger Fisher1	$m_E S80 + a_E$	$\chi^2_{p(p-1)/2}$
FSF2	Fouladi-Steiger Fisher2	$m_A S80 + a_A$	$\chi^2_{p(p-1)/2}$
RMAX	Test at reduced alpha		
FSSL	Fouladi-Steiger sumlog	$-2\sum_{i>j}\ln p_{ij}$	$\chi^2_{p(p-1)}$
FSSC	Fouladi-Steiger sumchi2	$\sum_{i>j}F^{-1}(1-p_{ij})$	$\chi^2_{p(p-1)/2}$

Note. $p_{ij} = \Pr(|r| \geqslant |r_{ij}| \,|\, \rho_{ij} = 0)$.

essary computations, this procedure has not been used by the general research community. Fouladi and Steiger (1995; Fouladi, 1996) suggested a procedure that is very similar to that of Mudholkar et al.; the key difference is that they proposed an additional initial linear transformation on B, which after further linear and nonlinear transformations yields an asymptotically normally distributed test statistic denoted herein as *FSN*.

Because the statistics based on the maximum-likelihood approach are all functions of the natural logarithm of the determinant of the sample correlation matrix, and because the natural logarithm of a nonpositive number is not defined in the set of real numbers, these test statistics are not defined under conditions when the determinant of the sample correlation matrix is nonpositive. As such, the sample correlation matrix must have a positive determinant for these statistics to be defined. To satisfy this condition, the maximum-likelihood-based statistics can only be used for N greater than p and for variables that are not linear combinations of each other.

Test Statistics Expressed as Functions of the Correlations. Browne (1977) described a very general procedure which, when applied to a test of the null hypothesis that all the correlations are zero in the population, yields the large-sample generalized least squares (*GLS*) test statistic detailed in Table 1. This statistic is asymptotically equivalent to the statistics based on methods of maximum likelihood but is computationally more efficient. The *GLS* test statistic is computationally equivalent to the statistic suggested by Lawley (1940) and described in Morrison (1990). This statistic is the product of $N - 1$ and the sum of the squared nonredundant correlations. *GLS* is distributed asymptotically in N as a χ^2 with $p(p - 1)/2$ degrees of freedom.

As an alternative, Bartlett (1950) suggested a statistic involving the application of the Bartlett multiplier to the sum of the squared nonredundant correlations. Though proposed by Bartlett, some texts (e.g., Morrison, 1990) refer to this as the "Lawley" test statistic (L), where L is distributed asymptotically in N as a χ^2 with $p(p - 1)/2$ degrees of freedom.

Burt (1952) proposed a statistic to be used for tests of residual correlations after extraction of factors. Taking this statistic and considering it under the condition of extracting no factors, one obtains a test that the correlation matrix has only unique factors, that is, represents p uncorrelated variables. The special case of this asymptotic χ^2 test statistic is computationally equivalent to the test statistic suggested by Steiger (1980a, 1980b).

Steiger (1980a, 1980b) suggested a statistic that capitalizes on the normalizing and variance-stabilizing properties of the Fisher transform. This statistic is computed as a simple function of the sum of squared Fisher transforms of the nonredundant correlations and the commonly used approximation for the variance of the Fisher transforms under a true null hypothesis, $(N-3)^{-1}$, suggested by Hotelling (1953). The test statistic, herein referred to as *S80*, is distributed asymptotically in N as a χ^2 with $p(p - 1)/2$ degrees of freedom, where z_{ij} is the Fisher transform of r_{ij}, that is, $z_{ij} = \tanh^{-1}(r_{ij}) = \frac{1}{2} \ln[(1 + r_{ij})/(1 - r_{ij})]$.

Generations of psychometricians and statisticians have believed the commonly used approximation for the variance of the Fisher transforms, $(N-3)^{-1}$, to be accurate enough for practical use; however, analysis and simulation studies have indicated that this is not quite the case (Konishi, 1978; Steiger & Fouladi, 1991b). Steiger and Fouladi (1991b; Fouladi, 1991) established that this approximation was not adequate for use as a multiplier for the sum of the squared Fisher transforms. They derived exact expressions for the moments of the Fisher transform and the squared Fisher transform under a true null hypothesis. For computational considerations, they also derived approximations to the exact moments. Using the exact and improved approximations to the moments, they developed two linear transformations of the Steiger procedure (*S80*). The application of their exact results obtained *SFF1* and the application of their approximation obtained *SFF2*.

Conceptually equivalent to the test of the hypothesis that all the correlations are zero is the test that the largest correlation is zero, *RMAX* (Fouladi, 1991, 1996; Moran, 1980). Thus, a test of the null hypothesis can be achieved by conducting a test on the largest correlation at an alpha level that will generate an acceptable familywise Type I error rate. Two possible alternatives are readily apparent; these include Bonferonni or Dunn-Sidak defined alphas,

$$\alpha_{\text{Bonferonni}} = \frac{\alpha_{\text{Family}}}{\dfrac{p(p-1)}{2}} \quad \text{and}$$

$$\alpha_{\text{Dunn-Sidak}} = 1 - \left(1 - \alpha_{\text{Family}}\right)^{2/p(p-1)}.$$

Lastly, Fouladi and Steiger (1995; Fouladi, 1991; Steiger & Fouladi, 1991a), using the results of Cameron and Eagleson (1985) and Geisser and Mantel (1962) on the asymptotic independence of correlation coefficients, suggested two additional tests of the identity correlation structure null hypothesis. These statistics are based on transformations of p_{ij}, $p_{ij} = \Pr(|r| \geqslant |r_{ij}| \,| \rho_{ij} = 0)$, where p_{ij} is the "p level" from the t test on r_{ij}. The first of these Fouladi-Steiger statistics, herein denoted *FSSL*, is given by the product of -2 and the sum of the natural logarithm of the p_{ij} of every nonredundant correlation; this statistic is distributed approximately as a χ^2 with $p(p - 1)$ degrees of freedom. The second of these statistics, herein denoted *FSSC*, is given by the sum of the value of the inverse cumulative distribution function, F^{-1} for a chi-square with 1 degree of freedom, of the $(1 - p_{ij})$'s of every nonredundant correlation; this statistic is distributed approximately as a χ^2 with $p(p - 1)/2$ degrees of freedom.

Testing Difference in Fit

Some covariance and correlation structure analysis techniques are available to test whether the fit of a nonidentity model is any better than the fit of an identity model; however, in general, these techniques, as currently discussed and implemented, are large-sample procedures and do not include any modifications to improve performance for small to moderate sample sizes.

Choosing a Procedure

So, how should a researcher address the question: Is there any relationship among the variables under study? Clearly, there are a wide variety of procedures available to address this one question.

There are a number of different issues that come into consideration when one chooses a procedure.

1. *Does One Know About It?* Clearly, if one does not know about it, one cannot choose it. But how does one learn of the existence of a procedure? One does this in many cases through graduate training, through "apprenticeship" under research supervisors, and through textbooks on quantitative methods. Yet, very few procedures actually make it from journal article to textbook. So, if one is not reading quantitative journals, one is not familiar with a large body of available techniques. Thus, there is a large void in many people's knowledge about the variety of procedures that are available. Of the class of procedures described previously, some of the maximum-likelihood-based tests (*ML, B,*

MTL), *GLS*, *L*, and *S80* have found their way into textbooks on multivariate data analytic techniques.

2. *Is It Easy to Use?* Many of the procedures we commonly use are ones that are included in large-scale statistical software packages. If a procedure does not have software implementation, the chances of its use are very slim. If the software implementation is difficult to use—cumbersome in any way—the probability that a procedure will be used is decreased. Of the class of procedures described previously, only Bartlett's statistic (*B*), *ML*, and *GLS* are readily available, though some of the other statistics (e.g., *FSSL*) can, with a small amount of effort, be easily implemented.

3. *Do Others Use It?* If there is no precedence in the literature for the use of a particular procedure, one is not likely to choose to use it. Of the class of procedures described previously, Bartlett's statistic (*B*) and tests of difference in fit are effectively the only procedures that have been applied in applied research.

4. *How Good Is the Statistic?* Even though the other three dimensions play into how we choose a procedure, the preferred guiding principle in making a decision whether to use a statistic should be the performance characteristics of the statistic in terms of its Type I error control, power, and robustness to assumption violations, where, ideally, one chooses the procedure that has the best performance profile. To find out about the performance profile of procedures, we can refer to the results of Monte Carlo studies.

Monte Carlo studies enable us to examine the performance profiles of statistical procedures under a range of conditions. For each condition, the computer generates a large number of random samples of given size from populations with specified characteristics. Each sample is referred to as a replication. For each replication, the value of the test statistic is computed and compared with its critical value for a particular alpha level. This alpha level is called *nominal alpha* or the nominal Type I error rate. It is the proportion of times that we expect the statistic to reject a true null hypothesis. The actual proportion of times that a particular statistic rejects the null hypothesis is called *empirical alpha* if the null hypothesis being tested is true, or *empirical power* if the null hypothesis is false. If a procedure has optimal Type I error control, then empirical alpha will be within sampling error of nominal alpha.

Bradley (1978) asserted that many researchers are unreasonably generous when defining acceptable departures of empirical alpha from the nominal level. He held that the departure of empirical alpha from the nominal level was "negligible" if empirical alpha was within $\alpha \pm \frac{1}{10}\alpha$ according to a "fairly stringent criterion," and $\alpha \pm \frac{1}{2}\alpha$ according to the "most liberal criterion that [he] was able to take seriously," which in the remainder of his article he referred to as the "liberal criterion." Robey and Barcikowski (1992) supplement the guidelines provided by Bradley with an "intermediate criterion" of $\alpha \pm \frac{1}{4}\alpha$ and a "very liberal criterion" of $\alpha \pm \frac{3}{4}\alpha$.

Relevant Monte Carlo Literature

Over the past few decades, a number of Monte Carlo studies have examined the performance profiles of procedures available to test the null hypothesis of identity correlation structure. These studies have characterized the statistics in terms of their Type I error control and power under various conditions.

Mudholkar and Subbaiah (1980/81) compared Bartlett's test (B) against several alternative tests; for the conditions examined, B had reasonable control of Type I error. Mudholkar et al. (1982) compared the performance of their normal approximation (MTL) to Bartlett's (B) procedure; their study showed MTL provided improved Type I error control over B.

Steiger (1980a) compared the performance of his statistic ($S80$) and Bartlett's test (B). Steiger found that $S80$ provided improved Type I error control over B for a range of small-sample conditions. This result was confirmed by Reddon (1987), Silver (1988), Silver and Dunlap (1989), and Wilson and Martin (1983).

Knapp and Swoyer (1967) provided some empirical results concerning the power of Bartlett's test (B). Mudholkar and Subbaiah (1980/81) examined the power of B and other test statistics;

few other studies have examined the power of alternative statistics.

Over the past decade, as part of our research program, we have sought to provide a comprehensive examination of the performance of procedures to test the null hypothesis of the presence of an identity correlation structure. Our studies, which in addition to assessing Type I error control and power, also examine robustness.

Fouladi (1991) examined the Type I error control and the power of B, $S80$, $FSF1$, $FSF2$, $FSSL$, L, and GLS under conditions of multivariate normality. Tests were conducted at nominal alpha of .05 and .01 on matrices based on 5, 10, and 15 variables for sample size to number of variables ratios of 2, 4, 10, 20, and 40. The empirical Type I error rate for each test statistic across 100,000 replications was assessed under each factorial condition. The empirical power for each test statistic across 10,000 replications under a number of conditions was also assessed.

Fouladi and Steiger (1995) examined the performance of B, $S80$, $FSF1$, $FSF2$, $FSSL$, $FSSC$, FSN, and the Dunn-Sidak version of $RMAX$ under conditions of multivariate normality and nonnormality. Tests were conducted at nominal alpha of .05 and .01 on matrices based on 5 and 10 variables for sample size to number of variables ratios of $(p + 1)/p$, 2, 4, 10, 20, and 40. The empirical Type I error rate for each test statistic across 200,000 replications was assessed for each factorial condition under conditions of multivariate normality. The empirical power for each test statistic across 25,000 replications was also assessed under a number of conditions. The empirical Type I error rate for each test was also assessed under conditions where all of the variables were uniformly nonnormal. The conditions of nonnormality of the variables examined included univariate skew of 0, .5, and 1.5 and univariate kurtosis of 5, 20, or 50.

The following sections provide a reexamination of some of our results using the Bradley, Robey, and Barcikowski guidelines described earlier for what constitutes acceptable departures of the empirical rejection rates from the nominal rejection rates. Here are some of the patterns we have observed in our studies.

Type I Error Control

Fouladi (1991). Using goodness-of-fit tests between the empirical Type I error rates and the nominal Type I error rates, Fouladi (1991) established that (1) none of the test statistics (B, $S80$, $FSF1$, $FSF2$, $FSSL$, L, GLS) control Type I error at the nominal level for the full range of sample sizes; (2) B, $S80$, $FSF1$, and $FSF2$ tend to have empirical rejection rates that are higher than the nominal level, whereas L and GLS tend to have empirical rejection rates that are lower than the nominal level; and (3) overall Type I error control was better for nominal alpha of .05 than nominal alpha of .01. Overall, Fouladi concluded that B, $S80$, L, and GLS had relatively poor small-sample performance, and $FSF1$, $FSF2$, and $FSSL$ had improved Type I error control.

A reexamination of those results using Bradley's (1978) and Robey and Barcikowski's (1992) guidelines for acceptable levels of departure of empirical alpha from nominal alpha indicates that, for the conditions examined, the patterns are different for testing at the nominal level of .05 versus .01. However, overall, (1) the $FSF1$, $FSF2$, and $FSSL$ procedures provide acceptable control of Type I error using the "liberal" criterion; (2) B and $S80$ provide acceptable control using the "very liberal" criterion; and (3) GLS and L do not provide acceptable control of Type I error. Table 2 provides an index of the departure of empirical alpha from nominal alpha as a percentage of nominal alpha under conditions of multivariate normality.

Focusing on the Bartlett (B) procedure, we see that B does not have very good control of Type I error for sample sizes that are two times the number of variables. We also see that at small $N:p$ the Type I error control of B deteriorates with increasing p. For nominal alpha equal to .05 and $N:p$ of 2, when p equaled 5, 10, and 15, the empirical rejection rates were 17%, 33%, and 48% higher than the nominal level, respectively. Assuming the trend continues for increasing numbers of variables, say a researcher conducts a study on 50 variables with 100 observations, the actual rejection rate would not be close to the expected level. The picture for B is even worse for nominal alpha equal to .01 and $N:p$ of 2; when p equaled 5, 10, and 15, the empirical rejection

Table 2 Fouladi (1991)—Departure of Empirical From Nominal Alpha as Percentage of Nominal Alpha, Under Conditions of Multivariate Normality

p	N	α = .05							α = .01						
		B	S80	FSF1	FSF2	FSSL	GLS	L	B	S80	FSF1	FSF2	FSSL	GLS	L
5	10	17	14	2	3	4	−90	−96	30	71	45	46	36	−50	−99
	20	2	7	1	1	1	−87	−70	2	38	23	23	18	−33	−82
	50	0	0	−3	−3	−3	−84	−36	−5	7	2	2	1	−22	−49
	100	−2	1	0	0	−1	−81	−19	1	7	5	5	4	−7	−26
	200	3	4	3	3	4	−80	−5	4	7	6	6	8	−2	−11
10	20	33	11	5	5	5	−84	−98	57	50	35	35	32	−22	−99
	40	5	6	3	3	3	−83	−79	6	22	15	15	15	−14	−86
	100	0	3	2	2	1	−80	−41	3	13	11	11	8	0	−47
	200	0	1	0	0	1	−81	−23	0	3	2	2	1	−4	−29
	400	1	1	1	1	2	−80	−11	−1	2	1	1	1	−1	−19
15	30	48	11	6	6	5	−83	−100	71	33	21	21	21	−15	−100
	60	6	4	1	1	2	−83	−88	2	8	3	3	3	−15	−94
	150	0	1	0	0	0	−80	−51	−1	7	5	5	4	−2	−62
	300	0	3	2	2	2	−79	−28	7	9	8	8	9	4	−29
	600	2	3	3	3	3	−79	−13	4	7	6	6	4	4	−16

rates were 30%, 57%, and 71% higher than the nominal level, respectively.

In contrast, the actual Type I error control of the other test procedures does not deteriorate in the same dramatic way for increasing numbers of variables. For example, with the *FSSL* procedure for nominal alpha equal to .05 and $N:p$ of 2, when p equaled 5, 10, and 15, the empirical rejection rates were 4%, 5%, and 5% higher than the nominal level, respectively. In the same way that *B*'s control of Type I error was better for .05 than .01 nominal alpha, so was the Type I error control by *FSSL* better for .05 than .01; for nominal alpha equal to .01 and $N:p$ of 2, when p equaled 5, 10, and 15, the empirical rejection rates of *FSSL* were 35.6%, 32.4%, and 21.3% higher than the nominal level, respectively.

Fouladi and Steiger (1995). In 1995, Fouladi and Steiger compared the performance of *FSN* and *RMAX* with *B*, *S80*, *FSF1*,

Table 3 Fouladi and Steiger (1995)—Departure of Empirical From Nominal Alpha as Percentage of Nominal Alpha Under Conditions of Multivariate Normality

p	N	B	S80	FSF1	FSF2	FSSL	FSSC	FSN	RMAX
					$\alpha = .05$				
5	6	194	17	5	9	7	4	2	−1
	10	15	15	3	4	4	2	0	0
	20	1	7	0	0	1	−1	0	1
	50	2	5	3	3	1	2	2	3
	100	0	2	1	1	1	1	1	2
	200	−1	0	−1	−1	−1	−1	0	−1
10	11	698	19	8	8	8	6	−1	0
	40	33	13	6	6	6	5	−1	2
	80	4	5	2	2	1	1	−1	−1
	200	1	3	1	1	0	1	0	0
	400	1	2	1	1	1	1	1	0
	800	1	2	1	1	1	1	1	2

Table 3 Continued

p	N	B	S80	FSF1	FSF2	FSSL	FSSC	FSN	RMAX
						$\alpha = .01$			
5	6	485	98	58	69	50	37	2	2
	10	23	68	40	41	37	28	−3	1
	20	2	33	21	21	17	14	−1	1
	50	1	16	10	10	8	7	−1	5
	100	2	9	7	7	6	6	1	2
	200	−7	−4	−5	−5	−5	−6	−8	−1
10	11	2228	78	50	50	47	41	−2	−1
	40	50	49	33	33	31	29	−3	4
	80	7	26	18	18	17	16	−1	0
	200	−4	6	3	3	5	3	−5	0
	400	1	4	3	3	3	2	1	1
	800	0	4	4	4	1	4	−1	0

FSF2, *FSSL*, and *FSSC*. Of the procedures examined, *B* and *S80* had decidedly worse small-sample-size performance than the other procedures. Table 3 provides an index of the departure of empirical alpha from nominal alpha as a percentage of nominal alpha under conditions of multivariate normality.

A reexamination of those results using Bradley's (1978) and Robey and Barcikowski's (1992) guidelines for acceptable levels of departure of empirical alpha from nominal alpha indicates that, for the conditions examined, overall, (1) *FSN* and *RMAX* provide acceptable control of Type I error using the "fairly stringent" criterion; (2) *FSSL* and *FSSC* provide acceptable control using the "liberal" criterion; (3) *FSF1* and *FSF2* provide acceptable control of Type I error using the "very liberal" criterion; and (4) *B* and *S80* do not provide acceptable control according to any of the Bradley-Robey-Barcikowski guidelines.

Overall, Type I error control was better for nominal alpha of .05 than for nominal alpha of .01. *FSF1*, *FSF2*, *FSSL*, and *FSSC* controlled Type I error at the stringent level for nominal alpha of .05; however, they did not do that for nominal alpha of .01. On the other hand, *FSN* and *RMAX* did. As such, *FSN* and *RMAX* were the only procedures that controlled Type I error close to the nominal level across the full range of sample sizes and levels of nominal alpha.

Power

Fouladi (1991). We examined the power of *B, S80, FSF1, FSF2, FSSL, L,* and *GLS* across an array of conditions with different proportions and magnitudes of nonzero correlations. We found that the procedures that showed the best control of Type I error (*FSF1, FSF2,* and *FSSL*) were relatively indistinguishable in terms of power.

Fouladi and Steiger (1995). We examined the power of our procedures (*B, S80, FSF1, FSF2, FSSL, FSSC, FSN,* and *RMAX*) across an array of conditions with different magnitudes of correlations. The *S80, FSF1, FSF2,* and *FSSL* procedures were indistinguishable in terms of power. These procedures were a little more powerful than *B, FSN,* and *RMAX*. Of the procedures that showed the best control of Type I error (*FSN* and *RMAX*), *FSN* tended to be the more powerful of the two. Table 4 provides an index of the empirical power as a function of the magnitude of the correlation coefficients in the population, the number of variables, the sample size, and nominal alpha.

Robustness

Robustness can be used to describe the imperviousness of a statistic to assumption violations or to the presence of outliers. The present discussion focuses on the robustness of procedures testing the identity correlation structure null hypothesis to the presence of nonnormality.

There are many ways in which multivariate nonnormality can be induced. The manner in which multivariate nonnormality was induced in the Fouladi and Steiger (1995) examination of tests of identity correlation structure was by varying the skewness and kurtosis of the distributions of the individual variables.

Table 4 Fouladi and Steiger (1995) — Power as a Function of ρ_{ij}, p, N, and Nominal Alpha

ρ_{ij}	p	N	B	S80	FSF1	FSF2	FSSL	FSSC	FSN	RMAX
						$\alpha = .05$				
.1	5	10	.07	.08	.08	.08	.08	.08	.06	.06
		20	.10	.12	.12	.12	.12	.12	.10	.08
		50	.22	.26	.26	.26	.27	.26	.22	.16
		100	.45	.51	.51	.51	.52	.51	.45	.29
		200	.80	.84	.84	.84	.85	.84	.80	.54
	10	20	.16	.23	.22	.22	.23	.23	.13	.09
		40	.30	.45	.45	.45	.45	.45	.29	.16
		100	.77	.89	.88	.88	.89	.88	.77	.38
		200	.99	1.00	1.00	1.00	1.00	1.00	.99	.72
		400	1.00	1.00	1.00	1.00	1.00	1.00	1.00	.98
.2	5	10	.13	.19	.18	.18	.19	.18	.12	.10
		20	.27	.37	.36	.36	.38	.37	.27	.20
		50	.71	.78	.78	.78	.79	.78	.71	.50
		100	.97	.98	.98	.98	.98	.98	.97	.84
		200	1.00	1.00	1.00	1.00	1.00	1.00	1.00	.99
	10	20	.44	.68	.68	.68	.69	.68	.39	.24
		40	.84	.95	.95	.95	.95	.95	.84	.52
		100	1.00	1.00	1.00	1.00	1.00	1.00	1.00	.95
		200	1.00	1.00	1.00	1.00	1.00	1.00	1.00	1.00
		400	1.00	1.00	1.00	1.00	1.00	1.00	1.00	1.00

Fouladi and Steiger (1995). For the conditions of multivariate nonnormality examined, increasing skew had little impact on empirical rejection rates; however, there was a significant main effect for kurtosis. We observed that increasing kurtosis resulted in an increasing departure of actual rejection rates from the expected level. Table 5 provides an index of the departure of empirical alpha from nominal alpha as a percentage of nominal alpha for different levels of kurtosis.

ρ_{ij}	p	N	B	$S80$	$FSF1$	$FSF2$	$FSSL$	$FSSC$	FSN	$RMAX$
						$\alpha = .01$				
.1	5	10	.02	.03	.02	.02	.03	.02	.01	.01
		20	.02	.05	.04	.04	.04	.04	.02	.02
		50	.08	.12	.12	.12	.12	.12	.08	.04
		100	.23	.31	.30	.30	.32	.30	.23	.10
		200	.61	.68	.68	.68	.70	.68	.61	.25
	10	20	.05	.11	.11	.11	.11	.11	.04	.02
		40	.13	.28	.28	.28	.28	.28	.12	.04
		100	.57	.77	.77	.77	.78	.77	.57	.13
		200	.97	.99	.99	.99	.99	.99	.97	.37
		400	1.00	1.00	1.00	1.00	1.00	1.00	1.00	.82
.2	5	10	.04	.09	.08	.08	.09	.08	.03	.02
		20	.11	.22	.21	.21	.22	.21	.11	.06
		50	.50	.63	.62	.62	.64	.62	.50	.22
		100	.91	.95	.95	.95	.95	.95	.91	.57
		200	1.00	1.00	1.00	1.00	1.00	1.00	1.00	.95
	10	20	.24	.54	.53	.53	.55	.54	.19	.07
		40	.68	.90	.90	.90	.90	.90	.67	.22
		100	1.00	1.00	1.00	1.00	1.00	1.00	1.00	.76
		200	1.00	1.00	1.00	1.00	1.00	1.00	1.00	1.00
		400	1.00	1.00	1.00	1.00	1.00	1.00	1.00	1.00

Table 4 Continued

We examined the robustness of B, $S80$, $FSF1$, $FSF2$, $FSSL$, $FSSC$, FSN, and $RMAX$ across an array of conditions. A reexamination of those results using Bradley's (1978) and Robey and Barcikowski's (1992) guidelines for acceptable levels of departure of empirical alpha from nominal alpha indicates that, for the conditions examined, none of the procedures provides overall control of Type I error. Though, if one uses the loose standard of robustness, for marginal kurtosis up to 5, $FSSL$, $FSSC$, FSN, and $RMAX$ would be declared as "robust" for tests at the nominal lev-

Table 5 Fouladi and Steiger (1995)—Departure of Empirical From Nominal Alpha as Percentage of Nominal Alpha Under Conditions of Marginal Kurtosis of 5, 20, and 50

κ	N	B	S80	FSF1	FSF2	FSSL	FSSC	FSN	RMAX
					$\alpha = .05$				
5	6	199	25	11	16	12	9	2	9
	10	22	27	14	14	10	10	6	23
	20	16	24	16	16	10	14	13	30
	50	17	19	16	16	11	15	17	33
	100	11	13	11	11	8	11	12	22
	200	5	4	4	4	2	4	6	12
20	11	229	74	59	63	38	47	15	75
	40	79	97	83	83	48	67	60	139
	80	82	94	86	86	52	76	81	167
	200	73	77	74	74	48	70	73	152
	400	56	58	56	56	37	55	57	121
	800	42	42	41	41	27	41	42	94
50	51	449	385	362	369	214	282	151	498
	100	307	336	319	320	190	265	283	509
	200	236	250	242	242	145	218	234	440
	500	177	182	179	179	113	171	177	348
	1000	135	137	136	136	87	132	135	284
	2000	112	113	112	112	75	110	112	235

el of .05 and .01. The worst performance is evidenced by *RMAX*. The best overall performance is exhibited by *FSSL*.

Conclusion

There are many procedures that can be used to test the identity correlation structure null hypothesis. Monte Carlo study results have shown that some procedures have better performance

Table 5 Continued									
κ	N	B	S80	FSF1	FSF2	FSSL	FSSC	FSN	RMAX
						$\alpha = .01$			
5	6	479	120	77	88	65	52	−1	10
	10	40	97	67	67	49	47	6	34
	20	33	73	57	57	40	46	27	69
	50	36	56	50	50	37	44	34	79
	100	29	36	34	34	24	32	28	57
	200	16	18	17	17	9	15	14	30
20	11	561	270	208	223	142	147	10	123
	40	163	320	269	270	165	198	117	316
	80	222	303	277	278	173	234	213	450
	200	236	266	257	257	172	238	234	466
	400	188	202	198	198	140	193	187	364
	800	145	152	150	150	109	147	143	275
50	51	1296	1486	1353	1391	719	925	245	1499
	100	975	1305	1220	1223	678	930	872	1700
	200	840	959	924	924	551	788	824	1545
	500	671	705	695	695	465	647	666	1254
	1000	536	551	548	548	379	522	533	1015
	2000	439	448	446	446	321	434	436	829

characteristics than others. When the assumption of multivariate normality holds, *FSN* and *RMAX* have the best Type I error control, where *FSN* is the more powerful of the two. When the assumption of multivariate normality does not hold, none of the available procedures controls Type I error at the nominal level; though, overall, *FSSL* provides better control than the other statistics. Thus, *FSN* and *RMAX* have the best performance profiles under conditions of multivariate normality, and *FSSL* has the best profile under conditions of multivariate nonnormality.

Regrettably, *FSN* is not presently available as a computer program for general use, and is far too complicated to compute by hand. However, *RMAX* and *FSSL* are easily calculated using any software package that yields p levels for each of the individual correlations and a simple hand calculator.

Under conditions of multivariate normality, *RMAX* controls Type I error close to the nominal level; however, because it is also the least powerful procedure, an obtained value that results in a rejection will be little doubted. Only when one fails to reject the null hypothesis would one be concerned about the lack of power.

Though *FSSL* does not control Type I error at the nominal level under conditions of nonnormality, *FSSL* provides better control than any of the other statistics examined. The key issue to keep in mind in using liberal procedures under conditions of nonnormality, it is only when one rejects the null hypothesis that one would be concerned. If one fails to reject the null hypothesis using procedures that are liberal under nonnormality, one has little cause for concern.

Two Closing Examples

Extremely small sample sizes are not uncommon in neurophysiology. Consider a situation in which a researcher obtains data from 10 brains, and computes the sample correlation matrix based on measurements of brain activity in five regions of each brain. In this example, $N = 10$ and $p = 5$. The sample correlation matrix is

$$\begin{bmatrix} 1.0 & & & & \\ .9 & 1.0 & & & \\ .5 & .8 & 1.0 & & \\ .2 & .4 & .7 & 1.0 & \\ .0 & .1 & .3 & .6 & 1.0 \end{bmatrix}.$$

For this example, *ML, GLS, B, S80, FSSL, FSSC*, and *RMAX* are computed; these procedures can be easily implemented using many software packages currently available, including EXCEL. The other test statistics are not computed because the required software is not widely available. To compute *ML, B, GLS, L, S80, FSSL, FSSC*, and *RMAX*, we need the natural logarithm of the determinant of the sample correlation matrix, the sum of the squared nonredundant correlations, and the sum of the squared Fisher transforms of those correlations; these equal -5.47, 2.84, and 5.23, respectively. We also need the two-tailed p levels from t tests on the significance of each correlation (from .9 to .0); these are .0004, .0055, .0242, .0667, .1411, .2521, .3997, .5796, and 1.0000.

Using the value of the natural logarithm of the determinant, ML and B yield observed χ^2 values of 49.25 and 35.57, respectively. Using the value of the sum of the squared correlations and the sum of the squared Fisher transforms, GLS, L, and $S80$ yield 25.56, 18.46, and 36.58, respectively. From the p levels, $FSSL$ yields an observed χ^2 value of 48.59, and $FSSC$ yields a value of 34.13.

At the .05 level, the critical values equal 18.31 for ML, B, GLS, L, $S80$, and $FSSC$, and 31.41 for $FSSL$. In each of these cases, because the observed values exceed the critical values, we reject the null hypothesis of an identity correlation structure in the population. For $RMAX$, we compare the p level corresponding to the largest element of the sample correlation matrix ($p = .0004$) to the Dunn-Sidak or Bonferroni defined alphas, which in this example are $1 - .95^{1/10} = .0051$ and $.05/10 = .0050$, respectively; because the observed p level is less than the Dunn-Sidak and Bonferroni defined alphas, we also reject the null hypothesis. For this example, ML, B, GLS, L, $S80$, $FSSL$, $FSSC$, and $RMAX$ yield converging conclusions; however, this need not always be the case, particularly if many of the correlations are small.

Here, each of the methods obtains a rejection of the null hypothesis for an identity structure for the population correlation matrix. Were this a real data set, we would wish to check whether the condition of multivariate normality is tenable. If multivariate normality is tenable, then we can be relatively assured of our results because we have obtained rejections of the null hypothesis with the most conservative procedures. However, if multivariate normality is not tenable, then we would interpret our results with caution because we could easily be making a false rejection of a true null hypothesis.

Consider a second example with the same sample size and the same variables, where the observed correlation between brain activity in the first and second brain region is still .9 (as in the first example); however, all other observed correlations are .4. In this case, the decision with *RMAX* is unchanged because the largest correlation is still .9. The observed values of *ML, B, GLS, L, S80, FSSL*, and *FSSC* are different, however; their values are 22.66, 16.37, 18.81, 13.59, 25.22, 37.76, and 24.08, respectively. All of the critical values stay the same; in this case, *ML, GLS, S80, FSSC, FSSL*, and *RMAX* yield rejections of the null hypothesis; however, *B* and *L* fail to reject the null hypothesis.

In this second example, we see that the most commonly recommended test for identity correlation structure, *B*, yields a different decision from the other procedures. These results emphasize the importance of using statistical procedures which, under small-sample conditions, maximize power while maintaining control over Type I error rates. With these considerations, this example reminds us that, though commonly recommended and offering substantial advantages over its large-sample counterpart, Bartlett's procedure, *B*, may not be the best procedure to use under small-sample-size conditions.

Final Note

Many have recommended the use of the test of the null hypothesis that the variables are uncorrelated in the population prior to confirmatory or exploratory covariance and correlation structure analysis; this is particularly relevant in small-sample situations. In this chapter, we reviewed a variety of the procedures that can be used to test this null hypothesis; we discussed Type I error control, power, and robustness under a range of sample size conditions.

Researchers involved in analyzing large-sample, normally distributed data sets are well advised to use Bartlett's test (*B*) or even the maximum-likelihood or generalized least squares statistics (*ML* or *GLS*) if their data sets are large enough; however, researchers, particularly those analyzing data sets based on a relatively small number of subjects or nonnormally distributed variables, will find that some of the alternative techniques reviewed in this chapter provide superior statistical decision making. Quite a number of the alternative procedures are easily implemented in current versions of software packages, such as EXCEL, SAS, SPSS, and Statistica.

Interested readers may direct inquiries regarding these tests of identity correlation structure to rachel.fouladi@mail.utexas.edu. Readers are referred to the Web sites http://www.edb.utexas.edu/-faculty/fouladi/index.htm and http://www.interchg.ubc.ca/steiger/-homepage.htm for announcements regarding the implementation of these and other procedures.

Author Note: We are grateful to the two anonymous reviewers and Rick H. Hoyle for their helpful comments and encouragement.

References

Bartlett, M. S. (1950). Tests of significance in factor analysis. *British Journal of Psychology, Statistical Section, 34*, 33–40.

Bartlett, M. S. (1954). A note on multiplying factors for various chi-squared approximations. *Journal of the Royal Statistical Society, B16*, 296–298.

Basilevsky, A. (1994). *Statistical factor analysis and related methods: Theory and application*. New York: Wiley.

Bollen, K. A. (1989). *Structural equations with latent variables*. New York: Wiley.

Box, G. E. P. (1949). A general distribution theory for a class of likelihood criteria. *Biometrika, 36*, 317–346.

Bradley, J. V. (1978). Robustness? *British Journal of Mathematical and Statistical Psychology, 31*, 144–152.

Browne, M. W. (1977). The analysis of patterned correlation matrices by generalized least squares. *British Journal of Mathematical and Statistical Psychology, 30*, 113–124.

Burt, C. (1952). Tests of significance in factor analysis. *British Journal of Psychology, 5*, 109–133.

Cameron, M. A., & Eagleson, G. K. (1985). A new procedure for assessing large sets of correlations. *Australian Journal of Statistics, 27*, 84–95.

Cohen, J., & Cohen, P. (1983). *Applied multiple regression/ correlation analysis for the behavioral sciences* (2nd ed.). Hillsdale, NJ: Erlbaum.

Cooley, W. W., & Lohnes, P. R. (1971). *Multivariate data analysis*. New York: Wiley.

Dziuban, C. D., & Shirkey, E. C. (1974a). When is a correlation matrix suitable for factor analysis? Some decision rules. *Psychological Bulletin, 81*, 358–361.

Dziuban, C. D., & Shirkey, E. C. (1974b). On the psychometric assessment of correlation matrices. *American Educational Research Journal, 11*, 211–216.

Fouladi, R. T. (1991). *A comprehensive examination of procedures for testing a correlation matrix and its elements*. Unpublished master's thesis, University of British Columbia, Canada.

Fouladi, R. T. (1996). *A study of procedures to examine correlation pattern hypotheses under conditions of multivariate normality and nonnormality*. Unpublished doctoral dissertation, University of British Columbia, Canada.

Fouladi, R. T., & Steiger, J. H. (1995, October). *Fixing Bartlett's test: An investigation of tests for an identity correlation structure*. Paper presented at the 36th annual meeting of the Society of Multivariate Experimental Psychology, Blaine, WA.

Geisser, S., & Mantel, N. (1962). Pairwise independence of jointly dependent variables. *Annals of Mathematical Statistics, 33*, 290–291.

Hotelling, H. (1953). New light on the correlation coefficient and its transforms. *Journal of the Royal Statistical Society, B15*, 193–232.

Knapp, T. R., & Swoyer, V. H. (1967). Some empirical results concerning the power of Bartlett's test of the significance of a correlation matrix. *American Educational Research Journal, 4*, 13–17.

Konishi, S. (1978). An approximation to the distribution of the sample correlation coefficient. *Biometrika, 65*, 654–666.

Lawley, D. N. (1940). The estimation of factor loadings by the method of maximum likelihood. *Proceedings of the Royal Society of Edinburgh, 60*, 64–82.

Mathai, A. M., & Katiyar, R. S. (1979). Exact percentage points for testing independence. *Biometrika, 66*, 353–356.

McDonald, R. P. (1985). *Factor analysis and related methods*. Hillsdale, NJ: Erlbaum.

Moran, P. A. P. (1980). Testing the largest of a set of correlation coefficients. *Australian Journal of Statistics, 22*, 289–297.

Morrison, D. F. (1990). *Multivariate statistical methods* (3rd ed.). New York: McGraw-Hill.

Mudholkar, G. S., & Subbaiah, P. (1980/81). Complete independence in the multivariate normal distribution. In G. P. Patil, C. Taillie, & B. Baldessari (Eds.), *Statistical distributions in scientific work* (Vol. 5, pp. 157–168). New York: Plenum.

Mudholkar, G. S., & Trivedi, M. C. (1980/81). A normal approximation for the multivariate likelihood ratio statistics. In G. P. Patil, C. Taillie, & B. Baldessari (Eds.), *Statistical distributions in scientific work* (Vol. 5, pp. 219–230). New York: Plenum.

Mudholkar, G. S., Trivedi, M. C., & Lin, C. T. (1982). An approximation to the distribution of the likelihood ratio statistic for testing complete independence. *Technometrics*, *24*, 130–143.

Reddon, J. R. (1987). Fisher's tanh^{-1} transformation of the correlation coefficient and a test for complete independence in a multivariate normal population. *Journal of Educational Statistics*, *12*, 294–300.

Robey, R. R., & Barcikowski, R. S. (1992). Type I error and the number of iterations in Monte Carlo studies of robustness. *British Journal of Mathematical and Statistical Psychology*, *45*, 283–288.

Silver, N. C. (1988). *Type I errors and power of tests of correlations in matrix*. Unpublished doctoral dissertation, Tulane University, New Orleans, LA.

Silver, N. C., & Dunlap, W. P. (1989). A Monte Carlo study of testing the significance of correlation matrices. *Educational Psychological Measurement*, *49*, 563–569.

SPSS 7.5 [computer software]. (1997). Chicago: SPSS.

Steiger, J. H. (1980a). Testing pattern hypotheses on correlation matrices: Alternative statistics and some empirical results. *Multivariate Behavioral Research*, *15*, 335–352.

Steiger, J. H. (1980b). Tests for comparing elements of a correlation matrix. *Psychological Bulletin*, *87*, 245–251.

Steiger, J. H., & Fouladi, R. T. (1991a). *A new simple test of multivariate independence*. Unpublished manuscript, University of British Columbia, Canada.

Steiger, J. H., & Fouladi, R. T. (1991b). *Squaring the Fisher transform: Some theoretical considerations*. Unpublished manuscript, University of British Columbia, Canada.

Tobias, S., & Carlson, J. E. (1969). Brief report: Bartlett's test of sphericity and chance findings in factor analysis. *Multivariate Behavioral Research*, *4*, 375–377.

Wilks, S. S. (1935). On the independence of *k* sets of normally distributed statistical variables. *Econometrica*, *3*, 309–326.

Wilson, G. A., & Martin, S. A. (1983). An empirical comparison of two methods for testing the significance of a correlation matrix. *Educational and Psychological Measurement*, *43*, 11–14.

8

Sample Size, Reliability, and Tests of Statistical Mediation

Rick H. Hoyle & David A. Kenny

STATISTICAL MEDIATION is present when it can be demonstrated that the causal influence of one variable on another is transmitted through one or more additional variables, referred to as mediators or intervening variables (Alwin & Hauser, 1975; Baron & Kenny, 1986; James & Brett, 1984; Rozenboom, 1956). Mediational analyses are important in the social and behavioral sciences because they concern mechanisms or processes that explain how or why one variable causes another. In this regard, mediational hypotheses and statistical tests are indicative of a maturing discipline or research literature, one that has demonstrated with reasonable confidence the direct causal connections between key variables and has turned to the challenging endeavor of explanation and theory testing regarding those connections (Reis & Stiller, 1992; Simon, 1992). Mediational analyses also can point to additional, undocumented causes of an outcome by implicating antecedents of a mediator other than the putative causal variable (Kimble, 1989). And mediational models and analyses have become central to the design and evaluation of prevention and treatment interventions (MacKinnon, 1998). As these virtues of mediational analyses have become apparent to social and behavioral scientists, the number of articles and chapters on when and how to test mediational hypotheses has steadily increased, and there is now a sizable didactic literature (e.g., Alwin & Hauser, 1975; Baron & Kenny, 1986; Dwyer et al., 1989; Holmbeck, 1997; James & Brett, 1984; Judd & Kenny, 1981; Kenny, Kashy, & Bolger, 1998; MacKinnon & Dwyer, 1993; Shadish & Sweeney, 1991; West, Aiken, & Todd, 1993) and a growing technical literature (e.g., Bollen, 1987; Finch, West, & MacKinnon, 1997; Fox, 1985; MacKinnon, Warsi, & Dwyer, 1995; Sobel, 1982, 1986, 1987; Stone & Sobel, 1990) on tests of statistical mediation.

The concern of this chapter is the integrity of statistical tests of simple mediation—one predictor, one mediator, and one outcome—under the less-than-ideal data-analytic conditions (e.g., relatively small samples, fallible measures of constructs) characteristic of social and behavioral science research. In particular, we focus on the influence of sample size, the unreliability of the mediator variable, and the strength of the association between the independent variable and the mediator on the accuracy of parameter estimates and the power of tests of statistical mediation. To keep our analysis focused and manageable, we assume that the independent variable and outcome are measured without error and that the model is correctly specified— there is no moderation and the outcome does not cause the mediator. In a Monte Carlo experiment, we vary sample size, degree of measurement error in the mediator, and degree of collinearity between the independent variable and the mediator in a complete factorial design. Under each set of conditions, we estimate a simple mediational model using two approaches to modeling the mediator variable: (1) Three fallible measures of the mediator are scored into a composite. (2) The measures are modeled as indicators of a latent variable. Statistical analyses focus on the effects of these factors on the estimates of path coefficients and the power of statistical tests of those co-efficients.

Conceptualization of a Mediational Model

Despite the appearance in high-profile journals of several instructive and illustrative articles on the development and testing of mediational hypotheses (e.g., Baron & Kenny, 1986; James & Brett, 1984), there is still evidence of confusion among applied researchers (e.g., Holmbeck, 1997). At the most general level, the confusion manifests as a lack of hypothesis validity—correspondence between a research hypothesis and the statistical test of it (Wampold, Davis, & Good, 1990). In some such instances, researchers develop a mediational hypothesis but, because of design shortcomings or inappropriate choice of statistical method, do not test it. In other instances, researchers develop other hypotheses that do not involve statistical mediation (e.g., moderator hypotheses) but label them as instances of mediation.

Simple mediation, on which our analysis focuses, can be profitably represented using a pair of path diagrams. The path diagram at the top of Figure 1 illustrates the direct effect of an independent variable, X, on an outcome, Y. The path coefficient, c, corresponds to a regression coefficient and indicates the strength and direction of the influence. In this two-variable model, path c reflects the total effect of X on Y. The path diagram in the middle of Figure 1 adds a mediator, or intervening variable, Z, and paths from the independent variable to the mediator, a, and the mediator to the outcome, b, to the model. In this model, the total effect of X on Y is partitioned into two components: the direct effect, reflected in path c', and the indirect effect, which we will denote as ab. The validity of this model rests on the assumption that there are no reverse casual effects (e.g., the outcome causes the mediator) or omitted variables (James & Brett, 1984; Kenny et al., 1998).

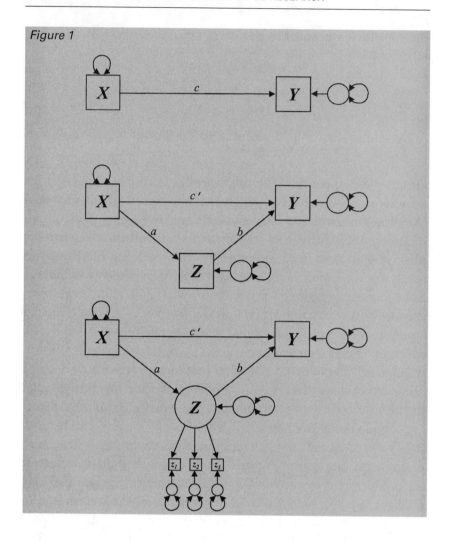

Figure 1

Technical Issues Concerning Tests of Mediation

Beyond the conceptual level are a variety of technical issues concerning statistical tests of mediation. Statistical evidence of mediation requires the following: (1) evidence of a causal influence of X on Y, reflected statistically as a nonzero value for c; and (2) a significant indirect effect of X on Y, reflected statistically as a nonzero value for ab (which is equivalent to $c - c'$), indicative of a decline in the direct effect of X on Y when the mediator is accounted for (i.e., $|c'| < |c|$).[1] If ab is significant but c' remains significant, then there is evidence of both direct and indirect effects of X on Y and, therefore, Z only partially mediates the effect. If ab is significant and c' is not, then Z fully mediates the effect of X on Y. These effects and the corresponding standard errors can be estimated using ordinary least squares (OLS) in a multiple-regression context or maximum likelihood (ML) in a structural equation modeling context.

The performance of these statistical tests is affected by a number of factors. We consider three: We first consider the effects of sample size on tests of mediation, for the most part focusing on the statistical power of the test. We then turn to collinearity between the independent and mediator variables and its effect on the statistical power of tests of mediation. Finally, we examine the effects of unreliability of the mediator on both the precision of path estimates and the statistical power of the test.

Sample Size

Applied researchers in the social and behavioral sciences rarely have the luxury of a large sample. Yet their hypotheses often concern detailed processes that require multivariate statistical methods (Hoyle, 1994). These seemingly incompatible realities have led methodologists to consider the practically important question: With how small a sample can a particular statistical strategy be used? Monte Carlo experiments that manipulate sample size now routinely consider sample sizes less than 100. And results indicate that even some large-sample strategies can be used with small samples for some hypothesis tests and types of data. Our concern is how tests of simple mediation perform with samples that comprise from 25 to 200 cases.

An immediate concern when contemplating small-sample statistical tests is statistical power. Although statistical power

---

[1] We emphasize the point that the effect of X on Y should be demonstrably causal. Nonlinear and nonrecursive influences are possible; however, the typical test involves linear relations in a recursive model (Baron & Kenny, 1986; James & Brett, 1984).

is affected by multiple characteristics of a research study, the effect of N is perhaps the most widely acknowledged. The effects of N on statistical power can be traced to the standard error, which forms the denominator of the statistical test. With least squares estimators such as OLS, the general form of the standard error, s, is the ratio of the standard deviation to the square root of N. Thus, as N increases, the denominator of this ratio increases, leading to smaller values of s and larger values of the test statistic.

With ML estimation, commonly used in applications of structural equation modeling, the effect of N on the standard error is less apparent but no less important. Maximum likelihood is a large-sample estimation method, which means that the underlying statistical theory presumes that the sample size is quite large. The problem for applied researchers is aptly captured in Sobel's (1982) statement, "Since one seldom knows when a sample is large enough, the application of [large sample] methods may be inappropriate in particularly small samples" (p. 308). Fortunately, a growing body of simulation research indicates that, under certain circumstances (e.g., normal distributions, well-specified model), large-sample methods such as ML perform acceptably in samples of 200 or less (e.g., Boomsma, 1983; Gerbing & Anderson, 1985; Tanaka, 1987).

For instance, consider the standard error most commonly used to test the statistical significance of the indirect effect, ab:

$$\sqrt{\left(s_a^2 b^2 + s_b^2 a^2\right)}. \tag{1}$$

This standard error was developed by Sobel (1982, 1986) using the multivariate-delta method (Rao, 1973), and has been integrated into widely used statistical packages for estimating structural equation models such as LISREL and EQS. In a simulation study of the effects of N on the performance of this standard error, Stone and Sobel (1990) concluded that, for a model with three independent variables and two mediators, a sample size of at least 100 is required (though $N \geqslant 200$ is recommended) when all variables are observed and at least 400 cases are required when the mediators are modeled as latent variables. MacKinnon et al. (1995) found that Sobel's standard error performed as expected in tests of a simple mediational model estimation with $N = 50$. MacKinnon et al. also found that, when the independent variable is continuous, there is little bias in the estimation of the standard error with Ns of 10 and 25. Thus, there is some evidence that simple mediated effects could be meaningfully tested when the sample size is quite small.

Collinearity Between Cause and Mediator

As we have shown, the mediational or indirect effect of X on Y involves two paths, a and b. Because b is most directly implicated in the estimation of c', evaluations such as ours rarely focus on the role of a in tests of mediation. Although this path has no direct effect on the estimation of c', it should affect the statistical power of the test of ab for reasons that concern the partitioning of variance in Z, the mediator. The more variance in Z accounted for by X (which is correlated with Y), the less variance in Z there is to contribute to the prediction of Y. Thus, we would expect the power associated with the test of b to decrease as a, the effect of X on Z (i.e., r_{xz}) increases. In fact, Kenny et al. (1998) indicated that the effective sample size for purposes of power calculations for tests of b and c' is $N(1 - r_{xz}^2)$. So, for instance, for a sample of size 100, the effective N when $r_{xz} = .3$ is 91, whereas for $r_{xz} = .5$ it is 75; as a increases, the N required to sustain a particular level of power for the test of b increases. The degree to which the power of the test of the indirect effect, ab, is affected by such collinearity is less clear because both a and b contribute to the indirect effect. By manipulating collinearity, we empirically evaluate this effect.

Unreliability of the Mediator

An important factor that typically is ignored in empirical tests of approaches to testing mediation is the reliability of the mediator. This factor is similarly ignored in standard statistical approaches such as multiple regression and analysis of variance. In a widely cited paper on testing mediation, Baron and Kenny (1986) spell out the detrimental effects of ignoring measurement error in the mediator, but the use of composite variables composed of fallible indicators of the mediator persists.

We can readily demonstrate the effects of unreliability on estimates of path coefficients. Consider the equation,

$$Y = bZ + c'X + u,$$

where X is the independent variable, Y is the outcome, and Z is the mediator. Thus, b corresponds to the path from the mediator to the outcome, and c' denotes the path from the independent variable to the outcome (see Figure 1). Our focus is on unreliability in the mediator, so we assume that the reliability of the independent variable, X, is perfect. We also assume that the true association between the independent variable and the mediator, a, is known. The question is, What will happen to b and c as the reliability of Z departs from 1.0? The observed correlation between the independent variable and the mediator, r_{xz}, is attenuated to the extent that the mediator is not perfectly reliable; $r_{xz} = a\sqrt{r_{zz}}$, where r_{zz} denotes the reliability of the mediator. The reliability of the mediator with the independent variable partialed out, $r_{zz'}$, is computed as $(r_{zz} - r_{xz}^2)/(1 - r_{xz}^2)$. The expected value of the observed influence of the mediator on the outcome is

$$r_{zz'}b, \tag{2}$$

where b denotes the population value of the path coefficient. And the expected value of the observed influence of the independent variable on the outcome, c', is

$$(1 - r_{zz'})ab + c, \tag{3}$$

where a, b, and c denote population values of the path coefficients. It should be apparent that, as the reliability of the mediator departs from 1.0 (toward zero), the observed effect of the mediator on the dependent variable, b, is underestimated and the observed effect of the independent variable on the dependent variable, c', is overestimated (assuming $ab > 0$). Thus, inasmuch as the reliability of measures used in the social and behavioral sciences rarely exceeds .90, and sometimes falls closer to .70, statistical approaches that ignore measurement error, such as multiple regression and analysis of variance, underestimate mediated effects when they are present. When the sample size is small and the mediator is measured with error, the available power to detect a mediated effect likely tends toward zero.

Latent Variable Modeling of Mediation

One means of overcoming the ill effects of unreliability in the measurement of the mediator is the use of structural equation modeling (Bollen, 1987; Hoyle, 1995) to estimate coefficients and standard errors. By partitioning unique variance and random error from variance shared by a set of measures of a variable, structural equation modeling permits the estimation of associations between latent variables, which are free of measurement error (Hoyle, 1991). A model in which the mediator is modeled as a latent variable is shown in path diagram form at the bottom of Figure 1. Note that variability in z_1, z_2, and z_3, indicators of the mediator (e.g., items of a scale, multiple scales, item parcels), is accounted for by a common source, Z, and a source unique to each indicator, represented by the small circles. By modeling the mediator in this way, uniqueness and random error are divorced from commonality in such a way that the reliability of the mediator is, in effect, 1.0.

Despite the clear appeal of structural equation modeling for tests of statistical mediation, a potential drawback is the relatively large samples recommended for applications of structural equation modeling. It is possible that any benefits in estimates of the path coefficients are offset by biases in the ML standard errors, which are based on large-sample theory. In the Monte Carlo experiment, we examine the feasibility of using structural equation modeling with the mediator modeled as a latent variable when N is small.

Monte Carlo Experiment

In a Monte Carlo experiment, we evaluated the effects of sample size, collinearity between the independent variable and the mediator, and unreliability of the mediator on parameter estimates and tests of statistical mediation when the mediator is modeled as either a composite or a latent variable. We investigated these effects in the context of the three-variable model shown in Figure 1. In the interest of focus, we chose not to investigate the effects of nonnormality (see Finch et al., 1997, for simulation work on this problem); we assumed normally distributed variables. Also, we considered only full mediation, that is, no direct effect of the independent variable on the dependent variable (i.e., $c' = 0$) when the indirect effect via the mediator is accounted for.

Design

The design of the experiment is a four-way factorial. We considered four samples sizes, 200, 100, 50, and 25, that fall within the range that is typical of social and behavioral science research. We examined three levels of reliability of the mediator: .60, .75, and .90. The lowest value falls beneath the recommended minimum, but would not be uncommon for short scales or broadband measures; the middle value is typical of applied research; and the highest value reflects a realistic ideal for research measures with a relatively small number of items (Nunnally & Bernstein, 1994). In a two-level factor, we varied the degree of collinearity between the independent variable and the mediator; levels were $r = .40$ and $r = .60$. Finally, we considered two approaches to modeling the mediator. In the composite model, illustrated in the path diagram in the middle of Figure 1, we treated the mediator as an observed variable, thereby not explicitly acknowledging unreliability in the model. In the latent variable model, displayed in path diagram form at the bottom of Figure 1, we specified three fallible measures as indicators of a latent variable, thereby explicitly incorporating unreliability into the model. In the context of this design, we compared mean estimates of selected parameter estimates and statistical power as a function of the four factors (Hauck & Anderson, 1984).

Technical Details

We used the Monte Carlo procedure in the SEPath module in Release 5.1 of STATISTICA for Windows (StatSoft, 1996) to simulate data for the 48 conditions.[2] We generated and analyzed data from 500 random samples per condition. From each analysis, we retained parameter estimates and standard errors for all free parameters, as well as diagnostic information relevant to convergence and permissibility of estimates. These data were then analyzed using SPSS for Windows, Release 7.5.1 (SPSS, 1996).

Random samples were generated from populations defined by covariance matrices, which varied according to level of reliability and collinearity between independent variable and mediator.[3] Parameters were estimated using the ML procedure in SEPath. For practical reasons and based on several trial runs, the maximum number of iterations was set at 150. Path coefficients and standard errors for the indirect effect, critical ratios for all parameters, and OLS standard errors were computed from SEPath output using SPSS.

Results

A preliminary check on the integrity of the simulated results revealed estimation problems for 522 (2%) of the 24,000 samples; these samples were excluded from subsequent analyses, rendering an analysis N of 23,478. The problems typically involved either impermissible values for parameters or standard errors ($n = 480$) or failure to converge within 150 iterations ($n = 20$). All but three problematic analyses arose in the latent variable model, and all but two occurred with Ns of 25 or 50 and reliability of .60. In the worst condition ($N = 25$; $r_{xx} = .60$), just under

---

[2] We gratefully acknowledge the guidance provided by James Steiger, author of the SEPath module in STATISTICA.

[3] Covariance matrices, STATISTICA input files, and raw data are available from the first author by request.

14% of the analyses were problematic. In summary, when the minimum conditions of $N = 100$ and $r_{zz} = .75$ were met, there were very few practical problems with estimation.

Parameter Estimates. The estimates of path a were relatively unaffected by the manipulations. The highly significant main effect of collinearity was confirmation of the manipulation of that characteristic of the model. Otherwise, there was a small but significant three-way interaction involving sample size, reliability, and model. Path a was overestimated when sample size was 25, reliability was .60, and the mediator was modeled as a latent variable ($Ms = .48$ and .66). Otherwise, mean estimates were within .02 of the population value.

Mean estimates of path b are displayed in Table 1. The strongest effect was a main effect of model, attributable to the consistent underestimation of b for the composite model. This effect was qualified by a significant Model × Reliability interaction. Whereas unreliability had relatively little influence on estimates of b in the latent variable model, it had a strong influence on estimates in the composite model. The Sample Size × Reliability interaction obtained, though the effect was relatively weak. Looking at the first two columns in the bottom half of Table 1, it is apparent that b is overestimated in the latent variable model when $N \leqslant 50$ and reliability is low or moderate. Although this pattern was not apparent for the composite model, the three-way interaction of model, sample size, and reliability was not significant. This null finding indicates that, in terms of parameter estimation, the ill effects of unreliability on path b are no more pronounced for small samples than for moderately large samples.

The pattern of means for the indirect effect, shown in Table 2, largely follows the pattern for path b (with the exception that the expected value differs as a function of the collinearity manipulation). The strong effect for model attests to the underestimation of ab when unreliability is ignored. Not surprisingly, this effect was moderated by reliability; as reliability decreases, the underestimation in the composite model was more pronounced. The highly significant main effect of collinearity simply reflects the manipulation; however, the collinearity differences varied as a function of model and reliability. The former is at-

Table 1 Maximum-Likelihood Parameter Estimates for the Path From the Mediator to the Outcome (Path *b*) as a Function of Sample Size, Modeling of Mediator, Collinearity of the Independent Variable and the Mediator, and Reliability of the Mediator

		Sample Size			
Condition	Equation 2	25	50	100	200
Composite Model					
Path *a* = .40					
Low reliability	.17	.17	.17	.17	.17
Moderate reliability	.21	.20	.22	.22	.22
High reliability	.26	.25	.26	.27	.27
Path *a* = .60					
Low reliability	.14	.15	.14	.15	.14
Moderate reliability	.20	.22	.19	.20	.20
High reliability	.26	.26	.27	.26	.25
Latent Variable Model					
Path *a* = .40					
Low reliability	.30	.38	.37	.32	.31
Moderate reliability	.30	.39	.37	.30	.30
High reliability	.30	.32	.33	.30	.30
Path *a* = .60					
Low reliability	.30	.37	.34	.33	.32
Moderate reliability	.30	.37	.31	.30	.29
High reliability	.30	.33	.31	.30	.30

Note. "Path *a*" is the path from the independent variable to the mediator. In all conditions, the population value of the parameter is .30.

tributable to a stronger effect of collinearity in the composite model compared to the latent variable model. And the latter, a small effect, is due to the fact that the collinearity differences decline as reliability declines, an effect that is largely limited to the composite model condition, giving rise to a weak but significant Model × Reliability × Collinearity interaction effect. The overestimation apparent in estimates of paths *a* and *b* in the latent variable model when N is small and reliability is low or moderate was less pronounced in estimates of ab in the latent variable model. Indeed, sample size was inconsequential in the analysis of the estimates of the indirect path coefficient.

Table 2 Maximum-Likelihood Parameter Estimates for the Indirect Path From the Outcome to the Independent Variable Through the Mediator (Path *ab*) as a Function of Sample Size, Modeling of the Mediator, Collinearity of the Independent Variable and the Mediator, and Reliability of the Mediator

Condition	a* (Equation 2)	Sample Size			
		25	50	100	200
Composite Model					
Path *a* = .40					
Low reliability	.07	.07	.07	.07	.07
Moderate reliability	.09	.08	.08	.09	.09
High reliability	.11	.10	.11	.11	.11
Path *a* = .60					
Low reliability	.09	.09	.08	.09	.09
Moderate reliability	.12	.13	.11	.12	.12
High reliability	.15	.15	.16	.16	.15
Latent Variable Model					
Path *a* = .40					
Low reliability	.12	.16	.13	.12	.12
Moderate reliability	.12	.14	.12	.12	.12
High reliability	.12	.13	.13	.12	.12
Path *a* = .60					
Low reliability	.18	.22	.19	.19	.19
Moderate reliability	.18	.20	.18	.18	.18
High reliability	.18	.20	.19	.18	.18

Note. "Path *a*" is the path from the independent variable to the mediator. In the "Path *a* = .40" condition, the population value of the parameter is .12. In the "Path *a* = .60" condition, the population value of the parameter is .18.

Displayed in Table 3 are means for path c'. As in the analysis of ab, sample size was not influential on estimation of path c'. As detailed in the introduction, estimates of c' and ab are inversely related, so it is not surprising that the pattern of significant results for c' mirror those for ab. Path c' is always overestimated in the composite model, but never departs more than .02 from the expected value in the latent variable model. The significant Model × Reliability interaction reflects the decline in overestimation as reliability increases. Significant interaction effects for Model × Collinearity and Reliability × Collinearity stem from stronger effects of collinearity in the composite model and with decreasing reliability, respectively. The three-way interaction of model, reliability, and collinearity is attributable to pronounced overestimation of path c' in the composite model when reliability is low.

Statistical Power. As with parameter estimation, our focus is not on path a; however, we briefly note the results of analyses of statistical power for tests against zero of path a across the 48 conditions. The two most prominent effects were a main effect for sample size and a main effect of collinearity. Reflecting basic tenets of statistical power analysis, power increased as sample size and size of the effect increased. There was also a nontrivial interaction of these two variables. Whereas for $a = .6$ power approached 1.0 with only 50 cases, regardless of unreliability, for $a = .4$, 100 cases were necessary to approach the maximum. In general, statistical power was acceptable except for $N = 25$ and $a = .4$.

Of greater interest is the statistical power associated with tests of b and ab. Estimates for tests of path b are presented in Table 4.[4] To provide information relevant to tests in a multiple-regression context, estimates of power when OLS standard errors are used in the composite model are presented in the top panel of

---

[4] To minimize the density of the tables, theoretical values are not presented in the tables displaying power estimates. The estimates shown in Tables 4, 5, and 6 correspond to values derived from statistical theory.

Table 3 Maximum-Likelihood Parameter Estimates for the Path From the Independent Variable to the Outcome (Path c') as a Function of Sample Size, Modeling of the Mediator, Collinearity of the Independent Variable and the Mediator, and Reliability of the Mediator

Condition	Equation 3	Sample Size			
		25	50	100	200
Composite Model					
Path a = .40					
Low reliability	.05	.05	.04	.05	.05
Moderate reliability	.03	.03	.03	.04	.03
High reliability	.01	.04	.02	.01	.01
Path a = .60					
Low reliability	.09	.10	.09	.10	.10
Moderate reliability	.06	.05	.07	.05	.06
High reliability	.03	.02	.03	.03	.03
Latent Variable Model					
Path a = .40					
Low reliability	.00	.00	−.01	.00	−.00
Moderate reliability	.00	−.02	.00	.01	.01
High reliability	.00	−.01	−.01	.00	.00
Path a = .60					
Low reliability	.00	.00	−.00	−.01	−.01
Moderate reliability	.00	−.02	−.00	.01	.01
High reliability	.00	−.02	−.01	.00	.00

Note. "Path a" is the path from the independent variable to the mediator. In all conditions, the population value of the parameter is .00.

the table.[5] The middle and lower panels contain power estimates based on testing with ML standard errors; estimates in these

---

[5] Ordinary least squares standard errors were derived from ML standard errors according to the formula

$$SE_{OLS} = SE_{ML}/[(N - 1 - k)/(N - 1)]^{1/2},$$

panels were compared in the four-factor design. The main effect of sample size was highly significant, owing to the higher levels of power with increasing N. As reliability increased, power increased as well. And power was lower when collinearity between independent variable and moderator was higher. In addition to the main effects, these three factors interacted to affect the statistical power of tests of b. The effect of sample size was strongest for the latent variable model with path a at .4. At the descriptive level, two properties of the values in Table 4 are worth noting. For the composite model, there is a slight power advantage for ML over OLS standard errors, though this advantage is negligible for Ns of 100 and 200. And power only attains desirable levels for samples of size 200.

The pattern of statistical power values for the tests of ab is displayed in Table 5. The effect of sample size was very strong, overshadowing all other effects. As would be expected, there was a power advantage associated with increased reliability of the mediator. Also, there was greater power when a was .4 than when it was .6. As closer examination of the pattern in Table 5 reveals, this effect for collinearity was moderated by sample size and reliability. At lower values of N, power was greater when a was larger, but this trend was reversed for higher values of N. Similarly, the higher value of a produced greater power when reliability was low, but lesser power when reliability was high. This pattern is best explained by the significant Sample Size $\times$ Reliability $\times$ Collinearity effect. The effect of collinearity on the power of the test of ab goes from positive to negative with a joint increase in sample size and reliability (the clearest instance of this effect is for $N = 100$ and the composite model). At the more general level, the wide range of power values is noteworthy. To achieve desirable levels of statistical power for the tests of the indirect effect, one would need a sample of at least 200 and a mediator with at least moderate reliability.

As noted earlier, the test of ab and the test of c' are inversely related. Thus, with decreasing values of statistical power for ab,

---

where k equals the number of predictors in the equation, one for a and two for b and c'.

Table 4 Statistical Power for Test of the Path From the Mediator to the Outcome (Path *b*) as a Function of Sample Size, Modeling of the Mediator, Collinearity of the Independent Variable and the Mediator, and Reliability of the Mediator

	Sample Size			
Condition	25	50	100	200
Composite Model (OLS)				
Path *a* = .40				
Low reliability	.18	.27	.53	.83
Moderate reliability	.20	.38	.68	.93
High reliability	.21	.42	.78	.98
Path *a* = .60				
Low reliability	.12	.19	.41	.67
Moderate reliability	.19	.25	.52	.85
High reliability	.17	.37	.62	.91
Composite Model (ML)				
Path *a* = .40				
Low reliability	.23	.31	.55	.84
Moderate reliability	.25	.43	.70	.93
High reliability	.27	.46	.79	.98
Path *a* = .60				
Low reliability	.16	.22	.43	.68
Moderate reliability	.24	.28	.53	.86
High reliability	.23	.40	.63	.91
Latent Variable Model				
Path *a* = .40				
Low reliability	.10	.20	.44	.82
Moderate reliability	.19	.36	.62	.91
High reliability	.33	.49	.76	.95
Path *a* = .60				
Low reliability	.05	.12	.30	.65
Moderate reliability	.14	.28	.48	.77
High reliability	.26	.38	.63	.89

Note. "Path *a*" is the path from the independent variable to the mediator. OLS = ordinary least squares. ML = maximum likelihood.

we would expect an increase in the instance of Type I errors for c'. This pattern is evident, particularly for the composite model, in the values shown in Table 6. Because $c' = 0$ in the population (i.e., there is full mediation), any significant effects for c' represent Type I error. Following convention, we would hope that the instance of such errors would not exceed 5%. The effect of sample size, though significant, was weak. The most pronounced effect on the means in Table 6 was model; the instance of Type I errors was higher for the composite model than for the latent variable model. This effect was moderated by reliability and collinearity. For the composite model, Type I errors increased as reliability decreased, particularly when path a was .6. The instance of Type I errors was near .05 at all levels of sample size, reliability, and collinearity for the latent variable model.

Discussion

In a Monte Carlo experiment, we investigated the effects of sample size, reliability, and collinearity of the independent variable and mediator on parameter estimates and statistical power for tests of simple mediation. We compared results using an analytic model that ignores unreliability by combining multiple measures of the mediator into a single score with a model that, using a latent variable approach, removes measurement error from the mediator prior to estimating path coefficients. Our findings indicate that, with samples of at least 50, the latent variable approach corrects for bias in the parameter estimates attributable to unreliability in the mediator. With regard to statistical power, our findings suggest a sample of at least 100 cases is needed to achieve modest power for tests of the path from the mediator to the outcome. Except when reliability of the mediator is high, at least 200 cases are required to achieve desirable levels of statistical power for tests of the effect of the independent variable on the outcome transmitted through the mediator. As with any Monte Carlo experiment, the conclusions are, to some degree, tied to the particular conditions we simulated; the findings should be applied cautiously to other conditions.

Table 5 Statistical Power for Test of the Indirect Path From the Independent Variable to the Outcome Through the Mediator (Path *ab*) as a Function of Sample Size, Modeling of the Mediator, Collinearity of the Independent Variable and the Mediator, and Reliability of the Mediator

| | Sample Size | | | |
Condition	25	50	100	200
Composite Model (OLS)				
Path $a = .40$				
Low reliability	.01	.07	.30	.74
Moderate reliability	.03	.11	.46	.90
High reliability	.04	.19	.65	.96
Path $a = .60$				
Low reliability	.05	.09	.35	.63
Moderate reliability	.09	.15	.48	.84
High reliability	.08	.29	.60	.90
Composite Model (ML)				
Path $a = .40$				
Low reliability	.01	.07	.30	.74
Moderate reliability	.03	.12	.47	.90
High reliability	.05	.21	.66	.96
Path $a = .60$				
Low reliability	.05	.10	.36	.64
Moderate reliability	.10	.17	.49	.84
High reliability	.12	.30	.60	.90
Latent Variable Model				
Path $a = .40$				
Low reliability	.01	.02	.14	.67
Moderate reliability	.01	.09	.40	.87
High reliability	.06	.20	.61	.93
Path $a = .60$				
Low reliability	.01	.03	.19	.57
Moderate reliability	.02	.12	.39	.74
High reliability	.13	.26	.59	.88

Note. "Path *a*" is the path from the independent variable to the mediator. OLS = ordinary least squares. ML = maximum likelihood. Standard error computed as in Equation 1.

Table 6 Type I Error for Test of the Direct Path From the Independent
Variable to the Outcome (Path c') as a Function of Sample
Size, Modeling of the Mediator, Collinearity of the
Independent Variable and the Mediator, and Reliability of
the Mediator

	Sample Size			
Condition	25	50	100	200
Composite Model (OLS)				
Path $a = .40$				
Low reliability	.04	.06	.06	.12
Moderate reliability	.06	.06	.05	.08
High reliability	.05	.06	.04	.05
Path $a = .60$				
Low reliability	.07	.09	.13	.26
Moderate reliability	.07	.08	.08	.09
High reliability	.04	.04	.04	.07
Composite Model (ML)				
Path $a = .40$				
Low reliability	.07	.07	.07	.13
Moderate reliability	.07	.06	.06	.08
High reliability	.07	.07	.04	.06
Path $a = .60$				
Low reliability	.13	.11	.15	.26
Moderate reliability	.09	.11	.08	.10
High reliability	.06	.05	.05	.07
Latent Variable Model				
Path $a = .40$				
Low reliability	.06	.05	.07	.04
Moderate reliability	.09	.07	.07	.07
High reliability	.07	.07	.06	.05
Path $a = .60$				
Low reliability	.06	.05	.06	.05
Moderate reliability	.09	.06	.08	.06
High reliability	.07	.05	.07	.06

Note. "Path a" is the path from the independent variable to the mediator. OLS = ordinary least squares. ML = maximum likelihood.

The analysis of the performance of latent variable models with samples as small as those we considered is rare, so our results are informative with regard to the question of how few cases are sufficient for such analyses. Our results argue against the use of latent variable modeling for simple mediational analyses with very small samples when the mediator is not measured reliably. Under conditions of high reliability, latent variable modeling essentially erased bias in parameter estimates regardless of sample size; however, under conditions of low and moderate reliability, ML estimates of the path from the mediator to the outcome were substantially overestimated when sample size was 50 or less. This pattern was less apparent for the coefficients for the indirect and direct paths, but it was not fully absent until N reached 100.

The performance of latent variable modeling with very small samples was problematic for other reasons, as well. With samples of size 25, there were considerable technical problems with parameter estimation; such problems were substantially less frequent, but still apparent, with 50 cases. With samples of 100 or more, such technical problems with estimation were rare. This outcome coupled with the findings for parameter estimates suggests that, for estimating simple mediational models with the mediator modeled as a latent variable, at least 100 cases are required when all variables are normally distributed.[6] When sample size is at least 100, reliability of the mediator is low to moderate, and collinearity between the independent variable and mediator is high, latent variable modeling provides superior parameter estimates with only a modest reduction in statistical power compared to multiple-regression analysis.

With regard to statistical power, our results underscore conventional wisdom regarding study design: More cases and more reliable measures lead to more statistical power (Cohen, 1977). With regard to tests of the indirect path, when reliability of the mediator is high samples of size 100 are sufficient to guarantee

---

[6] It is likely that a substantially larger minimum would be required for nonnormal data (Finch et al., 1997).

satisfactory statistical power; however, even with moderate, and typical, levels of reliability in the mediator, a sample size of at least 200 is necessary to provide sufficient statistical power for tests of the indirect effect.

In a departure from conventional wisdom, our results indicate that larger effects do not always give rise to greater statistical power. In particular, stronger effects of the independent variable on the mediator can compromise the power of tests of the path from the mediator to the outcome and the indirect path from the independent variable to the outcome. This effect was most pronounced for the path from the mediator to the outcome, for which power was lower when collinearity was higher regardless of sample size, reliability, or method of modeling the latent variable. This pattern reflects the fact that variability in the mediator that can account for variability in the outcome is reduced to the extent that the independent variable predicts the mediator. Viewed differently, in most circumstances, the maximum indirect effect, ab, equals the simple direct effect, c. Thus, as a increases, b must decrease, and as b decreases, the power to detect a significant effect decreases.

The pattern was somewhat more complicated for the statistical power of the test of the indirect effect. For samples of size 25 and 50, regardless of the degree of reliability of the mediator, a stronger effect of the independent variable on the mediator contributed to greater power of the test of the indirect effect. With sample sizes of 100, this pattern prevailed for low and moderate reliability, but reversed for high reliability—with a highly reliable mediator, a stronger association between the independent variable and the mediator led to a reduction in statistical power for the test of the indirect effect. For samples of size 200, power was always lower when the effect of the independent variable on the mediator was higher.

This influence of the relative magnitude of a and b on the test of ab can be described more formally. Assuming the use of Equation 1 to compute the standard error of the indirect effect and a particular value for the indirect effect, ab, the statistical power of the test of ab is maximized when a equals

$$\frac{\sqrt{(ab)^2 - \sqrt{(ab)^2 - (ab)^4}}}{2(ab)^2 - 1}.$$ (4)

It is apparent that, for a given value of a, $b = ab/a$. Thus, when $ab = .12$, as in our low-collinearity condition, Equation 4 yields an optimal value of .3284 for a; the corresponding value of b is .3654. When $ab = .18$, as in our high-collinearity condition, the optimal values of a and b are .3933 and .4577, respectively. This pattern suggests that the statistical power of tests of mediation is maximized when the effect of the mediator on the outcome exceeds the effect of the independent variable on the mediator, particularly when the indirect effect is strong.

This finding has implications for the design of research studies that will provide data for tests of statistical mediation. For instance, consider the spacing between assessments of the independent variable and mediator, and the mediator and outcome (Kenny et al., 1998). If information on the mediator is gathered close in time to observation or manipulation of the independent variable, then the magnitude of that effect will be maximized. If the time lapse between observation of the mediator and the outcome is longer, then a will be overestimated relative to b and the power of the test of ab will be reduced. Thus, from a statistical power perspective, the ideal spacing between observations of the independent variable and the mediator and the mediator and the outcome would ensure that path b equals or exceeds path a in magnitude.

Conclusions

Applied researchers in the social and behavioral sciences are increasingly motivated to explore the underlying processes and mechanisms that account for causal relationships. The statistical approach by which such exploration is accomplished involves evaluating the decline in the strength of the causal relationship when the putative process or mechanism is accounted for. Such tests of statistical mediation often are undertaken without regard for the quality of the operationalization of the mediator. Our findings indicate that unreliability in the measurement of the mediator has a dramatic effect on tests of statistical mediation. Statistical tests that ignore unreliability of the mediator produce biased parameter estimates that have a deleterious effect on statistical power and Type I error. With sufficiently large samples ($\geq$ 100), latent variable modeling is a viable approach to dealing with unreliability in the mediator, though any benefit in the way of increased statistical power is minimal. When possible, investigators should maximize sample size and reliability of the measure of the mediator and, if the sample is sufficiently large and the data reasonably normally distributed, model the mediator as a latent variable. Inferences based on mediational analyses that do not correct for unreliability in the mediator should be viewed with caution.

Author Notes: During the writing of this chapter, Rick Hoyle was supported by Grants DA05312 and DA09569 from the National Institute on Drug Abuse and Grant SP07967 from the Center for Substance Abuse Prevention. David Kenny was supported by grants from the National Science Foundation (DBS-9307949) and the National Institute of Mental Health (RO1-MH46567).

References

Alwin, D. F., & Hauser, R. M. (1975). The decomposition of effects in path analysis. *American Sociological Review, 40*, 37–47.

Baron, R. M., & Kenny, D. A. (1986). The moderator-mediator variable distinction in social psychological research: Conceptual, strategic, and statistical considerations. *Journal of Personality and Social Psychology, 51*, 1173–1182.

Bollen, K. A. (1987). Total, direct, and indirect effects in structural equation models. In C. C. Clogg (Ed.), *Sociological methodology* (pp. 37–69). San Francisco: Jossey-Bass.

Boomsma, A. (1983). *On the robustness of LISREL (maximum likelihood estimation) against small sample size and nonnormality*. Unpublished doctoral dissertation, University of Groningen, The Netherlands.

Cohen, J. (1977). *Statistical power analysis for the behavioral sciences* (Rev. ed.). New York: Academic Press.

Dwyer, J. H., MacKinnon, D. P., Pentz, M. A., Flay, B. R., Hansen, W. B., Wang, E. Y. I., & Johnson, C. A. (1989). Estimating intervention effects in longitudinal studies. *American Journal of Epidemiology, 130*, 781–795.

Finch, J. F., West, S. G., & MacKinnon, D. P. (1997). Effects of sample size and nonnormality on the estimation of mediated effects in latent variable models. *Structural Equation Modeling, 4*, 87–107.

Fox, J. (1985). Effect analysis in structural equation models: Calculation of specific indirect effects. *Sociological Methods and Research, 14*, 81–95.

Gerbing, D. W., & Anderson, J. C. (1985). The effects of sampling error and model characteristics on parameter estimation for maximum likelihood confirmatory factor analysis. *Multivariate Behavioral Research, 20*, 255–271.

Hauck, W. W., & Anderson, S. (1984). A survey regarding the reporting of simulation studies. *American Statistician, 38*, 214–216.

Holmbeck, G. N. (1997). Toward terminological, conceptual, and statistical clarity in the study of mediators and moderators: Examples from the child-clinical and pediatric psychology literatures. *Journal of Consulting and Clinical Psychology, 65*, 599–610.

Hoyle, R. H. (1991). Evaluating measurement models in clinical research: Covariance structure analysis of latent variable models of self-conception. *Journal of Consulting and Clinical Psychology, 59*, 67–76.

Hoyle, R. H. (1994). Introduction to the special section: Structural equation modeling in clinical research. *Journal of Consulting and Clinical Psychology, 62*, 427–428.

Hoyle, R. H. (Ed.) (1995). *Structural equation modeling: Concepts, issues, and applications*. Thousand Oaks, CA: Sage.

James, L. R., & Brett, J. M. (1984). Mediators, moderators, and tests for mediation. *Journal of Applied Psychology, 69*, 307–321.

Judd, C. M., & Kenny, D. A. (1981). Process analysis: Estimating mediation in treatment evaluations. *Evaluation Review, 5*, 602–619.

Kenny, D. A., Kashy, D. A., & Bolger, N. (1998). Data analysis in social psychology. In D. Gilbert, S. T. Fiske, & G. Lindzey

(Eds.), *Handbook of social psychology* (4th ed., pp. 233–265). New York: Academic Press.

Kimble, G. A. (1989). Psychology from the standpoint of a generalist. *American Psychologist, 44*, 491–499.

MacKinnon, D. P. (Organizer). (1998, March). *Conference on mediational models in prevention research: Statistical methods to determine how prevention programs achieve their effects.* Conference conducted at Arizona State University, Tempe.

MacKinnon, D. P., & Dwyer, J. H. (1993). Estimating mediated effects in prevention studies. *Evaluation Review, 17*, 144–158.

MacKinnon, D. P., Warsi, G., & Dwyer, J. H. (1995). A simulation study of mediated effect measures. *Multivariate Behavioral Research, 30*, 41–62.

Nunnally, J. C. & Bernstein, I. H. (1994). *Psychometric theory* (3rd ed.). New York: McGraw-Hill.

Rao, C. R. (1973). *Linear statistical inference and its applications.* New York: Wiley.

Reis, H. T., & Stiller, J. (1992). Publication trends in *JPSP*: A three-decade review. *Personality and Social Psychology Bulletin, 18*, 465–472.

Rozenboom, W. W. (1956). Mediation variables in scientific theory. *Psychological Review, 63*, 249–264.

Shadish, W. R., Jr., & Sweeney, R. B. (1991). Mediators and moderators in meta-analysis: There's a reason we don't let dodo birds tell us which psychotherapies should have prizes. *Journal of Consulting and Clinical Psychology, 59*, 883–893.

Simon, H. A. (1992). What is an "explanation" of behavior? *Psychological Science, 3*, 150–161.

Sobel, M. E. (1982). Asymptotic confidence intervals for indirect effects in structural equation models. In S. Leinhart (Ed.), *Sociological methodology* (pp. 290–312). San Francisco: Jossey-Bass.

Sobel, M. E. (1986). Some new results on indirect effects and their standard errors in covariance structure models. In N. B. Tuma (Ed.), *Sociological methodology* (pp. 159–186). San Francisco: Jossey-Bass.

Sobel, M. E. (1987). Direct and indirect effects in linear structural equation models. *Sociological Methods and Research, 16*, 601–606.

SPSS. (1996). SPSS for Windows (Release 7.5.1) [computer software]. Chicago: SPSS.

StatSoft. (1996). STATISTICA for Windows (Release 5.1) [computer software]. Tulsa, OK: StatSoft.

Stone, C. A., & Sobel, M. E. (1990). The robustness of estimates of total indirect effects in covariance structure models estimated by maximum likelihood. *Psychometrika, 55,* 337–352.

Tanaka, J. S. (1987). "How big is big enough?": Sample size and goodness of fit in structural equation models with latent variables. *Child Development, 58,* 134–146.

Wampold, B. E., Davis, B., & Good, R. H., III. (1990). Hypothesis validity of clinical research. *Journal of Consulting and Clinical Psychology, 58,* 360–367.

West, S. G., Aiken, L. S., & Todd, M. (1993). Probing the effects of individual components in multiple component programs. *American Journal of Community Psychology, 21,* 571–605.

9

Pooling Lagged Covariance Structures Based on Short, Multivariate Time Series for Dynamic Factor Analysis

John R. Nesselroade & Peter C. M. Molenaar

THE IMPORTANCE of multivariate, intraindividual designs for studying process is well appreciated by students of behavior and behavior change. Unfortunately, optimal research designs are often not implemented because of the difficulty and expense of collecting an abundance of repeated measurements on large, representative samples of participants. We propose a method for modeling multivariate process data that preserves the benefits of both intraindividual and group analysis while allowing design compromises that bring an encouraging line of inquiry within easier reach. The method involves evaluating statistically the validity of pooling the lagged covariance functions of multiple individuals' short time series for further dynamic analysis (e.g., Molenaar, 1985, 1994; Wood & Brown, 1994). We emphasize a focus on process, using idiographic information to pursue nomothetic laws, and the application of multivariate measurement and latent variable modeling.

A Focus on Process

The collection, analysis, and interpretation of data through which process can be modeled is an important aspect of contemporary behavioral research. Indeed, we find compelling the argument that behavioral phenomena cannot be properly understood until they can be cast in dynamic, change-process terms rather than the static, stability-oriented conceptions that have dominated not only psychology but science in general for the past couple of centuries (Gergen, 1977; Holling, 1973).

One fairly sturdy connotation of the term process is that pertinent data are temporally organized. Certain events precede others, changes in some of a system's parameters occur before others, and "recovery" of the system from perturbing outside forces may be rapid for some manifest variables, gradual for others. The feature of time-relatedness invokes special considerations in modeling repeated measurements.

Idiographic Emphases Within the Pursuit of Nomothetic Laws

A conceptually distinct, but nonetheless related emphasis to that on process involves the use of intensive information about individuals to build strong nomothetic relationships covering groups (Lamiell, 1981; Larsen, 1987; Nesselroade & Ford, 1985; Shoda, Mischel, & Wright, 1994; Zevon & Tellegen, 1982). The exploration of idiographic contributions to nomothetic relationships is consistent with a belief that group-based analyses and statements of relationship often are not very satisfying.

There are at least two reasons for dissatisfaction with group data. Analyses often lead to aggregating data over individuals who are qualitatively different from each other, distorting the aggregate into an entity that has no parallel in the group (Lamiell, 1988). This can be especially troubling when the sample is composed of distinct subsamples. Second, because of fiscal and temporal constraints, group analyses are often based on relatively superficial attributes of individuals; "important" attributes of individuals are not being represented in the data. A corollary of this sentiment is that characterizations of individuals based on intensive measurement schemes will provide a more fruitful basis for group analyses.

Measuring an individual day after day, for example, and studying the changes can yield a different picture of how behavior "works" than measuring a group of individuals at a single time and analyzing the differences found among them (Lamiell, 1988). The two kinds of "portraits," one based on within-person changes and the other based on among-persons differences, may or may not be mutually consistent.

Familiar tools for analyzing individual time series call for large numbers of repeated observations. Unfortunately, research designs often are not underwritten with sufficient financial resources to permit the measurement of many people on many variables at many occasions of measurement. One seeks to find an optimal configuration of design parameters that meshes well with the research objectives (McArdle & Woodcock, 1995). One can swap persons for occasions of measurements, for example, but there are realistic limits on how far this option can be taken. Thus, practicable longitudinal research designs often do not involve either enough repeated measurements for traditional time series analyses or enough replicate individuals for traditional, large-sample analyses. Methods for extracting process-relevant information rigorously from such data are at a premium.

Multivariate Measurement and Analysis

A third line of emphasis has to do with collecting multivariate data in order to model process in terms of latent variables rather than observable ones (Baltes & Nesselroade, 1973;

Bentler, 1980; Cattell, 1966; Horn & McArdle, 1980). In behavioral research, tools for analyzing data obtained from merging frequently repeated measurements and multivariate observations include multivariate time series analysis (e.g., Holtzman, 1963; Larsen, 1987; West & Hepworth, 1991), stationary components analysis (Millsap & Meredith, 1988), and P-technique factor analysis (Cattell, 1963; Nesselroade & Ford, 1985; Zevon & Tellegen, 1982).

P-technique factor analysis, used somewhat sparingly for its nearly 50 years (e.g., Cattell, Cattell, & Rhymer, 1947), involves fitting the common factor model to one individual's multivariate time series (Cattell, 1963). The difficulty of collecting appropriate data and the limitations of P-technique factor analysis have made some researchers disdainful of using it (Holtzman, 1963; Molenaar, 1985; Steyer, Ferring, & Schmitt, 1992).

Refinements of the basic P-technique factor analysis methodology have involved both design modifications (e.g., studying replicates more or less concurrently to answer questions of generalizability; Jones & Nesselroade, 1990; Lebo & Nesselroade, 1978; Nesselroade & Ford, 1985; Zevon & Tellegen, 1982) and changing factor model specification (e.g., representing the dynamics resident in frequently repeated measurements; McArdle, 1982; Molenaar, 1985; Wood & Brown, 1994). The model specification changes have resulted in some very promising data analysis tools; one of which—dynamic factor analysis (Molenaar, 1985, 1994; Wood & Brown, 1994)—will be discussed subsequently.

Statement of the Problem

Given a high level of interest in time-dependent, multivariate data structures and the infeasibility, in many cases, of collecting hundreds of repeated observations on many participants, a promising research tool is a rationale and procedure for both (a) pooling relatively short time series information across limited numbers of participants and (b) analyzing the pooled information for its dynamic, process-relevant elements. It is these matters that we address.

What Is Needed?

A formal procedure for combining information across experimental units requires both a determination of the appropriateness of pooling and a scheme for analyzing the pooled information. Such a method promises huge dividends by enabling researchers to exploit data that contain information about dynamics and change but which, because of limited numbers of repeated observations, do not permit the application of traditional methods of analyses.

Earlier Work on the Problem

Efforts to combine cross-sectional and time series data can be found in the literature of various disciplines (e.g., Caines, 1988; Shumway, 1988). Within psychology, chain P-technique factor analysis (Cattell, 1963; Cattell & Scheier, 1963) is an early approach to the pooling of intraperson change information across cases. It involves separately standardizing the multivariate time series of two or more individuals, pooling (chaining) the sets of standardized scores into one long multivariate time series for factor analysis. Unfortunately, these techniques do not include a direct test for assessing the propriety of "chaining" information over participants and empirical demonstrations suggest that the blind application of pooling methods can mislead seriously regarding the structural characteristics of the repeated measurements (e.g., Daly, Bath, & Nesselroade, 1974).

Pooling Dynamic Structures Rather Than Individuals' Time Series

In contrast to the "chaining" of individuals' score matrices as in the chain P-technique or averaging time series across several individuals, we focus on first determining the lagged covariance function of each individual's multivariate time series and then, if justified, pooling these lagged covariance functions. Therefore, our use of the term pooling has a rather specialized connotation that is elaborated in the next section.

Assessing the Poolability of Individual Covariance Structures: A Test of Ergodicity

We first present a formal means for assessing the appropriateness of pooling dynamic information across multiple individuals. Subsequently, we discuss a statistical model—dynamic factor analysis—for analyzing the process information in the pooled structural descriptions.

Ergodicity

Assessing the "poolability" of individual's dynamic information is cast in the statistical mechanics terminology *ergodicity* (Arnold & Avez, 1968; see also Molenaar, 1994). Consider a dynamical system that is started up under given initial conditions. The p-variate time series output of this system is a trajectory in some region of p-dimensional Euclidean space called the phase space of the system. The system's dynamics can be characterized by a functional analysis of this trajectory. In particular, if the system is stochastic then averages (moments) can be taken along this trajectory to apprehend the system's dynamics. In contrast, consider a (possibly infinite) set of identical dynamic systems, each of which is started up under some idiosyncratic set of initial conditions (or what amounts to the same situation, a single dynamic system that is repeatedly started up under different initial conditions). One thus obtains a population of trajectories in phase space. In this case, the system dynamics can be apprehended by taking averages over the density of trajectories in phase space.

The key question is: Is the characterization of the system dynamics based on averages along a single trajectory equivalent to that based on averages over the density of multiple trajectories in phase space? Systems for which this equivalence holds are called ergodic. Speaking heuristically, an ergodic system "forgets" the initial conditions from which it started. Consequently, the trajectory describing its output covers the phase space in the same way as the outputs of a collection of identical replicas started from different initial conditions would cover it.

More to the point, is the structure of dynamics at the individual level sufficiently homogeneous across individuals that one can treat these individual dynamics as representing a common structure? A related question is: Do the processes that represent how individuals change also account for how individuals differ from one another at a given point in time? Cattell (1963), for example, argued that factors "... should have a unity of growth (or fluctuation) as well as a unity of structure in terms of static individual differences" (p. 168). It was on this basis that he argued for a coherence of intraindividual change factors derived from P-technique analyses and interindividual difference factors derived from cross-sectional (R-technique) factor analyses.

To construct a test of the appropriateness of pooling information across multiple cases, we focus on the covariance functions of the individual time series. In relation to the preceding distinction, single-subject time series analysis is tantamount to taking averages along a given trajectory, whereas in ordinary longitudinal analysis (e.g., panel data analysis) averages are taken over the density of trajectories associated with the sample of subjects. Pooling of the covariance functions over multiple subjects is only justified if the behavioral system under scrutiny is ergodic.[1] Thus, the basic data with which we are concerned are in the form of N (persons) data matrices of order T_i (occasions for the ith person) by p (variables) and the lagged covariance functions derivable from them.

Lagged Relationships

Lag will be used in two different senses. One has to do with relationships among observed variables. The magnitude of re-

---

[1] In classical test theory, the true score of a subject is defined as the average over repeated applications of the test to this subject (Lord & Novick, 1968). This is reminiscent of taking an average along a single trajectory. However, it is concluded that such repeated measurement of a single subject is not feasible due to memory effects, fatigue, and so forth. Hence, averages are taken over a single application of the test to a collection of subjects. This is reminiscent of taking an average over phase space. Thus, it seems in practice, at least, that psychometry rests, to some extent, on a conception of ergodicity. Similar arguments could be made in reference to scaling methods in which one-time judgments of several participants are used in place of repeated judgments of a single participant.

lationships between two variables differs depending on whether the observations on one variable are concurrent with, or lagged by one or more occasions of measurement on the observations on the other variable. The data can be "played" by leading and lagging variables on each other to extract more of the information inherent in the repeated measurements. In contrast to this "correlational" sense of lag, there is also the notion that "causal" relationships (e.g., between latent factors and observed variables) are time referenced. A factor's effect on a variable may be immediately large and then dissipate gradually with time or it may be delayed, reaching its greatest magnitude several occasions of measurement later and then dissipating.

The Statistical Test of "Poolability"

The first step in assessing the "poolability" of N individuals' lagged covariance structures involves the construction of N specialized covariance matrices, one from the time series data of each participant. These N specialized covariance matrices are then tested for lack of equality. The covariance matrices, of a form known as block-Toeplitz matrices, are constructed as follows.

Let $\mathbf{z}_i(t)$, $t = 1, 2, 3, \ldots, T_i$, denote the p-variate time series (T_i occasions in length) of the ith participant ($i = 1, 2, \ldots, N$). Let $\mathbf{C}_i(u)$ denote the $p \times p$ matrix-valued covariance function of $\mathbf{z}_i(t)$ at lag u, $u = 0, 1, 2, \ldots, w$. Thus, $\mathbf{C}_i(0)$ is the $p \times p$ covariance matrix for the ith person with no (zero) lagging of the variables on themselves or each other. It is the matrix one would obtain by treating the T_i occasions for person i as though they were $N = T_i$ cases and covarying the p variables across the N cases. This matrix is the one factored in traditional P-technique factor analysis. $\mathbf{C}_i(1)$ is the $p \times p$ matrix of lag 1 covariances between variables (i.e., times t and $t + 1$) for the ith person. This matrix, which although square is ordinarily not symmetric, contains the lag 1 autocovariances of the variables in its principal diagonal. The remaining $\mathbf{C}_i(u)$ up to some maximum lag ($u = w$) are constructed in a similar manner.

The various $\mathbf{C}_i(u)$ are put together to form a block-Toeplitz covariance matrix, $\mathbf{S}_i(w)$, for each individual as follows:

$$\mathbf{S}_i(w) = \mathbf{C}_i(j - k), \qquad j, k = 0, 1, \ldots, w,$$

with $\mathbf{C}_i(-u) = \mathbf{C}_i'(u)$, and $'$ denoting matrix transposition. Thus, each $\mathbf{S}_i(w)$ is a supermatrix, the submatrices of which are the unlagged and lagged covariance matrices based on the ith participant's data. The construction of a block-Toeplitz matrix for $w = 4$ is illustrated in Figure 1. It contains $w + 1$ lag 0 portions (symmetric), w lag 1 portions (asymmetric), $w - 1$ lag 2 portions (asymmetric), ..., and one lag 4 portion (asymmetric). The diagonal entries of all submatrices represent autocovariances of the variables for the corresponding number of lags. For additional discussion of the nature of these block-Toeplitz matrices, see Wood and Brown (1994).

Testing the N block-Toeplitz matrices described previously for statistical equivalence requires the calculation of several intermediate values: $M = \sum_i M_i$, where $M_i = (T_i - 1) \times$

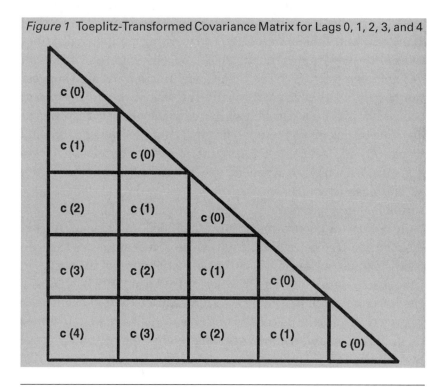

Figure 1 Toeplitz-Transformed Covariance Matrix for Lags 0, 1, 2, 3, and 4

$\ln\{\det[S(w)]\} - \ln\{\det[S_i(w)]\}$, $S(w) = \sum_I (T_i - 1) S_i(w) / \sum_I (T_i - 1)$, and T_i is the length of the time series, $\mathbf{z}_i(t)$, for the ith participant. Also required are the values: $a = \sum_i [1/(T_i - 1)]$, $b = [1/\sum_I (T_i - 1)]$, and

$$c = 1 - \left[\frac{2m^2 + 3m - 1}{6(m+1)(N-1)} \right] \cdot \left[\frac{1}{a} - \frac{1}{b} \right],$$

where N is the number of subjects and $m = p(w + 1)$, which, by the way, is also the order of the matrices $S(w)$ and $S_i(w)$.

Under the null hypothesis that the individual participants' lagged covariance functions do not differ from each other, the product $c \cdot M$ is distributed approximately as a chi-squared variable (see Morrison, 1990, p. 297). Ordinarily, the appropriate degrees of freedom would be $m(m+1)(N-1)/2$ for $m \times m$ matrices. In this case, however, because of the redundancies in the block-Toeplitz lagged covariance matrix, the appropriate degrees of freedom is computed as $[1/2p(p+1) + wp^2](N-1)$.

Caution is appropriate regarding the use of chi-squared statistics for testing and model fitting in this context. The work of Taniguchi and Krishnaiah (1987) concerning sampling distributions of the covariance functions of time series and the eigenvalues and eigenvectors of the covariance function at lag 0 suggest the possibility that asymptotically the statistics we use to test poolability are chi-squared distributed if the observed multivariate time series of each subject is Gaussian. However, it is only a suggestion concerning an asymptotic result. Extensive, large-scale simulation work is needed to evaluate this possibility in the special case in which we are interested—relatively short time series for each participant. Such simulations should compare both the use of pseudo-maximum likelihood and asymptotically distribution-free estimation and the use of test statistics that are robust against misspecification of the distribution of the observed time series data (see, e.g., Bentler & Dudgeon, 1996). Lacking the information that simulation studies are expected eventually to provide, we view the results of the empirical example to follow as preliminary and awaiting further evaluation of the proposed test of poolability.

If the value of the test statistic is not significant, pooling the lagged covariance functions for the N participants to provide an estimate of a single-population lagged covariance function is statistically justified. Structural models representing change processes (e.g., the dynamic factor analysis model, Molenaar, 1985; Wood & Brown, 1994) can then be fitted to the pooled covariance function, $\mathbf{S}(w)$.[2]

When a significant test statistic leads to rejection of the ergodicity hypothesis, one can try to create homogeneous subgroups by sequentially deleting the most "deviant" subject from the sample and reapplying the test. We have explored two ways to do this. The obvious way is to eliminate the person with the largest M_i value (defined previously) since M_i indicates the ith subject's contribution to the overall statistic (properly weighted by n_i). A given person's M_i value, however, is a function of the remaining $N - 1$ participants' data, so changes of only one person in the makeup of the sample can alter the relative size of a participant's M_i value. An alternative way to identify the most deviant subject has proven to be much more effective and is easily implemented. It involves eliminating each subject in turn, recalculating M for each subsample of $N - 1$ individuals. The subsample of $N - 1$ giving the smallest M is retained. If the test statistic is still significant, the procedure is repeated, calculating M for each possible subsample of $N - 2$. This algorithm can be repeated until either the test statistic is no longer significant or the original sample is decimated. When one subset of the sample has been selected as having "poolable" lagged covariance functions that subsample can be removed for dynamic factor analysis

---

[2] The test of equality of the individual block-Toeplitz matrices can be carried out using the multigroup option in LISREL. Each subject constitutes a group and one simply constrains the block-Toeplitz matrices to be invariant across groups. The chi-square goodness-of-fit statistic thus obtained is equivalent to M defined previously. Premultiplication by c can be carried out a posteriori. A drawback of the multigroup LISREL approach is that, as the number of variables increases, the computer memory requirements quickly become large and computation time is long. The LISREL-based ergodicity test makes clear that the chi-squared distribution for $c \cdot M$ is a likelihood ratio test where the numerator is the likelihood of the model constrained to be equal across groups and the denominator is the likelihood of the unconstrained set of block-Toeplitz matrices.

and the test procedure applied to the remainder of the sample to see if additional homogeneous subsets remain.

Dynamic Factor Analysis of Pooled, Lagged Covariance Functions

Dynamic factor analysis (Molenaar, 1985, 1994; Wood & Brown, 1994) is a merging of two important analytical tools—multivariate time series analysis and the common factor model. It was motivated by the potential value of factor analyzing multivariate time series coupled with the realization that the traditional common factor model did not fully exploit the information inherent in multivariate time series; indeed, that its application to time series data could be misleading with certain kinds of process information (Holtzman, 1963; Molenaar, 1985; Steyer et al., 1992).

The dynamic factor model (DFM) incorporating q factors and s lags of manifest variables on common factors (DFM[q, s]) is specified as

$$
\begin{aligned}
\mathbf{z}(t) = {} & \boldsymbol{\Lambda}(0) \cdot \boldsymbol{\eta}(t) + \boldsymbol{\Lambda}(1) \cdot \boldsymbol{\eta}(t-1) \\
& + \cdots + \boldsymbol{\Lambda}(s-1) \cdot \boldsymbol{\eta}(t-s+1) + \boldsymbol{\varepsilon}(t),
\end{aligned}
\tag{1}
$$

where $\mathbf{z}(t)$ is the observed or manifest p-variate time series, $\boldsymbol{\eta}(t)$ is the latent q-variate factor time series, $\boldsymbol{\varepsilon}(t)$ is a p-variate noise time series, and $\boldsymbol{\Lambda}(u)$, $u = 0, 1, \ldots, s - 1$, are $p \times q$ matrices of lagged factor loadings. Thus, the various $\boldsymbol{\Lambda}(u)$, $u = 0, 1, \ldots, s-1$, can differ from each other, signifying that the regressions of the variables on the factor vary with the amount of lag.

For the common factor model of lag 0 only, Equation 1 reduces to $\mathbf{z}(t) = \boldsymbol{\Lambda} \cdot \boldsymbol{\eta}(t) + \boldsymbol{\varepsilon}(t)$, which is the familiar P-technique factor model if both $\boldsymbol{\eta}(t)$ and $\boldsymbol{\varepsilon}(t)$ are white-noise series. The fuller model (Equation 1) indicates that the observed variables at time t are functions not only of the common factors at time t, but also of those same common factors up to $s - 1$ occasions earlier. In other words, the values of the common factors can influence the values of the observed variables both concurrently and in delayed fashion. Instead of being limited to immediate effects, the common factors influence on the variables can be exerted over several occasions.

Notice that the specific noise series $\varepsilon_j(t), j = 1, \ldots, p$, can be autocorrelated but the lagged cross-correlation between different specific noise series, for example, between $\varepsilon_j(t)$ and $\varepsilon_k(t+u), j \neq k$, is assumed to be zero for all u, including $u = 0$. Thus, analogous to the assumption of uncorrelated unique variances in the traditional common factor model, a lack of correlation between the unique series for all lags, including zero, is assumed.

Alternatives to these structures can be fitted to data, provided one has enough information to identify the parameters. A dynamic factor model for one factor, two manifest variables, and $s = 3$, DFM(1, 3), is schematized in Figure 2.

After a sufficient length of time (lag) all stationary auto- and cross-correlations decay to zero. Thus, if the occasion sam-

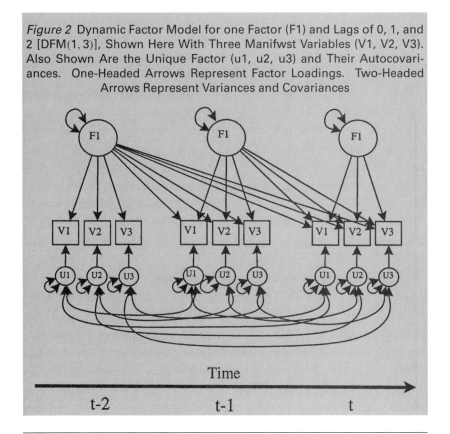

Figure 2 Dynamic Factor Model for one Factor (F1) and Lags of 0, 1, and 2 [DFM(1, 3)], Shown Here With Three Manifwst Variables (V1, V2, V3). Also Shown Are the Unique Factor (u1, u2, u3) and Their Autocovariances. One-Headed Arrows Represent Factor Loadings. Two-Headed Arrows Represent Variances and Covariances

pling frequency is low enough (i.e., if the time intervals are long enough), then the observed series will become white noise and appropriate for fitting by the traditional P-technique factor model.

An Empirical Example

The test of equality of lagged covariance functions and the follow-up dynamic factor analyses is demonstrated using a subset of data reported elsewhere (Eizenman, Nesselroade, Featherman, & Rowe, 1997; Kim, Nesselroade, & Featherman, 1996).

Data

The data are short, multivariate time series from a sample of 31 older adults. The mean age of the older adults who participated in the study was 77.5 years ($SD = 7.2$ years). They lived in a retirement community, Cornwall Manor, in central Pennsylvania. The participants, all of whom were volunteers, represent an above-average selection of individuals with regard to health status, education, and other demographic characteristics.

A subset of four cognitive performance and two biomedical variables was selected for the analyses reported here. Included are digit span forward (DSF), digit span backward (DSB), two trials on a delayed spatial recognition task called here Board Game 1 (BG1) and Board Game 2 (BG2), systolic blood pressure (SBP), and diastolic blood pressure (DBP). The SBP and DBP measurements are averages of multiple readings that were taken within each weekly session.

The subjects were measured each week for a period of 25 weeks. Subjects were "platooned" into a Monday, Wednesday, Friday group and a Tuesday, Thursday, Saturday group. Within those 3-day possibilities, measurement days were varied randomly across the 25-week period. Thus, a given individual in the MWF platoon might be measured on Monday of one week, Friday of the next week, and Wednesday of the next week, and so on. Measurements were done by personal interview between trained testers and participants. Usually, the measurements were made in the living quarters of the participant. For this analysis, we ignore the fact that the weekly measurements were not evenly spaced.

Testing the "Poolability" of the Participants' Covariance Functions

A block-Toeplitz matrix as defined previously was constructed from each individual's data. The values for M, a, b, and c were calculated and the product $c \cdot M$ for $w = 1$ (thus including lags of 0 and 1) was obtained. Due to the relatively short time series, for $w > 1$ many of the block-Toeplitz matrices, $\mathbf{S}_i(w)$, were singular and therefore unsuitable for testing ergodicity at lags larger than 1. The test statistic which, under the null hypothesis is distributed as chi-square, was 2,400.23 ($df = 1,710$), which is statistically significant well beyond the $p < .001$ level. Thus, the verdict was that, as a set, the lagged covariance functions of the $N = 31$ subjects were sufficiently different from each other that pooling them was not justified.

The iterative "search" analysis described previously identified a subsample of 10 individuals' lagged covariance functions that met the ergodicity criterion ($\chi^2 = 557.66$, $df = 513$, $p = .084$). More will be said in the discussion concerning the implications of finding that only 10 of 31 cases' data met the criterion for inclusion in the dynamic factor analysis.

The outcome of the dynamic factor analysis reported next will pertain to both the general ensemble and to 10 individual time series contributing information to the ensemble. On the one hand, the lagged loadings pertain to all 10 time series so, in that sense, the factor loading patterns are invariant across the individual cases. On the other hand, the factor series for each individual can be determined. Thus, when multiple common factors are involved, for instance, it is possible to detect individual differences in the patterning of relationships among factor series over time. Hence, pooling across subjects does not imply that idiographic characterization of each individual is irretrievably lost.

Fitting the Dynamic Factor Model to the Pooled Covariance Functions

A series of dynamic factor models was fitted to the block-Toeplitz matrix $S(w)$ derived from the pooled covariance function $C(u)$ of the 10 subjects. First, one-factor dynamic models with increasingly lagged loadings [DFM$(1, s)$, $s = 1, 2, 3, 4, 5$] were fitted.[3] Subsequently, we fitted a set of confirmatory, dynamic two-factor models with increasingly lagged loadings [DFM$(2, s)$, $s = 1, 2, 3, 4, 5$] to the block-Toeplitz matrix. For the two-factor models, the first latent factor series was specified with lagged loadings on the four manifest cognitive series and the second latent factor series with lagged loadings on the two manifest blood pressure series. Thus, in all the model fits to be reported later, $w = 4$, meaning that u takes on five values, 0, 1, 2, 3, and 4. Hence, given that the manifest series are six-dimensional, it follows that $S(4)$ is a 30×30 matrix.

We fit the series of models using LISREL 8 (Jöreskog & Sörbom, 1993). LISREL 8 requires the user to input the number of observations (NO) on which the input covariance matrix is based. We calculated NO as follows for this situation:

$$NO = \left[\frac{1}{u_{\max} + 1} \sum_{i=1}^{N_c} \sum_{u=0}^{u_{\max}} (T_i - u) \right] - c,$$

where N_c is the number of cases on which the block-Toeplitz matrix is based, T_i is the number of occasions of measurement for the ith individual, u is the lag, and c is a correction for missing data devised by us for this purpose as the average number of missing values across all p-component series for the N_c subjects.

The rationale for fitting a series of models rather than a single a priori model in dynamic factor analysis was discussed by Molenaar (1985) and Wood and Brown (1994). Suffice it to say that, at this point in the development of dynamic factor analysis, choosing an optimal configuration of the number of factors

---

[3] The reader is reminded that DFM$(1, 5)$, for example, specifies a one-factor model in which variables are lagged on factors with lags of 0, 1, 2, 3, and 4.

and the number of lags is not a matter of direct calculation but, rather, requires a systematic search process. Search methods certainly involve some risks (e.g., MacCallum, 1986), but, in the present case, the small sample size is compensated for somewhat by the fact that each participant was measured on 25 occasions. Formal characterizations of the roles of the number of participants and the number of occasions of measurement in ascertaining statistical power for this kind of modeling remain to be developed.

The series of model fits was evaluated by chi-square goodness-of-fit statistics and the derived Akaike's information criteria (AIC = chi-square − twice its df; cf. Bollen, 1989). The fit index values are presented in Table 1. It appears that DFM(1, 5) yields the best fit in terms of chi-square relative to its degrees of freedom. Interested readers can consult Molenaar (1985) for a discussion of how to adjust LISREL results for the redundancies in the block-Toeplitz matrices.

Estimates of Noise Series Parameters

Before presenting the factor loadings, we will briefly discuss the noise series that are also a part of this model. Let $\varepsilon_j(t)$ denote the specific noise time series for the jth manifest series and

Table 1 Dynamic Factor Model Fits to Pooled Covariance Functions Varying Number of Factors and Number of Lags (s)

| | Dynamic Factor Model | | | | | |
| | DFM($1, s$) | | | DFM($2, s$) | | |
s	χ^2	df	AIC	χ^2	df	AIC
1	336.06	129	78.06	336.06	128	80.06
2	303.39	123	57.39	290.87	122	46.87
3	270.30	117	36.30	242.58	116	10.58
4	229.98	111	7.98	236.92	110	16.92
5	206.52	105	−3.48	205.16	104	−2.84

let $c_j(u)$, $u = 0, 1, \ldots$, denote the lagged autocovariance function of $\varepsilon_j(t)$. Notice that it is assumed that the lagged cross-covariance function between $\varepsilon_j(t)$ and $\varepsilon_k(t - u)$ is zero if $j \neq k$. The estimates of $c_j(u)$, $u = 0, 1, 2, 3, 4$, are presented in Table 2.

The lag 0 autocovariances of the noise series for the manifest cognitive series tend to be larger than those of the noise series for the manifest physiological series. In addition, it can be seen that the noise series specific to the diastolic blood pressure series has larger lagged autocorrelations than the other series. These values are consistent with the systemic role of diastolic blood pressure in the functioning human organism.

Table 2 Estimates of the Specific Noise Series' Lagged Autocovariance Function for Lags of 0, 1, 2, 3, 4 and Factor Loadings for One-Factor, Five-Lag Model

	Lag(u)				
Variable	*u = 0*	*u = 1*	*u = 2*	*u = 3*	*u = 4*
Specific Noise Series Autocovariances					
Digit span forward	.95*	.18*	.09*	−.06	−.04
Digit span backward	.96*	−.07*	−.15*	−.02	.02
Board Game 1	.77*	−.28*	−.08	−.08	.02
Board Game 2	.97*	.11*	.09*	.04	−.16*
Systolic blood pressure	.76*	.11	−.04	.05	−.10
Diastolic blood pressure	.55*	.26*	.21*	−.36*	−.12
Factor Loadings					
Digit span forward	.18*	.09*	−.03	−.06	.06
Digit span backward	.00	.11*	.07	.08*	−.13*
Board Game 1	.28*	.26*	.20*	.21*	.05
Board Game 2	.12*	.07	.12*	.04	−.03
Systolic blood pressure	−.13*	−.16*	.31*	−.14*	.29*
Diastolic blood pressure	−.42*	.08	.44*	−.25*	−.08

Note. * indicates that the parameter value is greater than twice its estimated standard error.

Interpretation of the Lagged Factor Loadings

The estimated factor loadings for this model are presented in the lower panel of Table 2. The loading pattern is rather complex, with all lags having at least two statistically significant loadings. The concurrent loadings (lag $= 0$) tend to be greatest in magnitude for the cognitive variables with the notable exception of DSB. It is instructive to compare the entire loading pattern with the lag $= 0$ column only. The latter are the relationships captured by traditional P-technique factor analysis. Taken alone, these concurrent loadings reflect an inverse relationship between the cognitive series and the physiological series but the lagged loadings elaborate the nature of the relationships over time in a much more detailed pattern.

In our experience thus far, interpretation of factor loading patterns should not be based only on direct inspection of the loadings. Rather, one should also focus on the auto- and cross-correlation functions derived from these lagged loadings. Therefore, we next examine the analog of the common parts of the variables in the traditional factor model—the communal part of the selected DFM$(1, 5)$. The selected DFM$(1, 5)$ is given by

$$\mathbf{z}(t) = \boldsymbol{\Lambda}(0)\cdot\boldsymbol{\eta}(t) + \boldsymbol{\Lambda}(1)\cdot\boldsymbol{\eta}(t - 1) + \cdots + \boldsymbol{\Lambda}(4)\cdot\boldsymbol{\eta}(t - 4) + \boldsymbol{\varepsilon}(t).$$

We label the expected covariance function of $\mathbf{z}(t)$ based upon the latent factor series the communal covariance function of $\mathbf{z}(t)$. Hence, the "total" covariance function of $\mathbf{z}(t)$ consists of the sum of the communal covariance function and the covariance function of $\boldsymbol{\varepsilon}(t)$. Let $c(u, j, k)$ denote the communal covariance function at lag u between the jth and the kth component series of $\mathbf{z}(t), j, k = 1, 2, \ldots, 6$, and $u = -4, -3, -2, -1, 0, 1, 2, 3, 4$. Then $c(u, j, k)$ is estimated by

$$
\begin{aligned}
c(u, j, k) = E\big[\big[\lambda(0, j)\eta(t) &+ \lambda(1, j)\eta(t - 1) \\
&+ \cdots + \lambda(4, j)\eta(t - 4)\big] \cdot \big[\lambda(0, k)\eta(t + u) \\
&+ \lambda(1, k)\eta(t + u - 1) + \cdots + \lambda(4, j)\eta(t + u - 4)\big]'\big].
\end{aligned}
$$

Here, $\lambda(u, w)$ denotes the loadings at lag u of the wth component series of $\mathbf{z}(t)$ on the factor series. In the one-factor case, each

$\lambda(u, w)$ and each $\eta(t + u)$ is a scalar. For DFM(2, 5), for example, each $\lambda(u, w)$ would be a 1×2 row vector and each $\eta(t + u)$ would be a 2×1 column vector. For the DFM(2, 5) case, $c(u, j, k)$ is composed of 16 cross terms, but many of these can be zero because $E[\eta(t), \eta'(t + u)] = 0$, when lag $u \neq 0$. Only $E[\eta(t), \eta'(t)] \neq 0$. For DFM(1, 5), it is a scalar. For DFM(2, 5), it is a 2×2 correlation matrix with off-diagonal elements equal to the concurrent correlation between the two factor series. To illustrate specifically, consider $c(-3, i, j)$. This is given by

$$c(-3, j, k) = \lambda(3, j)V(\eta)\lambda'(0, k) + \lambda(4, j)V(\eta)\lambda'(1, k),$$

where $V(\eta) = E[\eta(t), \eta'(t)]$. The 21 communal correlation functions,

$$r(u, j, k) = \frac{c(u, j, k)}{\sqrt{c(0, j, j)}\sqrt{c(0, k, k)}},$$

and the standard deviations $\sqrt{c(0, k, k)}$ and $\sqrt{c(0, j, j)}$ for all j, k combinations are presented in Table 3. Notice that $r(u, j, k) = r(-u, k, j)$.

Several features of the elements in Table 3 are striking. One is the high correlation $(+.71)$ between the communal parts of DSF and DSB, with the former leading the latter by 1 week ($u = 1$). Note that the relationship is not symmetric. When DSB leads DSF by 1 week, the correlation is $-.06$. The substantial relationship between DSF and DSB suggests that the process represented by the latent factor series that induces a high score (or a low score) in DSF at a given occasion tends to induce a high score (or a low score) in DSB a week later. Also of particular interest is the relationship between BG2, SBP, and DBP. There is a strong positive correlation $(+.66)$ between BG2 and SBP with the former leading the latter by 2 weeks and a strong negative relationship $(-.48)$ between BG2 and DBP with the former trailing the latter by 2 weeks. If the three variables are changing as a "system," one might expect to see a substantial negative correlation between SBP and DBP at 4 weeks with the former leading the latter. Indeed, this is the case: $r = -.37$ at $u = -4$.

Table 3 Standard Deviations (SD) and Communal Correlation Functions $r(u, j, k)$ for Variables j and k at Lag u

j	k	$Sd(j)$	$Sd(k)$	Lag(u)								
				$u = -4$	$u = -3$	$u = -2$	$u = -1$	$u = 0$	$u = 1$	$u = 2$	$u = 3$	$u = 4$
1	1	.22	.22	.22	−.11	−.26	.24	1.00	.24	−.26	−.11	.22
2	1	.20	.22	.00	.15	−.05	−.06	−.11	.71	.54	.06	−.53
2	2	.20	.20	.00	−.36	−.01	.07	1.00	.07	−.01	−.36	.00
3	1	.48	.22	.16	−.01	−.11	.17	.49	.58	.53	.31	−.08
3	2	.48	.20	−.38	−.12	.15	.39	.68	.33	.20	−.06	.00
3	4	.48	.48	−.06	.20	.43	.67	1.00	.67	.43	.20	−.06
4	1	.19	.22	.17	−.07	−.01	.09	.48	.57	.62	.11	−.13
4	2	.19	.20	−.41	.01	−.04	.59	.61	.36	.06	−.09	.00
4	3	.19	.48	−.06	.24	.36	.74	.93	.57	.41	.04	−.09
4	4	.19	.19	−.10	.08	.38	.56	1.00	.56	.38	.08	−.10

Note. 1 = DSF, 2 = DSB, 3 = BG1, 4 = BG2, 5 = SBP, and 6 = DBP.

Table 3 Continued

j	k	Sd(j)	Sd(k)	Lag(u)								
				$u = -4$	$u = -3$	$u = -2$	$u = -1$	$u = 0$	$u = 1$	$u = 2$	$u = 3$	$u = 4$
5	1	.49	.22	−.07	−.02	.30	−.31	−.20	−.13	.32	.01	.48
5	2	.49	.20	.17	.10	−.63	.18	−.45	.48	.05	.32	.00
5	3	.49	.48	.03	−.08	−.32	.03	−.25	.29	.46	.15	.34
5	4	.49	.19	.04	−.00	−.33	−.12	−.04	−.03	.66	.04	.37
5	5	.49	.49	−.16	−.12	.30	.47	1.00	−.45	.30	−.12	−.16
6	1	.67	.22	−.17	.20	.23	−.56	−.49	.45	.40	−.36	−.10
6	2	.67	.20	.41	−.33	−.60	.20	.22	.18	−.25	−.07	.00
6	3	.67	.48	.06	−.29	−.28	.04	−.18	.22	.13	−.28	−.07
6	4	.67	.19	.10	−.15	−.48	.04	.00	.06	.20	−.28	−.08
6	5	.67	.49	−.37	.25	−.04	−.13	.58	−.45	−.13	.14	.03
6	6	.67	.68	.08	.22	−.54	−.20	1.00	−.20	−.54	.22	.08

In all, the factor loading patterns and corollary information suggest that the relationships represented by this modeling procedure are somewhat more complex than are usually encountered with applications of traditional factor models and their close relatives. Not surprisingly, some of the relationships that the dynamic factor model highlights are not at all evident on mere inspection of the total (raw) correlation functions. Distinguishing between the communal (common) parts and the unique parts of variables is the great strength of the common factor. It is in "prying apart" these very different constituents of observed variables across time that we begin to see order and regularity. Thus, the findings illustrate the potential value of this general approach for building a better understanding of change processes as well as the day-to-day functioning of the organism.

Discussion and Conclusions

Many of our more cherished interindividual differences concepts manifest short-term changes that ought not to be discarded as "noise." However, the limitations of traditional P-technique factor analysis, both strenuous data collection requirements and questions about the use of the common factor model, have severely restricted its application to perplexing issues that might be usefully attacked from an intraindividual variability standpoint. The procedure we have presented here alters this situation in promising ways.

From a research design perspective, our proposals make it feasible to design research on process and change without going to the extreme of using only one participant to generate long series of observations. Investigators are more apt to collect time series data if they can aim for 25–50 repeated observations per experimental unit than if they must collect 100–500 observations. Obviously, the number of subjects and the number of occasions must be played off against each other in optimal ways that will have to be determined in part by trial and error, but the point is that methods such as we have presented make the systematic study of intraindividual variability a much more feasible and manageable prospect than it has been.

Analyses required to "parse" data of the kind used here are neither quick nor easy. However, the computational machinery is available (e.g., Wood & Brown, 1994), and it can be implemented on rather ordinary computing facilities. Today's bigger, faster computers allow the incorporation of more variables and lags in the analyses, so providing adequate representation of variables, occasions, and persons is not a barrier in design and analyses.

Making the pooling of information across participants an explicit, rational procedure eases concerns about aggregation fallacies. The procedures can be applied to a range of repeated measures situations from short multivariate time series to full-scale P-technique data collected on multiple participants. The fact that we found only 10 of 31 cases' data met the test of ergodicity is troubling in some respects, of course, but it may be telling us to search for general lawfulness at a more abstract level than is typically done. More to the point, perhaps, the lack of generality should be equally troubling to investigators who pool information across participants without mustering statistical support for their actions.

Substantively, the outcomes reinforce the notion that linkages between physiological and behavioral domains may not be captured well by looking only at direct, concurrent indications of relationships; rather order and organization may lie in more abstract, complicated, time-lagged relationships. Designing fruitful investigations of more complex relationship patterns will likely involve some trial and error regarding choice of intervals, number of occasions, and so forth, but the theorizing and empirical work of the past couple of decades should help.

Process information is hidden in streams of behavior, rather than in single-occasion or widely separated repeated measurements. It underlies the workings of a collection of manifest variables rather than in the observable action of a few and generality across persons and contexts is a hope yet to be realized. The tools we have presented are aimed at helping us rigorously extract information from relatively short time series of multiple experimental units. They promise to help nudge open a little farther the door to the understanding of process; a door that now seems only barely ajar.

Author Notes: The John D. and Catherine T. MacArthur Foundation's Research Network on Successful Aging and the Max-Planck-Institute for Human Development, Berlin, Germany, supported the conceptual and empirical work presented here. We also thank Jack McArdle and Chris Hertzog for their valuable comments on an earlier version of the manuscript.

References

Arnold, V. I., & Avez, A. (1968). *Ergodic problems of classical mechanics*. New York: Benjamin.

Baltes, P. B., & Nesselroade, J. R. (1973). The developmental analysis of individual differences on multiple measures. In J. R. Nesselroade & H. W. Reese (Eds.), *Life-span developmental psychology: Methodological issues* (pp. 219–251). New York: Academic Press.

Bentler, P. M. (1980). Multivariate analysis with latent variables: Causal modeling. In M. R. Rosenzweig & L. W. Porter (Eds.), *Annual review of psychology* (Vol. 31, pp. 419–456). Palo Alto, CA: Annual Reviews.

Bentler, P. M., & Dudgeon, P. (1996). Covariance structure analysis: Statistical practice, theory, and directions. *Annual review of psychology* (Vol. 47, pp. 563–592). Palo Alto, CA: Annual Reviews.

Bollen, K. A. (1989). *Structural equations with latent variables*. New York: Wiley.

Caines, P. E. (1988). *Linear stochastic systems*. New York: Wiley.

Cattell, R. B. (1963). The structure of change by P-technique and incremental R-technique. In C. W. Harris (Ed.), *Problems in measuring change* (pp. 167–198). Madison: University of Wisconsin Press.

Cattell, R. B. (1966). Guest editorial: Multivariate behavioral research and the integrative challenge. *Multivariate Behavioral Research, 1*, 4–23.

Cattell, R. B., Cattell, A. K. S., & Rhymer, R. M. (1947). P-technique demonstrated in determining psycho-physiological source traits in a normal individual. *Psychometrika, 12,* 267–288.

Cattell, R. B., & Scheier, I. H. (1961). *The meaning and measurement of neuroticism and anxiety.* New York: Ronald Press.

Daly, D. L., Bath, K. E., & Nesselroade, J. R. (1974). On the confounding of inter- and intraindividual variability in examining change patterns. *Journal of Clinical Psychology, 30,* 33–36.

Eizenman, D. R., Nesselroade, J. R., Featherman, D. L., & Rowe, J. W. (1997). Intra-individual variability in perceived control of older adults: The MacArthur Successful Aging Studies. *Psychology and Aging, 12,* 489–502.

Gergen, K. J. (1977). Stability, change and chance in understanding human development. In N. Datan & H. Rheese (Eds.), *Life span developmental psychology: Dialectic parspectives* (pp. 135–157). New York: Academic Press.

Holling, C. S. (1973). Resilience and stability of ecological systems. *Annual Review of Ecology and Systematics, 4,* 1–23.

Holtzman, W. H. (1963). Statistical models for the study of change in the single case. In C. W. Harris (Ed.), *Problems in measuring change.* Madison: University of Wisconsin Press.

Horn, J. L., & McArdle, J. J. (1980). Perspectives on mathematical/statistical model building (MASMOB) in research on aging. In L. W. Poon (Ed.), *Aging in the 1980s.* Washington, DC: American Psychological Association.

Jones, C. J., & Nesselroade, J. R. (1990). Multivariate, replicated, single-subject designs and P-technique factor analysis: A selective review of intraindividual change studies. *Experimental Aging Research, 16,* 171–183.

Jöreskog, K. G., & Sörbom, D. (1993). *LISREL 8: Structural equation modeling with the SIMPLIS command language.* Hillsdale, NJ: Erlbaum.

Kim, J., Nesselroade, J. R., & Featherman, D. L. (1996). The state component in self-reported world views and religious beliefs of older adults: The MacArthur Successful Aging Studies. *Psychology and Aging, 11,* 396–407.

Lamiell, J. T. (1981). Toward an idiothetic psychology of personality. *American Psychologist, 36,* 276–289.

Lamiell, J. T. (1988, August). *Once more into the breach: Why individual differences research cannot advance personality theory.* Paper presented at the annual meeting of the American Psychological Association, Atlanta, GA.

Larsen, R. J. (1987). The stability of mood variability: A spectral analytic approach to daily mood assessments. *Journal of Personality and Social Psychology, 52*, 1195–1204.

Lebo, M. A., & Nesselroade, J. R. (1978). Intra-individual differences dimensions of mood change during pregnancy identified in five P-technique factor analyses. *Journal of Research in Personality, 12*, 205–224.

Lord, F. M. & Novick, M. R. (1968). *Statistical theories of mental test scores.* Reading, MA: Addison-Wesley.

MacCallum, R. C. (1986). Specification searches in covariance structure modeling. *Psychological Bulletin, 100*, 107–120.

McArdle, J. J. (1982). *Structural equation modeling of an individual system: Preliminary results from "A case study in episodic alcoholism."* Unpublished manuscript, University of Denver.

McArdle, J. J., & Woodcock, R. W. (1995). *Modeling developmental components of change from time-lagged, test-retest data.* Unpublished manuscript, University of Virginia.

Millsap, R. E., & Meredith, W. (1988). Component analysis in cross-sectional and longitudinal data. *Psychometrika, 53*, 123–134.

Molenaar, P. C. M. (1985). A dynamic factor model for the analysis of multivariate time-series. *Psychometrika, 50*, 181–202.

Molenaar, P. C. M. (1994). Dynamic latent variable models in developmental psychology. In A. von Eye & C. C. Clogg (Eds.), *Latent variables analysis: Applications for developmental research* (pp. 155–180). Thousand Oaks, CA: Sage.

Morrison, D. F. (1990). *Multivariate statistical methods* (3rd ed.). New York: McGraw-Hill.

Nesselroade, J. R., & Ford, D. H. (1985). P-technique comes of age: Multivariate, replicated, single subject designs for research on older adults. *Research on Aging, 7*, 46–80.

Shoda, Y., Mischel, W., & Wright, J. C. (1994). Intra-individual stability in the organization and patterning of behavior: Incorporating psychological situations into the idiographic analysis of personality. *Journal of Personality and Social Psychology, 67*, 674–687.

Shumway, R. H. (1988). *Applied statistical time series analysis.* Englewood Cliffs, NJ: Prentice-Hall.

Steyer, R., Ferring, D., & Schmitt, M. (1992). States and traits in psychological assessment. *European Journal of Psychological Assessment, 8*, 79–98.

Taniguchi, M., & Krishnaiah, P. R. (1987). Asymptotic distributions of functions of the eigenvalues of sample covariance matrix and canonical correlation matrix in multivariate time series. *Journal of Multivariate Analysis, 22,* 156–176.

West, S. G., & Hepworth, J. T. (1991). Statistical issues in the study of temporal data: Daily experiences. *Journal of Personality, 59,* 609–662.

Wood, P. K., & Brown, D. (1994). The study of intraindividual differences by means of dynamic factor models: Rationale, implementation, and interpretation. *Psychological Bulletin, 116,* 166–186.

Zevon, M. A., & Tellegen, A. (1982). The structure of mood change: An idiographic/nomothetic analysis. *Journal of Personality and Social Psychology, 43,* 111–122.

10

Confirmatory Factor Analysis: Strategies for Small Sample Sizes

Herbert W. Marsh & Kit-Tai Hau

IN THIS CHAPTER, we address specific strategies for conducting confirmatory factor analysis (CFA) and structural equation modeling (SEM) in small sample-size (N) research. Whereas we agree that it is always better to have a larger N, there are a variety of circumstances that require researchers to limit themselves to smaller Ns than might otherwise be desirable (Tanaka, 1987). Particularly in small-N research, solutions do not always converge to a completely proper solution (i.e., variance estimates < 0, factor correlations > 1). Hence, a major focus of this chapter is to evaluate strategies proposed to avoid this problem.

Proposed Strategies

More Items Is Better

Here we evaluate the proposal that "more is better" in terms of both N and, particularly when N is small, the number of indicators per factor. In CFA, there are vague and sometimes contradictory guidelines about the desirable amount of data. The number of data points is the product of N and the number of indicators (p). There is general agreement that, in term of N more is better. For example, Boomsma (1982; also see Anderson & Gerbing, 1984; Boomsma, 1985; Gerbing & Anderson, 1987, 1993; Guadagnoli & Velicer, 1988) found that the percentage of proper solutions, accuracy of parameter estimates, sampling variability in parameter estimates, and the appropriateness of the χ^2 test statistic were all favorably influenced by having larger Ns, recommending $N > 100$, but also noting the desirability of $N > 200$.

Although there is general agreement that larger N is always desirable, there seems to be much confusion about what minimum N is desirable under what circumstances. Guidelines offered to applied researchers (e.g., rules about the minimum ratio of N/p or N per number of parameter estimates) imply that a large number of indicators should only be considered when N is very large. In the case of the optimal ratio of number of indicators per factor (p/f), there seems to be broad agreement that at least three indicators per factor are desirable, but that under some circumstances two may be sufficient (see the discussion by Bollen, 1989). The guidelines about ratios of N to measured variables or estimated parameters, however, imply that researchers should limit p/f, particularly when N is small. From this, it would follow that small-N researchers should try to limit the number of measured variables or estimated parameters. This is, of course, in direct opposition to implications derived from classical test theory that suggest that it is better to have more indicators per factor in that reliability (and thus validity) tend to increase as does the precision of estimates.

Velicer and Fava (1987, 1989; also see Guadagnoli & Velicer, 1988) reviewed a variety of such recommendations, but they also concluded that there was no support for rules positing a minimum N as a function of p and that convergence to proper solutions and goodness of fit were favorably influenced by increasing N, p/f, and saturation (factor loadings). Rules positing minimum ratios of N to p or t (number of estimated parameters) were also violated by Marsh and Bailey's (1991) CFA study of multitrait-multimethod data. Anderson and Gerbing (1984), Boomsma (1982, 1985), Ding, Velicer, and Harlow (1995), and Gerbing and Anderson (1987) reported that the likelihood of fully proper solutions increased with increasing p/f, N, and saturation. Gerbing and Anderson (1987) also reported smaller standard errors of parameter estimates when N and p/f were larger.

Inferential approaches to fit indices, the construction of confidence intervals, and power estimates (MacCallum, Browne, & Sugawara, 1996) provide another basis of support for the "more is better" strategy. As emphasized by MacCallum et al., power estimates and precision (i.e., the narrowness of confidence intervals about fit indices) increase monotonically with N and the df. Because the df increases as the number of indicators per factor increases (i.e., when p increases, $p(p+1)/2$ increases more rapidly than the number of estimated parameters), more indicators per factors provide a more powerful, precise test than a comparable model with fewer indicators per factor. Their mathematical derivations demonstrate a compensatory relation between N and model size in which large N and large df is best, but that small N can be compensated for by large df, leading them to conclude that "adequate power for the recommended test can be achieved with relatively moderate levels of N when d [df] is not small" (p. 144). Hence, in the small-N research emphasized here, adequate power can only be achieved in large models.

Item Parcels

We briefly examine the use of item parcels, in which a potentially very large number of indicators for each latent factor are combined to form a much smaller number of measured variables.

The logic of using item parcels is that each parcel is likely to be more strongly related to the latent factor, is less likely to be influenced by the idiosyncratic wording and method effects associated with individual items, and is more likely to meet the typical assumptions of normality in maximum-likelihood approaches to CFA. The use of item parcels can also reduce substantially the number of indicators per factor and, subsequently, the number of estimated parameters.

Equal-Loading Strategy

Particularly if researchers are using well-validated measures in which it can be assumed that all measured variables have moderately high and reasonably homogeneous relations to the underlying latent factor, it may be possible to improve the quality of the solution by fitting models in which all the factor loadings for a given latent variable are constrained to be equal, thereby substantially reducing the number of estimated parameters. This logic underlying the equal-loading strategy, of course, is not new (e.g., Dawes, 1979; Wainer, 1976). Wainer, in particular, argued that equal weights may be better (when items vary along a similar scale and are reflected so that they all vary in the same direction) than empirically estimated weights, because the estimated weights are often suboptimal due to capitalization on chance in estimation from a sample (particularly when N is small). The implementation of this equal-loading strategy is also consistent with the widely noted emphasis on model parsimony in CFA (Mulaik et al., 1989; but also see Marsh & Hau, 1996) in that models with invariant factor loadings are more parsimonious than those with freely estimated factor loadings.

Convergence, Proper Solutions, and N

Confirmatory factor analysis is based on a sample covariance matrix $\mathbf{S}$ with elements s_{ij} for sample size N and p measured variables (e.g., Bollen, 1989). The population covariance matrix Σ

with elements σ_{ij} is hypothesized to be generated by q true but unknown parameter estimates that can be expressed as a function of a $q \times 1$ vector Θ. Thus,

$$\sigma_{ij} = f(\Theta)$$

is a model of the covariance structure, where f relates the parameters in Θ to the elements σ_{ij}. Because Σ and Θ are unknown, it is necessary to estimate population parameters, resulting in Θ_E and Σ_E such that

$$\sigma_E = f(\Theta_E).$$

The issue of goodness of fit is to determine whether $\mathbf{S}$ and Σ_E are sufficiently close to justify the claim that the model used to generate Σ_E fits the data (Marsh, Balla, & McDonald, 1988). A number of different fitting functions can be used to minimize this difference, but we consider the maximum-likelihood function (F_{ML}), which is the most widely used function in CFA studies. Under appropriate conditions, $(N - 1)F_{ML}$ is approximately distributed as the χ^2 test statistic with $p(p + 1)/2 - t$ degrees of freedom, where t is the number of parameters in the model and can be used for evaluating the statistical significance of the lack of fit.

In CFA, iterative processes are used to minimize the difference between $\mathbf{S}$ and Σ_E in relation to a particular fitting function. Nonconvergence occurs when the estimation algorithm is unable to meet the criterion within a specified number of iterations (see Bollen, 1989, p. 254; Jöreskog & Sörbom, 1988, p. 269) and is likely to be a function of the data or the model rather than the number of iterations or starting values (Velicer & Jackson, 1990). Even when there is convergence, however, the solution may be improper such that one or more of the parameter estimation matrices is not positive definite (Wothke, 1993). Thus, for example, a variance or residual variance estimate may be negative (typically called a Heywood case) or a factor correlation (standardized factor covariance) may have an absolute value greater than 1.0. Following van Driel (1978), Marsh, Hau, and Balla (1997) also classified as improper those solutions where standard errors (SEs) were so large that no interpretations are warranted.

Marsh, Hau, and Balla (1997) Study

This chapter is based substantially on the Marsh et al. (1997) Monte Carlo study that we summarize in detail. They evaluated whether "more is ever too much" for the number of indicators per factor (p/f) in CFA by varying the sample size ($N = 50-1,000$) and p/f (2–12 items per factor). Three-factor congeneric models were constructed in which each indicator loaded on one and only one factor. Five levels of p/f were considered in which all factors for a given generating model had 2, 3, 4, 6, or 12 items per factor. All factor correlations were .30 and each indicator had factor loadings and uniquenesses of .60 and .64, respectively.

Convergence Behavior

Marsh et al. (1997) reported that the likelihood of fully proper solutions was substantially related to larger Ns and larger p/f. Thus, for example, only 14% of the solutions based on $N = 50$ and $p/f = 2$ were proper (57% failed to converge at all), whereas solutions based on $N = 50$ and $p/f = 12$ or $N = 1,000$ and $p/f = 2$ converged to proper solutions most of the time (100% and 93%, respectively). These results suggested a compensatory effect of N and p/f. For $p/f = 2$, it was important to have very large Ns—at least $N = 400$; however, for $p/f = 6$ or 12, $N = 50$ was sufficient. These results support a "more is better" conclusion for both N and p/f. Whereas Boomsma's (1982) recommendation of a minimum $N = 100$ seems reasonable when $p/f = 3$ or 4, it did not generalize to solutions where p/f was smaller ($p/f = 2$) or larger ($p/f = 6$ or 12) in the Marsh et al. study. Likewise, whereas it may be undesirable to have $p/f = 2$, this situation was less unacceptable when N was sufficiently large. Finally, the results offered at least one strong refutation of the generality of guidelines focusing on minimum ratios of N to p or t. For each N considered by Marsh et al., the likelihood of convergence to a proper solution improved with increasing p/f (and t).

Marsh et al. (1997) extended and combined a classification of solutions (fully proper, boundary, nonboundary, large SE improper, large *SE* proper, and nonconverged) adapted from van Driel (1978) and a classification of parameter estimates (proper, nonoffending, offending related, and offending) adapted from Gerbing and Anderson (1987). In their study and consistent with previous research, goodness of fit for the fully proper solutions did not differ significantly from any classification of (converged) improper solutions. Nonoffending parameter estimates from different types of improper solutions were similar to those based on the fully proper solutions, particularly when there were at least three items per factor. In contrast, offending uniquenesses were consistently too small, whereas the corresponding factor loadings were too large. These results suggest that, even when solutions converge to an improper solution, estimates of the goodness of fit and parameter estimates not involving the offending parameter may be reasonable, although appropriate caution in interpretations is clearly warranted.

Effects of Number of Indicators and N in Confirmatory Factor Analysis

Marsh et al. (1997) evaluated parameter estimate variability, factor reliability, and goodness of fit based on only the fully proper solutions in a 5 (levels of p/f: 2, 3, 4, 6, 12) × 5 (levels of N: 50, 100, 200, 400, 1,000) analysis of variance (ANOVA). Mean parameter estimates for all cells were reasonably consistent although estimates from two-indicator solutions—particularly those with smaller Ns—appeared to differ systematically from population values. The combined effects of p/f, N, and their interaction accounted for only 0.7%, 2%, and 3% of the variance in factor loadings, uniquenesses, and factor correlations, respectively. In contrast, factor reliability estimates increased steadily with increasing p/f. The *SD*s for all parameter and reliability estimates decreased substantially with increases in N and p/f, accounting for 31%, 32%, and 30% of the variance in factor loadings, uniquenesses, and factor correlations, respectively. Although the effects of N and p/f were large, their interaction explained only about 1% of the variance in each set of estimates.

A Comparison of Parcel and Item Solutions

Marsh et al. (1997) constructed 2, 3, 4, and 6 parcels from the 12 items in the $p/f = 12$ data. Thus, the 12 items per factor were divided into 2 parcels (of 6 items), 3 parcels (of 4 items), 4 parcels (of 3 items), and 6 parcels (of 2 items). Hence, each latent construct reflected all 12 items, but the actual number of parcels used in the CFA varied. Solutions based on 2, 3, 4, or 6 parcels were more likely to be fully proper than solutions based on 2, 3, 4, or 6 items, but the trends were similar in that the likelihood of a proper solution increased systematically with N and the number of indicators (items or parcels); however, it is important to reiterate that all the parcel solutions were based on responses to 12 items and that the 12-item solutions resulted in 100% fully proper solutions for all Ns. When the number of parcels was small and N was small to moderate, parcel solutions were more likely to result in improper solutions than the 12-item solution. Hence, at least in terms of obtaining fully proper solutions for these data, there were some potential disadvantages in using parcels instead of the individual items.

Mean factor loadings and correlations were almost unaffected by N or p/f, but the comparisons were complicated by the change in metric produced by forming parcels. For analyses done in the (untransformed) covariance metric, the factor loadings remained constant whereas the uniquenesses (error variance) decreased as the number of items in each parcel increased. However, the reliability of each factor was nearly unaffected because all parcel solutions and the 12-item solutions were all based on responses to the same 12 items.

The SDs of parameter estimates and reliability estimates all declined with increasing N. The effect of the number of parcels on the SDs was complicated by the change in metric of the analyses. The SDs of the correlations and reliability estimates, however, were nearly independent of the number of parcels. That is, because all latent constructs are inferred from responses to all 12 original items no matter how many parcels were included in the analysis, inferences about the latent constructs were similar for item and parcel solutions.

In summary, the Marsh et al. (1997) results suggested that the number of indicators used to infer a latent construct is more important than whether latent constructs were inferred with items or parcels. In relation to their question of whether or not it is better to parcel, for their data it seems that it did not make much difference as long as the number of parcels and N were adequate. However, if N was small or the number of items was not sufficient to construct at least 3 or 4 parcels per factor, then it may be better to conduct analyses at the item level. There are, of course, many other considerations that may impact on the efficacy of parcels (e.g., nonnormal response distributions, method effects that are idiosyncratic to particular items, size and consistency of saturations for each item) that were beyond the scope of the Marsh et al. study. The results based on the parcel solutions provided additional support for a "more is better" conclusion. Having more items to begin with was better whether analyses were done at the item or parcel level, item solutions were somewhat better behaved than parcel solutions, and solutions based on more parcels were somewhat better behaved than solutions based on fewer parcels. One practical recommendation is that if a researcher obtains an improper solution using parcels, then the use of more parcels per factor or analyses at the item level may resolve the problem.

Extensions

In an attempt to "push" the limits of the "more is better" conclusion, Marsh et al. (1997) examined a possibly critical barrier where the number of estimated parameters exceeded N ($t > N$). [LISREL (Jöreskog & Sörbom, 1993) gives an explicit warning that results should be interpreted cautiously when this occurs.] This only occurred for $p/f = 12$ ($t = 75$) for $N = 50$, but the results for that cell of the Marsh et al. design suggested no dire consequences. These solutions seemed better behaved than $p/f = 6$ solutions (with $t = 39$) that did not cross this barrier and there were no apparent discontinuities in the trends observed across all five p/f ratios based on $N = 50$ and $N = 100$. To further explore this conclusion, Marsh et al. conducted supplemental simulations for $p/f = 12$ for Ns between 70 and 80 (i.e., Ns slightly above and slightly below $t = 75$), but again found no discontinuities in the pattern of results (convergence to proper solutions, fit statistics, and parameter estimates). Although further research is clearly warranted, these supplemental analyses suggested that there may be nothing special about crossing the $N = t$ barrier despite LISREL's dire warning! These supplemental results also supported the generality of conclusions that more is better for conditions considered by Marsh et al.

Study 1: The Effects of Measured Variable Saturation, Number of Indicators, and N

The Marsh et al. (1997) study was based on a population generating model that had a particularly simple structure in which the saturation for all measured variables was constant (i.e., the population factor loadings were .6 in all generating models). This feature is potentially worrisome in that other research (e.g., Anderson & Gerbing, 1984; Boomsma, 1982, 1985; Ding et al., 1995; Gerbing & Anderson, 1987; Velicer & Fava, 1987) suggests that the behavior of CFA solutions varies as a function of the saturation. In Study 1, we test the replicability of the earlier results—particularly in relation to the effects of p/f—and extend the results in terms of variation in the size of factor loadings (saturation).

Methods

Study 1 is based on a 5 (levels of N: 50, 100, 200, 400, 1,000) × 3 (levels of p/f: 3, 6, 9) design with three-factor congeneric models in which each indicator loaded on one and only one factor. One third of the factor loadings in each solution were .4, .6, and .8, respectively (with uniquenesses of .84, .64, and .36). Thus, for example, the population generating models with 3, 6, and 9 indicators per factor had 1, 2, and 3 indicators with population factor loadings of .4, .6, and .8, respectively. All the data were generated and analyzed using EQS (Version 5.3, Bentler & Wu, 1995) such that: the factor variances were fixed at unity; factor correlations, factor loadings, and uniquenesses were all freely estimated; and the maximum number of iterations was set to 500. All models tested in this study are "true" in that the pattern of free and fixed parameters was the same in the generating model used to generate the simulated data and the approximating model used to fit the data. Hence, to the extent that the χ^2 is behaving appropriately, the mean χ^2/df ratio should not differ systematically from 1.0, and the mean p value associated with the χ^2 test statistic should not differ significantly from .50. (Because the df associated with different models varies substantially, the χ^2 should differ substantially as a function of the number of measured variables and so it is less useful for our present purposes.) Because the purpose of the present investigation was not to evaluate different fit indices per se, we do not present results for a variety of subjective indices of fit (e.g., Marsh et al., 1988; McDonald & Marsh, 1990) other than the χ^2/df results.

Results

Convergence to Proper Solutions. We did not consider models with only two indicators per factor in Study 1 and so there were not nearly so many improper solutions as in the Marsh et al. (1997) study. Nevertheless, it is useful to note the pattern of relations between p/f, N, and obtaining fully proper solutions. For $N = 50$, the percentage of fully proper solutions was 41%, 98%, and 99% for $p/f = 3$, 6, and 9, respectively. Particularly for a small fixed N, the likelihood of a fully proper solution increases dramatically as p/f increases. The corresponding percentages for $N = 100$ (72%, 99%, and 100%), $N = 200$ (91%, 100%, and 100%), and $N = 400$ (99%, 100%, and 100%) support this trend to lessening degrees. For $N = 1,000$, all three levels of p/f resulted in 100% proper solutions. Whereas large N and large p/f are best, it is better to have larger p/f when N is small and to have larger N when p/f is small. In this way, large p/f and large N complement each other, replicating the findings of Marsh et al. (1997).

Parameter Estimates. The size of parameter estimates—factor loadings, uniquenesses, and factor correlations (see Tables 1 and 2)—are relatively unaffected by the p/f, N, or their interaction. Factor reliability is, however, substantially and positively related to p/f, although factor reliability is relatively unaffected by N or its interaction with p/f. The variability of parameter estimates—factor loadings, uniquenesses, and factor correlations—decreases systematically with increases in p/f and in N. Hence, these results replicate those of the Marsh et al. study, but also indicate that the effects of p/f on the variability of factor loadings (and uniquenesses) vary with the size of the population factor loading (and uniqueness). For items with low saturation (population factor loadings of .4), the decrease in variability with increases in p/f is small, but the effect is systematically larger for medium saturation (population factor loading of .6) and even larger for high saturation. In this respect, the results of Study 1 extend those of Marsh et al. (1997).

Study 2: The Effect of Imposing Equality Constraints to Improve the Behavior of Factor Solutions With Small N

In Study 2, we extend the results of Marsh et al. (1997) and Study 1 in several new directions. A comparison of the mixed-saturation condition (factor loadings of .4, .6, and .8) in Study 1 with the constant-saturation (all factor loadings = .6) condition in the Marsh et al. study suggests that equal factor loadings resulted in more fully proper solutions. Hence, one objective is to test this observation more fully.

Our main objective, however, is to explore the efficacy of our equal-loading strategy (see earlier discussions). In Study 2, we consider both constant- and mixed-saturation conditions (for the population generating models) and compare the behavior of approximating models in which the estimated factor loadings are constrained to be equal (equal-loading strategy) or are freely estimated. We expect this equal-loading strategy to be beneficial for the constant-saturation condition, which is consistent with

Table 1 Study 1: Parameters and Factor Reliability Estimates by Sample Size and Number of Indicators

| | Factor Loading | | | | | | Uniqueness | | | | | |
| | Popu = .40 | | Popu = .60 | | Popu = .80 | | Popu = .84 | | Popu = .64 | | Popu = .36 | |
p	M	SD	M	SD	M	SD	M	SD	M	SD	M	SD
					Sample Size = 50							
3	.435	.167	.638	.165	.763	.167	.791	.185	.570	.191	.400	.199
6	.395	.150	.595	.141	.797	.133	.814	.172	.625	.145	.348	.120
9	.401	.146	.599	.139	.796	.126	.818	.170	.624	.139	.353	.097
					Sample Size = 100							
3	.409	.118	.618	.124	.782	.132	.819	.129	.603	.141	.369	.168
6	.395	.106	.596	.098	.798	.091	.823	.120	.632	.102	.354	.082
9	.402	.101	.602	.098	.799	.090	.829	.119	.630	.100	.356	.068
					Sample Size = 200							
3	.400	.085	.606	.086	.797	.098	.831	.089	.623	.096	.354	.131
6	.395	.074	.598	.068	.799	.064	.828	.086	.636	.070	.357	.056
9	.402	.072	.603	.069	.801	.061	.833	.084	.634	.071	.358	.048

Table 1 Continued

| | Factor Loading | | | | | | | | Uniqueness | | | |
| | Popu = .40 | | Popu = .60 | | Popu = .80 | | Popu = .84 | | Popu = .64 | | Popu = .36 | |
p	M	SD	M	SD	M	SD	M	SD	M	SD	M	SD
					Sample Size = 400							
3	.397	.059	.602	.062	.799	.072	.836	.063	.629	.070	.354	.096
6	.396	.053	.598	.049	.800	.045	.831	.060	.637	.050	.358	.039
9	.403	.051	.603	.049	.801	.043	.835	.059	.636	.050	.359	.034
					Sample Size = 1,000							
3	.398	.035	.602	.038	.798	.047	.838	.039	.632	.048	.359	.063
6	.396	.034	.598	.029	.800	.029	.832	.038	.639	.033	.359	.024
9	.403	.032	.603	.030	.802	.029	.837	.038	.638	.032	.360	.022

Table 1 Continued								
	Fac Corr		Reliability		χ^2/df		p value	
p	M	SD	M	SD	M	SD	M	SD
				Sample Size = 50				
3	.353	.213	.651	.085	1.026	.297	.476	.287
6	.297	.162	.777	.046	1.192	.147	.159	.200
9	.295	.151	.839	.037	1.307	.102	.009	.034
				Sample Size = 100				
3	.313	.145	.642	.064	1.005	.282	.491	.285
6	.298	.113	.778	.031	1.083	.129	.321	.268
9	.297	.102	.841	.025	1.119	.083	.150	.188
				Sample Size = 200				
3	.303	.100	.641	.044	.996	.315	.510	.306
6	.300	.077	.779	.022	1.039	.124	.411	.285
9	.297	.073	.842	.017	1.053	.080	.318	.262
				Sample Size = 400				
3	.300	.069	.641	.032	1.015	.313	.494	.302
6	.300	.052	.779	.016	1.016	.128	.461	.297
9	.298	.050	.842	.012	1.020	.078	.431	.279
				Sample Size = 1,000				
3	.302	.042	.640	.020	1.010	.284	.486	.285
6	.300	.034	.779	.010	1.003	.117	.489	.276
9	.298	.030	.842	.007	1.001	.071	.495	.265

Note. p = number of indicators. Popu = population value. Values are based only on fully proper solutions. The means and standard deviations of the three types of indicators are listed separately. Population value for factor correlation is .30.

this constraint (i.e., population factor loadings actually are constant); however, the efficacy of this strategy may be less clear for the mixed-saturation condition, which is inconsistent with this constraint. On the one hand, at least some of the factor loadings

Table 2 Study 1: Effects of Sample Size and Number of Indicators on Parameter Estimates, Factor Reliability, and Goodness-of-Fit Indices

	Effect					
	Number of Indicators		Sample Size		Indicator $\times$ Size	
	E	r	E	r	E	r
Parameter Estimates						
Factor loading						
Indicator (.40)	.05	−.03	.05	−.04	.07	.06
Indicator (.60)	.07	−.06	.04	−.03	.08	.06
Indicator (.80)	.06	.06	.06	.05	.06	−.05
Uniqueness						
Indicator (.84)	.03	.03	.09	.08	.05	−.04
Indicator (.64)	.10	.09	.11	.10	.08	−.07
Indicator (.36)	.06	−.05	.04	−.02	.10	.07
Factor correlation	.07	−.07	.05	−.04	.09	.07
Parameter Variability (Standard Errors)						
Factor loading						
Indicator (.40)	.05	−.05	.50	−.49	.04	.04
Indicator (.60)	.13	−.13	.49	−.48	.05	.04
Indicator (.80)	.21	−.21	.47	−.46	.05	.04
Uniqueness						
Indicator (.86)	.03	−.03	.51	−.49	.03	.03
Indicator (.64)	.15	−.14	.48	−.47	.07	.06
Indicator (.36)	.39	−.38	.40	−.39	.12	.11
Factor correlation	.14	−.14	.51	−.49	.09	.09
Factor reliability	.91	.91	.02	.02	.02	.01
Goodness-of-Fit Indices						
χ^2/df	.17	.17	.29	−.26	.20	−.19
p value	.29	−.28	.33	.32	.24	.23

Note. For each estimate, a 5 (levels of N) × 3 (levels of p/f) ANOVA was conducted. Effect size for each main and interaction effect is summarized by $\eta[E = (SS_{effect}/SS_{total})^{1/2}]$ and the linear effect (r) of log N, log p/f, and their interaction. Values are based only on fully proper solutions. The effects on the three different types of indicators are listed separately.

(and corresponding uniquenesses) based on the constraint will be systematically biased (some positively, some negatively) and the size of this bias will vary with the extent of variation in the factor loadings in the mixed-saturation conditions. It is unclear, however, how this intentional biasing of factor loadings and uniquenesses will affect the convergence behavior of solutions. Because the solutions based on the equal-loading strategy are more parsimonious—requiring many fewer estimated parameters—it may be that the equal-loading strategy will result in more fully proper solutions even when parameter estimates are systematically biased. It is also unclear whether the estimation of the factor correlations—which are a major focus of this research—will be systematically affected by this equal-loading strategy.

Methods

A 4 (N: 50, 100, 200, 1,000) × 3 (saturation condition: constant, low-mixed, high-mixed) × 2 (factor loading constraints: free or equal) design was considered. The three population generating models differed in the factor loading (saturation) disparities (constant: .6, .6, .6; low-mixed: .5, .6, .7; and high-mixed: .4, .6, .8). Two different approximating models were used to fit the data, one where all factor loading estimates were constrained to be equal (the equal-loading strategy) and one in which factor loading estimates were freely estimated with no invariance constraints. All population generating models had three congeneric factors and each factor had three indicators (i.e., a total of nine measured variables). All factors and indicators had unit variance and all factor correlations were .30. Data were generated and results analyzed with PRELIS 2 and LISREL 8 (Jöreskog & Sörbom, 1993, 1996).

All models with the free factor loadings (or factor loadings constrained to be equal when population factor loadings are equal) are "true" in that the pattern of free and fixed parameters was the same in the generating model used to generate the simulated data and the approximating model used to fit the data. Hence, to the extent that the χ^2 test is behaving appropriately, the mean χ^2/df ratio should not differ systematically from 1.0

and the mean p value associated with the χ^2 should not differ significantly from .50. All models in which the approximating model constrains the factor loadings to be equal in the mixed-saturation conditions are "false" and the extent of misfit is larger in the high-mixed condition than in the low-mixed condition.

Initially, we evaluated the convergence behavior of solutions in each cell of the design. Analysis of variance was then used to estimate the effects of these variables on parameter estimates (factor loadings, uniquenesses, factor correlations), parameter estimate variability, and goodness of fit (χ^2/df, p value). Because of the very large sample size, we evaluate effect sizes defined as $\eta = (SS_{\text{effect}}/SS_{\text{total}})^{1/2}$ based on results of fully proper solutions.

Results

Convergence to Proper Solutions. The effects of N, saturation (mixed or constant factor loading disparity), and estimation constraint strategy (free versus equal factor loadings) are all substantial in the convergence behavior of solutions in this study (Table 3). As found in earlier research, the percentage of fully proper solutions increases substantially with larger N. As suggested from the juxtaposition of the results of Study 1 and the Marsh et al. (1997) study, however, convergence to a proper solution is much more likely in the constant-saturation condition. Thus, for example, the percentages of fully proper solutions (Table 3) for $N = 50$ and $N = 100$ drops from 58% and 89% (constant saturation) to 53% and 84% (low-mixed saturation) to 39% and 67% (high-mixed saturation).

The major new finding is the dramatic improvement in the behavior of solutions with equality constraints imposed on the factor loadings. In contrast to the substantial number of improper solutions when factor loadings are freely estimated (particularly when $N = 50$ or 100), improper solutions are nearly eliminated. Even when $N = 50$, the percentage of fully proper solutions is greater than 98% for all cells and is 100% for all other cells with $N \geqslant 100$. Although the superior performance of this equal-loading strategy was expected in the constant-saturation condition (where the equality constraint is consistent with the

Table 3 Study 2: Percentages of Different Convergence Behavior by Sample Size, Degree of Factor Loading Disparity, and Condition of Loading Equality Constraint

Loading Disparity		Equality Constraint								
		No				Yes				
	$N =$	50	100	200	1,000	50	100	200	1,000
Constant, population loading = .6 .6 .6		58.2	88.6	98.6	100.0	98.5	100.0	100.0	100.0
Low-mixed, population loading = .5 .6 .7		53.3	84.2	97.8	100.0	98.3	100.0	100.0	100.0
High-mixed, population loading = .4 .6 .8		39.5	66.7	89.8	100.0	98.1	100.0	100.0	100.0

population generating model), the percentage of fully proper solutions is essentially the same for the two mixed-saturation conditions. Hence, at least in terms of the goal of fostering convergence to fully proper solutions—particularly when N is small—the results of Study 2 suggest that the equal-loading strategy is potentially useful in small-N research and very successful for the data considered here.

These results demonstrate a very interesting feature. Not only did the equal-loading strategy work, but it actually worked better when the underlying assumption of equal factor loadings was *false*. Furthermore, the "more wrong" the assumption became (i.e., the misfit between population generating and approximating model increased), the better it worked. These possibly paradoxical results are due to the fact that increasing variability in factor saturations leads to more improper solutions when factor loadings are freely estimated, whereas increasing differences in factor saturation has little effect on convergence behavior for solutions based on the equal-loading strategy. Hence, we observed substantial advantages for the equal-loading strategy in relation to this one very important criterion—convergence to a fully proper solution—even when (or especially when) the assumption of equal factor loadings was false. We now turn to potential disadvantages of this strategy in terms of parameter estimates.

Estimates of Factor Loadings. We present the results for only the second indicator of the second factor that had a common population value (.6), which was the point of symmetry for factor loadings in all three population generating models (i.e., .6, **.6**, .6; .5, **.6**, .7; and .4, **.6**, .8). The mean factor loading in each cell at least approximates the common population value as shown by the small effect sizes in the three-way ANOVA used to summarize these results (Table 4). None of the three main effects nor any of their interactions even approaches $\eta = .1$ (i.e., 1% of the variance explained). The only exceptions to this pattern (see Table 5) are for the $N = 50$ cells with no equality constraints where the mean estimated parameter estimates are somewhat too high. It should be recalled, however, that many improper solutions (more than 50% overall) were excluded from this particular cell and this may account for this apparently idiosyncratic finding. In contrast to the mean factor loadings, there are substantial effects on the variability (*SE*s) of the factor loadings, with large effects of N ($\eta = .82$), the approximating model ($\eta = .48$), and their interaction ($\eta = .21$). As expected, the *SE*s decline substantially as N increases, but the *SE*s are also systematically smaller when equality constraints are imposed—particularly when N is small.

In evaluating these effects on the factor loadings, it needs to be emphasized that we have only considered estimates for the indicator with a .6 population factor loading, which is common to all cells in the design. The sizes of estimated factor loadings do vary substantially as a function of the approximating model for the mixed-saturation conditions. Thus, for example, for the high-mixed-saturation condition (.4, .6, and .8, factor loadings), estimated factor loadings approximate the population values when there are no equality constraints but have a mean of approximately .6 when equality constraints are imposed. Hence, the equality constraint results in a systematic positive bias in the smallest factor loadings and a systematic negative bias in the largest factor loadings.

Estimates of Measured Variable Uniquenesses. In illustrating these effects, we focus on the uniquenesses for only the second indicator of the second factor that has a common population value (.64) across all cells in the design. Inspection of the effect sizes (Table 4) and the mean uniqueness estimates (Table 5) indicates that the effects of the generating model, the approximating model, and N are all small. However, to illustrate the size of the bias of the equality constraints in factor loadings on the other uniquenesses, we also examined the effects on the uniqueness of the first indicator that had population values of .64 (the same as the other measured variables), .75, and .84 in the three different population generating models. When the equality constraints for the factor loadings were reasonable (i.e., the population values were equal), the uniquenesses for the first two indicators were similar; however, when the factor loadings were constrained to be equal and the population values were not equal, there were systematic biases in the estimated uniqueness for the first measured variable. Thus, for example, whereas the population uniqueness is

Table 4 Study 2: Effects (η) of Sample Size, Degree of Loading Disparity, and Condition of Loading Equality Constraint on Parameter Estimates and Goodness of Fit

	Main Effects			Interaction Effects			
	Sample Size (N)	Loading Disparity (D)	Equality Constraint (E)	$N \times D$	$N \times E$	$D \times E$	$N \times D \times E$
Parameter Estimates							
Factor loading	.01	.02	.05	.01	.08	.03	.04
Uniqueness	.08	.07	.04	.03	.08	.01	.03
Factor correlation	.04	.01	.03	.03	.07	.01	.01
Parameter Variability (Standard Error)							
Factor loading	.82	.00	.48	.00	.21	.00	.00
Uniqueness	.88	.01	.18	.01	.08	.01	.01
Factor correlation	.94	.04	.11	.01	.09	.03	.01
Goodness-of-Fit Indices							
χ^2/df	.36	.34	.34	.38	.38	.33	.38
p value	.05	.25	.36	.12	.13	.25	.12

Note. $\eta = (SS_{effect}/SS_{total})^{1/2}$. Parameter variability is estimated both by the *SE* of the parameters as well as by the differences between two corresponding indicators in two factors (e.g., loading variability = difference between loadings of indicators 2 and 5, both are the middle indicator in their factors). When the effect of an interaction was large, post hoc comparisons were performed and are described in the text.

Table 5 Study 2: Parameter Estimates, Variability, and Goodness-of-Fit Indices by Sample Size, Degree of Loading Disparity (Constant, Low mixed, High mixed), and Condition of Loading Equality Constraint

	N = 50				N = 100				N = 200				N = 1,000			
	Equality Constr.				Equality Constr.				Equality Constr.				Equality Constr.			
	Without		With		Without		With		Without		With		Without		With	
Loading Disparity	M	SD	M	SD	M	SD	M	SD	M	SD	M	SD	M	SD	M	SD
Factor Loading: Mean																
Constant	.61	.17	.59	.14	.60	.13	.60	.07	.60	.09	.60	.05	.60	.04	.60	.02
		(1164)		(1969)		(886)		(1,000)		(493)		(500)		(100)		(100)
Low mixed	.62	.18	.59	.15	.60	.13	.60	.08	.60	.09	.60	.05	.60	.04	.60	.02
		(1065)		(1966)		(842)		(1,000)		(489)		(500)		(100)		(100)
High mixed	.64	.18	.57	.22	.62	.12	.60	.09	.61	.09	.61	.05	.60	.04	.61	.02
		(789)		(1962)		(667)		(1,000)		(449)		(500)		(100)		(100)
Factor Loading Variability (Standard Error)																
Constant	.17	.02	.10	.01	.12	.01	.07	.00	.09	.01	.05	.00	.04	.00	.02	.00
Low mixed	.17	.03	.10	.01	.12	.01	.07	.00	.09	.01	.05	.00	.04	.00	.02	.00
High mixed	.17	.03	.10	.01	.12	.01	.07	.00	.09	.01	.05	.00	.04	.00	.02	.00

Table 5 (Continued)

Uniqueness: Mean

Constant	.61	.19	.64	.16	.63	.14	.64	.12	.64	.10	.64	.08	.64	.04	.64	.04
Low mixed	.60	.20	.64	.16	.63	.14	.64	.12	.64	.10	.64	.08	.65	.04	.64	.04
High mixed	.57	.19	.62	.16	.61	.14	.62	.12	.63	.10	.62	.08	.65	.04	.62	.04

Uniqueness Variability (Standard Error)

Constant	.19	.05	.16	.03	.14	.03	.12	.02	.10	.01	.08	.01	.04	.00	.04	.00
Low mixed	.20	.05	.16	.03	.14	.03	.11	.02	.10	.01	.08	.01	.04	.00	.04	.00
High mixed	.19	.05	.16	.03	.14	.03	.11	.02	.10	.01	.08	.01	.04	.00	.04	.00

Factor Correlation: Mean

Constant	.34	.23	.30	.24	.30	.16	.30	.16	.30	.11	.30	.11	.30	.05	.30	.05
Low mixed	.34	.23	.30	.25	.31	.16	.30	.17	.30	.11	.30	.11	.30	.05	.30	.05
High mixed	.33	.24	.28	.27	.32	.14	.31	.17	.30	.10	.31	.11	.30	.05	.31	.05

Factor Correlation Variability (Standard Error)

Constant	.19	.03	.22	.04	.14	.01	.15	.02	.10	.01	.11	.01	.05	.00	.05	.00
Low mixed	.19	.02	.22	.04	.14	.01	.15	.02	.10	.01	.11	.01	.05	.00	.05	.00
High mixed	.18	.02	.22	.04	.13	.01	.15	.02	.09	.01	.11	.01	.04	.00	.05	.00

Table 5 (Continued)

Goodness-of-Fit Indices: χ^2/df

Constant	1.05	.30	1.10	.28	1.03	.29	1.04	.27	1.02	.29	1.02	.25	.99	.30	1.00	.26
Low mixed	1.06	.30	1.16	.30	1.02	.29	1.17	.29	1.02	.29	1.28	.31	.99	.30	2.31	.47
High mixed	1.06	.30	1.35	.34	1.02	.28	1.56	.37	1.02	.29	2.05	.44	.99	.30	6.20	.85

Goodness-of-Fit Indices: p value

Constant	.45	.29	.40	.28	.47	.29	.45	.29	.48	.29	.48	.29	.51	.29	.50	.28
Low mixed	.44	.29	.34	.28	.47	.28	.33	.27	.48	.29	.24	.24	.52	.29	.00	.01
High mixed	.44	.29	.20	.23	.47	.29	.10	.16	.48	.29	.02	.05	.51	.29	.00	.00

Note. For the three factor loading disparity conditions, factor loadings were: .6, .6, .6 (constant); .5, .6, .7 (low mixed), and .4, .6, .8 (high mixed). Population values for the summarized parameter estimates are: factor loading = .6, factor correlation = .30, uniqueness = .64. Number of subjects (N) are shown in parentheses for mean factor loadings only, but are the same for all other parameter estimates.

.75 in the low-mixed-saturation condition, the estimated uniqueness is .69 (systematically larger than the .64 value for the middle uniqueness, but systematically smaller than the true population value). The direction of these biases, of course, is expected and merely reflects the inappropriateness of the equality constraints on factor loadings when the population values are not equal.

In contrast to the mean values of the uniquenesses, there are systematic effects on the *SE*s of the uniqueness estimates. There is a substantial effect of *N* such that the *SE*s decrease substantially with increasing *N*. It is also important to note, however, that the *SE*s tend to be somewhat smaller when equality constraints are imposed. Furthermore, this increased precision associated with the equality constraints does not vary with the factor generating model (and thus the extent of misfit due to the equality constraint).

Estimates of Factor Correlations. The mean factor correlation in each cell approximates the common population value as shown by the small effect sizes in the three-way ANOVA (Table 4) and parameter estimates (Table 5). None of the three main effects nor any of their interactions had $\eta > .07$ (i.e., 0.49% of the variance explained). The only exceptions to this pattern are for the $N = 50$ cells with no equality constraints where the mean estimated factor correlations are somewhat too high (and where more than half of the replicates were excluded due to "missing data" associated with improper solutions). In contrast to the mean factor correlations, there are substantial effects on the variability of the factor correlations. Particularly for the *SE*s, there is a huge effect of *N* ($\eta = .89$), a small effect of the approximating model ($\eta = .12$), and a marginal effect of their interaction ($\eta = .05$). As expected, the *SE*s decline substantially as *N* increases, but the variability of factor correlations also tends to be slightly higher for solutions in which factor loadings are constrained to be equal—particularly when *N* is smaller and the saturation is mixed.

Goodness of Fit. For both indices of fit (χ^2/df and *p* values; see Table 4), there are substantial effects of all the independent variables. This is, of course, expected in that the approximating model is "true" for all conditions in which no equality constraints are imposed and for the constant-saturation condition when equality constraints are imposed. In contrast, the approximating model is false in mixed-saturation conditions when the equal loading strategy is implemented. Consistent with the design of the study, the χ^2/df approximates the expected value of 1.0 for all conditions in which the approximating model is true, but is systematically higher when the approximating model is false. Also, as expected, the sizes of the mean χ^2/df ratios for false models increases systematically with N and with the variability of the population factor loadings (the size of the misfit in the design).

Conclusions, Implications, Limitations, and Directions for Future Research

The purpose of this study was to examine a variety of strategies that are particularly relevant for studies where it is necessary to use small N. Although we hope that our findings have some practical implications for researchers in this situation, we must preface our remarks with the strong caveat that the use of small N is never desirable. It is always better to have larger Ns—particularly in relation to the small Ns emphasized in this monograph. Hence, our first recommendation—and the one we offer with the greatest confidence—is that in small-N studies researchers should try to increase their Ns if at all possible.

The use of item parcels has intuitive appeal in small-N studies. Marsh et al. (1997) evaluated some limited aspects of this strategy—particularly whether solutions based on item parcels were more or less likely to result in proper solutions than the corresponding solutions based on items. They found that solutions based on a given number of parcels consistently did better than solutions based on the same number of items, but that parcels made up of various combinations of the 12 items (i.e., two 6-item parcels, three 4-item parcels, etc.) never did better than solutions based on the 12 items used to construct these parcels. These limited results suggested that it may not make much difference whether solutions are based on items or parcels as long as there are enough parcels or N is at least moderate. It is, of course, important to reiterate that they evaluated only a very limited range of relevant variables. The use of nonnormal data, mixed saturations, more complicated data structures, various levels of misfit, and so forth would greatly complicate studies of the effectiveness of item parcels, but might also show advantages of item parcels over items—particularly when N is small. Hence, there is a clear need for further research comparing the advantages and disadvantages under a much wider set of conditions.

The main finding of the Marsh et al. (1997) study was that solution behavior steadily improved (more proper solutions, more accurate parameter estimates, greater reliability) with increasing p/f for all Ns that they considered. There was a compensatory relationship between N and p/f such that large p/f compensated for small N and large N compensated for small p/f, even though large N and large p/f was best. They concluded that, for conditions in their simulation study, traditional "rules" implying fewer indicators should be used for smaller N may be inappropriate and CFA researchers should consider using more indicators per factor than is evident in current practice. Whereas it would seem that there may be some upper limit beyond which the use of increasing numbers of indicators may be counterproductive or leads to identification problems, the exploratory extensions of the Marsh et al. study suggest that even this conclusion should not be accepted without further research.

In Study 1, we extended the Marsh et al. (1997) study by using different procedures to generate and analyze the data and by evaluating the effects of varying the level of saturation. The results of Study 1 largely replicated the Marsh et al. study, thus supporting the generality of the conclusions over variations in the two studies. Study 1 also showed, however, that the increased precision of factor loadings with increasing p/f ratios found by Marsh et al. was even larger for indicators with greater saturation.

The juxtaposition of the Marsh et al. results based on a constant-saturation condition (all factor loadings of .6) and Study 1 with a mixed-saturation condition (factor loadings of .4, .6, and .8) also suggested that the saturation variability may be an important feature. Consistent with these conjectures, the results of Study 2 showed that the percentage of improper solutions increased substantially as the variability of the factor loadings in the mixed-saturation conditions increased.

The major focus of Study 2 was on the efficacy of an equal-loading strategy whereby all factor loadings on the same latent construct were constrained to be equal. Not unexpectedly, this strategy was very effective when the population factor loadings really were equal. Particularly for small $N = 50$, the percentage of fully proper solutions rose from 58% to 98%. However, somewhat unexpectedly, the strategy was even more successful—at least in terms of resulting in fully proper solutions—when the population factor loadings did not conform to the equality constraint. Thus, for example, whereas the percentage of fully proper solutions remained at about 98% for all conditions at $N = 50$ when the equality constraint was imposed, the corresponding values dropped from 58% to 43% to 39% in the constant-, low-mixed-, and high-mixed-saturation conditions when no equality constraints were imposed. Whereas the equality constraints clearly led to a poorer fit when the constraint was false and biased estimates of the largest and smallest factor loadings, estimates of the intermediate factor loadings were reasonably accurate and less variable than when the factor loadings were not constrained. More important, perhaps, this strategy appeared to have little or no detrimental effects on the estimation of the factor correlations that were a major emphasis in this study. At least in terms of the conditions considered here, there seemed to be relatively few drawbacks to the equal-loading strategy—particularly in relation to the dramatic increase in the percentage of proper solutions.

The equal-loading strategy seems to be potentially valuable for small-N research, but a number of potential limitations of Study 2 needs to be considered. In particular, the generality of the results needs to be evaluated in a much wider variety of conditions for simulated and real data. Even within Study 2, for example, the advantages of the equal-loading strategy declined dramatically with increasing N in that there were 100% fully proper solutions for all conditions for $N = 1,000$. Hence, the potential advantages of this strategy seem most relevant to small-N research. We are comfortable recommending routine use of the equal-loading strategy in combination with models that do not impose equality constraints. If the solution with no equality constraints is fully proper and fits the data significantly better than the corresponding solution based on the equal-loading strategy, then it is usually better to use the solution with no equality constraints. When this occurs, it may still be useful to compare the results of the two solutions to see if there are any substantively meaningful differences (other than the differences in the factor loadings and uniquenesses associated with the equality constraints). If, however, the solution with no equality constraints fails to converge to a fully proper solution and the solution based on the equal-loading strategy is fully proper, then it is probably preferable to use the solution with equality constraints. Whereas the use of the equal-loading strategy may complicate model comparisons, it should not pose a problem for the comparison of *nested* models in which all comparisons are between models with the same equality constraints. Based on the results presented in this chapter and our general experience, it seems likely that the solution with no equality constraints results in improper solutions with sufficient frequency in small-N research to warrant the routine use of the equal-loading strategy as one of the alternatives to be considered.

Finally, we reiterate that, as with all simulation studies, our major aim is to shed light on an area where "rules of thumb" and typical practice may be misleading. Studies in this chapter and the Marsh et al. (1997) study show that common advice to limit the number of indicators is inappropriate under the conditions that we investigated, and raises the same concern in other contexts. Similarly, our research may call into question the intuitively plausible practice of using a small number of item parcels (2 or even 3) instead of a larger number of items in small-N research under at least one set of conditions. Also, the results of Study 2 demonstrated that for conditions in that study the imposition of the equal-loading strategy resulted in many more fully proper solutions than an approximating model with no equality constraints—even when the equality constraint was known to be false. For the Ns considered, much of the behavior exhibited would seem to be preasymptotic, but these Ns reflect common practice. For the same reasons, the mathematics available for investigating such issues more comprehensively may not be available and obtaining exact general results in relation to a technique of estimation whose roots lie in asymptotic maximum-likelihood theory we suspect will prove very difficult. In such an unexplored environment, simulations have an important role to play, provided that their results are always qualified by their specificity.

In conclusion, based in part on the results of our research, we would like to offer some recommendations for researchers conducting small-N CFA studies:

1. If at all possible, increase the N.
2. Particularly in small-N research, be sure to use lots of good indicators—a minimum of four or five good indicators per factor, but more is probably better.
3. Particularly in small-N research, researchers should conduct pilot studies to evaluate the psychometric properties of their measures so that they are confident that all the indicators are strong (standardized factor loadings $> .6$). This should also help avoid the problems associated with highly mixed saturations and low saturations that seem to be particularly troublesome in small-N research.
4. Although not a focus of this chapter (see Marsh et al., 1997), even when a solution is an improper solution, there is some evidence to suggest the meaningfulness of goodness-of-fit statistics and, perhaps, even the parameter estimates not associated with the offending parameters. This strategy may be reasonable when the improper solution is part of a series of nested or partially nested sequences in which most of the models did converge to fully proper solutions. However, the research summarized here suggests that the imposition of the equal-loading strategy may result in a fully proper solution that may help circumvent some of these problems.
5. In small-N research, routinely implement the equal-loading strategy in addition to the typical approximating models with no such invariance constraints. With the equal-loading strat-

egy, the factor correlations (or path coefficients) can be trustworthy, particularly when all items are reasonably good. On the other hand, the estimated factor loadings can be systematically biased, the severity of which depends on the degree of disparities in loading saturation (e.g., in pilot measures consisting of good and bad items).

Author Notes: The authors would like to thank Alexander Yeung and David Grayson for helpful comments on earlier versions of this chapter. Correspondence in relation to this study should be sent to Professor Herbert W. Marsh, Faculty of Education, University of Western Sydney, Macarthur, PO Box 555, Campbelltown, NSW 2560 Australia. Electronic mail may be sent via the Internet to h.marsh@uws.edu.au.

References

Anderson, J. C., & Gerbing, D. W. (1984). The effect of sampling error on convergence, improper solutions, and goodness-of-fit indices for maximum likelihood confirmatory factor analysis. *Psychometrika*, *49*, 155–173.

Bentler, P. M., & Wu, E. J. C. (1995). *EQS for Windows user's guide*. Encino, CA: Multivariate Software.

Bollen, K. A. (1989). *Structural equations with latent variables*. New York: Wiley.

Boomsma, A. (1982). Robustness of LISREL against small sample sizes in factor analysis models. In K. G. Jöreskog & H. Wold (Eds.), *Systems under indirect observation: Causality, structure, prediction* (Part I, pp. 149–173). Amsterdam: North-Holland.

Boomsma, A. (1985). Nonconvergence, improper solutions, and starting values in LISREL maximum likelihood estimation. *Psychometrika*, *50*, 229–242.

Dawes, R. M. (1979). The robust beauty of IMPROPER linear models in decision making. *American Psychologist*, *34*, 571–582.

Ding, L., Velicer, W. F., & Harlow, L. L. (1995). The effects of estimation methods, number of indicators per factor and improper solutions on structural equation modeling fit indices. *Structural Equation Modeling*, *2*, 119–144.

Gerbing, D. W., & Anderson, J. C. (1987). Improper solutions in the analysis of covariance structures: Their interpretability and a comparison of alternate respecification. *Psychometrika*, *52*, 99–111.

Gerbing, D. W., & Anderson, J. C. (1993). Monte Carlo evaluations of goodness-of-fit indices for structural equation models. In K. A. Bollen & J. S. Long (Eds.), *Testing structural equation models* (pp. 40–65). Newbury Park, CA: Sage.

Guadagnoli, E., & Velicer, W. F. (1988). Relation of sample size to the stability of component patterns. *Psychological Bulletin*, *103*, 265–275.

Jöreskog, K. G., & Sörbom, D. (1988). *LISREL 7: A guide to the program and applications* (2nd ed.). Chicago: SPSS.

Jöreskog, K. G., & Sörbom, D. (1993). *LISREL 8: Structural equation modeling with the SIMPLIS command language*. Chicago: Scientific Software.

Jöreskog, K. G., & Sörbom, D. (1996). *PRELIS2 user's reference guide* (3rd ed.). Chicago: Scientific Software.

MacCallum, R. C., Browne, M. W., & Sugawara, H. M. (1996). Power analysis and determination of sample size for covariance structure modeling. *Psychological Methods*, *1*, 130–149.

Marsh, H. W., & Bailey, M. (1991). Confirmatory factor analyses of multitrait-multimethod data: A comparison of alternative models. *Applied Psychological Measurement*, *15*, 47–70.

Marsh, H. W., Balla, J. R., & McDonald, R. P. (1988). Goodness-of-fit indexes in confirmatory factor analysis: The effect of sample size. *Psychological Bulletin*, *103*, 391–410.

Marsh, H. W., & Hau, K.-T. (1996). Assessing goodness of fit: Is parsimony always desirable? *Journal of Experimental Education*, *64*, 364–390.

Marsh, H. W., Hau, K.-T., & Balla, J. (1997, March). *Is more ever too much: The number of indicators per factor in confirmatory factor analysis*. Paper presented at the Annual Meeting of the American Educational Research Association, Chicago.

McDonald, R. P., & Marsh, H. W. (1990). Choosing a multivariate model: Noncentrality and goodness of fit. *Psychological Bulletin*, *107*, 247–255.

Mulaik, S. A., James, L. R., Van Alstine, J., Bennett, N., Lind, S., & Stilwell, C. D. (1989). Evaluation of goodness-of-fit indices for structural equation models. *Psychological Bulletin*, *105*, 430–445.

Tanaka, J. S. (1987). "How big is big enough?": Sample size and goodness of fit in structural equation models with latent variables. *Child Development, 58*, 134–146.

van Driel, O. P. (1978). On various causes of improper solutions in maximum likelihood factor analysis. *Psychometrika, 43*, 225–243.

Velicer, W. F., & Fava, L. L. (1987). An evaluation of the effects of variable sampling on component, image, and factor analysis. *Multivariate Behavioral Research, 22*, 193–209.

Velicer, W. F., & Fava, L. L. (1989, November). *The effects of variable and subject sampling on factor pattern recovery: An evaluation of the effects of variable sampling on component, image, and factor analysis.* Paper presented at the Annual Meeting of the Society for Multivariate Experimental Psychology, Oahu, HI.

Velicer, W. F., & Jackson, D. N. (1990). Component analysis versus common factor analysis: Some issues in selecting an appropriate procedure. *Multivariate Behavioral Research, 25*, 1–28.

Wainer, H. (1976). Estimating coefficients in linear models: It don't make no nevermind. *Psychological Bulletin, 83*, 213–217.

Wothke, W. (1993). Nonpositive definite matrices in structural equation modeling. In K. A. Bollen & J. S. Long (Eds.), *Testing structural equation models* (pp. 256–293). Newbury Park, CA: Sage.

11

Small Samples in Structural Equation State Space Modeling

Johan H. L. Oud, Robert A. R. G. Jansen, &
Dominique M. A. Haughton

THE STATE SPACE APPROACH, which is at the core of modern control theory (Caines, 1988), has become increasingly popular in other fields as well. It covers a very general class of dynamic models. In fact, all nonanticipative longitudinal models (models with no causal arrows heading backward in time) can be represented in state space form. For example, both the Box-Jenkins autoregressive moving average ARMA model and the extended ARMAX model, which adds exogenous or input variables to the ARMA model, are easily formulated as special cases of the discrete-time, time-invariant state space model (Caines, 1988; Deistler, 1985; Ljung, 1985). The state space model also covers longitudinal latent factor and path analysis models and allows the optimal estimation of the latent states or factor scores (Oud, van den Bercken, & Essers, 1990; Oud, van Leeuwe, &

Jansen, 1993). Latent state estimation is performed by two important results of the state space approach: the Kalman filter and the Kalman smoother (Jazwinski, 1970; Lewis, 1986; Oud & Jansen, 1996; Rauch, Tung, & Striebel, 1965). In fact, the use of the Kalman filter or smoother often motivates state space modeling.

In this chapter, the state space model is formulated in terms of structural equation modeling (SEM). Both models allow a measurement equation to be part of the model, allowing for measurement errors in the observed variables. Parameter estimation in SEM takes place on the basis of a sample of independently identically distributed (i.i.d.) multivariate observations, usually originating from multiple subjects. In contrast to the traditional $N = 1$ case, where the lack of independent observations makes it necessary to assume time-invariant parameters and the model as a whole to be asymptotically stable, SEM state space model parameter estimation allows the parameters to be arbitrarily time varying and, in particular, does not require asymptotic stability. A special feature of SEM state space modeling is that random subject effects may be specified as part of the model. These random subject effects cause subjects to regress toward their own mean instead of toward the mean of the population under investigation.

Structural equation modeling analysis might be limited as regards sample size. To obtain valid results in SEM, a sample size of $N \geqslant 400$ is often mentioned. Although $N \geqslant 400$ may be safe as a general recommendation, it depends, however, on the model, the kind of data collected, and the purpose of the analysis whether such a sample is necessary. At one extreme, there is the example mentioned by Jöreskog (1973, p. 88): a dynamic model including lagged endogenous variables observed with measurement errors, where the data are taken as N overlapping stretches from the same time series. The maximum-likehood (ML) method produces not only biased results, but, because of the dependence in the data, loses even its maximum-likelihood property. The parameter estimates are consistent, but a huge sample might be necessary to obtain useful results. At the other extreme is the simple-regression model, which, estimated as a special case of SEM by means of an SEM program and the ML method, yields the same unbiased, maximum likelihood and consistent parameter estimates as given by the classical ordinary least squares method (Jöreskog & Sörbom, 1989, p. 143). Structural equation modeling regression analysis allows the same small sample sizes as in classical regression analysis. Apart from a minor correction for degrees of freedom in the denominator, even the standard errors are correct in SEM regression analysis.

In this chapter, a simulation study is presented, evaluating the use of small samples of $N = 50$ and 100 in SEM state space model estimation for multinormal i.i.d. observations. In addition to these small sample sizes, the study includes the sample size of $N = 400$ for comparison. For checking, consistency sample sizes of $N = 1,000$ and $5,000$ were also investigated, but these results are not reported in tabular form. Three true models, and for each true model four analytic models covering the true parameter values but differing in the number and type of freely estimated parameters, were entertained. The true models increased in complexity. Starting from the true state space model I with observed state variables, measurement errors were added in true model II, and additionally random subject effects in true model III. For each of the 15 sample size and true model combinations, 500 sample moment matrices were generated to be analyzed by the SEM program. Each series of 500 sample moment matrices was analyzed by the four analytic models.

The quality of the parameter estimates in each series of 500 samples was assessed by the bias of the estimates themselves and of the associated standard errors. The bias of the standard errors enables one to evaluate whether the t tests based on these standard errors are correct, conservative, or liberal. Also the bias of the model fit χ^2 value and of the associated p value was investigated as well as the percentage of Heywood cases in each series.

State Space Modeling by Means of Structural Equation Modeling

The discrete-time, time-varying linear stochastic state space model consists of two equations:

$$\mathbf{x}_t = \mathbf{A}_{t-1}\mathbf{x}_{t-1} + \kappa + \mathbf{B}_{t-1}\mathbf{u}_{t-1} + \mathbf{w}_{t-1}$$
$$\text{with } \text{cov}(\mathbf{w}_{t-1}) = \mathbf{Q}_{t-1}, \tag{1}$$
$$\mathbf{y}_t = \mathbf{C}_t\mathbf{x}_t + \mathbf{D}_t\mathbf{u}_t + \mathbf{v}_t$$
$$\text{with } \text{cov}(\mathbf{v}_t) = \mathbf{R}_t. \tag{2}$$

The dynamic part, or state equation (Equation 1), describes the dependence of the m latent state variables in $\mathbf{x}_t$ on their lagged values in $\mathbf{x}_{t-1}$, possibly also on r fixed input variables in $\mathbf{u}_{t-1}$, and it allows random subject effects κ to be part of $\mathbf{x}_t$. The matrix $\mathbf{A}_{t-1}$ specifies the autoregressive and cross-lagged effects between the state variables at successive discrete time points t and $t-1$. The static part, or output equation (Equation 2), connects the latent state variables and possibly the fixed input variables to the p observed variables in $\mathbf{y}_t$. $\mathbf{C}_t$ contains the loadings of the p observed output variables in $\mathbf{y}_t$ on the latent state variables. Note the time subscripts of all matrices in Equations 1 and 2, indicating that parameter values may change arbitrarily over time.

The process errors in successive vectors $\mathbf{w}_{t-1}$, the measurement errors in successive vectors $\mathbf{v}_t$, and the elements of κ are assumed to have zero expectations. Except possibly for nonzero covariances within vectors ($\mathbf{Q}_{t-1}$ and $\mathbf{R}_t$ may be nondiagonal), the errors are assumed to have zero covariances with one another, with the initial state $\mathbf{x}_{t_0}$, and with κ. Finally, the errors, $\mathbf{x}_{t_0}$ and κ are assumed to be jointly multinormally distributed.

Nonconstant mean trajectories $E(\mathbf{x}_t)$ and $E(\mathbf{y}_t)$ result from the specification of input variables and input effects $\mathbf{B}_{t-1}\mathbf{u}_{t-1} \neq \mathbf{0}$ and $\mathbf{D}_t\mathbf{u}_t \neq \mathbf{0}$. In one case, only a single, so-called unit input variable, is specified ($\mathbf{u}_t = 1$ for all t), which is constant over time points as well as over subjects in the sample. Here the vectors $\mathbf{b}_{t-1}$ represent latent growth intercepts and the vectors $\mathbf{d}_t$ location parameters (origins) of the measurement scales. $\mathbf{C}_t$ relates the measurement scale units to those of the latent state variables. The model implies a mean trajectory that is common to all subjects in the sample. In another case, the input variables are all constant over time ($\mathbf{u}_t = \mathbf{u}_{t-k}$ for all t and $k > 0$) but, apart from the unit input variable, varying over subjects (gender, socioeconomic status, etc.). Finally, additional input variables may be specified that vary over time points as well as over subjects.

Random subject effects $\kappa \neq \mathbf{0}$ lead to a model that became very popular in econometric panel analysis (see, e.g., Baltagi, 1995). Because of their constancy over time, the added normally distributed variables in κ with $E(\kappa) = \mathbf{0}$ are sometimes called "trait" variables. A trait variable may be specified for each of the state variables. It can be characterized as a random (but constant over time) intercept term, to be contrasted to the fixed (but possibly time varying) intercept associated with the unit input variable. Within the "state-trait" model, each subject is allowed to have its own subject-specific mean trajectory, toward which its state regresses instead of toward the one of the population or subpopulation of which the subject happens to be a member. Subject-specific mean trajectories can also be specified by means of fixed effects but, in the case of a large sample, this easily leads to nonidentification and an excessive loss of degrees of freedom (Baltagi, 1995, pp. 10–13).

The trait variables can be viewed as a special kind of (unobserved and constant over time) state variable. For model estimation by means of SEM, the trait variables in κ are added as extra elements to the state vector. The extended initial state covariance matrix $\mathbf{\Phi}_{t_0}$ becomes

$$\mathbf{\Phi}_{t_0} = \begin{bmatrix} \mathbf{\Phi}_{x t_0} & \mathbf{\Phi}_{x t_0, \kappa} \\ \mathbf{\Phi}_{\kappa, x t_0} & \mathbf{\Phi}_{\kappa} \end{bmatrix}.$$

Significance tests on the existence of constant random subject effects ("unobserved heterogeneity") can easily be performed in SEM: Both the variances of the trait variables in $\mathbf{\Phi}_{\kappa}$ and their covariances with the initial state variables in $\mathbf{\Phi}_{\kappa, x t_0}$ are testable quantities, required to be different from zero (Baltagi, 1995, p. 125).

Using the reformulated state vector, the state space model in Equations 1 and 2 may be written as an SEM model as follows. Let $\mathbf{u}$ denote the (fixed) input vector, which combines all input variables over all time points but specifies the constant (e.g., the unit input variable) and other exactly linearly related input variables only once, and define

$$
\begin{aligned}
\eta &= [\mathbf{u}'\ \mathbf{x}']' & \text{with } \mathbf{x} &= [\mathbf{x}'_{t_0}\ \mathbf{x}'_{t_0+1}\ \cdots\ \mathbf{x}'_{t_0+T-1}]', \\
\zeta &= [\mathbf{u}'\ \mathbf{w}']' & \text{with } \mathbf{x} &= \left[\left[\mathbf{x}_{t_0} - E(\mathbf{x}_{t_0})\right]'\ \mathbf{w}'_{t_0+1}\ \cdots\ \mathbf{w}'_{t_0+T-1}\right]', \\
\mathbf{y} &= [\mathbf{u}'\ \mathbf{y}'_0]' & \text{with } \mathbf{y}_0 &= [\mathbf{y}'_{t_0}\ \mathbf{y}'_{t_0+1}\ \cdots\ \mathbf{y}'_{t_0+T-1}]', \\
\varepsilon &= [\mathbf{0}'\ \mathbf{v}']' & \text{with } \mathbf{v} &= [\mathbf{v}'_{t_0}\ \mathbf{v}'_{t_0+1}\ \cdots\ \mathbf{v}'_{t_0+T-1}]'.
\end{aligned}
\tag{3}
$$

Then the SEM form of Equations 1 and 2 is

$$
\begin{bmatrix} \mathbf{u} \\ \mathbf{x} \end{bmatrix} = \begin{bmatrix} \mathbf{0} & \mathbf{0} \\ \bar{\mathbf{B}} & \bar{\mathbf{A}} \end{bmatrix} \begin{bmatrix} \mathbf{u} \\ \mathbf{x} \end{bmatrix} + \begin{bmatrix} \mathbf{u} \\ \mathbf{w} \end{bmatrix},
$$
$$
\eta \ \ = \ \ \mathbf{B} \quad \eta \ + \ \zeta,
$$
$$
\begin{bmatrix} \mathbf{u} \\ \mathbf{y}_0 \end{bmatrix} = \begin{bmatrix} \mathbf{I} & \mathbf{0} \\ \bar{\mathbf{D}} & \bar{\mathbf{C}} \end{bmatrix} \begin{bmatrix} \mathbf{u} \\ \mathbf{x} \end{bmatrix} + \begin{bmatrix} \mathbf{u} \\ \mathbf{v} \end{bmatrix},
$$
$$
\mathbf{y} \ \ = \ \ \Lambda \quad \eta \ + \ \varepsilon,
$$

where all parameter matrices $\mathbf{A}_{t-1}$, $\mathbf{B}_{t-1}$, $\mathbf{C}_t$, and $\mathbf{D}_t$ are put on the appropriate places in $\bar{\mathbf{A}}$, $\bar{\mathbf{B}}$, $\bar{\mathbf{C}}$, and $\bar{\mathbf{D}}$, respectively. Notice that in $\mathbf{x}$ the initial state $\mathbf{x}_{t_0}$ gets zero rows in $\bar{\mathbf{A}}$ but extra parameters in $\bar{\mathbf{B}}$ in the column corresponding to the unit input variable for modeling and estimating nonzero elements in $E(\mathbf{x}_{t_0})$. $E(\mathbf{x}_{t_0})$ is therefore subtracted from $\mathbf{x}_{t_0}$ in $\mathbf{w}$ (see Equation 3) and leads to the initial state covariance matrix Φ_{t_0} in $\Psi = E(\zeta\zeta')$. The value and identifiability of $E(\mathbf{x}_{t_0})$ depend on the choice of $E(\mathbf{x}_{t_0})$ as well as of the factor loading matrix $\mathbf{D}_{t_0}$. The latter additionally determines the value and identifiability of Φ_{t_0}. In fact, these choices determine the measurement scales (origins and scale units) of the latent state variables, which need to be maintained across the whole time range by special identification techniques (Oud et al., 1993, pp. 15–16).

For maximum-likelihood fitting of the SEM model to the data in $\mathbf{Y}' = [\mathbf{U}'\ \mathbf{Y}'_0]'$, we define the augmented moment matrix (augmented with the fixed input variables)

$$\Sigma = E(\mathbf{y}\mathbf{y}') = \Lambda(\mathbf{I} - \mathbf{B})^{-1}\Psi(\mathbf{I} - \mathbf{B}')^{-1}\Lambda' + \Theta, \tag{4}$$

where $\Theta = E(\varepsilon\varepsilon')$, and the corresponding sample matrix

$$\mathbf{S}_{(q+p_0)\times(q+p_0)} = \frac{1}{N}\mathbf{Y}\mathbf{Y}' = \begin{bmatrix} \frac{1}{N}\sum_{i=1}^{N}\mathbf{u}_i\mathbf{u}_i' & \frac{1}{N}\sum_{i=1}^{N}\mathbf{u}_i\mathbf{y}_{0i}' \\ \frac{1}{N}\sum_{i=1}^{N}\mathbf{y}_{0i}\mathbf{u}_i' & \frac{1}{N}\sum_{i=1}^{N}\mathbf{y}_{0i}\mathbf{y}_{0i}' \end{bmatrix}, \tag{5}$$

where q is the number of (fixed) elements in $\mathbf{u}$ and $p_0 = pT$ the number of elements in observed random vector $\mathbf{y}_0$. SEM programs usually employ the following fitting function in terms of the moment matrices defined in Equations 4 and 5:

$$F_{\mathrm{ML}} = \log|\Sigma| + \mathrm{tr}(\mathbf{S}\Sigma^{-1}) - \log|\mathbf{S}| - (q - p_0).$$

One of the benefits of the recursive state space specification in Equations 1 and 2 is that the Kalman filter can be applied for the optimal estimation of each subject's constant trait value in addition to the changing values of the state variables. The Kalman filter estimates of the constant trait value become more precise as time proceeds. Like the polynomial random effects model (Bryk & Raudenbush, 1987; Willett & Sayer, 1994), the state-trait model allows different kinds of random subject effects to be specified, tested, and their variances and covariances as well as their values estimated. In contrast to the descriptive nature of polynomial curve fitting, however, the state-trait model has a causal dynamic orientation.

Simulation Study

In the simulation, three true state space models were entertained that increased in complexity. Each true model was analyzed by means of four analytic models. These also increased in complexity in the sense that a following analytic model had more parameters freed than a previous one. The analysis results of the small sample sizes, $N = 50$ and 100, are expected to be acceptable for the simpler models but to show increasing bias for the more complex models. First, the nature of the true models is explained, then the nature of the analytic models is detailed, and, finally, the simulation procedure is described.

A true model has all parameters fixed and is used to generate sample moment matrices to be analyzed by the analytic models that have one or more parameters free. Consider the state space model shown in Figure 1. This type of model is frequently encountered in practice and consists of two state variables that have some predictability over time because of the specification of autoregressive effects. The first state variable is additionally allowed to have a cross-lagged effect on the second one. In this way, it can be tested whether longitudinal causal effects exist, thereby controlling for the autoregression effects. The model in Figure 1 corresponds to true model I. The most important aspect of true model I is that no measurement equation is specified, meaning that the eight state variables are supposed to be observed. It should be mentioned that the cross-lagged effects (a_{41}, a_{63}, a_{85}) in Figure 1 were specified to be zero in true model I. In this way, the differences between the situations of estimating and not estimating these effects for the quality of the other parameter estimates

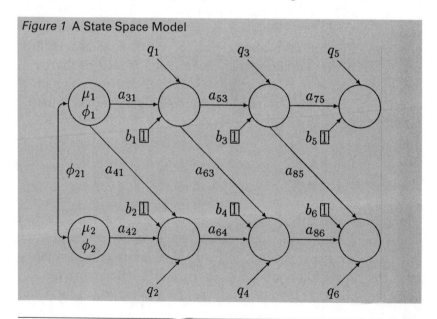

Figure 1 A State Space Model

could be evaluated. The latent intercepts b_i were specified to be zero also, but estimated in all analytic models as time-varying parameters. Time-varying means that the parameters are allowed to take on different values at different points in time. The values given to the parameters of true model I are displayed in Table 1.

True model II only differs from true model I in the addition of a measurement model. The extra time-invariant parameters, in LISREL notation λ_{ij} (factor loadings), ν_i (measurement origins of the observed variables), and θ_i (measurement error variances), are specified for each of the 16 observed variables, 2 observed variables for each of the 8 latent state variables: $i = 1, \ldots, p_0$, $j = 1, \ldots, m$. The parameter values in true model II are shown in Table 2 except for the factor loadings ($\lambda_{11}, \lambda_{32}, \lambda_{53}, \lambda_{74}, \lambda_{95}, \lambda_{11,6}, \lambda_{13,7}, \lambda_{15,8}$), which, for identification purposes, were fixed to unity. Finally, in true model III, random subject effects (traits) are additionally specified with the extra parameters $\phi_{\kappa_1}, \phi_{\kappa_2}, \phi_{1,\kappa_1}, \phi_{2,\kappa_2}$. ϕ_{κ_1} and ϕ_{κ_2} are the trait variances and ϕ_{1,κ_1} and ϕ_{2,κ_2} are their covariances with state variables 1 and 2, respectively.

In the most restrictive analytic model 1, all time-invariant parameters of the true model were constrained to be time invariant (except for the latent intercepts b_i, which were always estimated as time varying). In analytic model 2, these equality constraints were relaxed to evaluate the effect of a time-varying specification on the quality of the parameter estimates. Analytic models 3 and 4 were equal to analytic models 1 and 2 except that additionally cross-lagged effects between the state variables were estimated, as time-invariant parameters in model 3 and as time-varying ones in model 4.

The procedure of the simulation study was as follows:

1. The model implied moment matrices $\Sigma = \Lambda \Phi \Lambda' + \Theta$ were computed for the true models I, II, and III by means of the LISREL program (Jöreskog & Sörbom, 1993), fixing all parameters at the true values.

2. The LISREL program was used to compute the lower triangular matrices $\mathbf{T}$ such that $\Sigma = \mathbf{T T'}$ (see the procedure in Jöreskog & Sörbom, 1993, pp. 7–8) for the true models I, II, and III.

Table 1 Bias Values for the Simulations on the Basis of True Model I: Observed Variables

Parameter	True Value	Estimates			Standard Errors		
		$N = 50$	100	400	50	100	400
Model 1: Time-Invariant, No Cross-Lagged Effects							
a_{31}	.75	.002	−.006	−.003	.000	−.002	−.002
a_{42}	.50	−.011	−.009	.000	−.004	−.002	.001
ϕ_1	60	−3.582	−.800	−.311	−.607	1.050	.133
ϕ_2	80	2.545	.337	−.575	−.902	−1.419	.261
ϕ_{21}	.50	.225	.030	−.014	1.775	−.132	−.201
q_1	20	−.653	−.318	−.105	−.023	−.211	−.007
q_2	30	−.957	−1.002	−.088	−.072	−.069	.095
μ_1	12	.018	−.067	−.017	−.001	−.078	−.008
μ_2	10	−.216	−.216	.010	−.056	.063	.016
b_1	0	.032	−.067	−.013	−.023	.024	−.004
b_2	0	−.137	−.003	.015	.046	.029	.033
df	29						
$\chi^2 - df$	0	2.549	1.581	2.192			
$p(\chi^2)$	.10	.134	.108	.114			
$p(\chi^2)$	.05	.078	.056	.064			
Model 2: Time-Varying, No Cross-Lagged Effects							
a_{31}	.75	.012	.005	−.003	−.002	−.003	.000
a_{42}	.50	−.002	−.005	.000	−.014	−.001	.000
ϕ_1	60	−3.582	−.800	−.311	−.607	1.050	.133
ϕ_2	80	2.545	.337	−.575	−.902	−1.419	.261
ϕ_{21}	.50	.225	.030	−.012	1.775	−.132	−.201
q_1	20	−.778	−.539	−.179	.329	.183	.071
q_2	30	−2.143	−1.508	.003	.225	.151	.173
μ_1	12	.018	−.067	−.017	−.001	−.078	−.008
μ_2	10	−.216	−.216	.010	−.056	.063	.016
b_1	0	.027	−.066	−.013	−.021	.021	−.004
b_2	0	−.125	.003	.015	.020	.019	.034

Table 1 Continued

Parameter	True Value	Estimates			Standard Errors		
		$N = 50$	100	400	50	100	400
df	21						
$\chi^2 - df$	0	1.394	.685	1.557			
$p(\chi^2)$	.10	.162	.102	.150			
$p(\chi^2)$	.05	.088	.042	.102			
Model 3: Time-Invariant, Cross-Lagged Effects							
a_{31}	.75	.002	−.006	−.003	.000	−.002	−.002
a_{42}	.50	−.012	−.011	.000	−.004	−.001	.001
ϕ_1	60	−3.582	−.800	−.311	−.607	1.050	.133
ϕ_2	80	2.545	.337	−.575	−.902	−1.419	.261
ϕ_{21}	.50	.225	.030	−.105	1.775	−.132	−.201
q_1	20	−.653	−.318	−.012	−.023	−.211	−.007
q_2	30	−1.124	−1.109	−.113	−.075	−.086	.096
μ_1	12	.018	−.067	−.017	−.001	−.078	−.008
μ_2	10	−.216	−.216	.010	−.056	.063	.016
b_1	0	.032	−.067	−.013	−.023	.024	−.004
b_2	0	−.132	.001	.015	.043	.026	.034
a_{41}	0	−.004	.001	−.000	.005	−.003	.000
df	28						
$\chi^2 - df$	0	2.697	1.461	2.177			
$p(\chi^2)$	.10	.134	.102	.126			
$p(\chi^2)$	.05	.094	.042	.056			
Model 4: Time-Varying, Cross-Lagged Effects							
a_{31}	.75	.012	.005	−.003	−.002	−.003	.000
a_{42}	.50	−.002	−.006	−.001	−.014	−.001	.000
ϕ_1	60	−3.582	−.800	−.311	−.607	1.050	.133
ϕ_2	80	2.545	.337	−.575	−.902	−1.419	.261
ϕ_{21}	.50	.225	.030	−.012	1.775	−.132	−.201

Table 1 Continued

Parameter	True Value	Estimates			Standard Errors		
		$N = 50$	100	400	50	100	400
q_1	20	−.778	−.539	−.179	.329	.183	.071
q_2	30	−2.689	−1.841	−.064	.117	.197	.173
μ_1	12	.018	−.067	−.017	−.001	−.078	−.008
μ_2	10	−.216	−.216	.010	−.056	.063	.016
b_1	0	.027	−.066	−.015	−.021	.021	−.004
b_2	0	−.134	.011	.015	.016	−.001	.036
a_{41}	0	.011	.001	.002	−.001	−.006	.002
df	18						
$\chi^2 - df$	0	2.340	1.100	2.623			
$p(\chi^2)$	.10	.142	.106	.136			
$p(\chi^2)$	.05	.076	.072	.086			

3. The PRELIS program (Jöreskog & Sörbom, 1993, pp. 8–10) was used to generate five sets (sample sizes 50, 100, 400, 1,000, 5,000) of 500 sample moment matrices of 8 (true model I) or 16 (true models II and III) multinormally distributed variables on the basis of **T**. This was repeated for the true models I, II, and III.

4. Each sample moment matrix in each of the 15 sets of 500 moment matrices was analyzed by means of the four analytic models 1, 2, 3, 4, using the LISREL program. The LISREL output files of the parameter estimates, standard errors, and goodness-of-fit indices were collected for each set of 500 samples.

5. The LISREL output files were checked for Heywood cases (negative estimates of measurement error variances) and other abnormal results.

Parameter	True Value	Estimates			Standard Errors		
		$N = 50$	100	400	50	100	400
Model 1: Time-Invariant, No Cross-Lagged Effects							
a_{31}	.75	−.002	−.002	−.002	−.003	.001	.001
a_{42}	.50	.000	−.003	.000	−.002	−.002	.000
ϕ_1	60	−1.938	−1.328	−.338	−1.049	−.044	.240
ϕ_2	80	−1.185	−.440	.012	.104	−.499	.106
ϕ_{21}	.50	−.662	−.318	−.115	−.310	.232	−.149
q_1	20	−.493	−.626	−.039	−.054	−.049	−.015
q_2	30	−1.236	−.686	−.094	.250	.023	−.016
μ_1	12	.005	.031	−.020	−.026	.004	.002
μ_2	10	−.004	−.041	−.003	.068	−.039	−.025
b_1	0	−.020	.013	−.001	−.029	−.010	−.008
b_2	0	−.022	−.008	.006	−.031	−.010	.002
λ_{21}	1.2	.005	.004	.001	−.006	.001	.001
λ_{42}	.8	.009	.002	.000	.001	−.002	.000
ν_2	0	−.050	.030	−.004	.006	.006	.002
ν_4	0	−.007	.003	.008	−.001	−.008	.000
θ_1	8	−.220	.012	.062	.163	.003	.008
θ_2	10	−.197	.180	−.076	.105	.006	.006
θ_3	4	.305	−.058	.005	.024	−.034	−.016
θ_4	6	−.372	−.030	.002	.000	−.040	−.002
df	129						
$\chi^2 - df$	0	16.702	8.116	.903			
$p(\chi^2)$	.10	.387	.211	.110			
$p(\chi^2)$	.05	.268	.135	.044			
% Heywood cases	3.8	.6	.0				
Model 2: Time-Varying, No Cross-Lagged Effects							
a_{31}	.75	.016	.005	.000	−.003	.011	−.001
a_{42}	.50	.018	.011	.001	.003	−.004	−.001

Table 2 Bias Values for the Simulations on the Basis of True Model II: Measurement Errors

Table 2 Continued

Parameter	True Value	Estimates			Standard Errors		
		$N = 50$	100	400	50	100	400
ϕ_1	60	−3.584	−1.236	−.521	−1.630	.065	.160
ϕ_2	80	1.338	−1.279	−.224	−.757	−.470	.049
ϕ_{21}	.50	.462	−.711	−.058	.672	.240	−.200
q_1	20	−1.056	−.446	−.103	−.004	−.071	−.067
q_2	30	−3.281	−1.681	−.411	.029	.221	−.123
μ_1	12	.250	.102	−.021	.037	−.038	.001
μ_2	10	−.015	−.038	.006	.143	−.057	−.024
b_1	0	−.019	.016	−.003	.034	−.024	−.009
b_2	0	−.048	−.028	.005	−.065	−.007	.001
λ_{21}	1.2	.028	.011	.003	−.004	.001	−.001
λ_{42}	.8	.017	.015	.002	.023	.006	.002
ν_2	0	−.063	.025	−.007	−.013	.002	.003
ν_4	0	−.018	−.009	.008	.011	−.005	.001
θ_1	8	−.472	.228	.060	.468	.002	−.029
θ_2	10	−.385	.636	.152	.812	.018	−.099
θ_3	4	1.145	.848	.236	2.047	1.062	.175
θ_4	6	−1.208	−.719	−.201	1.365	.567	.117
df	103						
$\chi^2 - df$	0	12.794	8.078	−.083			
$p(\chi^2)$	.10	.394	.229	.081			
$p(\chi^2)$	.05	.260	.141	.041			
% Heywood cases	79.2	54.6	6.6				
Model 3: Time-Invariant, Cross-Lagged Effects							
a_{31}	.75	−.001	−.002	−.002	−.003	.001	.001
a_{42}	.50	−.002	−.005	.000	−.002	−.002	.000
ϕ_1	60	−1.959	−1.356	−.338	−1.061	−.059	.239

Table 2 Continued

		Estimates			Standard Errors		
Parameter	True Value	N = 50	100	400	50	100	400
ϕ_2	80	−1.187	−.452	.014	.078	−.496	.106
ϕ_{21}	.50	−.663	−.310	−.115	−.314	.237	−.150
q_1	20	−.486	−.624	−.039	−.053	−.049	−.016
q_2	30	−1.473	−.788	−.123	.201	−.012	−.017
μ_1	12	.003	.030	−.020	−.027	.004	.002
μ_2	10	−.004	−.040	−.002	.068	−.038	−.023
b_1	0	−.021	.013	−.001	−.029	−.010	−.009
b_2	0	−.006	−.008	.007	−.035	−.009	.002
a_{41}	0	−.002	−.002	.001	−.001	−.001	.000
λ_{21}	1.2	.005	.004	.001	−.006	.001	.001
λ_{42}	.8	.009	.002	.000	.001	−.003	.000
ν_2	0	−.051	.030	−.004	.006	.007	.002
ν_4	0	−.008	.003	.008	−.001	−.008	.000
θ_1	8	−.224	.013	.062	.162	.000	.008
θ_2	10	−.207	.180	−.077	.094	.004	.006
θ_3	4	.315	−.068	.005	.025	−.046	−.016
θ_4	6	−.376	−.023	.003	.002	−.048	−.002
df	128						
$\chi^2 - df$	0	16.574	8.108	.897			
$p(\chi^2)$	.10	.388	.215	.118			
$p(\chi^2)$	.05	.267	.133	.046			
% Heywood cases	4.0	.4	.0				
Model 4: Time-Varying, Cross-Lagged Effects							
a_{31}	.75	.024	.005	.000	−.001	.010	−.000
a_{42}	.50	.020	.009	.001	−.003	−.006	−.001
ϕ_1	60	−3.719	−1.130	−.489	−2.101	.148	.155
ϕ_2	80	−.108	−1.513	−.267	−.536	−.652	.040

Table 2 Continued

Parameter	True Value	Estimates			Standard Errors		
	$N = 50$	100	400	50	100	400
ϕ_{21}	.50	.131	−.732	−.049	−.926	.210	−.197
q_1	20	−.663	−.430	−.098	.387	.038	−.069
q_2	30	−3.226	−1.485	−.506	.759	.225	−.138
μ_1	12	.268	.107	−.023	.078	−.019	.001
μ_2	10	−.107	.013	.006	.236	−.019	−.026
b_1	0	−.047	.021	−.001	.017	−.016	−.007
b_2	0	−.053	−.019	.005	−.068	.005	.000
a_{41}	0	.003	−.006	−.001	.006	−.008	.000
λ_{21}	1.2	.024	.010	.003	−.004	.000	−.001
λ_{42}	.8	.017	.014	.003	.018	.006	.002
ν_2	0	−.058	.024	−.006	.019	.002	.003
ν_4	0	−.006	−.008	.008	−.007	−.012	−.001
θ_1	8	−.643	.212	.053	.453	−.059	−.030
θ_2	10	.232	.619	.163	.822	.004	−.099
θ_3	4	1.518	.809	.251	2.071	1.082	.178
θ_4	6	−1.373	−.728	−.208	1.397	.621	.116
df	100						
$\chi^2 - df$	0	14.803	7.236	−.168			
$p(\chi^2)$	.10	.423	.229	.076			
$p(\chi^2)$	.05	.299	.126	.045			
% Heywood cases	80.6	57.2	7.4				

Results of the Simulation Study

The quality of the model estimates in each of the 15 series of 500 samples was assessed by the bias of the parameter estimates (mean parameter estimate in the series minus true parameter value) and of the standard errors (mean standard error in the series minus standard deviation of parameter estimates in the series). The results for true models I and II are shown in Tables 1 and 2. No table is given for true model III, the results of which are only summarized in the text. If a set of time-invariant parameters in a true model is estimated as time varying in the analytic model (analytic models 2 and 4), only the first parameter in the set is displayed. Also the bias of the model fit χ^2 value (mean χ^2 value minus degrees of freedom of the model df) and correctness of the p value (empirical error rates for nominal $\alpha = .10$ and $\alpha = .05$) are evaluated. $\chi^2 - df$ is an estimate of the noncentrality parameter but, as all analytic models cover the true parameter values, its mean values should invariably be zero. For true model II in Table 2, the percentages of Heywood cases (one or more negative measurement error variance estimates in the analysis) are given. Heywood cases are present, the information in the table is based on the remaining cases analyses.

Results for the Simulation on the Basis of True Model I: Observed State Variables (See Table 1)

The parameter estimates in the four analytic models showed consistency in the sense of the biases of estimates and standard errors becoming extremely small with increasing sample sizes of $N = 50, 100, 400, 1,000,$ and $5,000$ except for ϕ_{21}. The estimate bias of ϕ_{21} in all four models reached the same value 0.152 with $N = 5,000$, which is quite considerable in view of this parameter's true value of 0.500. Apparently, in spite of the identification of the analytic models in Table 1, there is something difficult in estimating this relatively small initial covariance between the two state variables with the relatively large initial variances of 60 and 80, respectively. Remarkably, in the smaller sample sizes, this isolated consistency problem with ϕ_{21} tends to show up more clearly in the standard errors than in the estimates.

Table 1 al͞ hows that the biases increase with decreasing sample sizes; however, generally the biases are still quite acceptable for the sample size of $N = 100$—and even for the sample size of $N = 50$, especially if viewed in relation to the true parameter values. Especially good is the performance with regard to the autoregression parameters (a_{31}, a_{42}, etc.). Also, there is no clear tendency for the biases of the standard errors to have the same sign and, therefore, for t testing of the parameters to be generally conservative or liberal. Comparing the results across the analytic models, it is interesting and reassuring that the biases of the parameters not involved in the model extension do not change or only little in the more extended model. So, it is simply not true, in general, that the more complex analytic model leads necessarily to more bias. For as far as bias is involved, there does not seem to be reason to refrain from adding extra parameters for estimation. An important result is that the biases in the cross-lagged effects (a_{41}, a_{63}, a_{85}) in models 3 and 4 are quite small, even for the small sample sizes. Changing from the time-invariant to the time-varying model (from model 2 to model 4), the quality of the estimates generally deteriorates as well as the standard errors involved (a_{ij}, q_i); however, the effect is quite small in most cases. Furthermore, χ^2 has an acceptable distribution for $N = 100$, which in this simulation happens to be even better than for $N = 400$, but it is not acceptable for $N = 50$. The reason for the relatively bad χ^2 performance with $N = 400$ is not clear, especially as it is not replicated in Table 2. Generally, there is a clear tendency for the χ^2 value to be too large (only two very small negative biases occurred with values of -0.120 and -0.084, respectively, in analytic models 1 and 3 for $N = 1,000$). In general, formal χ^2 testing rejects the model too often with almost all sample sizes.

Results for the Simulation on the Basis of True Model II: Measurement Errors (See Table 2)

Apart from the consistency problem with ϕ_{21}, which affects all sample sizes, the small sample sizes of $N = 50$ and 100 are particularly poor in estimating time-varying measurement error variances θ_i in analytic models 2 and 4. These lead to huge numbers of Heywood cases and, although the remaining cases show good estimates of the λ_{ij} and ν_i, autoregressive and cross-lagged parameters, other parameter estimates suffer. The χ^2 values are particularly bad. We conclude that sample sizes of $N = 400$ and higher give acceptable results both in parameter estimation and χ^2 testing for all four analytic models. We further conclude that the sample size of $N = 100$ and to a lesser degree that of $N = 50$ is acceptable in parameter estimation when the time-invariant measurement error variances can be estimated time invariant as in models 1 and 3. Finally, we conclude that the sample size of $N = 50$ is unacceptable for all four models in χ^2 testing. Attention should be drawn to the particularly small biases for the autoregression and cross-lagged effects as well as for the factor loadings in Table 2 for each sample size.

Results for the Simulation on the Basis of True Model III: Measurement Errors and Traits (Random Subject Effects)

The introduction of the four new trait parameters (trait variances ϕ_{κ_1}, ϕ_{κ_2}, and trait-state covariances ϕ_{1,κ_1}, ϕ_{2,κ_2}) in true model III has a predictable biasing effect on the estimates of all parameters. The same pattern and problems occur as in Table 2 but more markedly. The trait parameters themselves seem to be particularly difficult to be estimated unbiasedly. In the case of time-varying parameters in models 2 and 4, even the sample size of $N = 400$ seems to be not large enough. We conclude that in the case of a model with both measurement errors and traits the small sample sizes of $N = 50$ and 100 should be avoided and that a sample of $N = 400$ should be used only with time-invariant parameters. One positive aspect to be mentioned as regards true model III is that the consistency problem of parameter ϕ_{21} is much less serious than under true models I and II. The $N = 5,000$ estimate bias, which under true model I was 0.152, shrinks to a value between -0.056 and -0.060 under model III.

Conclusion and Discussion

Previously, we observed that the question of how small the sample size may be depends on the type of model used and the purpose of the SEM analysis. On the basis of the simulation results, the question with regard to SEM state space modeling can be answered as follows: For unbiasedly estimating trait variances and trait covariances in a state-trait model, a sample size of at least $N = 400$ is needed. Clearly, the important benefits of the specification of random subject effects, mentioned in the literature, have to be paid for by a large sample size; however, $N = 100$ and even $N = 50$ is acceptable for parameter estimation in models without traits and measurement errors. The same is true in models that include measurement errors but no traits, in which case the parameters are assumed to be time invariant. The latter assumption becomes less important if interest is only focused on autoregression effects, cross-lagged effects, or factor loadings. We found a positive bias in the χ^2 value, even in the larger sample sizes of $N > 400$. χ^2 testing turns out to be particularly vulnerable to bias and should therefore, in general, not be done below a sample size of $N = 400$. We found an exception for $N = 100$ in the observed variables model (no measurement errors and no traits). As regards the analytic models, differences between them were rather small under true model I (observed variables). For true models II (measurement errors) and III (traits), clear differences were found between the time-varying models (analytic models 2 and 4) and time-invariant models (models 1 and 3). The larger biases within the time-varying models were concentrated in the variance and covariance parameters.

As the main emphasis of the simulation study was on the effect of decreasing sample size on bias, we employed the usual assumptions of normality and correctly specified models (zero noncentrality parameter). These assumptions could be dropped, however, in future SEM state space modeling simulation studies. Problems with formal χ^2 testing have been pointed out by many authors also in large samples and have led to alternative ways of using the χ^2 value as, for example, in many model fit measures; these should also be evaluated in small samples. It should further be stressed that the absence of bias for a small sample size does not mean that the sample is large enough to obtain a significant result, as, for example, in t testing. So, a large sample may be necessary for reasons other than bias. Finally, attention should be drawn to the usefulness of a simulation study such as the one presented here in detecting inconsistently estimated parameters that otherwise would remain unnoticed.

References

Baltagi, B. H. (1995). *Econometric analysis of panel data*. Chichester, England: Wiley.

Bryk, A. S., & Raudenbush, S. W. (1987). Application of hierarchical linear models to assessing change. *Psychological Bulletin, 101*, 147–158.

Caines, P. E. (1988). *Linear stochastic systems*. New York: Wiley.

Deistler, M. (1985). General structure and parametrization of ARMA and state-space systems and its relation to statistical problems. In E. J. Hannan, P. R. Krishnaiah, & M. M. Rao (Eds.), *Handbook of statistics: Vol. 5. Time series in the time domain* (pp. 257–277). Amsterdam: North-Holland.

Jazwinski, A. H. (1970). *Stochastic processes and filtering theory*. New York: Academic Press.

Jöreskog, K. G. (1973). A general method for estimating a structural equation system. In A. S. Goldberger & O. D. Duncan (Eds.), *Structural equation models in the social sciences* (pp. 85–112). New York: Seminar.

Jöreskog, K. G., & Sörbom, D. (1989). *LISREL 7: User's reference guide*. Mooresville, IN: Scientific Software.

Jöreskog, K. G., & Sörbom, D. (1993). *New features in LISREL*. Chicago: Scientific Software.

Lewis, F. L. (1986). *Optimal estimation: With an introduction to stochastic control theory*. New York: Wiley.

Ljung, L. (1985). Estimation of parameters in dynamical systems. In E. J. Hannan, P. R. Krishnaiah, & M. M. Rao (Eds.), *Handbook of statistics: Vol. 5. Time series in the time domain* (pp. 189–211). Amsterdam: North-Holland.

Oud, J. H. L., & Jansen, R. A. R. G. (1996). Nonstationary longitudinal LISREL model estimation from incomplete panel data using EM and the Kalman smoother. In U. Engel & J. Reinecke (Eds.), *Analysis of change: Advanced techniques in panel data analysis* (pp. 135–159). New York: de Gruyter.

Oud, J. H. L., van den Bercken, J. H. L., & Essers, R. J. (1990). Longitudinal factor scores estimation using the Kalman filter. *Applied Psychological Measurement, 14*, 395–418.

Oud, J. H. L., van Leeuwe, J. F. J., & Jansen, R. A. R. G. (1993). Kalman filtering in discrete and continuous time based on longitudinal LISREL models. In J. H. L. Oud & A. W. van Blokland-Vogelesang (Eds.), *Advances in longitudinal and multivariate analysis in the behavioral sciences* (pp. 3–26). Nijmegen, The Netherlands: ITS.

Rauch, H. E., Tung, F., & Striebel, C. T. (1965). Maximum likelihood estimates of linear dynamic systems. *AIAA Journal, 3,* 1445–1450.

Willett, J. B., & Sayer, A. G. (1994). Using covariance structure analysis to detect correlates and predictors of individual change over time. *Psychological Bulletin, 116,* 363–381.

12

Structural Equation Modeling Analysis With Small Samples Using Partial Least Squares

Wynne W. Chin & Peter R. Newsted

STRUCTURAL EQUATION MODELING (SEM) techniques as represented by software such as LISREL, EQS, AMOS, SEPath, CALIS, and RAMONA have become very popular among social scientists in the past decade. Viewed as a coupling of two traditions: an econometric perspective focusing on prediction and a psychometric emphasis that models concepts as latent (unobserved) variables that are indirectly inferred from multiple observed measures (alternately termed as indicators or manifest variables), SEM essentially offers social scientists the ability to perform path-analytic modeling with latent variables. This approach, in turn, has led some to describe it as an example of "a second generation of multivariate analysis" (Fornell, 1987).

The primary advantage that SEM-based procedures have over first-generation techniques such as principal components analysis, factor analysis, discriminant analysis, or multiple regression is the greater flexibility that a researcher has for the interplay of theory and data. Overall, SEM-based approaches provide researchers with the flexibility to perform the following:

- Model relationships among multiple predictor and criterion variables.
- Construct unobservable latent variables.
- Model errors in measurements for observed variables.
- Statistically test a priori substantive/theoretical and measurement assumptions against empirical data (i.e., confirmatory analysis).

Essentially, second-generation multivariate techniques such as SEM involve generalizations and extensions of first-generation procedures. Applying certain constraints or assumptions on one or more particular second-generation techniques would result in a first-generation procedure with correspondingly less flexibility in modeling theory with data.

Yet, a number of factors, including sample size, tend to preclude the use of the predominate technique of covariance-based SEM. The objective of this chapter is to elaborate on a lesser known approach for SEM analysis called partial least squares (PLS). Rather than view PLS as a competing method, it will be shown as complementary in terms of research objectives, data conditions, and modeling. In addition to considering sample size, this chapter begins by outlining the factors that should be considered in choosing one approach over the other. The specific algorithm is then covered in a nontechnical fashion. Finally, the results of a Monte Carlo simulation are presented to see how PLS performs under varying levels of sample size and model complexity with the extreme case being 21 latent variables, 672 indicators, and a sample size of 20.

Contrasting Partial Least Squares and Covariance-Based Structural Equation Modeling

The *covariance-based approach* for SEM dates back to the original development by Jöreskog (1973), Keesling (1972), and Wiley

(1973). Its widespread popularity is due in a large part to the availability of the LISREL III program developed by Jöreskog and Sörbom in the mid-1970s and subsequent updates (see Preface, Jöreskog and Sörbom, 1989). Typically, using a maximum-likelihood (ML) function, covariance-based SEM attempts to minimize the difference between the sample covariances and those predicted by the theoretical model (i.e., $\Sigma - \Sigma(\Theta)$). Therefore, the parameter estimation process attempts to reproduce the covariance matrix of the observed measures.

Along with the benefits discussed earlier, the use of covariance-based SEM (hereafter CBSEM) involves constraints in the form of parametric assumptions, sample size, model complexity, identification, and factor indeterminacy. In order to use this approach, it is assumed that the observed variables follow a specific multivariate distribution (normality in the case of the ML function) and that observations are independent of one another. Possibly more critical is the sample size requirement, which is often beyond the range of researchers. Small samples that are not "asymptotic" in characteristics can lead to poor parameter estimates and model test statistics (Chou & Bentler, 1995; Hu & Bentler, 1995). In fact, inadmissible solutions in the form of negative variances and out-of-range covariances often occur as sample size decreases (e.g., Anderson & Gerbing, 1984; Boomsma, 1983; Dillon, Kumar, & Mulani, 1987; Gerbing & Anderson, 1987; MacCallum, 1986; van Driel, 1978). When the latent variates are dependent, fit indices tend to overreject models at sample sizes of 250 or less (Hu & Bentler, 1995, p. 95).

Equally critical with small sample sizes is the potential for Type II error, whereby a poor model can still falsely achieve adequate model fit. According to MacCallum, Browne, and Sugawara (1996), sample sizes less than 200 are inadequate to achieve the standard .80 level for a test of close fit when models have degrees of freedom at 55 or lower. Using their alternative test of "not close fit," models at samples sizes of 200 need to be even more restrictive (i.e., degrees of freedom greater than 80). Furthermore, under exploratory conditions with small-to-moderate sample sizes (i.e., 100 to 400), MacCallum (1986) demonstrated that final models derived via post hoc modifications should not be trusted.

Complex models also can be problematic relative to fit indices and computation. As the degrees of freedom increase with increasing number of indicators and latent variables, various model fit indices tend to be positively biased relative to simpler models (Mulaik et al., 1989). Pragmatically, current software packages begin to slow down or possibly fail to run as the number of indicators approaches 50 or 100 (approximately 20 to 30 in the case of distribution-free estimation).

Covariance-based SEM analysis typically requires indicators in a *reflective* mode. Under this condition, indicators are viewed as being influenced or affected by the underlying latent variable. Yet, an alternative conceptualization has the indicators in a *formative* mode. In this situation, indicators are viewed as causing rather than being caused by the latent variable. According to Bollen and Lennox (1991), such formative indicators "do not conform to the classical test theory or factor analysis models that treat indicators as effects of a construct" (p. 305). As an example, Cohen, Cohen, Teresi, Marchi, and Velez (1990) used the latent variable of socioeconomic status (SES) with education, occupational prestige, and income as indicators. In this instance, the indicators determine an individual's SES. If one of the indicators increases, the other ones need not do so. Yet, an increase in any one indicator (e.g., income) will lead to an increase in the latent variable SES. Another example of formative indicators would be job loss, divorce, recent accident, and death in the family for the latent variable life stress. Although a CBSEM analysis generally requires all latent variables to have reflective indicators, researchers may unknowingly incorporate formative ones. As Cohen et al. (1990, Table 1, p. 186) showed in a survey of 15 articles that performed CBSEM analysis, a sizable number of latent variables were indeed inappropriately modeled, treating formative indicators as reflective. Finally, as MacCallum and Browne (1993) demonstrated, any attempts to model formative indicators in a CBSEM analysis can lead to identification problems, implied covariances of zero among some indicators, and/or the existence of equivalent models. Although these problems can be managed, MacCallum and Browne (1993) argue that this would involve "altering the original model in terms of its substantive meaning or parsimony, or both" (p. 540).

There is also an inherent indeterminacy in the CBSEM procedure. In other words, case values for the latent variables cannot be obtained in the process. Thus, it is not possible to estimate scores for the underlying latent variables in order to predict the observed indicators. In fact, an infinite set of possible scores can be created that are not only consistent with the parameter estimates, but need not be correlated. This may or may not be viewed as problematic depending on the objectives (see Maraun, 1996, and the two rounds of commentary). The CBSEM approach is ideal if the goal is to obtain population parameter estimates for explaining covariances with the assumption that the underlying model is correct. However, this procedure was not developed for predictive purposes where the researcher desires parameter estimates (i.e., weights for each individual indicator) in order to create latent variable scores that can be used to predict its own indicators or other latent variables. As will be explained in more detail later, this is the primary goal of partial least squares: predicting the variances of latent and manifest variables.

Identification problems pertaining to a unique set of estimates can also occur either algebraically or empirically under conditions where the number of indicators per construct is low, the correlation among factors is zero, or both (Rindskopf, 1984). Thus, it is generally necessary to have three or more indicators per latent variable in order to avoid identification problems in CBSEM analysis.

A final issue to consider when using a CBSEM procedure is the role theory plays in the analyses of the data. At this point, very little has been done to examine the influence of model misspecification on parameter estimates. Being a full information approach, the parameter estimates in one part of a model (e.g., loadings for one latent variable) may be unduly influenced by misspecifications in some other part of the model (e.g., missing structural paths or poor indicators for another construct). This is less of an issue for a large percentage of CBSEM studies, which follow a confirmatory mode whereby the analyses are done under strong theory and use measures that were developed from prior studies—typically via a series of exploratory factor analyses. When the theory is still relatively tentative or the measures for each latent variable are new, however, greater emphasis may need to be placed on the data relative to the theory.

In the case of CBSEM, it has been argued that theory is given more influence in estimating parameters as opposed to the partial least squares approach to SEM analysis. For example, if a correlated two-factor model was specified, the estimated correlation between the two abstract latent variables tends to go up as the correlations among observed indicators go down. Given a specific theoretical model, the only logical deduction for situations with low observed correlations is that there is a large amount of random error/noise affecting each indicator. According to Fornell (1989),

> ... consistent with the specification of reflective indicators, the abstract model specification plays a large role in determining the results; almost to the point that it "overrides" the data .... Thus, it is here that the researcher must make a decision about the relative weight that should be given to data vs. theory .... Fortunately, alternatives to covariance structure analysis are available when the analyst is unwilling to depart too far from the data and wants to obtain a different balance between theory and observation. One such alternative is partial least squares (PLS) developed by Herman Wold. (pp. 165–166)

As an alternative to covariance-based SEM analysis, the variance-based approach of PLS shifts the orientation from causal model/theory testing to component-based predictive modeling. Rather than focusing on building models that are meant to explain the covariances of all the observed indicators, the objective of PLS is prediction. As such, latent variables are defined as the sum of their respective indicators. The PLS algorithm attempts to obtain the best weight estimates for each block of indicators corresponding to each latent variable. The resulting component score for each latent variable based on the estimated indicator weights maximizes variance explained for dependent variables (i.e., latent, observed, or both).

Partial least squares can be a powerful method of analysis because of the minimal demands on measurement scales (i.e., categorical to ratio level indicators can be used in the same model), sample size, and residual distributions (Wold, 1985). Although PLS can be used for theory confirmation, it can also be used to suggest where relationships might or might not exist and to suggest propositions for later testing. Being closer to the data and a limited estimation procedure, misspecifications in one part of a model have less influence on the parameter estimates in other parts of the model. Compared to the better known CBSEM, the component-based PLS avoids two serious problems: inadmissible solutions and factor indeterminacy (Fornell & Bookstein, 1982). Because the iterative algorithm performed in a PLS analysis generally consists of a series of ordinary least squares analyses, identification is not a problem for recursive models, nor does it presume any distributional form for measured variables. Furthermore, the computational efficiency of the algorithm lends itself to estimating large complex models on the order of hundreds of latent variables and thousands of indicators. The utility of the PLS method has been documented elsewhere (Falk & Miller, 1992, p. xi) as possibly more appropriate for a large percentage of the studies and data sets typically used among researchers.

In summary, if the hypothesized structural and measurement model is correct in the sense of explaining the covariation of all the indicators and the data/sample size conditions are met, the covariance-based procedure provides optimal estimates of the model parameters. It is ideal for model confirmation and estimation of the "true" underlying population parameters. However, depending on the researcher's objectives and epistemic view of data to theory, properties of the data at hand, or level of theoretical knowledge and measurement development, the PLS approach can be argued to be more suitable. Table 1 provides a summary of the key differences between PLS and CBSEM.

Table 1 Comparison of Partial Least Squares and Covariance-Based Structural Equation Modeling

Criterion	PLS	CBSEM
Objective:	Prediction oriented	Parameter oriented
Approach:	Variance based	Covariance based
Assumptions:	Predictor specification (nonparametric)	Typically multivariate normal distribution and independent observations (parametric)
Parameter estimates:	Consistent as indicators and sample size increase (i.e., consistency at large)	Consistent
Latent variable scores:	Explicitly estimated	Indeterminate
Epistemic relationship between a latent variable and its measures:	Can be modeled in either formative or reflective mode	Typically only with reflective indicators
Implications:	Optimal for prediction accuracy	Optimal for parameter accuracy
Model complexity:	Large complexity (e.g., 100 constructs and 1,000 indicators)	Small to moderate complexity (e.g., less than 100 indicators)
Sample size:	Power analysis based on the portion of the model with the largest number of predictors. Minimal recommendations range from 30 to 100 cases.	Ideally based on power analysis of specific model—minimal recommendations range from 200 to 800.

The Standard Partial Least Squares Algorithm

The basic PLS design was completed in 1977 (see Wold, 1982, p. 35) and has subsequently been extended in various ways. Lohmöller (1984, 1989) covered various inner weighting schemes. Wold (1982) discussed nonlinearities among latent variables, whereas Hui (1978, 1982) used a fixed-point PLS method to model nonrecursive (i.e., interdependent) relationships. In accord with this chapter's objective of providing a simple introduction to the PLS method, the following discussion is restricted to the basic design involving recursive models.

As discussed earlier, the objective of PLS is to help the researcher obtain determinate values of latent variables for prediction. The formal model (to be described later) explicitly defines latent variables as linear aggregates of their observed indicators. The weight estimates to create the latent variable component scores are obtained based on how the inner (i.e., structural) and outer (i.e., measurement) models are specified. As a result, the residual variances of dependent variables (both latent and observed variables) are minimized.

The parameter estimates obtained via PLS can be viewed as falling into three categories. The first category is the weight estimates, which are used to create the latent variable scores. The second reflects the path estimates connecting latent variables and between latent variables and their respective block of indicators (i.e., loadings). The third category pertains to the means and location parameters (i.e., regression constants) for indicators and latent variables. In order to come up with these three sets of parameter estimates, the PLS algorithm follows a three-stage process with each stage used to obtain each set of estimates, respectively. Therefore, the first stage results in obtaining the weight estimates. The second stage provides estimates for the inner model (i.e., structural relations among latent variables) and outer model (i.e., reflective or formative measurement paths). And the third stage yields the means and location estimates. In the first two stages, the indicators and latent variables are treated as deviations from their means. In the third stage, should the researcher wish to obtain estimates based on the original data metrics, the weight and path estimates from the previous two stages are used for calculating the means and location parameters.

Stage 1 represents the heart of the PLS algorithm. It consists of an iterative procedure that almost always converges to a stable set of weight estimates. Essentially, component score estimates for each latent variable are obtained in two ways. The outside approximation represents a weighted aggregate of its own indicators. The inside approximation refers to a weighted aggregate of other component scores that are related to it in the theoretical model. During each iteration, the inner model estimates are used to obtain the outside approximation weights, whereas the outer model estimates are used to obtain the inside approximation weights. The procedure stops when the percentage change of each outside approximation weight relative to the previous round is less than 0.001. Thus, both the theoretical and the measurement portions of the model contribute in the estimation process. This is contrasted to a two-step approach where the measurement model is derived first before it is used at the structural level (see Fornell & Yi, 1992, for further discussion relating the one- and two-step approach toward modeling).

Multiblock Example

To illustrate the stage 1 process PLS goes through, let's look at the model provided in Figure 1. As depicted, the measures are partitioned into four blocks (two exogenous ξs and two endogenous ηs). As a starting point, the algorithm does an initial outside approximation estimation of the latent variables (LVs) by summing the indicators in each block with equal weights. The weights, in each iteration, are scaled to obtain unit variance for the latent variable scores over the N cases in the sample. Using the estimated scores for each LV as given, an inside approximation estimate of the LVs is performed.

There have been three primary "inside approximation" weighting schemes developed thus far for combining "neighboring" LVs to obtain an estimate for a specific LV: centroid, factor, and path

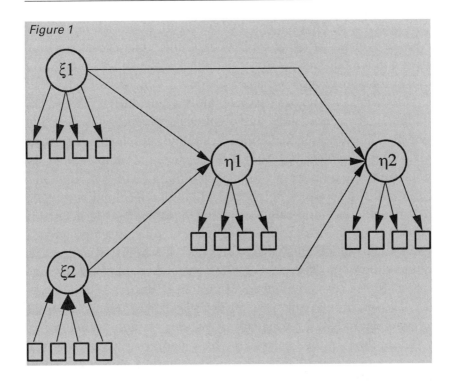

Figure 1

weighting. Although each weighting scheme follows a particular logic, it has been noted that the choice tends to have little influence on the results: .005 or less for structural paths and .05 or less for measurement paths (Noonan & Wold, 1982).

The centroid weighting scheme was the original procedure used by Wold. It only considers the sign of the correlations between the LV and the neighboring LVs. The strength of the correlations and the direction of the structural model are not taken into account. It is computationally simple because the resulting estimates are obtained by adding up all connected LVs with either weights of $+1$ or -1 depending on the sign of their correlation, which leads each LV to become similar to the centroid factor (Lohmöller, 1989). Thus, if a structurally linked LV is correlated $-.30$, the weight assigned to it would be -1. This approach is considered advantageous (relative to the path weighting scheme) when the LV correlation matrix is singular because the weights are based only on the bivariate correlations among component scores. A disadvantage arises when an LV correlation is close to zero and thus may oscillate during iterations from a small positive to a small negative and back. Under this situation, these values are magnified by the corresponding $+1$ and -1 weights.

The factor weighting scheme, therefore, uses the correlation coefficients between the focal LV and its neighboring LVs as the weights. The LV becomes the "principal component" of its neighboring LVs. According to Lohmöller (1989), the factor weighting scheme maximizes the variance of the principal component of the LVs when the number of LVs goes to infinity.

Finally, the path weighting scheme differentially weights neighboring LVs depending on whether they are antecedents or consequents of the focal LV. This scheme, thus, attempts to produce a component that ideally can both be predicted and at the same time be a good predictor for subsequent dependent variables. To do this, all independent variables influencing the target LV are weighted by the multiple-regression coefficients, whereas all dependent LVs are weighted by the correlation coefficients. In a sense, the focal LV becomes the best mediating LV between the source and target LVs. As the only procedure among the three that takes into account the directionality of the structural model, the path weighting scheme is often used for models with hypothesized causal relations. If, on the other hand, no propositions are made regarding the associations among the LVs, the factor weighting scheme would be the logical choice.

If a factor weighting scheme were used in this example, the inside approximation estimate for ξ_1 would be the sum of the outside approximation estimates for η_1 and η_2 weighted by their respective correlation coefficients with ξ_1. ξ_2 is not included in the estimate because there is no link between it and ξ_1. η_1, on the other hand, is a weighted estimate of the other three LVs because it has structural paths with all three.

Under a path weighting scheme, there are three different inside approximation situations. As both ξ_1 and ξ_2 are exogenous constructs, they are weighted by correlation coefficients. So, for example, the estimate for ξ_1 would follow the same procedure as under the factor weighting scheme. In the case of η_2, being a pure endogenous (dependent) variable, a multiple regression is performed with the outside approximation estimates for $\xi_1, \xi_2,$

and η_1 on the outside approximation estimate of η_2. The multiple-regression coefficients are then used as the weights for combining the outside approximation estimates of ξ_1, ξ_2, and η_1 to obtain the inside approximation estimate for η_2. Finally, the estimate for η_1 uses both multiple-regression coefficients and correlation coefficients as weights. η_1 is regressed on ξ_1 and ξ_2 to obtain weights for ξ_1 and ξ_2 and the simple correlation between η_1 on η_2 is taken for the weight of η_2.

Given the LV estimates from the inside approximation, a new set of weights from a new round of outside approximations can be obtained. Taking the inside approximation scores as fixed, either simple or multiple regression is performed depending on whether the block of indicators is in a reflective mode (termed mode A) or a formative mode (termed mode B) mode. Because ξ_1, η_2, and η_1 are modeled as mode A with arrows directed toward the indicators, each indicator in each block would be individually regressed on its respective LV estimate (i.e., inside approximation score). In the case of ξ_2, being in mode B with arrows directed toward the LV, a multiple regression of the estimate of ξ_2 on its indicators is performed. The simple- or multiple-regressions coefficients are then used as new weights for an outside approximation of each LV. Figure 2 depicts the logical flow of this iterative process.

Once the latent variable scores from stage 1 are estimated, the path relations are immediately estimated by ordinary least squares regression in stage 2. Each dependent variable in the model (either endogenous LVs or indicators in a reflective mode) is regressed on its respective independent variables (i.e., other LVs or indicators in a formative mode). When the final paths are estimated in stage 2 and it makes substantive sense (e.g., differences in the means, scale, and variances are meaningful), the means and location parameters for the indicators and LVs are estimated in stage 3. To do this, the means for each indicator are first calculated based on the original data. Then, using the weights derived in stage 1, the means for each LV are calculated. Given means for the LVs and path estimates from stage 2, the location parameter for each dependent LV is simply calculated as the difference between the just obtained mean and the systematic part accounted for by the independent LVs that influence it.

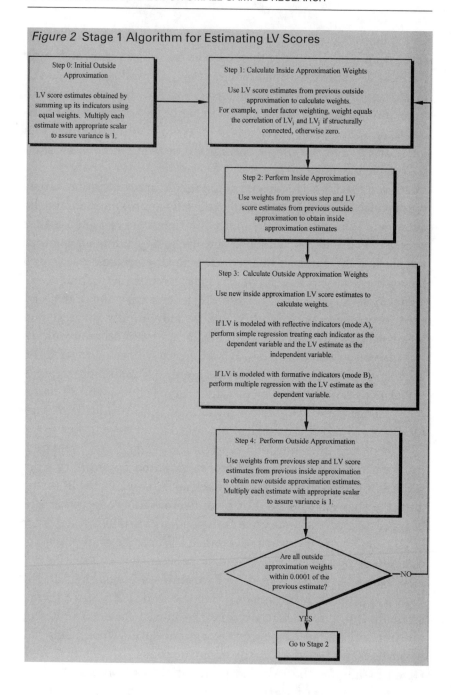

Figure 2 Stage 1 Algorithm for Estimating LV Scores

Likewise, the location parameter for a reflective indicator is simply the difference between its mean and the estimate based on its underlying LV and path loading.

Formal Specification of the Partial Least Squares Model

Having covered the PLS estimation procedure, the formal model specification that guides the process is now presented. As noted, the latent variable path models in PLS consist of three sets of relations: (1) the inner model, which specifies the relationships between LVs; (2) the outer model, which specifies the relationships between LVs and their associated observed or manifest variables (MVs); and (3) the weight relations upon which case values for the LVs can be estimated. Without loss of generality, it can be assumed that LVs and MVs are scaled to zero means and unit variances so that location parameters (i.e., constant parameter terms) can be eliminated in the following equations.

Inner Model

The inner model (also referred to as the inner relations, structural model, substantive theory) depicts the relationship among latent variables based on substantive theory:

$$\eta = \beta_0 + \beta\eta + \Gamma\xi + \zeta, \tag{1}$$

where η represents the vector of endogenous (i.e., dependent) latent variables, ξ is a vector of the exogenous latent variables, and ζ is the vector of residual variables (i.e., unexplained variance).

Because the basic PLS design assumes recursive relations (i.e., one-way arrows) among LVs, each dependent latent variable η_j in this often termed "causal chain system" of LVs can be specified as follows:

$$\eta_j = \sum_i \beta_{ji}\eta_i + \sum_h \gamma_{jh}\xi_h + \zeta_j, \tag{2}$$

where β_{ji} and γ_{jh} are the path coefficients linking the predictor endogenous and exogenous latent variables ξ and η over the range specified by the indices i and h, and ζ_j is the inner residual variable.

The inner model (Equation 1) is subject to predictor specification (Wold, 1988):

$$E(\eta_j \mid \forall \eta_i, \xi_h) = \sum_i \beta_{ji}\eta_i + \sum_h \gamma_{jh}\xi_h.$$

Thus, it is assumed that each LV is a linear function of its predictors and that there are no linear relationship between the predictors and the residual,

$$E(\zeta_j \mid \forall \eta_i, \xi_h) = 0 \qquad \text{and} \qquad \text{Cov}(\zeta_j, \eta_i) = \text{Cov}(\zeta_j, \xi_h) = 0$$

for the indices i and h ranging over all predictors.

The structural form of the inner model can be also be written in reduced form by subtracting $\beta\eta$ from both sides of Equation 1 and premultiplying by $(I - \beta)^{-1}$ yielding:

$$\begin{aligned}
\eta &= (I - \beta)^{-1}\Gamma\xi + (I - \beta)^{-1}\zeta \\
&= \beta^*\xi + \zeta^*,
\end{aligned}$$

where β^* represents the total effect of the exogenous latent variable ξ.

To make predictor specification possible for both the structural and the reduced forms, the assumption is made that $E(\zeta_j^* \mid \forall \xi_h) = 0$ for all j endogenous LVs as they relate to the exogenous LVs impacting in the first j relations given in the structural form given in Equation 2.

Outer Model

The outer model (also referred to as outer relations or measurement model) defines how each block of indicators relates to its latent variable. The MVs are partitioned into non-overlapping blocks. For those blocks with reflective indicators, the relationships can be defined as

$$x = \Lambda_x \xi + \varepsilon_x,$$
$$y = \Lambda_y \eta + \varepsilon_y,$$

where x and y are the MVs for the exogenous and endogenous LVs ξ and η, respectively. Λ_x and Λ_y are the loadings matrices representing simple regression coefficients connecting the LV and their measures. The residuals for the measures ε_x and ε_y, in turn, can be interpreted as measurement errors or noise.

Predictor specification, as in the case for the inner model, is assumed to hold for the outer model in reflective mode as follows:

$$E[x \mid \xi] = \Lambda_x \xi,$$
$$E[y \mid \eta] = \Lambda_y \eta. \tag{3}$$

For those blocks in a formative mode, the relationship is defined as:

$$\xi = \Pi_\xi x + \delta_\xi,$$
$$\eta = \Pi_\eta y + \delta_\eta,$$

where ξ, η, x, and y are the same as those used in Equation 3. Π_x and Π_y are the multiple-regression coefficients for the LV on its block of indicators and δ_x and δ_y are the corresponding residuals from the regressions. Predictor specification is also in effect as

$$E[\xi \mid x] = \Pi_\xi x,$$
$$E[\eta \mid y] = \Pi_\eta y.$$

As opposed to the weight relations to be discussed next, the formative specification for outer relations refer to the MV and the true LV. This, in turn, provides the basis for the manner in which the weights are determined within the PLS estimation algorithm estimating the LV.

Weight Relations

Although the inner and outer models provide the specifications that are followed in the PLS estimation algorithm, the weight relations need to be defined for completeness. The case value for each LV is estimate in PLS as follows:

$$\hat{\xi}_h = \sum_{kh} w_{kh} x_{kh},$$

$$\hat{\eta}_i = \sum_{ki} w_{ki} y_{ki},$$

where w_{kh} and w_{ki} are the k weights used to form the LV estimates of ξ_h and η_i.

Thus, the LV estimates are linear aggregates of their observed indicators whose weights are obtained via the PLS estimation procedure as specified by the inner and outer models where η is a vector of the endogenous (i.e., dependent) latent variables, ξ is a vector of the exogenous (i.e., independent) latent variables, ζ is a vector of residuals, and B and Γ are the path coefficient matrices.

Predictor Specification

Predictor specification (Presp), therefore, forms the basis for PLS modeling. Whereas the covariance-based ML estimation rests on the assumptions of a specific joint multivariate distribution and independence of observations, the PLS approach does not make these hard assumptions. Instead, the PLS technique of model building uses very general, soft distributional assumptions, which often lead to this approach being termed "soft modeling." Thus, as Lohmöller (1989, p. 64) noted, "it is not the concepts nor the models nor the estimation techniques which are 'soft,' only the distributional assumptions."

Presp "is imposed on relations that the investigator wants to use for prediction, be it in theoretical or estimated form, and Presp provides the ensuing predictions" (Wold, 1988, p. 589).

Lohmöller (1989) further states that Presp "starts with the purpose of prediction (not primarily a structural explanation) [and] sets up a system of relations preferably linear, where the structure of the relations must be founded in the substance of the matter, and the predictive purpose should not jeopardize a structural-causal interpretation of the relation (causal-predictive relation)" (p. 72). Presp adopts the statistical assumptions for a linear conditional expectation relationship between dependent and independent variables, which can be summarized as

$$y = \alpha + Bx + v, \qquad \hat{y} \equiv E[y \mid x] = \alpha + Bx$$
$$\Rightarrow E[v] = 0$$
$$\Rightarrow \text{Cov}[x, v] = \text{Cov}[\hat{y}, v] = 0 \tag{4}$$
$$\Rightarrow \text{Cov}[x, y] = \text{Cov}[x, \hat{y}] = B \, \text{var}[x],$$

where y and x are $m \times 1$ and $n \times 1$ matrices of dependent and independent variables, v is an $m \times 1$ matrix of residuals, and B the $m \times n$ matrix of coefficient relations between y and x. The implications are that, for a given x and y:

1. x is a predictor (cause or stimulus) of y, and not the other way around (i.e., nonreversability).
2. $\hat{y}$ is the systematic part of y, with respect to x.
3. The systematic part, $\hat{y}$, is a linear function of x.

The observational or empirical representation of Equation 4 would follow simply by including the index n for observations $1, \ldots, N$:

$$y = \alpha + \beta x_n + v_n, \qquad \hat{y}_n \equiv E[y_n \mid x_n] = \alpha + \beta x_n$$
$$\Rightarrow E[v_n] = 0$$
$$\Rightarrow \text{Cov}[x_n, v_n] = \text{Cov}[\hat{y}_n, v_n] = 0$$
$$\Rightarrow \text{Cov}[x_n, y_n] = \text{Cov}[x_n, \hat{y}_n] = \beta \, \text{var}[x_n].$$

Therefore, it should be noted that identical distributions are not assumed. For any two cases, say n and $n+1$, no assumption is made that the residuals v_n and v_{n+1} have the same distribution. Nor is independence of cases required because no specification was made regarding the correlation between two different cases (i.e., $\text{Cov}[\nu_n, \nu_{n+1}]$). In general, a sufficient condition for consistency of least squares estimates is that, as the number of observations approaches infinity, the sum of the correlations between cases must stay below infinity (i.e., $\sum_i |\text{cor}(\nu_n, \nu_{n+1})| < \infty$; Wold, 1988).

Thus, predictor specification can be viewed as a least squares counterpart to the distributional assumptions of ML modeling. It avoids the assumptions that observations follow a specific distributional pattern and that they are independently distributed. Therefore, no restriction is made on the structure of the residual covariances and, under least squares modeling, the residual variance terms are minimized. In summary, Wold (1988) states that Presp "provides a general rationale for (i) LS [least squares] specification and (ii) LS estimation, and thereby also for the application of (iii) the cross-validation test for predictive relevance ... and (iv) the assessment of SEs by Tukey's jackknife" (p. 587), which are used for model evaluation.

Sample Size Requirements Based on the Inside and Outside Approximations

With the formal model specification and the basic PLS estimation process described, the requirements for sample size become reasonably clear for all three stages. As our previous example demonstrates, either simple or multiple regressions are performed, depending on the mode for each block of indicators and the inner weighting scheme. Due to the partial nature of the estimation procedure, where only a portion of the model is involved at any one time, only that part that requires the largest multiple regression need be found. Although stages 2 and 3 are equivalent in sample size requirements, stage 1 may not require as large a sample size contingent on which inner approximation is selected.

Overall, for an initial sense of the sample size required at stages 2 and 3, one simply looks at the model specification or, equivalently, the graphical model such as that depicted in Figure 1 and finds the largest of two possibilities: (1) the block with the largest number of formative indicators (i.e., largest measurement equation) or (2) the dependent LV with the largest number of independent LVs influencing it (i.e., the largest structural equation). If one were to use a regression heuristic of 10 cases per predictor, the sample size requirement would be 10 times either (1) or (2), whichever is greater.

Ideally, for a more accurate assessment, one needs to specify the effect size for each regression analysis and look up the power tables provided by Cohen (1988) or Green's (1991) approximation to these tables. Using Figure 1 as an example, the only block with formative indicators consists of four indicators influencing ξ_2. The dependent LV with the largest number of independent LVs influencing it is η_2, with three paths going into it. Thus, the largest regression at any one time consists of four independent variables. Assuming a medium effect size as defined by Cohen (1988), a minimum sample size of 84 is needed to obtain a power of .80. With a large effect size, the sample requirement drops to 39.

For stage 1, the use of a path weighting scheme would result in the same sample requirements as necessary for stages 2 and 3. However, with the use of a factor or a centroid weighting scheme, only simple regressions between the LVs are performed in calculating the weights to be used for the inside approximation. In this situation, only the measurement model with formative indicators becomes the critical factor in sample size requirements. Had all latent variables been modeled as reflective (mode A), the use of either a factor or a centroid weighting scheme would entail only a series of simple regressions during the entire stage 1 process, resulting in minimum sample size requirements of 53 and 24 for medium and large effect sizes, respectively.

In fact, the minimum sample size required to assess component loadings for reflective indicators is likely even smaller. Given that the standard requirement for loadings is normally set at .60 or above, the effect size of component loadings is larger than what is considered large in regression power analysis (i.e., f^2 of .35, Cohen, 1988). For example, a .60 loading represents an f^2 effect size of .56 and requires a sample size of 15 to obtain a power of .80 for detection. This situation is demonstrated partly in the Monte Carlo study to follow, wherein sample sizes of 20 could not detect structural paths of .40, but easily detected loadings of .60 and .80.

Model Evaluation

As noted, PLS makes no distributional assumption (other than predictor specification) in its procedure for estimating parameters. Thus, traditional parametric-based techniques for significance testing/evaluation would not be appropriate. Instead, Wold (1980, 1982) argued for tests consistent with the distribution-free/predictive approach of PLS. In other words, rather than based on covariance fit, evaluation of PLS models should apply prediction-oriented measures that are also nonparametric. To that extent, the R^2 for dependent LVs, the Stone-Geisser (Stone, 1974; Geisser, 1975) test for predictive relevance, and Fornell and Larcker's (1981) average variance extracted measure are used to assess predictiveness, whereas resampling procedures such as jackknifing and bootstrapping are used to examine the stability of estimates. Readers interested in more detail regarding statistical tests, with examples of their use, can consult Barclay, Higgins, and Thompson (1995), Chin (1998), Chin and Gopal (1995), and Mathieson, Peacock, and Chin (1996).

Partial Least Squares Estimates: The Issue of Consistency at Large

Although one of the benefits of the PLS procedure can be argued to be its ability to estimate LV case values, these scores can lead to biased parameter estimates. Essentially, the case values for the LVs are "inconsistent" relative to the CBSEM model due to the fact that they are aggregates of the observed variables, which in part include measurement error. This bias tends to manifest itself in higher estimates for component loadings (outer model relations) and lower estimates at the structural level (inner model relations). The estimates will approach the "true" latent variable scores as both the number of indicators per block and the sample size increase. This limiting case is termed "consistency at large" (Wold, 1982, p. 25). Intuitively, the larger the number of indicators in a block, the more the "essence" of the LV is confirmed by the data. However, the sample size also needs to increase, as in the usual asymptotic notion of consistency, in order for the sample covariance matrix to become a better estimate of the population covariance matrix. Thus, in PLS, better estimates cannot simply be obtained by increasing the sample size. Both more indicators and more cases are needed. Furthermore, increasing the block size not only results in estimates that approach the "true" parameter scores, but also lowers the standard errors, which have been shown to vary inversely with the square root of the block size (Lyttkens, 1966, 1973).

Although closed-form solutions for estimating the amount of bias are not available for multiblock heterogeneous loading conditions, formulas for estimating the bias of PLS estimates relative to the parameter-oriented CBSEM ML estimates in the single- and two-block models have been provided (for derivations, see Lohmöller, 1989, pp. 207–212). In these situations, it was shown that the bias decreases as the loadings become more reliable, and the bias decreases as the number of indicators increases. For the simple two-block model, it was also demonstrated that the predicted correlation between indicators from different blocks is unbiased because the loading and correlation biases cancel each other out. The general proof that this canceling effect occurs even under conditions of unequal block sizes, weights, and loadings has been given by Areskoug (1982). Therefore, we again see the distinction between prediction orientation versus parameter orientation. The parameter estimation accuracy of the PLS procedure relative to the covariance-based ML procedure increases under consistency at large.

Yet, it can be argued that PLS estimates are consistent under the formal PLS model. The bias measures just discussed were calculated relative to CBSEM ML estimation, which presupposes that the underlying model that generates the data is covariance based. Schneeweiss (1990) has suggested that the consistency at large notion is really a "justification for using PLS as an estimation method to estimate CBSEM parameters in cases where the number of manifest variables is large" (p. 38). Instead, Schneeweiss argues that PLS can be seen as a consistent estimator of parameters and latent variables as long as we determine which population parameters we are attempting to estimate. If we are estimating the parameters for the population model as defined by PLS, then we have the advantage of "treating PLS as a method for defining descriptive parameters in situations where blocks of manifest variables are related to each other" (p. 38), even if the data cannot be regarded as stemming from a CBSEM model. In this situation, the PLS estimation method will estimate the PLS parameters consistently. If, on the other hand, the data are generated from a covariance-based model, the PLS estimates will result in inconsistent estimates.

Therefore, while PLS can be used in a confirmatory sense following a covariance-based orientation, it can also be used for testing the appropriateness of a block of indicators in a predictive sense and for suggesting potential relations among blocks without necessarily making any assumptions regarding which LV model generated the data. As Wold (1980) noted, an initial PLS model is:

> ... usually tentative since the model construction is an evolutionary process. The empirical content of the model is extracted from the data, and the model is improved by interactions through the estimation procedure between the model and the data and the reactions of the researcher. Consequently, the researcher should begin with a generous number of observables-indicators in the various blocks. To use many observables makes for rich empirical content of the model and is favorable to the accuracy of the PLS estimation procedure. In the interaction between the data and the original model it will become apparent which indicators are relevant and which should be omitted (p. 70).

Monte Carlo Simulation

In this section, the results of two Monte Carlo studies are summarized.[1] The studies were designed to examine how well the PLS algorithm performs in recovering the "true" population parameters under varying numbers of latent variables, indicators, and sample cases. More specifically, the estimates for structural paths and component loadings were examined under conditions (as discussed earlier) that are normally out of the range of CBSEM analysis. Although the distinction in generating data conforming to a PLS model versus a CBSEM model and its impact on the notion of consistency was made, a CBSEM-based model was nonetheless applied in order to see how well PLS performs under the notion of consistency at large. In terms of structural path recovery, PLS was also compared to simple path-analytic regression using a simple summation of the indicators. No attempt was made in these studies to compare the PLS estimates to CBSEM estimates. The sample size and model complexity tested in these studies were, by and large, beyond the scope of current CBSEM programs. The data were generated using PRELIS 2.14 and tested using PLS-Graph, Version 2.91.

In the first Monte Carlo study, the three treatments consisted of sample sizes (20, 50, 100, 150, and 200 cases), number of connected latent variables (2, 4, 8, 12, and 16), and number of indicators attached to each latent variable (4, 8, 12, 16, or 32 indicators). For each of the 125 cells in the design, 100 replications were made. Figure 3 represents the model tested. In this model, a focal exogenous latent variable is connected to m endogenous latent variables with standardized paths of .40. As with the other m LVs, the focal LV has n indicators. Consistent with CBSEM models, all latent variables were modeled with reflective indicators. In all runs, the "true" loadings for each LV were kept heterogeneous with the first 25% of indicators set at standardized loadings of .20, the next 25% at .60, and the last 50% at 0.80.

---

[1] Due to page limitations, results of the Monte Carlo studies are not presented in tabular form. Tabled results can be obtained from either author, the editor, or on the World Wide Web at http://disc-nt.cba.uh.edu/chin/sage/appendix.htm.

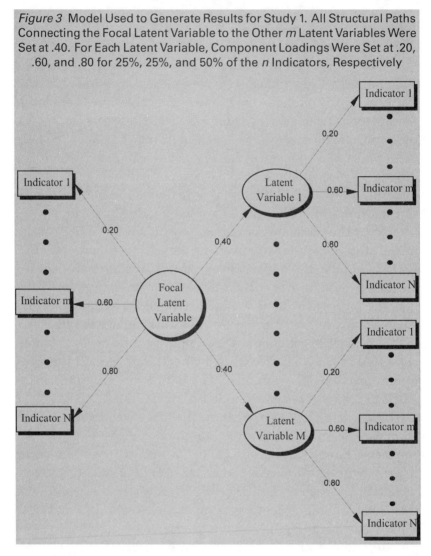

Figure 3 Model Used to Generate Results for Study 1. All Structural Paths Connecting the Focal Latent Variable to the Other *m* Latent Variables Were Set at .40. For Each Latent Variable, Component Loadings Were Set at .20, .60, and .80 for 25%, 25%, and 50% of the *n* Indicators, Respectively

Essentially, this represents a situation in which one fourth of the indicators for each LV are useless, one fourth adequate, and one half considered good.

The impact of consistency at large on loading estimates was clear. Specifically, increasing sample size alone does not provide a better approximation to the population value. Instead, the number of indicators also has to increase. As an example, for the .80 loading in the 150 sample size analysis, a substantial improvement occurs when the number of indicators increases from four to eight, whereupon it starts to plateau. As expected, increasing sample size lowered standard errors. At the extreme, the very small loading of .20 was not detected until sample sizes of 150 and 200 were reached. However, as discussed earlier, it was possible to successfully estimate and detect path loadings of .60 and .80 at the small sample size of 20, albeit with reasonably large standard errors.

Interestingly, the number of connected latent variables did not seem to help the loading estimates. At best, the standard error dropped slightly as the number of LVs increased, but only when the number of indicators was at four or eight. For example, using the 100 sample size analysis with four indicators, the standard error for the .60 loading drops from .07 to .05 as the number of LVs increases from 2 to 16. Similarly, the standard error for the .80 loading goes from .04 to .02. It is possible that a more significant LV influence may occur if a structural path larger than the .40 had been specified.

Partial least squares always performed better than the simple summed regression approach, although it did best at lower numbers of indicators. As discussed earlier, the minimum sample size for a medium effect size, which .40 represents, is 53. Thus, it was not surprising to find nonsignificant results for the $N = 20$ analysis and less accurate estimates for the $N = 50$ analysis. For the $N = 200$ analysis, both the PLS and regression estimate improved as the number of indicators increased. However, the PLS estimate was approximately .05 closer to the population parameter for four- and eight-indicator conditions. The gap dropped to .03 as the number of indicators increased. For sample sizes of 150 or 200, the mean PLS estimate yielded the population parameter at indicator levels of 16 and 32 with the regression estimate being quite close. Overall, with 16 or more indicators, the regression approach might be preferred because it obtains similar results at a simpler level of computation. At the more realistic level for social science research (i.e., four or eight indicators), however, the more accurate estimates would suggest using PLS.

In the second study, treatments consisted of sample sizes (50, 100, and 200), number of connected latent variables (2, 8, and 16), and number of indicators attached to each latent variable (4, 8, 16, or 32 indicators). Heterogeneous loadings were set in the same fashion as in the first study. In addition to restricting the scope of the treatments, the model was modified by adding four independent exogenous LVs impacting our focal LV (all with standardized paths of .40). Thus, the focal LV becomes a mediator between four exogenous LVs and m endogenous LVs. Figure 4 depicts the model analyzed.

Figure 4 Model Used to Generate Results for Study 2. All Structural Paths Connecting the Focal Latent Variable to the Other Latent Variables Were Set at .40. There Are Four Exogenous Latent Variables and m Endogenous Latent Variables Connected to the Focal Latent Variable. For Each Latent Variable, Component Loadings Were Set at .20, .60, and .80 for 25%, 25%, and 50% of the n Indicators, Respectively

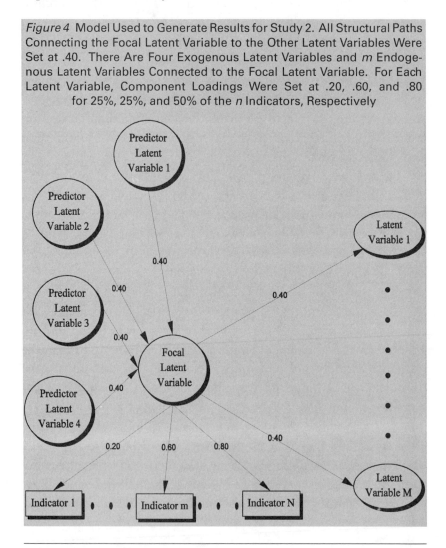

The results of Study 2 essentially corroborated the results obtained in the first study. Earlier, it was noted that a regression involving four independent variables and medium effect sizes would need a minimum sample size of 80. Interestingly, the analysis at sample size 50 still generated significant results. The standard errors, as expected, dropped as sample size increased. Though not as strong, the PLS estimates again performed best relative to the simple summed regression approach with four and eight indicators; the difference in the standardized beta was approximately .02 or .03. With greater numbers of indicators, the PLS and regression estimates were essentially the same.

Overall, the results show that the PLS approach can provide information about the appropriateness of indicators at sample size as low as 20. Furthermore, it performed better than the simple summed regression approach with four or eight indicators. Computationally, the most complex model in this study, which involved 672 indicators, 21 latent variables, and 200 cases, took approximately 1.5 minutes to run on a 166-MHz Pentium computer. Such an analysis would not be possible using CBSEM.

Summary

As mentioned at the beginning of this chapter, by far the most common approach for SEM has been covariance-based procedures. Yet, the PLS procedure may be more suitable under certain circumstances. The PLS model and estimation procedure covered in this chapter revealed many differences between CBSEM and PLS.

Programs such as LISREL, EQS, AMOS, SEPath, CALIS, and RAMONA use covariance-based procedures with the objective of obtaining optimal parameter accuracy. The level of theoretical/substantive knowledge that the researcher brings to the study is a major factor inasmuch as any given model becomes the basis for explaining the covariances among all the indicators. To obtain consistent parameter estimates, the empirical conditions of the data require a multivariate normal distribution (under an

ML function) and independence of observations. Finally, indicators are typically required to be modeled as reflective and unique case values for LVs cannot be obtained (i.e., factor indeterminacy).

Partial least squares was developed as a counterpart to CBSEM analysis. In general, it can be viewed as complementary to CBSEM because its main objective is prediction. The focus of PLS, under predictor specification, is on the variance of dependent variables and no assumptions are made regarding the joint distribution of the indicators or the independence of sample cases. Because of its prediction orientation, factors are determinate and unique case values for the LVs are estimated. Indicators can be modeled as either formative or reflective.

Sample size requirements under PLS can be quite minimal relative to a CBSEM analysis. Computationally, PLS is an order of magnitude faster given that its procedure involves only a series of least squares estimations. By virtue of the fact that, at any moment, only a subset of the parameters is being estimated, PLS can handle much larger/complex models with many LVs and indicators in each block. Models consisting of over 1,000 indicators can be easily executed. Furthermore, as the number of indicators per block increases along with the sample size, the PLS estimates tend to become more stable as they converge to the "true" parameter values.

In summary, PLS should not be viewed as simply a distribution-free alternative to CBSEM. Rather, it represents a different approach to empirical modeling—a descriptive, prediction-oriented one. As Falk and Miller (1992) state, using the terms "soft" and "hard" modeling for PLS and CBSEM, respectively:

> A wide gulf exists between predictive relationships and causal relationships. While causal relationships are predictive, predictive relationships need not be even remotely causal. With soft modeling the researcher is forced to adopt a more predictive, therefore descriptive, stance.
>
> If hard modeling procedures cannot be used because of study limitations, then soft modeling procedures cannot be expected to answer hard modeling questions about

statistical inferences. On the other hand, we reject the notion that study limitations should prevent data from being analyzed. Our position is that many research questions can and should be answered without making causal inferences. In our view this is the role of soft modeling. (pp. xi–xii)

We agree that the PLS methodology will likely grow in usage in the future. The approach is congruent with a large percentage of social science research where:

- The objective is prediction, and/or
- The phenomenon in question is relatively new or changing and the theoretical model or measures are not well formed, and/or
- The model is relatively complex with large numbers of indicators and/or LVs, and/or
- There is an epistemic need to model the relationship between LVs and indicators in different modes (i.e., formative and reflective measures), and/or
- The data conditions relating to normal distribution, independence, and/or sample size are not met.

Author Note: The assistance of Robert Willis in running the Monte Carlo simulations reported in this chapter is gratefully acknowledged.

References

Anderson, J. C., & Gerbing, D. W. (1984). The effect of sampling error on convergence, improper solutions, and goodness-of-fit indices for maximum likelihood confirmatory factory analyses. *Psychometrika, 49*, 155–173.

Areskoug, B. (1982). The first canonical correlation: Theoretical PLS analysis and simulation experiments. In K. G. Jöreskog and H. Wold (Eds.), *Systems under indirect observation: Causality, structure, prediction* (Part 2, pp. 95–118). Amsterdam: North-Holland.

Barclay, D., Higgins, C., & Thompson, R. (1995). The partial least squares (PLS) approach to causal modeling: Personal computer adoption and use as an illustration (with commentaries). *Technology Studies, 2*, 285–323.

Bollen, K. A., & Lennox, R. D. (1991). Conventional wisdom on measurement: A structural equation perspective. *Psychological Bulletin, 110*, 305–314.

Boomsma, A. (1983). *On the robustness of LISREL (maximum likelihood estimation) against small sample size and nonnormality.* Amsterdam: Sociometric Research Foundation.

Chin, W. W. (1998). The partial least squares approach for structural equation modeling. In G. A. Marcoulides (Ed.), *Modern methods for business research* (pp. 295–336). Mahwah, NJ: Erlbaum.

Chin, W. W., & Gopal, A. (1995). Adoption intention in GSS: Relative importance of beliefs. *The Data Base for Advances in Information Systems, 26*, 42–64.

Chou, C.-P., & Bentler, P. M. (1995). Estimates and tests in structural equation modeling. In R. H. Hoyle (Ed.), *Structural equation modeling: Concepts, issues, and applications* (pp. 37–55). Newbury Park, CA: Sage.

Cohen, J. (1988). *Statistical power analysis for the behavioral sciences* (2nd ed.). Hillsdale, NJ: Erlbaum.

Cohen, P., Cohen, J., Teresi, J., Marchi, M., & Velez, C. N. (1990). Problems in the measurement of latent variables in structural equations causal models. *Applied Psychological Measurement, 14*, 183–196.

Dillon, W. R., Kumar, A., & Mulani, N. (1987). Offending estimates in covariance structure analysis: Comments on the causes of and solutions to Heywood cases. *Psychological Bulletin, 101*, 126–135.

Falk, R. F., & Miller, N. B. (1992). *A primer for soft modeling.* Akron, OH: University of Akron Press.

Fornell, C. (1987). A second generation of multivariate analysis: Classification of methods and implications for marketing research. In M. J. Houston (Ed.), *Review of marketing* (pp. 407–450). Chicago: American Marketing Association.

Fornell, C. (1989). The blending of theoretical and empirical knowledge in structural equations with unobservables. In H. Wold (Ed.), *Theoretical empiricism* (pp. 153–173). New York: Paragon.

Fornell, C., & Bookstein, F. (1982). Two structural equation models: LISREL and PLS applied to consumer exit-voice theory. *Journal of Marketing Research, 19,* 440–452.

Fornell, C., & Larcker, D. (1981). Evaluating structural equation models with unobservable variables and measurement error. *Journal of Marketing Research, 18,* 39–50.

Fornell, C., & Yi, Y. (1992). Assumption of the two-step approach to latent variable modeling. *Sociological Methods and Research, 20,* 291–320.

Geisser, S. (1975). The predictive sample reuse method with applications. *Journal of the American Statistical Association, 70,* 320–328.

Gerbing, D. W., & Anderson, J. C. (1987). Improper solutions in the analysis of covariance structures: Their interpretability and a comparison of alternative respecifications. *Psychometrika, 52,* 99–111.

Green, S. B. (1991). How many subjects does it take to do a regression analysis. *Multivariate Behavioral Research, 26,* 499–510.

Hu, L.-T., & Bentler, P. M. (1995). Evaluating model fit. In R. H. Hoyle (Ed.), *Structural equation modeling: Concepts, issues, and applications* (pp. 76–99). Newbury Park, CA: Sage.

Hui, B. S. (1978). *The partial least squares approach to path models of indirectly observed variables with multiple indicators.* Unpublished doctoral dissertation, University of Pennsylvania, Philadelphia.

Hui, B. S. (1982). On building partial least squares models with interdependent inner relations. In K. G. Jöreskog & H. Wold (Eds.), *Systems under indirect observation: Causality, structure, prediction* (Part 2, pp. 249–272). Amsterdam: North-Holland.

Jöreskog, K. G. (1973). A general method for estimating a linear structural equation system. In A. S. Goldberger & O. D. Duncan (Eds.), *Structural equation models in the social sciences* (pp. 85–112). New York: Academic Press.

Jöreskog, K. G., & Sörbom, D. (1989). *LISREL 7: A guide to the program and applications.* Chicago: SPSS.

Keesling, J. W. (1972). *Maximum likelihood approaches to causal analysis.* Unpublished doctoral dissertation, University of Chicago.

Lohmöller, J.-B. (1984). *LVPLS program manual: Latent variables path analysis with partial least-squares estimation.*

Cologne, Germany: Zentralarchiv für empirische Sozial-forschung.

Lohmöller, J.-B. (1989). *Latent variable path modeling with partial least squares.* Heidelberg, Germany: Physica-Verlag.

Lyttkens, E. (1966). On the fix-point property of Wold's iterative estimation method for principal components. In P. R. Krishnaiah (Ed.), *Multivariate analysis: Proceedings of an international symposium held in Dayton, Ohio, June 14–19, 1965* (pp. 335–350). New York: Academic Press.

Lyttkens, E. (1973). The fixed-point method for estimating interdependent systems with the underlying model specification. *Journal of the Royal Statistical Society, A136,* 353–394.

MacCallum, R. C. (1986). Specification searches in covariance structure analyses. *Psychological Bulletin, 100,* 107–120.

MacCallum, R. C., & Browne, M. W. (1993). The use of causal indicators in covariance structure models: Some practical issues. *Psychological Bulletin, 114,* 533–541.

MacCallum, R. C., Browne, M. W., & Sugawara, H. M. (1996). Power analysis and determination of sample size for covariance structure modeling. *Psychological Methods, 1,* 130–149.

Maraun, M. D. (1996). Metaphor taken as math: Indeterminacy in the factor analysis model. *Multivariate Behavioral Research, 31,* 517–538.

Mathieson, K., Peacock, E., & Chin, W. (1996). *Extending the technology acceptance model: The influence of perceived user resources.* Working Paper WP 96–18, Faculty of Management, University of Calgary, Alberta, Canada.

Mulaik, S. A., James, L. R., Van Alstine, J., Bennett, N., Lind, S., & Stillwell, C. D. (1989). An evaluation of goodness-of-fit indices for structural equation models. *Psychological Bulletin, 105,* 430–445.

Noonan, R., & Wold, H. (1982). PLS path modeling with indirectly observed variables: A comparison of alternative estimates for latent variables. In K. G. Jöreskog & H. Wold (Eds.), *Systems under indirect observation: Causality, structure, prediction* (Part 2, pp. 75–94). Amsterdam: North-Holland.

Rindskopf, D. (1984). Structural equation models: Empirical identification, Heywood cases, and related problems. *Sociological Methods and Research, 13,* 109–119.

Schneeweiss, H. (1990). Models with latent variables: LISREL versus PLS. *Contemporary Mathematics, 112,* 33–40.

Stone, M. (1974). Cross-validatory choice and assessment of statistical predictions, *Journal of the Royal Statistical Society*, *B36*, 111–133.

van Driel, O. P. (1978). On various causes of improper solutions in maximum likelihood factor analysis. *Psychometrika*, *43*, 225–243.

Wiley, D. E. (1973). The identification problem for structural equation models with unmeasured variables. In A. S. Goldberger & O. D. Duncan (Eds.), *Structural equation models in the social sciences* (pp. 69–83). New York: Academic Press.

Wold, H. (1980). Model construction and evaluation when theoretical knowledge is scarce: Theory and application of partial least squares. In J. Kmenta & J. B. Ramsey (Eds.), *Evaluation of econometric models*. New York: Academic Press.

Wold, H. (1982). Soft modeling: The basic design and some extensions. In K. G. Jöreskog & H. Wold (Eds.), *Systems under indirect observations: Causality, structure, prediction* (Part 2, pp. 1–54). Amsterdam: North-Holland.

Wold, H. (1985). Partial least squares. In S. Kotz & N. L. Johnson (Eds.), *Encyclopedia of statistical sciences* (Vol. 6, pp. 581–591). New York: Wiley.

Wold, H. (1988). Specification, predictor. In S. Kotz & N. L. Johnson (Eds.), *Encyclopedia of statistical sciences* (Vol. 8, pp. 587–599). New York: Wiley.

Author Index

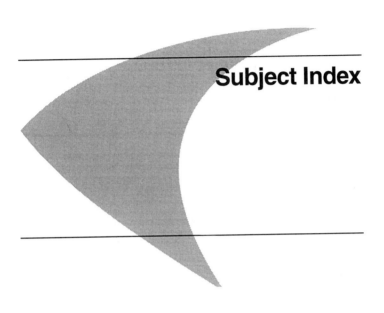

Subject Index

About the Contributors

Wai Chan (Ph.D., University of California at Los Angeles, 1995) is Assistant Professor of Psychology at the Chinese University of Hong Kong. He is a psychometrician, and his primary research interests are in the area of structural equation modeling and bootstrap methods. He has published methodological articles in *Sociological Methods and Research* and *Multivariate Behavioral Research*.

Wynne W. Chin (Ph.D., University of Michigan, 1992) is Associate Professor in the College of Business Administration at the University of Houston. As part of his research on casual models related to IT adoption and GSS meeting processes, he developed *PLS-Graph*, a Windows-based software program for performing partial least squares analyses. His efforts have resulted in publications in journals such as *Information Systems Research*, *MIS Quarterly*, *Journal of Management Information Systems*, and *Decision Sciences*.

Rachel T. Fouladi (Ph.D., University of British Columbia, 1996) is Assistant Professor of Educational Psychology at the University of Texas at Austin. Her interests include issues of pedagogy and use of elementary and multivariate statistical procedures, in particular, covariance and correlation structure analysis techniques, under a variety of distributional conditions, assumption violations, and reduced sample sizes.

John W. Graham (Ph.D., University of Southern California, 1983) is Professor of Biobehavioral Health at Pennsylvania State University, and is Associate Director of the NIDA-funded Center for the Study of Prevention Through Innovative Methodology. His research interests include (a) social influence and health-related behavior in adolescents and adults and (b) development and application of research methodology, including missing-data analysis, structural equation modeling, and detection/correction of self-report biases.

Samuel B. Green (Ph.D., University of Georgia, 1975) is Professor and Chair of the Department of Psychology and Research in the School of Education at the University of Kansas. His interests are in applied issues in statistics, psychometrics, and research methods.

Kit-Tai Hau (Ph.D., University of Hong Kong, 1992) is Lecturer on the Faculty of Education at the Chinese University of Hong Kong. His research interests include developmental psychology, moral development, achievement motivation, causal attribution, and self-concept.

Dominique M. A. Haughton (Ph.D., Massachusetts Institute of Technology, 1984) is Associate Professor of Statistics in the Mathematical Sciences Department at Bentley College. Most of her publications are about information criteria for model selection in various fields.

Scott L. Hershberger (Ph.D., Fordham University, 1990) is Assistant Professor of Quantitative Psychology in the Department of Psychology at the University of Kansas. His research interests include latent variable modeling, developmental behavioral genetics, and the development of sexual orientation.

Rick H. Hoyle (Ph.D., University of North Carolina at Chapel Hill, 1988) is Associate Professor of Psychology and Director of Methodology and Statistics at the Center for Prevention Research at the University of Kentucky. He currently serves as Associate Editor of *Journal of Personality*. His research interests include self and identity, personality and social processes in problem behavior, and research methods.

Robert A. R. G. Jansen (Ph.D., University of Nijmegen, The Netherlands, 1997) is Statistical Researcher at the Department of Trade, Transport and Services of the Central Statistical Office, The Netherlands. His research interests include redesign of economic statistics, simulation, and structural equation and latent state space modeling.

David A. Kenny (Ph.D., Northwestern University, 1972) is Professor of Psychology at the University of Connecticut. His initial research area was the analysis of nonexperimental data, and his book *Correlation and Causality* was one the early presentations of structural equation modeling to a social science audience. More recently, he has investigated person perception in naturalistic contexts. He is the author of *Interpersonal Perception: A Social Relations Analysis*. He has published 5 books and over 70 articles and chapters.

Sharon H. Kramer is a doctoral candidate in the Department of Psychology at Harvard University. Her interests include both theoretical and applied areas of social psychology as well as issues of statistical methodology. Her most recent research examines the relationship between group interaction and group problem-solving effectiveness as well as research on the methodology of meta-analysis. Recent publications include a chapter on meta-analytic research synthesis in *Comprehensive Clinical Psychology*.

Janet G. Marquis (Ph.D., University of Kansas, 1983) is Director of the Research Design and Analysis Unit in the Institute for Life Span Studies at the University of Kansas. Her research interests are experimental design and the analysis of data in longitudinal studies.

Herbert W. Marsh (Ph.D., University of California at Los Angeles, 1974) is Research Professor of Education at the University of Western Sydney-Macarthur in Australia. His research spans a broad array of methodological (research design, statistical analysis, psychological measurement, multitrait-multimethod analyses, covariance structural modeling) and substantive (students' evaluations of teaching effectiveness, self-concept, school effectiveness, gender differences, sports psychology) concerns, and he has published widely in these areas. He is the author of several psychological instruments, including the set of self-concept instruments, the Self Description Questionnaires (SDQ) I, II, and III, Physical Self Description Questionnaire (PSDQ), and the Academic Self Description Questionnaire (ASDQ), as well as the student evaluation instrument, Students' Evaluations of Educational Quality (SEEQ).

Scott E. Maxwell (Ph.D., University of North Carolina at Chapel Hill, 1977) is Professor of Psychology at the University of Notre Dame. His research interests include experimental design and power analysis. He served as Associate Editor of the Quantitative Methods in the Psychology section of *Psychological Bulletin* from 1994 to 1996.

Cyrus R. Mehta (Ph.D., Massachusetts Institute of Technology, 1974) is Adjunct Associate Professor in the Department of Biostatistics at the Harvard School of Public Health. During the past 15 years, he has focused his research activities on developing permutational algorithms that can be applied to categorical data analysis, nonparametric tests, power and sample size calculations, the analysis of contingency tables, and, more generally, to inference concerning the parameters of regression models for categorical data. He has published more than 65 papers in journals such as *Journal of the American Statistical Association*, *Biometrika*, and *Biometrics*.

Peter C. M. Molenaar (Ph.D., University of Utrecht, The Netherlands, 1981) is Professor of Psychology at the University of Amsterdam. His areas of expertise include dynamic factor analysis, applied nonlinear dynamics, adaptive filtering techniques, spectrum analysis, psychophysiological signal analysis, artificial neural network modeling, covariance structure modeling, mathematical psychology and behavior genetics modeling (emphasizing applications to cognitive development) brain-behavior relationships, brain maturation and cognition, genetical influences on EEG during the life span, and optimal control of psychotherapeutic processes.

John R. Nesselroade (Ph.D., University of Illinois at Urbana-Champaign, 1967) is Hugh Scott Hamilton Professor of Psychology at the University of Virginia. His primary areas of research include intraindividual variability, development, and change in personality and human ability measures across the life span, developmental research methodology, and multivariate design and data analysis.

Peter R. Newsted (Ph.D., Carnegie-Mellon University, 1971) is Professor of Management Information Systems at the University of Calgary. Currently, he is serving as area chair of the MIS area after 5 years as Associate Dean (Academic) for the Faculty. His interests, which include the more human side of data processing, stem from his joint background in information processing and psychology. He has published in *Behavioral Science, International Journal of Man-Machine Studies, Information and Management, Behaviour and Information Technology*, and *Information Systems Research*. He is working on a full-text digital library for information systems, the dissemination on the Web of information about MIS surveys, and the use of PCS to administer surveys.

Johan H. L. Oud (Ph.D., University of Nijmegen, The Netherlands, 1978) is Associate Professor of Longitudinal Assessment Methods in the Department of Special Education at the University of Nijmegen, The Netherlands. His primary research interests are in SEM state space modeling and Kalman filtering and smoothing, as well as the construction of monitoring systems based on these approaches. His applications are in the fields of education, family relations, juvenile delinquency, and rehabilitation. He co-authored the Dutch pupil monitoring system LISKAL.

Nitin R. Patel (Ph.D., Massachusetts Institute of Technology, 1973) is Vice President and cofounder of Cytel Software Corporation and Visiting Professor of Management Science at the Sloan School of Management at M.I.T. His primary research interest is in developing procedures and algorithms for inference in small samples. In the past, he has served as president of the

Operational Research Society of India and as a vice president of the International Federation of Operations Research Societies.

Robert Rosenthal (Ph.D., University of California at Los Angeles, 1956) is Edgar Pierce Professor of Psychology at Harvard University. His substantive research interests are in the areas of interpersonal expectancy effects, nonverbal communication, and dyadic interaction. His methodological interests include sources of artifact in behavioral research, experimental design and analysis, contrast analysis, and meta-analysis.

Joseph L. Schafer (Ph.D., Harvard University, 1992) is Assistant Professor of Statistics at Pennsylvania State University, and a principal investigator at the NIDA-funded Center for the Study of Prevention Through Innovative Methodology. His research interests include statistical methods for incomplete data, analysis of longitudinal data, computational algorithms, and software development.

James H. Steiger (Ph.D., Purdue University, 1976) is Professor of Psychology at the University of British Columbia. His primary research interests are in factor analysis, covariance structure analysis, and correlational testing. He is a former editor of *Multivariate Behavioral Research* and has authored a number of commercial and academic computer programs for multivariate analysis, including the SEPATH (Structural Equations and PATH modeling) module in *Statistica*.

Anre Venter (Ph.D., University of Notre Dame, 1996) is Director of Undergraduate Studies in the Department of Psychology at the University of Notre Dame. His research interests include the social comparison process, impression formation, and experimental design.

Dennis D. Wallace (Ph.D., University of North Carolina at Chapel Hill, 1993) is Assistant Professor of Biostatistics in the Department of Preventive Medicine at the University of Kansas Medical Center. His primary research interests are in statistical methods for the analyses of longitudinal and correlated data and application of statistical techniques to epidemiologic and clinical research.

Yiu-Fai Yung (Ph.D., University of California at Los Angeles, 1994) is Assistant Professor of Psychometrics at the University of North Carolina at Chapel Hill. His research interests deal with multivariate analysis, especially in factor analysis and structural equation modeling. Previous and ongoing research work includes mixture models for confirmatory factor analysis, information in mean and covariance structures, and bootstrap applications to structural equation models. Some of his work appears in *British Journal of Mathematical and Statistical Psychology*, *Journal of Educational and Behavioral Statistics*, and *Psychometrika*.

DATE DUE

The Library Store #47-0119